UNFINISHED BUSINESS

UNFINISHED BUSINESS

Evolving Capitalism in the World's Largest Democracy

NANDINI VIJAYARAGHAVAN

BUSINESS
An imprint of Penguin Random House

PENGUIN BUSINESS

USA | Canada | UK | Ireland | Australia
New Zealand | India | South Africa | China

Penguin Business is part of the Penguin Random House group of companies whose addresses can be found at global.penguinrandomhouse.com

Published by Penguin Random House India Pvt. Ltd
4th Floor, Capital Tower 1, MG Road,
Gurugram 122 002, Haryana, India

First published in Penguin Business by Penguin Random House India 2023

10 9 8 7 6 5 4 3 2 1

ISBN 9780670097371

Typeset in Adobe Caslon Pro by MAP Systems, Bengaluru, India
Printed at Replika Press Pvt. Ltd, India

www.penguin.co.in

Contents

Foreword

Writing a foreword for Nandini Vijayaraghavan's well-researched book encouraged my mind to wander over the last fifty-five years of my association with corporations. India is reported to have 63 million enterprises—one man, family, small, medium, large, all kinds. Of these, only 19,000 have a capital of over ₹10 crore; 5000 are publicly listed and, about 50 account for the dominant proportion of total market capitalization. These numbers make one wonder if the Indian enterprise 'jungle' has only a handful of consequential species, surrounded by a seemingly infinite variety of inconsequential creatures. India needs more sustainable and honest enterprises—SHEs, as I like to call them—to revitalize the economy.

There seem to exist a variety of entrepreneurship nurtured by governments, regulators, lenders and investors alike that causes irreversible loss of livelihoods and capital that a developing country like India can ill-afford. Nandini Vijayaraghavan terms this 'Icarus Entrepreneurship'.

While serving Unilever and Tata, I've had the opportunity to interact closely with sustainable businesses and those characterized by Icarus entrepreneurship. While most companies struggle at the time of inception and during the growth phase, how do regulators, investors and lenders separate the grain from the chaff? This is the question Nandini attempts to answer.

Categorizing a company as a product of Icarus entrepreneurship can be conveniently done post facto, after its failure. There is a behavioural aspect to certain entrepreneurs. Nandini argues, using real-life examples, how founders' or management's proclivities, the companies' operating and financial performance and the nature of interactions with regulators and government underpin sustainability.

Companies characterized by Icarus entrepreneurship could, initially, appear successful, and may even be market leaders or dominant players in their respective industries. These companies may report profits and/or their share prices may appreciate. Often, these companies are heavily indebted and are hard put to pay dividends.

Yet, the media often portrays the founders of such companies as trailblazing visionaries. Equity investors, both the supposedly well-informed institutional investors and ill-informed retail investors, rush to buy shares of these companies in invariably overpriced Initial Public Offerings (IPOs). Financiers have no compunction about lending to these companies, notwithstanding their weak financials and inflated values of assets offered as collateral. Regulatory approvals are easily availed courtesy the friends these Icarus entrepreneurs may have among politicians.

When companies characterized by Icarus entrepreneurship invariably encounter stress or fail, pandemonium ensues. Their hitherto unknown failings become immediately evident to the universe at large. The former trailblazers are reviled for gross mismanagement, weak financials, poor stock performance and sometimes, much worse—fraud. Credit rating agencies (CRAs) are accused of wilful professional negligence. Are regulators, CRAs, lenders, and equity investors unable to unearth these failings till these companies implode?

Nandini Vijayaraghavan uses four instances of corporate failures in India to illustrate that the seeds of downfall of companies characterized by Icarus entrepreneurship are embedded in their DNAs.

Building sustainable companies that enhance the well-being of stakeholders—employees, vendors, customers, lenders, investors, regulators, government, and the environment—is a community initiative. Nandini, through a realistic and unbiased analysis of the four corporate failures, highlights what the six stakeholders in the development of corporates—entrepreneurs, investors, lenders, CRAs, regulators, and the government—must do to minimize, if not eradicate, the recurrence of Icarus entrepreneurship.

Valuation expert and Professor of Finance at New York University's Stern School of Business, Aswath Damodaran, goes so far as to warn, 'I believe that ESG (environmental, social and governance factors-based investing) is, at its core, a feel-good scam that is enriching consultants, measurement services and fund managers, while doing close to nothing for the businesses and investors it claims to help, and even less for society.'

When Raghuvir Srinivasan, the editor of *The Hindu BusinessLine*, introduced me to Nandini and her writings, I thought *Unfinished Business* was yet another relevant account of corporate failures. However, through the narration of four corporate collapses, interspersed with humour, Nandini has gone one step further. She provides actionable recommendations to identify and arrest Icarus entrepreneurship. These recommendations, if implemented, will facilitate the creation of a fairer and a more efficient business ecosystem.

Unfinished Business has takeaways for entrepreneurs, governments, regulators, CRAs, investors, lenders, students of business and aficionados of business books.

R. Gopalakrishnan
Author and business commentator
Mumbai

Prologue

Business historians would credit the British government with creating the world's first sovereign perpetual bond. Consols, as these perpetual bonds were called, were first issued in 1751 and carried an interest of 3.5 per cent. After more than three-and-a-half centuries, the UK government redeemed all consols in 2015.

However, the world's first issue of perpetual debt is probably documented in Indian mythology. Vishnu, one among the Hindu trinity, who is considered the protector of the universe, incarnated on earth as a commoner named Venkateswara. He and Padmavati, a princess, fell in love. As Venkateswara did not have the wherewithal to organize a wedding that befit Padmavati and the royal and divine guests, he borrowed 14 lakh (1.4 million) '*rama mudras*'—gold coins that bore the seal (mudra) of Rama from Kubera, the god of wealth.

Venkateswara agreed to pay interest on this loan through Kali Yuga, the fourth and final era in the Hindu concept of time that spans a period of 4,32,000 years. The principal is repayable at the end of Kali Yuga.[1] The loan agreement was scribed by the borrower, Venkateswara. The other two gods of the Hindu trinity—Brahma, the creator, and Shiva, the destroyer—attested the loan agreement as witnesses.

Vishnu and his two consorts, Lakshmi and Padmavati, are deified at the Tirupati temple located amidst the Tirumala hills in the south Indian state of Andhra Pradesh.

The Tirupati temple is supposedly the richest religious organization in the world in terms of daily donations received.

The temple reportedly receives donations worth ₹3.18 crore ($432,000) every day, or ₹1161 crore ($158 million) per annum. The Tirumala Tirupati Devasthanam, which falls under the jurisdiction of the state government of Andhra Pradesh, oversees the temple administration and the numerous educational institutions and hospitals it has set up over the years.

Of the four protagonists of this book—V.G. Siddhartha (VGS), Vijay Mallya, Naresh Goyal and Anil Ambani—at least two, Mallya and Ambani, are supposedly ardent devotees of Lord Venkateswara.[2,3] Every aircraft purchased by Mallya's Kingfisher Airlines was first taken to the Tirupati airport for the lord's blessings before commencing commercial operations.[4] Sadly, unlike the deity in whom Mallya and Ambani reposed so much faith, timely debt servicing was not their forte. Neither was it the strength of VGS or Naresh Goyal.

The four gentlemen belonged to a rarefied club of entrepreneurs who could raise sizeable quantum of debt with ease despite their businesses not generating adequate cash flows to punctually repay principal and interest and, not possessing sufficient assets to pledge as collateral. This is in India, where banks are dominant providers of debt to corporates, and the bond market is not as large and liquid as it is in the US and UK. Bureaucratic state-owned and private sector banks can reduce credit-worthy small-, mid-caps and individuals seeking a modest quantum of debt and willing to pledge assets, whose market value is more than the loan, to tears.

So, what competitive advantage did the guild of Indian entrepreneurs who had preferential and seemingly limitless access to debt possess? Understanding India's dynamic political landscape is essential to unravelling the puzzle of preferential credit access.

Political Churn

Narendra Damodardas Modi, leader of the Bharatiya Janata Party (BJP) and the former chief minister of Gujarat, which

"The documents are in order. But loan approval is subject to due diligence."

"Please take the loan now! Send your documents later for due diligence."

Cartoon: Ravikanth Nandula

also happens to be home to Dhirubhai Ambani, Gautam Adani and Mohandas Karamchand Gandhi, was sworn in as India's fourteenth prime minister in 2014. Although his party led the National Democratic Alliance (NDA) coalition, in the 2014 general elections it had single-handedly won 282 seats; 10 more than the 272 seats that constitute a majority in the 543-seat Lok Sabha, the lower house of the Indian parliament. This was more than double the 116 seats the BJP had won in the 2009 general elections.

The Congress party, which spearheaded the moderate faction of the Indian independence movement and had remained in power for nearly fifty-five years—as of 2022—since India became a sovereign nation seventy-five years ago, was completely routed. It won just 44 seats, down 79 per cent from 206 seats in the 2009 general elections.

From May 2004 to May 2014, the Congress party had led a coalition called the United Progressive Alliance (UPA). With former Reserve Bank of India (RBI) governor and Union finance minister Dr Manmohan Singh as prime minister, the Indian economy witnessed its most robust growth phase since attaining Independence on 15 August 1947.

Gross Domestic Product (GDP) growth, which accelerated in the last two years of the Atal Bihari Vajpayee-led BJP government to 7.86 per cent in FY2003[5] and 7.92 per cent in FY2004, sustained its momentum during the run up to the 2007–08 Global Financial Crisis (GFC). Even in FY2008, India's real GDP grew by 3.09 per cent and bounced back to 7.86 per cent in FY2009 and 8.50 per cent in FY2010. By May 2014, when Dr Singh completed his second five-year term as prime minister, he had presided over one of the fastest growing phases of the Indian economy. India was ranked the world's second-fastest growing major economy, after China.

Why then did the Congress receive such a drubbing at the polls, despite the impressive macroeconomic performance? The public had lost confidence in the party. Rahul Gandhi, who was anointed general secretary of the Congress, was increasingly projected as the face of party and given credit for populist schemes. However, he was no match for Modi's alpha male personality.

Credit: Gujarat Cooperative Milk Marketing Federation Ltd. (Amul)

Further, India's decelerating GDP growth between FY2011 and FY2013 was a contributing factor. With crude oil prices spiking to over $100 per barrel during 2011 to 2013, energy-importing India's current account deficit was elevated. High borrowing costs and delays in securing government approvals stalled corporate investments and constrained cash flows, while high inflation and slower hiring weakened consumer confidence and forced households to cut spending.[6] However, the primary reason for the public's loss of support and the party's poll defeat was corruption.

Despite being led by the personally upright Dr Singh, UPA's tenure, particularly during the five-year period following the 2009 general elections, was marred by frauds and bribery. Scams relating to the sale of 2G spectrum (2008), Commonwealth Games (2010), Adarsh Housing Society for war widows in Mumbai, chopper sales, and the Tatra truck sales (2012) facilitated the BJP-led NDA's resounding victory in the 2014 elections and consolidation of power in the 2019 elections. The upheaval was, however, not restricted to India's political landscape.

Corporate Upheavals

India's corporate sector too witnessed cataclysmic changes that continued into the second decade of the twenty-first century. India's inherently chaotic financial sector turned tumultuous when borrowings of Indian corporates, especially those headed by well-connected entrepreneurs, increased exponentially. Delays in obtaining land and environmental clearances and rising finance costs made it difficult for corporates to repay debt. Fortunes and reputations, which had taken decades to build, were lost in the blink of an eye. Careers of India's one-time iconic CEOs, like Subrata Roy, Nirav Modi, Naresh Goyal, Vijay Mallya, VGS, Anil Ambani, Chanda Kochhar, Rana Kapoor and Ravi Parthasarathy, came to naught.

In 2014, for instance, Subrata Roy, the promoter-CEO of India's largest residuary non-banking finance company, Sahara India Financial Corporation (SIFC), was arrested. After the RBI debarred the Sahara Group's flagship entity, the unlisted SIFC, from raising fresh deposits from the public way back in 2008, Roy floated multiple companies that announced ₹40,000 crore (over $9.0 billion) issues of optionally fully convertible debentures (OFCD).[7] The terms and conditions of these OFCDs contravened Securities and Exchange Board of India (SEBI) norms. Further, defaults by multiple Sahara group entities, some of which were listed, opened a can of worms that led to Roy's arrest in 2014. However, following his mother's demise, he was granted parole from prison in May 2016.[8,9] Indian courts extended Roy's parole multiple times and he has not returned to prison since 2016.

Diamantaire Nirav Modi, and his uncle, the jeweller Mehul Choksi, in connivance with employees of state-owned Punjab National Bank (PNB) generated fraudulent letters of credit (LCs) worth ₹13,600 crore (around $2.0 billion in 2017) for over a decade.[10] The uncle and nephew duo had used these fake LCs to make business purchases and siphon money into their personal accounts held outside India. Modi and Choksi fled India in January 2018 before their scam was uncovered. Modi's flagship entity was the unlisted Firestar International Private Limited and Choksi was the CEO of the listed Gitanjali Gems. Modi was arrested in London in March 2019 and is awaiting extradition to India. Mehul Choksi lived in Antigua after obtaining citizenship of the island nation until May 2021, when he was reported missing. Later, he was arrested in Dominica and is undergoing court proceedings for his extradition to India. India's Central Bureau of Investigation (CBI) has tied up with INTERPOL to apprehend Choksi.

Veerappa Gangaiah Siddhartha or VGS as we refer to him in this book, a first-generation entrepreneur, was born in a family that had owned coffee plantations for over a century. He introduced the newly-liberalized India of the 1990s to the café culture.

His Café Coffee Day outlets, the dominant business of Coffee Day Enterprises Limited (CDEL), is India's largest café chain. VGS was also a renowned tech investor who had reaped handsome profits by investing in IPOs of IT companies, including those of Infosys and Mindtree. The son-in-law of former Karnataka chief minister, S.M. Krishna, the then sixty-year-old VGS died by suicide in July 2019. He stated in his suicide note that pressure from private equity investors and harassment from a former director general (DG) of Income Tax had driven him to this decision.

Naresh Goyal, born in modest circumstances, began his career as an employee in his uncle's travel agency. How he acquired the wealth to launch one of post-independent India's earliest private sector airlines is subject to much conjecture and controversy. Goyal acquired a deep understanding of the airline industry, the network to raise vast sums of money for financing the capital-intensive airline business and the ingenuity to influence the government to structure legislation to benefit Jet Airways, and sometimes to the detriment of India's flag carrier, Air India. Yet, Jet Airways' failure to repay the vast debt it had accumulated resulted in Goyal's ouster. The airlines' equity investors witnessed a substantial diminution in the value of their investments.

In stark contrast to Naresh Goyal, Vijay Mallya was the scion of one of India's most profitable conglomerates, the United Breweries (UB) Group, and a successful liquor baron in his own right. He attempted to operate Kingfisher Airlines as a top-end, full-service airline priced at par with budget carriers. The investment he made in Kingfisher Airlines paled in comparison to the astronomical debt the airline incurred. It was unable to generate adequate cash flows to pay its employees and vendors and service its debt. Caught in a bind, Mallya, who was also a Member of Parliament (MP), surreptitiously flew to the UK using his diplomatic passport.[11,12] Despite Kingfisher Airlines' lenders seizing some of his stake in UB, the value of his remaining holdings in UB and personal wealth enable Mallya to continue leading a lavish life. In July 2021, a UK court declared Mallya bankrupt, enabling lenders to freeze his assets worldwide and secure repayment of the defunct Kingfisher Airlines' borrowings.[13]

Equally dramatic is Anil Ambani's riches-to-reported rags story. Soon after the demise of Reliance Group founder-CEO, Dhirubhai Ambani, in 2002, it became apparent that Anil Ambani and his older brother, Mukesh Ambani, did not see eye to eye. In 2005, the Reliance Group was divided between the two brothers, with Mukesh Ambani getting the lion's share. The exact quantum of cash that Mukesh paid Anil to make good the difference in the size of their bequests is subject to much speculation.[14,15] Anil began his empire-building spree with a bang. In addition to overseeing the expansion of the telecom, finance and power companies he had inherited, he made forays into defence and entertainment. The blockbuster Reliance Power IPO in 2008 made him the sixth richest man in the world with a net worth of $42 billion, which was just a billion short of the net worth of the world's fifth most affluent man—Mukesh Ambani.

Yet, Reliance Power's dependence on Mukesh's Reliance Industries for natural gas supplies, the siblings' conflict-ridden relationship and Anil's failure to generate sufficient earnings from his capital-intensive businesses to repay the sizeable debt did him in.

These developments did not go unnoticed. India's FY2017 Economic Survey observed, 'In a span of just three years, from 2004–05 to 2008–09, the amount of non-food credit doubled . . . By 2013, nearly one-third of corporate debt was owed by companies with an interest coverage ratio of less than 1, many of them in the infrastructure (especially power generation) and metals sector . . . In 2016, more than four-fifths of the non-performing assets were in the public sector banks, where the NPA ratio had reached almost 12 per cent.'

The inability of the excessively-indebted corporates to repay their debt resulted in banks accumulating non-performing assets (NPAs). The RBI applied prompt corrective action (PCA) norms to the weaker state-run banks that curtailed their ability to lend. This opened a window of opportunity for private sector banks and non-banking finance companies (NBFCs), whose share of lending for corporate investments and retail consumption increased. With India's annual GDP growth decelerating to below 7 per cent between 2016 and 2018, and dipping to 5.95 per cent in 2019, the original twin balance sheet problem, encompassing banks and corporates, had exacerbated to a four-balance-sheet challenge. NBFCs and property companies were also under stress.

However, it was not just a macroeconomic slowdown that landed certain banks and NBFCs in trouble. Their CEOs overlooked the wilful lending to counterparties, whose debt servicing ability was weak, if not non-existent. Of course, they personally benefitted from these transactions. The decisions of Yes Bank's Rana Kapoor, ICICI Bank's Chanda Kochhar and Infrastructure Leasing and Financial Services' (IL&FS) Ravi Parthasarathy caused monetary and reputational losses to their respective organizations. Legal action was initiated against these high-profile CEOs in 2018 and 2019.

This is not an exhaustive account of business failures in India during the first two decades of the twenty-first century. It is a narrative of the outcomes of the confluence of corporate head honchos, politicians, and regulators, some of whom possess certain distinguishing characteristics. What happens when CEOs who rush to build empires unmindful of their businesses' performance have preferential access to ignorant/ power hungry/venal politicians and are overseen by regulatory agencies that do not have adequate industry representation/were not proactive/possibly lethargic?

Lender Lapses: Financial institutions like ICICI Bank, Yes Bank and IL&FS, are subject to regulatory oversight. Rana Kapoor, Chanda Kochhar and Ravi Parthasarathy were intimately involved in providing strategic direction to the organizations they helmed, upholding governance standards and ensuring that their organizations were financially stable. Lending to high-risk borrowers and engaging in transactions that involved conflicts of interest was an inside job that debilitated their organizations' reputations and financial profiles.

Unlisted Corporates: The flagship enterprises of Nirav Modi and Subrata Roy were unlisted enterprises that had a contractual obligation to repay their borrowers. The terms and conditions that governed other equity investors' investments, if any, in their enterprises are not available in the public domain.

Listed Corporates: Anil Ambani, Naresh Goyal, VGS and Vijay Mallya, the subjects of this book, share some interesting similarities. They were promoter-CEOs who had invested their personal wealth into their businesses. Hence, they had much more skin in the game than executive CEOs of listed companies, whose compensation includes stock options. They were CEOs of listed corporates that were contractually duty bound to repay lenders and they had a fiduciary duty to preserve and augment shareholders' investment. They were also born within a decade of each other—Naresh Goyal in 1949, Vijay Mallya in 1955 and Anil Ambani and V.G. Siddhartha in 1959. These men were at a relatively early stage in their careers when India's economic liberalization occurred in the early 1990s. They had to contend with less red tape and had more access to financing than previous generations of entrepreneurs.

Yet, they stumbled.

Unfinished Business is a chronicle of contemporary Indian corporate history narrated through the professional trajectories of Anil Ambani, Naresh Goyal, VGS and Vijay Mallya. They were by no means unique in their proclivity for debt and penchant for politics. What caused their enterprises to struggle, while other similar organizations whose CEOs share these attributes seem to survive and even flourish?

How did India's pecuniary ecosystem—regulation, lenders' underwriting practices, investor due diligence, and the ease of doing business—influence the organizations that this quartet helmed? *Unfinished Business* explores the takeaways for entrepreneurs, regulators, lenders and investors.

Part 1: Coffee King

Chapter 1

At the Netravati

On the morning of Monday 28 July 2019, sixty-year-old Veerappa Gangaiah Siddhartha Hegde, popularly known as V.G. Siddhartha, or VGS, left his home in India's garden city and IT capital, Bengaluru, after informing his family that he was heading out to office and then to his family home at Sakleshpur in Hassan district, 221 kilometres from Bangalore.

VGS was, among other things, the founder of Café Coffee Day, India's largest chain of home-grown coffee cafés, and a famed investor in Indian technology companies, including Infosys, the second-largest listed company by market capitalization, and Mindtree. Born into a family that had owned coffee plantations for 140 years and was in the coffee business, in 1989, VGS married Malavika Hegde, the daughter of former Karnataka chief minister, S.M. Krishna. The couple have two sons—Amartya and Ishaan.

On this fateful day, VGS left home for office earlier than usual, at 8.00 a.m. rather than his usual 9.30 a.m. But Malavika and Krishna were not surprised. They knew VGS loved to visit his hometown and father's coffee estate. VGS left his office for Sakleshpur at 11.00 a.m. Along the way, VGS instructed his chauffeur, Basavaraj Patil, to steer the black Toyota Innova to Mangaluru instead, about 130 kilometres further down from Sakleshpur. The drive from Karnataka's capital city to Sakleshpur along the scenic NH75 highway would have usually taken around four to five hours. This detour entailed an additional three to four hours' drive.

One would have thought that VGS, at worst, would have been in a cautiously optimistic frame of mind. He had sold his stake in Mindtree for a consideration of ₹3269 crore ($435 million) in March 2019, thereby reaping a handsome profit of ₹2858 crore ($380 million).[1]

In filings made to the Bombay Stock Exchange (BSE) and the National Stock Exchange (NSE), VGS's flagship company, Coffee Day Enterprises Limited (CDEL) had stated that proceeds from the Mindtree stake sale would be used to 'pare down the Coffee Day Group's debt'.[2] CDEL's consolidated debt as of 31 March 2019 was a sizeable ₹7269 crore ($1.0 billion),[3] more than double the proceeds received from the sale of the Mindtree stake.

By 7.00 p.m., the Toyota Innova had reached the Ullal bridge that spans the Netravati river on the outskirts of Mangaluru. VGS instructed Patil to drop him off at the bridge and return an hour later. When Patil returned, there was no sign of VGS. He called his employer several times, but VGS's mobile was switched off. Panicking, Patil called VGS's family in Bengaluru, who immediately instructed him to lodge a complaint at the local police station.

In his statement recorded with the police, Patil stated that VGS had called around 15–20 people while being driven to Mangaluru and apologized to them. The chauffeur acknowledged that VGS had sounded upset. The police initiated a search operation amidst intense media scrutiny. On 29 July 2019, a typed letter, purportedly a suicide note, found its way on social media.

Suicide Note Goes Viral

This note that bore VGS's signature indicates the despondent state of mind of a man under pressure. Some of the statements in the note were, 'I have failed to create the right profitable business model despite my best efforts; I gave up as I could not take any more pressure from one of the private equity partners forcing me to buy back shares; Tremendous pressure from other lenders led to me succumbing to the situation; There was a lot of harassment from the previous DG[4] income tax in the form of attaching our shares on two separate occasions to block our Mindtree deal and then taking *position*[5] of our Coffee Day shares, although the revised returns have been filed by us; My team, auditors and senior management are totally unaware of my transactions. The law should hold me and only me accountable as I have withheld this information from everybody including my family.'

Expectedly, the letter went viral on social media. Kiran Mazumdar Shaw, the high-profile founder-CEO of the Indian biopharmaceutical firm, Biocon, tweeted, 'It [the note] seems to indicate that the Private Equity fund manager acted like a money lender 'n seems to have caused unbearable stress—needs to be investigated.'[6] 'Black letter day for start-ups & entrepreneurship in India!' tweeted Amit Ranjan, the co-founder of SlideShare.[7] A tweet from fugitive liquor baron and founder of Kingfisher Airlines, Vijay Mallya, read, 'I am indirectly related to VG Siddhartha. Excellent human and brilliant entrepreneur. I am devastated with the contents of his letter. The Govt Agencies and Banks can drive anyone to despair . . . Vicious and unrelenting.'[8] Mallya's stepbrother, Umesh Hingorani, is married to Malavika Hegde's sister, Shambhavi.

While the media was quick to point out that the Income Tax department had raided the residence and offices of VGS in 2017, CDEL's board of directors and the tax department questioned the veracity of the letter.[9] CDEL's board of directors stated that the data quoted in the letter was outdated and that it was uncharacteristic of VGS to write such a detailed note. The tax department opined that VGS's signature in the letter did not match the one in their records.

A Family Grieves

On 30 July 2019, as the search operation continued, a fisherman claimed to have sighted a man jumping off Ullal Bridge into the Netravati river the previous evening. Teams of the National Disaster Response Force, Coast Guard, Home Guard, fire services and coastal police, along with local fishermen, scoured the swollen Netravati river. The intense search had to be halted at nightfall and was resumed the following morning.[10]

At around 6.30 a.m. on 31 July 2019, a local fisherman found a body, later identified as VGS, that had washed ashore near Ullal, 500 metres away from the bridge, off which he had apparently jumped into the river. The mortal remains were moved to Wenlock Hospital at Chikkamagaluru for an autopsy. Crowds thronged the Wenlock Hospital to pay homage to the deceased son of the soil. VGS's mortal remains were subsequently handed over to his family and the 36-hour-long search operation came to an end.

In Bengaluru, politicians cutting across party lines made a beeline to the VGS residence. These included B.S. Yeddyurappa, then the chief minister of Karnataka's BJP-led government, Congress leader Siddaramaiah, Congress functionaries D.K. Shivakumar and B.L. Shankar, former prime minister of India and Janata Dal (Secular) leader, H.D. Deve Gowda and his son H.D. Kumaraswamy, former Karnataka chief minister.

VGS's mortal remains were subsequently transported from the family's coffee estate at Cheekanahalli village (near Chikkamagaluru) to the office premises of Amalgamated Bean Coffee, a Coffee Day group company, so that the public could pay their last respects. A voluntary 'bandh' was observed across Chikkamagaluru with commercial establishments shutting down as a mark of respect to VGS.

The media reported that at least 10,000 people were present at the family's estate during the funeral.

Figure 1: VGS's letter, dated 27 July 2019, to the CDEL board and employees[11]

V.G. Siddhartha

To our Board of Directors and Coffee day family,

After 37 years, with strong commitment to hard work, having directly created 30,000 jobs in our companies and their subsidiaries, as well as another 20,000 jobs in technology company where I have been a large shareholder since its founding, I have failed to create the right profitable business model despite my best efforts.

I would like to say I gave it my all. I am very sorry to let down all the people that put their trust in me. I fought for a long time but today I gave up as I could not take any more pressure from one of the private equity partners forcing me to buy back shares, a transaction I had partially completed six months ago by borrowing a large sum of money from a friend. Tremendous pressure from other lenders lead to me succumbing to the situation. There was a lot of harassment from the previous DG income tax in the form of attaching our shares on two separate occasions to block our Mindtree deal and then taking position of our Coffee Day shares, although the revised returns have been filed by us. This was very unfair and has led to a serious liquidity crunch.

I sincerely request each of you to be strong and to continue running these businesses with a new management. I am solely responsible for all mistakes. Every financial transaction is my responsibility. My team, auditors and senior management are totally unaware of all my transactions. The law should hold me and only me accountable, as I have withheld this information from everybody including my family.

My intention was never to cheat or mislead anybody, I have failed as an entrepreneur. This is my sincere submission, I hope someday you will understand, forgive and pardon me.

I have enclosed a list of our assets and tentative value of each asset. As seen below our assets outweigh our liabilities and can help repay everybody.

Regards,
V.G. Siddhartha

Source: 'I've failed, sorry to let you all down: V.G. Siddhartha's last letter found', The Economic Times, 30 July 2019

A Management Rejig

CDEL's board of directors swiftly swung into action. S.V. Ranganath, an independent director and retired civil servant, was appointed interim chairman, while Malavika was appointed as CEO. Ranganath had been the chief secretary, the senior-most executive role in the government of Karnataka, and was the chairman of the Coffee Board of India. The chairperson of CDEL's realty arm, Tanglin Developments, Nitin Bagamane, was appointed interim chief operating officer (COO). The board also constituted an executive committee comprising Ranganath, Bagamane and the chief finance officer, R. Ram Mohan, to manage the unforeseen crisis.

However, this management rejig did not stem the precipitous drop in CDEL's share price or avert a credit rating downgrade. CDEL's share price, which closed at ₹191.75 ($2.72) on 29 July 2019, almost halved in four days to ₹99.45 ($1.41) on 2 August 2019. Further, on 30 July 2019, ICRA, the Indian subsidiary of Moody's Investor Services, the international credit rating agency (CRA), placed CDEL's 'BBB+' investment grade rating on watch with negative implications. A week later, on 8 August, ICRA downgraded the rating by three notches to BB+ with a negative outlook. The rating rationale was stated as 'The rating revision considers the heightened refinancing risk for CDEL and group companies following developments due to the unexpected demise of the group's promoter—Mr. V.G. Siddhartha.' CDEL's credit rating was now in the non-investment grade territory on the domestic credit rating scale.

A month later, ICRA downgraded CDEL's rating by nine notches to 'D', the lowest on the credit rating scale denoting default or imminent default. ICRA opined, 'Coffee Day Global Limited, the flagship subsidiary of CDEL has delayed debt servicing for the month of August. Further, the Sical group of companies, which are part of the Coffee Day group have also witnessed delays in debt servicing.'[12]

The fate of the expansive conglomerate VGS founded hung in the balance.

On 25 August 2019, less than a month after VGS's demise, his father Gangaiah Hegde, who had been in a coma when his son passed away, took his last breath.

Chapter 2

Way to Wealth

Folklore has it that an Indian Muslim ascetic, Shah Janab Allah Magatabi, popularly known as Baba Budan, discovered the wonders of coffee during his pilgrimage to Mecca. He hid seven coffee beans in his beard and smuggled them from Yemen to Mysuru in India. It was then illegal to transport green coffee beans out of Arabia. Baba Budan planted the coffee beans on the Chandragiri hills in the Chikkamagaluru district of present-day Karnataka, the birthplace of coffee in India. Systematic cultivation of coffee started in 1670 CE, soon after Baba Budan planted the first coffee beans. Chandragiri was renamed Baba Budan Giri (*giri* means 'hill' in Kannada). Coffee cultivation soon spread to the adjoining areas of Wayanad (now in Kerala), Shevaroys and Nilgiris (in present-day Tamil Nadu).

The two most commonly consumed varieties of coffee globally—Arabica and Robusta—are cultivated here, and within 10 degrees north and south of the equator, in a region known as the 'coffee belt'. India is the seventh largest producer of coffee in the world, while Brazil is the largest.

The three southern states—Karnataka, Kerala and Tamil Nadu—account for more than 90 per cent of India's coffee output. While almost 80 per cent of India's coffee is exported, its consumption is widespread in Karnataka and Tamil Nadu, two states united in their passion for 'filter' coffee and deeply divided over the sharing of the waters of the Cauvery river. The rest of India remains predominantly a tea-drinking nation.

The Kannadigas and Tamilians, as those native to Karnataka and Tamil Nadu are known as, are passionate about their 'filter' coffee. The filter refers to a set of two cylindrical containers, one of which is perforated and placed on top of the other. Ground coffee powder is placed in the perforated cup and boiling hot water is poured over it. The deep brown, hot decoction that drips into the cup placed below is mixed with boiling hot milk and sugar in a stainless steel or silver glass known as tumbler. The boiling hot coffee is then swiftly poured into a flat-base cup known as *dabara*, and from the dabara back to the tumbler. This process is repeated a few times in quick succession to work up a froth and dissolve the sugar. The filter coffee is then consumed piping hot. The ratio of roasted 'pea berry' and 'A' coffee beans ground to form the coffee powder, whether or not chicory is added, and the creaminess of milk used determine the flavour, fragrance and consistency of the coffee. Filter coffee is also known as Mysuru filter coffee, Madras (now known as Chennai) filter coffee, Mylapore filter coffee, and Kumbakonam degree coffee. Mysuru, Madras, Mylapore, and Kumbakonam are cities, towns, and suburbs in Karnataka and Tamil Nadu renowned for their filter coffees.

VGS was born in a family that owned coffee plantations for over a century in Chikkamagaluru. Chikkamagaluru means younger daughter's town. This town (*uru*) is said to have been given as a dowry to the youngest (*chikka*) daughter (*magal*) of a local chieftain. VGS's paternal family had been growing coffee in India since 1870. Following a split in the family in 1956, VGS's father, Gangaiah Hegde, established his own enterprise that cultivated and traded coffee by acquiring an abandoned 479-acre (approximately 194 hectares) coffee estate in Chikkamagaluru.[1] Gangaiah's plantations prospered and so did the family's fortunes.

The only son of his parents, the 1959-born VGS did his BA Economics at St Aloysius College at nearby Mangaluru.

K.V. Kamath, the former CEO of ICICI Bank, K.K. Venugopal, India's attorney general since July 2017 and Arvind Adiga, author and Man Booker prize-winning author of *The White Tiger* are among the alumni of the Jesuit-run college, which was established in 1880.

While Gangaiah wanted his son to join the family business, VGS wanted to enlist in the Indian Army. He was a member of his college unit of the National Cadet Corps (NCC), a voluntary organization affiliated to India's armed forces that recruits cadets from schools and colleges and trains them to use basic arms and participate in parades. This experience evoked in VGS the desire to enlist for active military service. However, admission to India's National Defence Academy (NDA) requires passing a rigorous entrance examination, which VGS was unable to clear. Fate, obviously, had other plans for him.

Later, as a young entrepreneur, VGS confessed in an interview to the magazine *Outlook Business* that 'after failing to secure admission at the NDA, Economics slowly grew on me.'[2] He was drawn to the Communist Party of India's (CPI) public library situated close to Aloysius College. For a modest membership fee of ₹10 (less than US$1.0), members could borrow a book a week. Deeply impressed by Karl Marx's *Das Kapital*, VGS was convinced that communism was the way forward. However, he was soon disillusioned when he learnt that Stalin and his coterie 'lived like kings'.

This disillusionment kindled his interest in business. VGS stated, 'I wanted to be Robin Hood—rob the rich and give to the poor! But then I realized India was a really poor country. There was nothing to rob, really. It was better to make your own money—to get into business.'[3]

Gangaiah continued to try and persuade VGS to assist him in managing the family's extensive coffee plantations. VGS, however, had other ideas. Armed with a degree in economics, he was keen to head to Bombay—as India's financial capital Mumbai was then known—and embark on a career in share trading.

As an amateur investor while still in college, VGS had avidly followed stock market developments and the titans who dominated the Bombay Stock Exchange (BSE), the oldest stock exchange in Asia. Mahendra Kampani, who helmed the then decade-old home-grown investment banking firm JM Financial & Investment Consultancy Services, popularly known as JM Financial, was his idol.

JM Financial was the investment banking arm of Jamnadas Morarjee Securities, one of India's oldest stockbroking firms. It was set up in 1875, the same year as the BSE. The founding family's scions, Mahendra Kampani and his cousin, Nimesh Kampani, co-founded JM Financial in 1973, and it went on to become one of the most innovative firms on Dalal Street, the financial nerve centre of the city and home to the BSE. The company had, by 1980, filed the first offer document for listing securities of an Indian client with FSA, London, and had floated the first fully convertible debentures in India. JM Financial would go on to manage India's maiden equity warrant and deep discount bond issues; incorporate one of the country's earliest private sector mutual funds—JM Financial Asset Management—and list itself on the Bombay, Ahmedabad and Delhi Stock Exchanges by the mid-1990s. The International Finance Corporation (IFC) acquired a 15 per cent stake in JM Financial at the time of the latter's listing in 1992. In 1999, Morgan Stanley became a joint venture partner of JM Financial; the partnership lasted eight years. JM Financial bought out Morgan Stanley in 2007.

Mahendra Kampani went on to be widely regarded as a pioneer in stock market reforms, specifically online trading in India, and even served as the president of the BSE for one term, 1987 to 1988. He would later become a partner in his family's stockbroking firm, Jamnadas Morarjee Securities, while his more famous cousin Nimesh Kampani retained majority ownership of JM Financial. Mahendra Kampani tragically died at barely fifty-eight years of age in 2013, when a speeding taxi struck him as he was returning home from a routine early morning walk.

Keen to learn the tricks of the trade from the Kampanis, VGS persuaded his father to allow him to embark on a career in finance in Bombay.

In 1983, VGS travelled to Mumbai, located 885 kilometres north-west of Chikkamagaluru, by taking two buses—the first to Belgaum, a city located 400 kilometres north, and then another to Mumbai. He checked into a modest hotel in the Fort area, a stone's throw from Nariman Point, the business district of Mumbai. The rent for a room with a shared toilet at Hotel Midland was ₹120 ($12.20) per night. The following day, he headed to the offices of JM Financial at Nariman Point. Unfamiliar with elevators, VGS climbed six floors to the JM Financial office and requested for a meeting with Mahendra Kampani. He had not scheduled an appointment.

Fortunately for VGS, Kampani's secretary, a Tamil-speaking man from Bengaluru, allowed him to meet Kampani. Mahendra *bhai* ('brother' in Hindi), as VGS would come to address Kampani, graciously offered VGS a seat, water to drink and heard his eager spiel. Impressed with the young man's sincerity, Kampani asked VGS to observe the work of the research department and meet him again in the evening. When VGS met Kampani that evening, he was recruited as a management trainee in JM Financial's research division. It was a dream come true.

VGS would start working at 7.00 a.m. and would be the last to leave office, along with Kampani, after 9.00 p.m. He had no qualms about carrying Kampani's files and lunch box to the car. VGS found trading in stocks exciting and considered Kampani his 'guru' who taught him 'everything about investing'. It was during this period that VGS forged close friendships with leading traders and investors in Mumbai.

He worked for two years at JM Financial. It was an intense time during which VGS learnt the intricacies of stock trading and business operations. By 1985, he felt he had learnt enough and resigned. VGS then returned to Chikkamagaluru and persuaded his father for capital to start his own venture in Bengaluru.

He promised Gangaiah that if he did not succeed, the loss would be worth only about 100 acres of coffee estate, a fraction of the family's plantation. However, if he did, he would give jobs to the youth of Chikkamagaluru.

Gangaiah, while providing his only son the seed capital of ₹7.50 lakhs ($61,325), told him, 'When you lose it, you can come home!'

VGS used the money to purchase a plot of land for ₹5 lakhs ($40,900) and invested the rest in incorporating his own stock trading firm, Sivan Securities, in Bengaluru. His rationale was that the land was bound to appreciate in value in five years and would enable him to repay his father, even if Sivan Securities were to fail.

The BSE Sensex, India's first stock index, which comprises thirty of the nation's large-cap and most liquid stocks, was constituted in 1986, almost a year after the founding of Sivan Securities. In the 1980s, stock trading and investing in India was restricted to a clutch of stockbrokers, affluent individuals who traded and invested through their stockbrokers, corporates, banks, and government-owned institutions like the Unit Trust of India, Employees Provident Fund Organisation (EPFO), Life Insurance Corporation of India (LIC), General Insurance Corporation of India (GIC), and four non-life insurance companies.[4] Mutual funds were non-existent; India's first mutual fund—Kothari Pioneer Mutual Fund—was established in 1993. Retail participation in capital markets was much lower than it is in 2021, when retail activity surged thanks to the Covid-19 induced lockdown. According to Reserve Bank of India (RBI) estimates, 57 per cent of Indian households' financial assets were invested in bank deposits, 23 per cent in life insurance, 14 per cent in currency, and 7 per cent in mutual funds. As of March 2020,[5] households' direct investments in listed bonds and stocks was not even 1 per cent of households' financial assets; it was close to non-existent in 1985.

This situation, for VGS and Sivan Securities, had two implications. First, the practical absence of retail investors meant there was less 'noise' in the stock markets. Thus, stock traders and investors did not have to anticipate the actions of thousands of retail investors with varying degrees of knowledge while making trading and investment decisions. It was theoretically easier to anticipate the actions of the supposedly better-informed institutional investors. Second, low retail participation in stock markets meant there was a large untapped market that Sivan Securities could service. This translated into favourable growth prospects.

The BSE Sensex appreciated by 75 per cent over a five-year period to 1048 points in December 1990 from 598 points in January 1986. VGS's inherent interest in stock markets, training and close contacts with Mumbai's leading stock traders and brokers enabled him to profit from a rising stock market.

VGS recalled those heady days and described his market performance with the following words, 'My God, those were some days, such easy trades. The inter-market arbitrage was so high that I could make tons of money and that's what I did, thanks to my friends in Bombay. Buy something for ₹10 in Bombay, sell for ₹11 in Bengaluru, ₹11.50 in Jaipur and so on . . . Those were the days of quick gains and quick losses. There was never a dull day. I was lucky to have made my money in stocks . . . none of it involved any higher order thinking—they were just easy trades.'[6]

In an interview with web portal Rediff, VGS quipped, 'I was a very smart trader. I made money almost every day on the stock market. And with whatever money I made, I kept buying coffee plantations in Chikkamagaluru. My family background was such that I had a mindset that the new economy might not be the greatest, and that solid, tangible, physical assets like land were the best to own.'[7]

In spite of his success and increasing wealth, VGS remained firmly rooted in his community and simple in his ways. He always spoke respectfully with everyone and regularly participated in social events like weddings and house-warming ceremonies in Chikkamagaluru. The rising entrepreneur developed a reputation for having his heart in the right place.

In 1989, the thirty-year-old VGS was married to twenty-year-old Malavika Krishna, the younger daughter of Somanahalli Mallaiah Krishna or S.M. Krishna, who was by then an influential Congress politician. It was a marriage arranged by their two families. It was also the year Krishna became speaker of the Karnataka state legislative assembly. India was stumbling towards liberalization, which would open a floodgate of opportunities for VGS.

Chapter 3

The Rise

The year 1991 was a watershed moment in India's political and economic history. The Gulf War that waged from August 1990 to February 1991 between a coalition of thirty-five nations led by the US against Iraq's invasion and conquest of Kuwait, resulted in a 30 per cent increase in the average annual price of Dubai crude from $15.70 per barrel (bbl) in 1989 to $20.46 per bbl in 1990.[1] India, a major importer of crude oil, by end-June 1991, witnessed a precipitous decline in foreign exchange reserves to less than $1.0 billion, barely adequate to meet three weeks of imports.

During this crisis, international CRAs like Moody's and Standard & Poor's (S&P) downgraded India's sovereign credit rating to Ba2 and BB+ respectively. International lenders were unwilling to lend money without collateral to the Indian sovereign, which was rated non-investment grade. RBI was put in an embarrassing situation of having to pledge 67 tonnes of its gold to raise a $2.2 billion emergency loan from the IMF.

Most adult Indians who lived through this period are likely to attribute India's 1991 economic crisis to the Gulf War and the resultant hike in crude oil prices. While the sharp spike in crude oil prices was the proverbial last straw on the camel's back, the seeds of the 1991 economic crisis were sown in Government of India's fiscal mismanagement from, at least, 1979. A sharp and progressive deterioration of the fiscal and current account deficits financed by government borrowing pushed India into what economists Vijay Joshi and IMD Little call a 'policy-induced crisis par excellence'.[2]

The chaos the nation was experiencing was exacerbated by the assassination of former prime minister and Congress party's president, Rajiv Gandhi, amidst campaigning for the ongoing elections in May 1991. The 1991 general elections effectively comprised two sub-elections: the Congress party's performance during the first phase of polling, which had occurred before the assassination, was lacklustre; the sympathy factor herded a higher voter turnout and enabled Congress to make a clean sweep of the second and third phases.

The Congress, as the single largest party, formed a minority government even though it was 41 seats short of the 273-seat majority. Veteran Congress politician, P.V. Narasimha Rao, was elected prime minister, and former RBI governor and Cambridge- and Oxford-educated economist, Dr Manmohan Singh, was appointed finance minister.

Dr Singh, the seventh finance minister in six years, presented India's 'Epochal Budget' in July 1991, which kickstarted the country's economic liberalization.[3] This budget overhauled India's restrictive import-export policies, slashed import licensing and actively promoted exports. One of the industries to be liberalized in this budget was coffee.

The Call of Coffee

Did VGS foresee India's economic liberalization? He had started buying coffee plantations in 1985, and, by 1993, had accumulated almost 3,000 acres (1,200 hectares). VGS articulated the reason for doing so as follows.[4] 'Between 1985 and 1992, I made a killing in the stock market. It was during these years that I began purchasing coffee plantations that were being sold at distress rates of ₹6,000—₹20,000 per acre in the Chikmagalur area. What goes down must go up, that was my reading. Indian growers were then earning 35 cents per pound of coffee, when internationally, traders

Credit: Gujarat Cooperative Milk Marketing Federation Ltd. (Amul)

earn $1.20 per pound. But the situation was bound to improve, for India was in the throes of globalisation and I knew instinctively that we would be forced to learn to market our produce better, or sink.'

VGS set up the Amalgamated Bean Coffee Trading Company Limited (ABCL) in 1993 to process and trade coffee beans. The timing was fortuitous: a frost in Brazil had caused coffee output to decline and international coffee prices to double in 1994. By 1995, ABCL had become India's largest unroasted coffee exporter.

The Infosys IPO

In 1981, seven engineers—including N.R. Narayana Murthy and Nandan Nilekani—resigned from Patni Computers to start their own software company, Infosys Consultants Private Limited, in Pune. Infosys's seed capital of ₹10,000 ($250) was provided by Sudha, Narayana Murthy's wife, as a loan to her husband. These seven engineers shifted the headquarters of their start-up to Bengaluru in 1983. Infosys steadily built a solid franchise in providing software solutions to banking, insurance and manufacturing companies. It also differentiated itself from other Indian corporates by upholding high standards of ethics, governance and transparency since its inception.

Infosys, hitherto a privately-held company, launched an IPO in February 1993 to list its shares on Indian stock exchanges. Unfortunately, Mumbai was rocked by thirteen bomb explosions in March, engineered by mobster Dawood Ibrahim, in retaliation for the demolition of the Babri Masjid in December 1992. At the time, the Indian stock markets were yet to completely recover from the $1.0 billion securities scam— perpetrated by 'Big Bull' Harshad Mehta—that had unravelled in April 1992.

In these circumstances, investor sentiment was understandably tepid, due to which the Infosys IPO was undersubscribed. Underwriters are responsible for selling a company's shares to retail and institutional investors and are contractually bound to purchase the unsubscribed portion of the IPO. The Infosys IPO's underwriter, US investment bank Morgan Stanley, purchased a 13 per cent stake in the software company. Two other investors bought sizeable stakes in Infosys: VGS, who had by then befriended Nandan Nilekani, and the Mumbai-headquartered Enam Securities, an investment firm headed by one of India's star investors, Vallabh Bhansali. Thus, the Infosys IPO barely managed to mobilize the quantum of funds it had targeted to raise.

However, Infosys's equity investors were in for a pleasant surprise. On the day of its listing in June 1993, the company's share price opened at ₹145, which was 53 per cent higher than the ₹95 IPO price. The share price has, since, continued to rise and create history.

One can only speculate as to why investors behaved quixotically by not purchasing Infosys shares at the lower price of ₹95, but within a matter of weeks were scrambling to buy them at substantially higher prices. Was it a belated recognition of the company's strong fundamentals and robust prospects? Had investors finally shaken off the pessimism that had set in after the Harshad Mehta scam and the Bombay bomb blasts? Or was it FOMO (fear of missing out)?

Six months later, VGS sold his Infosys stake. At the time, the company's share price was trading at six times its IPO price.

He made a profit, but it was a decision he regretted later. By June 2019—a month before VGS's demise—Infosys's shares had generated a return of over 1600 per cent during the twenty-five-year period since listing, equal to an annual return of over 64 per cent.[5] Nevertheless, in the mid-1990s, VGS was a happy man courtesy the bumper profits from his Infosys investment and with ABCL flourishing. There was just one fly in the ointment.

The price of coffee, as a commodity, is volatile across the world and changes in response to multiple factors, including weather, geo-politics and exchange rate fluctuations. Therefore, the profits of companies that rely entirely on cultivating and selling coffee beans tend to fluctuate, in line with the price of coffee beans in international markets. For instance, $5.98, the peak average annual Arabica coffee price per kilogram in 2011, was close to 7.5 times the trough of $0.81 in 1963 during the sixty-year period from 1960 to 2020. As a coffee cultivator and trader, VGS realized that branding ABCL's coffee was essential for product differentiation and stabilizing profits.

Figure 1: Trend in Annual Coffee Prices[6]

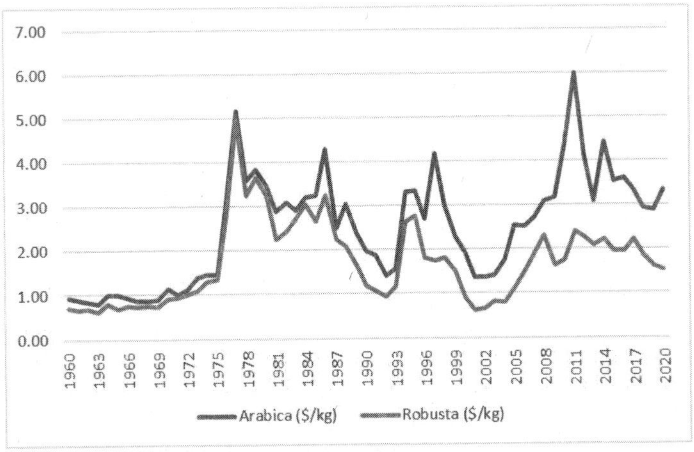

Source: World Bank Commodity Price Data

A Brand is Born

Two incidents strengthened VGS's conviction to enter the branded coffee business. The first was in 1994, when VGS met a representative of Tchibo GmbH, a German chain of coffee retailers and cafés and Europe's second largest processor of coffee, over dinner. Tchibo GmbH was already a customer of ABCL. Discussions during dinner made it evident to VGS that he could scale up his business and render it less susceptible to commodity price volatility by transforming ABCL into an integrated coffee player. In other words, he could start coffee cafés, retail branded coffee powder and hot beverage vending machines: businesses that would purchase coffee from the plantations at a price that ensured a reasonable profit. These 'downstream' businesses that would purchase coffee beans from ABCL would partially insulate the company from volatile international coffee prices and provide it with an assured clientele.

VGS quickly set up 450 small retail outlets in Karnataka and Tamil Nadu to sell freshly ground coffee powder.[7] These outlets were named 'Coffee Day Fresh & Ground'. Thus was born the 'Coffee Day' brand, which was designated as India's second most exciting food services brand in 2012 by *Brand Equity*, a publication of *The Economic Times*.

VGS then came up with the idea of setting up a coffee café on Brigade Road, Bengaluru's premier commercial centre and shopping district. He sought advice from friends. One of them rubbished the venture. The friend pointed out that piping hot, fresh filter coffee was available at ₹5 ($0.16) per cup at numerous budget and mid-market restaurants across Bengaluru. So, why should customers be willing to pay ₹25 ($0.80) for a cappuccino? Dissuaded, VGS dropped the plan, but the idea lingered around in his mind.

The idea of evolving into an integrated coffee player with businesses operating at all points of the coffee value chain such as cultivation, processing, distribution, and retailing, gained further credence during a visit to Singapore, six months later. The internet cafés in the city-state, where customers could access high-speed internet, socialize and snack, left an indelible mark on VGS. He was keen to replicate the model in India. When he informed the friend of his decision, the latter dissuaded him once again. Yet, this time, VGS held his ground. He shot back, 'We'll experiment. It should cost us ₹1.50 crore[8]—we'll try. No sweat even if we fail. I (will) put in ₹50 lakh[9] in deposit, ₹50 lakh for furnishing and ₹50 lakh for computers.'[10]

In the 1990s, IBM computers were expensive, as was internet connectivity. But VGS had it all worked out. In 1996, he inaugurated the first Café Coffee Day (CCD) outlet at Brigade Road with much fanfare. CCD was an instant hit, courtesy the chic interiors, a lip-smacking menu comprising a wide range of coffees and 'continental' snacks, and a tag line that summed it all—'Anything can happen over coffee'. The café offered a 64bps free wi-fi connection at a time when internet was accessible to just 10,000–15,000 IT professionals in India.

VGS's friend had clearly overlooked a burgeoning class of consumers—India's aspirational youth—who were exposed to global consumption trends in the aftermath of the 1991 liberalization and the fact that high-speed internet was still unavailable to most Indian households. VGS had not. He quipped later, 'You can't expect anything better than linear thinking from MBA folks.'

VGS was ecstatic with CCD's success. Most evenings, after finishing work at around 7.00 p.m., VGS and his wife would occupy a table by the window at the top floor of the CCD outlet. The couple would observe passers-by and try to guess who would step into their popular café.

Expansion

The flagship store's success spurred VGS to expand. By 2000, he had set up twenty-two cafés in south India. Though CCD was a novel concept, it could be easily replicated as there were no entry barriers. Soon, competitors had set up at least ten cafés each in Mumbai and New Delhi. Dismayed that competitors were replicating his idea and, in some instances, performing better than CCD, VGS decided to embark on an all-India roll out of CCD.

In 2000, VGS estimated that setting up stores across India would cost around ₹54 crore ($12.0 million). Guided by bankers, he availed US$12.0 million equity from the US-headquartered multinational insurance and finance conglomerate, AIG.

Nandan Nilekani disagreed with VGS's move to raising equity. When the two friends met for lunch at Bengaluru's Taj West End, Nilekani asked VGS if he could not have financed the expansion by liquidating his investments. He also questioned VGS about the necessity to dilute his promoter's stake and, if he had decided to list CCD, though the company was in its infancy.

VGS concurred with Nilekani's view that prematurely diluting his stake in CCD when he could monetize his personal investments to finance the expansion was unnecessary. The very next day, VGS reportedly took a flight to Hong Kong and negotiated with AIG to buy back the equity. In April 2003, VGS bought back AIG's equity stake in CCD at a price that he believed ensured a 'reasonable return' for the latter.

By 2004, 200 CCD outlets had been rolled out across India and the company steadily expanded thereafter. VGS later confessed that there was no need to raise $12 million equity from AIG. He remarked, 'Nandan has always been my go-to man for clarity in business. For moral support, Durgesh (a friend) is standing by. For everything else, but business, Malavika is always there.'[12]

The Tech Investor

VGS was a people's person. This, along with a fascination for tech firms, impelled him to invest in three IT start-ups in 1999: Ivega Corp, Kshema Technologies and, what would emerge as the jewel in the CCD Group's crown by 2019, Mindtree Limited.[13] VGS provided these start-ups with financial backing and gave the promoters a free hand. He reaped profits when the US-based

TCG Software purchased Ivega Corp for $5.0 million and the Bengaluru-headquartered Mphasis Limited purchased Kshema Technologies for $21.0 million.

Founder of Ivega, Giri Devanur, reminisced at the time of VGS's demise, 'Ivega was technically started in Coffee Day on Brigade Road due to the internet there. He was curious that a bunch of youngsters were using its internet. I got introduced to him there. He invested ₹10 crore[14] in Ivega. The discussions were done verbally on a Friday, we got the money on Monday before even the term sheet was signed.'[15]

Ashok Soota, former president of Wipro Infotech, along with nine other professionals, incorporated the IT firm, Mindtree Limited, in 1999. VGS was among the first investors in Mindtree. He acquired a 6.6 per cent stake in Mindtree by investing ₹44 crore ($10.2 million) in 1999. In 2011, he invested ₹85 crore ($18.2 million) and ₹40 crore ($8.6 million) for incremental stakes of 5.75 per cent and 2.05 per cent, respectively.[16] By 31 March 2019, VGS's 19.95 per cent stake in Mindtree had exceeded the promoters' stake of 13.32 per cent.[17] Retail and institutional shareholding in Mindtree was 66.63 per cent.

Mindtree's executive chairman, Krishnakumar Natarajan, opined in a February 2019 interview with Rediff, 'While as founders of the company, we have a lot more emotional intensity in the company, Siddhartha also has an equal level of commitment because in a way, he has also grown with the company.'[18]

Diversification

VGS's empire building aspirations were evident in the speed with which he incorporated numerous businesses. In 2000, he set up a financial advisory, research and broking firm, Way2Wealth Securities. The firm offered online accounts for retail and institutional investors to trade in bonds, stocks, mutual funds, derivatives and currencies. Way2Wealth Securities acquired Sivan Securities, the first enterprise VGS had incorporated in 1985.

In 2005, CCD's first overseas outlet was inaugurated at Vienna. In 2006, VGS founded the Global Village Tech Park, a state-of-the-art software technology park located in a lush 120-acre campus with a total built-up area of 3.3 million square feet, 13 kilometres away from Bengaluru central (railway) station. Several leading corporates moved into this facility including Accenture, Crompton Greaves, MPhasis, Sonata Software and Texas Instruments. Mindtree Limited also relocated its headquarters to this technology park.

The year 2006 also marked VGS's foray into the hospitality business with the inauguration of the upmarket resort, The Serai, at Chikkamagaluru. Perched on a verdant hillock in the Western Ghats, just 30 kilometres away from Karnataka's highest peak, Mullayanagiri, and 250 kilometres away from Bengaluru, The Serai (Chikkamagaluru) is a plush weekend getaway. Two more high-end resorts in Karnataka—The Serai Bandipur and The Serai Kabini—and one in Andaman Islands, Barefoot at Havelock, followed.

From coffee plantations to coffee cafés with internet to IT companies to hospitality, VGS wanted it all. In a move towards backward integration, VGS started a furniture unit around 2009, to capitalize on the huge depository of full-grown silver oak, teak, rosewood and mahogany trees from his 15,000 acres (6070 hectares) of coffee plantations in Chikkamagaluru.[52] The unit designed multi-purpose furniture for home, kitchen, office, hotels and retail outlets. It also manufactured multiple kinds of plywood, wood boards, panel sheets and beadings, making use of wood waste and saw powder. The furniture arm served a captive clientele of CCD outlets and The Serai resorts.

VGS's gaze then turned to offshore and multimodal logistics for cargo. In 2011, CDEL acquired a 20 per cent stake in Chennai-based SICAL Logistics—an integrated logistics company with a fifty-six-year track record—for approximately ₹100 crore

($21.43 million). VGS progressively increased his stake in SICAL Logistics, an entity listed on BSE and NSE, to 55.18 per cent by March 2019.

In 2011, VGS also leased 4.57 million acres (1.85 million hectares) of Amazonian forestland on a thirty-year lease from the Republic of Guyana to start a furniture business in India. The royalty VGS would pay the Guyanese government was not disclosed. VGS proposed to transport cut logs on chartered ships from the Guyanese capital, Georgetown, to the Mangaluru Port and then ferry them via road to his furniture plant in Chikkamagaluru.

Media reported VGS's intention to float a new venture, Dark Forest Furniture Company, whose product offerings would encompass modern, classic, ethnic furniture for homes, retail, offices, and lounges and lifestyle and entertainment furniture. The incumbent players in India's furniture industry—Godrej, Wipro, Featherlite, Reliance, Zuari and Durian—mostly focused on office furniture and/or relied on imported furniture.

The Altruistic Streak

There was more to VGS than being an entrepreneur. He felt a sense of responsibility and desire to give back to society. Even while expanding his horizons, VGS was committed to Chikkamagaluru. In 2002, he founded the SVGH Education Trust as a not-for-profit organization, dedicated to providing affordable premium quality education. One of the initiatives of this trust was the founding and management of a residential school, the Amber Valley School, in Chikkamagaluru.

Conscious of India's colossal unemployment problem, especially among the youth in semi-urban and rural areas, he set up an institute that offered training in the hospitality sector for the youth in Chikkamagaluru district. The Yuva Institute was set up under the aegis of the VGS-managed SVGH Trust at a sprawling campus in Muguthihalli on the outskirts of Chikkamagaluru. The institute offers a one-year certificate course in hospitality management, culinary skills and commercial operations in the hospitality sector. In addition to free education, food and accommodation, students are paid ₹1750 (around $25) per month as stipend.

By 31 March 2015, CDEL had reported consolidated assets of ₹6000 crore ($971 million). VGS, who had started his entrepreneurial journey in 1985 with a seed capital of ₹7.50 lakh (around $61,325) received from his father, had achieved an 80,000-fold growth in assets over a period of three decades.

Now, the conquistador in him was keen to catapult CDEL from a mid-sized conglomerate to a blue chip, for which listing the stock was essential.

Chapter 4

The Listing

CDEL's exponential expansion was fuelled by VGS's vision, his wide circle of well-connected friends and his ability to rope in experienced people with great networks to helm key positions in his companies.

A key person on his management team was Sakalespur Vishweswaraiya Ranganath (S.V. Ranganath), who took charge of the company following VGS's sudden death. Ranganath was appointed as an independent non-executive director on CDEL's board of directors ahead of the company's listing. A 1975-cadre officer of the highly competitive Indian Administrative Services (IAS), Ranganath had held several high-profile bureaucratic positions, including senior-most roles in Karnataka's bureaucracy. He was the state's chief secretary (2009–2013), principal secretary to the chief minister of Karnataka and the chairman of the Indian Coffee Board. After his retirement from government service, Ranganath was appointed as the non-executive chairman of the state-owned development finance institution, IFCI Ltd (2014–2017). The media described Ranganath as an honest bureaucrat. On weekends, he would not use his official car with chauffeur and instead preferred local transport. He reportedly used auto rickshaws to accompany his grandkids for outings in Bengaluru.

Another business associate of VGS was Mangalore Devadas Mallya (M.D. Mallya), who was earlier the chairman and managing director of the state-owned Bank of Baroda. Like Ranganath, he was appointed as an independent non-executive director on CDEL's board before the company's listing. He held this role till his demise in November 2018. Bank of Baroda's lending to CDEL is documented since its 2015 IPO.

Poornima Jairaj was a key person who headed Global Technology Ventures—CDEL's private equity arm. She is married to senior bureaucrat, K. Jairaj, former additional chief secretary of Karnataka. Subroto Bagchi, a co-founder of Mindtree and former chief executive of IT major Wipro's global R&D division, was a trustee of Amber Valley School. So were Poornima Jairaj and Javagal Srinath, a cricketer who represented India during 1991–2003.

The Nexus of Business and Politics

VGS's two high-profile friends were Nandan Nilekani and Dodalahalli Kempegowda Shivakumar, popularly known as D.K. Shivakumar. VGS considered Nilekani, who was four years older than him, an elder brother and mentor. Nilekani later succeeded Murthy as Infosys CEO and went on to become the chairman of the Unique Identification Authority of India (UIDAI), a Government of India (GoI) initiative that designed and implemented the world's largest biometric identity system, Aadhaar.

On the other hand, Shivakumar, a politician affiliated to the Congress party, was a minister in the Karnataka state government for energy, medical education and water resources between 2014–2019. In March 2020, Shivakumar was elected president of the Karnataka Pradesh Congress Committee, the state unit of the Congress party. He was a protégé of Krishna, VGS's father-in-law. All three men and H.D. Deve Gowda, India's former prime minister, belonged to Karnataka's closely knit Vokkaliga caste. The Vokkaligas and the Lingayats, a Kannadiga sect who worship Shiva, together constitute around a quarter of Karnataka's population and dominate the state's political landscape.

VGS's political connections brought him a fair share of adverse media coverage. Accusations of land grabbing and using his political connections to further his business grew in tandem with his acquisition of coffee plantations and real estate. VGS vehemently refuted these charges. In a July 2000 interview with Rediff, he stated, 'I had already bought most of my coffee plantations before my marriage, which took place in 1989.' VGS was even alleged to have played a role in the release of Karnataka's matinee idol, Rajkumar, after he was kidnapped by sandalwood smuggler Veerappan.

A Forest Brigand

The 1929-born Singanalluru Puttaswamaiah Muthuraj, popularly known by his stage name Dr Rajkumar, is the only film star to have won both the Dada Saheb Phalke award, India's highest award for acting, and the National Award for singing. He was also the recipient of the Padma Bhushan, India's third-highest civilian award. On 30 July 2000, Rajkumar, his son-in-law Govindaraju, and two others were abducted from the actor's home at his birthplace, Gajanur, a village in Tamil Nadu close to the state's border with Karnataka. The kidnapping was masterminded by the notorious brigand, Veerappan, who operated from the forests bordering the two states and engaged in sandalwood smuggling, poaching, abduction and banditry.

As ransom, Veerappan demanded the release of his associates who were imprisoned under the now defunct Terrorism and Disruptive Activities (Prevention) Act (1985–1995) and Prevention of Terrorism Ordinance, 2001. The Karnataka and Tamil Nadu governments were about to release Veerappan's associates when the Supreme Court of India, in response to a public interest litigation, forbade the state governments from doing so.

Rajkumar was in Veerappan's custody for 108 days, during which time civil unrest broke out in Karnataka and a bandh was announced on 22 September. The police force and S.M. Krishna, as Karnataka's sitting chief minister, sought assistance from M. Karunanidhi, then Tamil Nadu chief minister. The state dispatched R. Gopal, the editor of Tamil magazine *Nakkheeran*, to negotiate with Veerappan. Gopal had conducted several such discussions with Veerappan before and his videotaped interviews with Veerappan were telecast on national TV. Rajkumar and his associates were finally released unharmed in November 2000.

In November 2002, Konark Publishers published a book penned by C. Dinakar, *Veerappan's Prize Catch: Rajkumar*.[1] Dinakar, whom certain Bangalore-based journalists describe as a loose cannon, was Karnataka's director general of police (DGP) during Rajkumar's abduction. He alleged that the Karnataka government had paid Veerappan a ransom of ₹20 crore ($3.40 million) and that VGS, the deputy inspector general of police (DIG) T. Jayaprakash, and Rajkumar's wife, Parvathamma, had ferried the cash in instalments to M. Karunanidhi's residence in Chennai.[2]

Gopal refuted Dinakar's allegation, though we will never know if the denial was to buttress his role as the sole negotiator in this escapade. The Delhi High Court, in February 2007, dismissed the defamation case that VGS had filed against Dinakar, calling it frivolous. In September 2014, the court dismissed VGS's appeal.[3]

The Allure of Private Equity

Media coverage of VGS's activities after the Veerappan–Rajkumar episode was mostly related to his businesses, which started attracting international attention. By 2010, CCD had emerged as the largest café chain in India. Rising incomes, a burgeoning middle class and a large, aspirational population of youth meant that CCD could consolidate its market leadership thanks to its first mover advantage. Its growth prospects were favourable.

In March 2010, two US private equity (PE) firms, Kohlberg Kravis Roberts & Co (KKR) and New Silk Route Partners (NSR), and the UK-headquartered Standard Chartered Private Equity

(SCPE) announced their intended investment of ₹960 crore ($210 million) in CDEL—the company that owned VGS's coffee, financial services and hospitality businesses.[4] It was then known as Coffee Day Resorts; and was renamed Coffee Day Enterprises Limited during its 2015 listing. This was Coffee Day Resorts' largest financing since inception.

SCPE was the private equity arm of Standard Chartered Bank, which the bank had spun out in December 2018 as an independent private equity firm. Affirma Capital, KKR and NSR have interesting antecedents. KKR was founded by three bankers—Jerome S. Kohlberg Jr., Henry Kravis and George Roberts—who quit the US investment banking firm Bear Stearns to start a leveraged buyout (LBO) firm.

In his book *Merchants of Debt*, George Anders chronicles KKR's emergence as the pre-eminent firm that facilitated over 200 LBOs with a lean organization structure and minimal equity invested by its founders. Anders writes, 'KKR is famous for leading America on a daredevil dash into high-debt finance in the 1980s. The firm remains in the headlines, even today, having nimbly recast itself as a time-tested leader in what is now referred to as the global private-equity business.'[5]

NSR was founded by the India-born Rajat Gupta, McKinsey & Company's first foreign-born managing director; Raj Rajaratnam, former managing director of the hedge fund, Galleon Group; Parag Saxena, former managing director of Invesco Capital and Mark Schwartz, the chairman of Goldman Sachs Asia.[6] When Gupta and Rajaratnam were embroiled in insider trading allegations and subsequently convicted, the duo was replaced by Victor Menezes, Citigroup's former vice chairman. NSR is focused on investing in India and other high-growth Asian economies.

PE investors tend to undertake riskier investments than banks. They invest in companies with promising business models that are not necessarily profitable. PEs earn the bulk of their profits by selling their shares in investee companies at the time of the latter's IPOs. In other words, retail and institutional investors acquire stakes in investee companies at substantially higher share prices than the prices at which the PEs invested, thereby providing PEs profitable exits. The handsome profits PEs make while exiting their successful investments cover their unsuccessful investments, operating expenses and distributions to the entities that invest in PEs. KKR's George Roberts' quote sums up the PE investment philosophy best—'I don't think you should ever fall in love with anything except your wife and kids.'[7]

VGS's thirst for growth and the need to stymie the mushrooming of CCD clones prompted him to avail of PE financing.

Of the ₹960 crore ($210 million) investments that the Coffee Day Group secured from the three private equity companies, only 9 per cent (₹88 crore, $19 million) was equity. While KKR practically made the entire equity investment, NSR made a nominal investment of ₹1.77 lakh ($3,900). The balance 91 per cent was in the form of hybrid securities. SCPE had subscribed to ₹240 crore ($52 million) of compulsorily convertible preference shares (CCPS). NSR and KKR also invested in compulsorily convertible debentures worth ₹360 crore ($79 million) and ₹272 crore ($59 million) respectively.

By virtue of its equity investment, KKR became CDEL's part-owner. KKR nominated Sanjay Omprakash Nayar, the CEO of KKR India Advisors, as a non-executive director to CDEL's board. He remained on the CDEL board until November 2019, three months after VGS's demise.

The CCD Juggernaut Continues to Roll

Armed with the PE firm-financed war chest, VGS's expansionary spree continued. His first purchase after obtaining PE financing was in November 2010—a 52.8 per cent stake in the Chennai-headquartered listed logistics firm, SICAL Logistics, for

₹200 crore ($44 million). SICAL, an investment that consumed 21 per cent of CDEL's PE financing, was meant to cater to supply chain requirements of both the Coffee Day Group and external clients. This logistics firm had a delivery network that encompassed an exclusive walk-in berth at Chennai port for ships carrying bulk cargo; a container terminal at Tuticorin port; and 225,000 square feet of storage across 17 warehouses. SICAL owned and regularly contracted a fleet of more than 1,000 transport vehicles and container freight stations at three locations across India.

SICAL's chairman, Ashwin Muthiah, was a scion of the promoter family and the founder M.A. Chidambaram's grandson. In March 2007, IDFC Private Equity had acquired a 13.28 per cent stake in SICAL for ₹116 crore ($28 million). By 2010, the cash-strapped Ashwin Muthiah was looking to raise funds to repay ₹223 crore ($50 million) debt falling due in March–April 2011.[8]

IDFC Private Equity exited its investment in SICAL at a loss when it sold its stake to Jupiter Capital Pvt Ltd, an investment company owned by Bengaluru-based entrepreneur-politician, Rajeev Chandrasekhar. IDFC sold its stake at ₹83.40 ($1.82) per share, less than half the price of ₹222 ($5.37) per share it had paid in March 2007. For Jupiter Capital, this acquisition was a purely financial investment and it declined to assume the two board seats IDFC Private Equity had in the company. Four years later, Sudhakar Gande, a director at Jupiter Capital stated, 'We have no plans to raise our stake in Sical either.'[9]

We do not know if IDFC Private Equity sold its SICAL stake at a loss due to business considerations or if there was some behind-the-scene action to ensure VGS had a free hand in running SICAL.

Storm Clouds?

On 29 October 2012, the UK-based newspaper, The *Guardian*, reported, 'During the past ten days, sweaty queues of up to

50 people have formed outside an old colonial building in downtown Mumbai, while a security guard operates a one-in-one-out policy. These hopefuls are not trying to get into an edgy new nightclub or shake hands with a visiting politician. They are waiting for up to an hour to go to Starbucks.' This was the flagship Starbucks café, inaugurated on 19 October 2012, at the historic Elphinstone Building in Mumbai. It is a stone's throw away from Bombay House, the headquarters of Tata Sons, the Tata Group's holding company. Tata Starbucks Limited, a 50:50 joint venture between Starbucks and Tata Global Beverages, the non-alcoholic beverages arm of the Tata Group, was formed to oversee Starbucks' India franchise.

VGS, by 2012, was known as India's Howard Schultz, the iconic CEO of Starbucks Coffee Company. Schultz, who was Starbucks' CEO from 1986 to 2000, was responsible for the evolution of Starbucks into a global brand. Schultz quit Starbucks in 2000 but returned in 2008 to rejuvenate the company, which had turned into a desultorily performing behemoth. Schultz was Starbucks' CEO till 2017, during which time he streamlined the company and masterminded Starbucks' business strategy for the predominantly tea-drinking nations of China and India.

Starbucks India's foray served to intensify VGS's competitive spirit. Unlike in the US, where Starbucks is a high street chain, Tata Starbucks positioned the Starbucks cafés in India as premium outlets. The price of food and beverages at Starbucks' Indian outlets were two to three times higher than those at CCD. This was completely lost on VGS. Unmindful of Starbucks' positioning as an upmarket café chain, the mid-market-focused CDEL unnecessarily intensified its expansion spree.

By 31 December 2014, CDEL was operating 1,488 CCDs, 590 Coffee Day Xpress Kiosks, 28,777 vending machines, and 424 'Fresh and Ground' outlets. India's second-largest café chain, Barista, which was founded in 2000, was a distant second with 169 outlets, including 25 franchised outlets.

Growth versus Profits

So, how was this expansion financed? CDEL's IPO prospectus dated 25 June 2015 and its FY2015 annual report shed light on the company's financial performance for the six-year period from 1 April 2009 to 31 March 2015. The company had reported post-tax losses in four of the six years—FY2010, FY2013, FY2014 and FY2015. The aggregate losses of ₹167 crore ($29 million) were almost five times the aggregate profits of ₹37 crore ($8 million) in FY2011 and FY2012.

This meant that CDEL was raising external capital—debt, equity and hybrid securities—to finance its operations and expansion. From FY2010 to FY2015, debt had more than doubled to a staggering ₹4,662 crore ($754 million). L&T Finance—the subsidiary of the engineering conglomerate Larsen & Toubro Limited (L&T), which would, in 2019, launch India's first hostile acquisition bid for an IT company, Mindtree Limited—was also a lender to CDEL, albeit with a low loan outstanding of ₹125 crore ($20 million).

Sizeable and recurring losses had eaten into CDEL's net worth, which is equity share capital plus post-tax profits minus dividends. Despite the company also raising ₹696 crore ($138 million) equity ahead of its IPO, net worth had only marginally increased to ₹1058 crore ($171 million) as of March 2015 from ₹976 crore ($204 million) in March 2010.[10]

Thus, the ratio of net worth to consolidated assets, a metric that measures owners' investment in a company relative to its total assets, had more than halved to 9 per cent in FY2015 from 22 per cent in FY2010. In other words, the share of equity, a relatively safer though dilutive source of capital from the owners' point of view, was low and declining.

But neither VGS nor the PE investors were willing to allow weak financial performance to come in the way of what they thought was a good (investment) story. They decided to proceed with the listing of CDEL.

The Bonus Issue

In June 2015, CDEL filed its IPO prospectus with India's securities and commodity markets regulator, the Securities and Exchange Board of India (SEBI). The IPO targeted to raise ₹1,150 crore ($179 million). A ₹318 ($4.96) premium was ascribed to a share of ₹10 ($0.16) face value, translating to a share price of ₹328 ($5.11).

Kotak Investment Banking, Citigroup, Morgan Stanley, Axis Capital, Edelweiss Financial Services and Yes Bank were appointed lead managers to the IPO. CDEL's IPO, which was the largest IPO in India in three years, opened on 14 October and closed on 16 October 2015.

A group of marquee investors, including Nandan Nilekani, Rakesh Jhunjhunwala, Radhakishan Damani, Ramesh Damani and, Ketan and Sonal Sheth, together purchased ₹100 crore ($15.59 million) worth equity shares ahead of CDEL's IPO. Of this ₹100 crore, Nilekani invested the lion's share of ₹75 crore ($11.69 million) in his individual capacity. Roping in marquee investors ahead of the IPO was an astute move to ensure that it received a favourable response.

Rakesh Jhunjhunwala, one of India's most prominent equity investors, considers the two Damanis, renowned investors on Dalal Street who are not related, his mentors. Radhakishan Damani, also known as India's retail king, is the founder of the listed Avenue Supermarts Limited which runs the D-Mart retail chain. In 2020, Forbes ranked Radhakishan Damani as the fourth richest Indian and seventy-eighth in its global billionaires list. Ramesh Damani is the chairman of Avenue Supermarts.

Interestingly, another early investor in CDEL was Bennett, Coleman & Company, a media conglomerate, also known as the Times Group. Bennett, Coleman publishes India's most widely circulated English newspaper, The *Times of India*. In October 2012, Bennett Coleman purchased 1,71,038 shares in CDEL for ₹45 crore ($8.42 million).

By May 2015, five months before CDEL's October 2015 IPO, VGS and his family, KKR, NSR, Bennett, Coleman, Nilekani, Jhunjhunwala, the two Damanis and the Sheths, had collectively invested ₹481 crore.

On 8 May 2015, CDEL's shareholders approved a 1:7 bonus issue. This meant that a shareholder owning 100 shares would receive 700 shares free of cost. Shareholders benefitted from this bonus issue on two counts. First, a bonus issue enabled the company to reward its shareholders with higher dividends without them having to buy more shares. Second, and more importantly, when a company allocates bonus shares ahead of its IPO, the gains or losses the early investors earn or incur when share prices appreciate or decline after listing are amplified or reduced.

An example will facilitate understanding the second point. Let's assume an investor, X, purchases one share of an unlisted company at ₹800. This company undertakes a 1:7 bonus issue, due to which X receives seven more shares. So, X now has eight shares for ₹800, thereby reducing her average cost of buying one share to ₹100. Let's also assume the company lists its shares through an IPO and the listing price is ₹800 per share. If the share price were to appreciate to ₹900 per share, X's eight shares would be worth ₹7200. Hence X's gain will be ₹6400, i.e., ₹7200 less ₹800. In the absence of the bonus issue, X's gain would have been ₹100. X will make a loss only if the share price were to decline to ₹99, i.e., the share price crashes by almost 88 per cent! In this instance, X would have incurred a ₹8 loss as the market value of her portfolio will be ₹792, which is lower than the ₹800 she spent on buying one share.

This example also explains why amateur investors who replicate the investment decisions of the likes of Warren Buffet and Rakesh Jhunjhunwala seldom earn the stratospheric returns these legendary investors do. The timing of an investment decision, be it purchase or sale of shares, is as critical as stock picking. Access to a network of market participants—issuers, brokers, investors—is also essential to be able to trade stocks legally at attractive prices.

CDEL generously awarded bonus shares to the promoters (VGS and family), PE investors and the marquee investors to ensure that the market value of their stakes appreciated considerably on listing day. The bonus issue was the sweetener that incentivized the astute Jhunjhunwala and Damanis to invest in the loss-making and highly indebted CDEL. Pre-IPO bonus issues, though legal and by no means unique to CDEL, enable pre-IPO investors to profit at the expense of retail and institutional IPO investors.

Interestingly, VGS and his family had invested in CDEL shares at a price of ₹22.83 ($0.36 in 2015), which was 93 per cent lower than the IPO price of ₹328 per share ($5.11). Similarly, the private equity investors—KKR and NLS—had invested at a share price that was 33 per cent lower than the IPO price. While Bennett, Coleman had more or less invested at par, the rest of the marquee investors had invested at a price that was close to 11 per cent higher than the IPO price! One wonders if the marquee investors buying CDEL shares at a price higher than the IPO price is a reflection of their confidence in CDEL or the Indian capital markets or they had hedged their purchases using derivatives.

Now let's return to the chronicle of CDEL's IPO.

Litmus Test

The IPO elicited subscription orders for 1.8 times the number of shares offered.[11] While retail and non-institutional categories were subscribed only 90 per cent and 53 per cent respectively, sizeable orders from institutions resulted in the IPO being oversubscribed. Strong institutional demand was a testimony to VGS's close relationships with banks and other financial institutions and the marketing skills of the issue's lead managers.

Another disappointment awaited VGS on 2 November 2015, the listing day. CDEL's share price opened at ₹313 ($4.88), touched a high of ₹318 ($4.96), a low of ₹270 ($4.21), and closed at ₹270.15; almost 18 per cent below the ₹328 ($5.11) offer price.

Figure 1: Pre-IPO Equity Allotment

Investors	Period of Investment	Shares Including Bonus Issue	Investment (₹ Crore)	Average Price (₹)	(Discount) / Premium to IPO Price
VGS & Family	June 15 2008 - May 18 2015	108,604,712	247.91	22.83	-93.04%
KKR Mauritius PE Investments	Mar 30 2010 - May 18 2015	4,000,000	88.40	221.00	-32.62%
NLS Mauritius LLC	Mar 31 2010 - May 18 2015	800	0.02	221.00	-32.62%
Bennett Coleman & Company Limited	Oct 11 2012 - May 18 2015	1,368,304	45.00	328.88	0.27%
Nandan Nilekani	Mar 2 - May 18 2015	2,068,960	75.00	362.50	10.52%
Rare Enterprises, Rakesh Jhunjhunwala	Mar 2 - May 18 2015	275,856	10.00	362.50	10.52%
Derive Investments, Radhakishan Damani	Mar 2 - May 18 2015	275,856	10.00	362.50	10.52%
Ramesh Damani	Mar 2 - May 18 2015	82,752	3.00	362.50	10.52%
Ketan Sheth & Sonal K Sheth	Mar 2 - May 18 2015	55,168	2.00	362.50	10.52%
Total		**116,732,408**	**481.32**	**41.23**	**-87.43%**

Source: CDEL IPO Prospectus, 25 June 2015

Market observers attributed several reasons for the stock's poor performance. Some analysts felt that the shares were over-priced. 'We thought ₹275–285 ($4.29–4.44) would have been the ideal price range for this IPO. I think companies should learn from this case and try to keep the pricing attractive, by leaving enough on the table for investors,' Amisha Vora, joint managing director of Mumbai-headquartered brokerage firm, Prabhudas Lilladher, said,[12] 'The Sensex has fallen for six straight sessions, losing 3.32%, over the period, as investors gave the thumbs down to lacklustre corporate earnings,' observed the Indian financial daily, *Mint*.[13] Other reasons cited were the impending results of the Bihar state elections, CDEL's complex organization structure that encompassed multiple diverse businesses resulting in a conglomerate discount, the company's weak financial performance, and a probable decline in overall confidence in the Indian economy.

While all these reasons may be valid, one cannot help but benchmark CDEL's IPO performance with that of Interglobe Aviation Ltd, which operated the low-cost air carrier IndiGo. Interglobe Aviation's IPO, which was more than twice as large as CDEL's at ₹3018 crore ($470 million), was floated a fortnight later. The IPO was 5.15 times oversubscribed. On its listing day, Interglobe Aviation's share price appreciated by almost 15 per cent over its listing price of ₹765 ($11.92) and closed at ₹878 ($13.69).[14]

Most of the marquee investors, including Rakesh Jhunjhunwala, Radhakishan Damani and Ramesh Damani, had sold their stake in CDEL by March 2016. Bennett Coleman too sold its stake by March 2018. The marquee investors had sold the CDEL shares at a loss despite the 1:7 bonus issue. As the private equity investors had invested in CDEL at close to 11 per cent discount to the IPO price, there was no erosion in the market value of their investment till VGS's demise in July 2019. Within days of VGS's demise, the CDEL share price fell much below ₹100 ($1.42) or more than 50 per cent of the ₹221 ($3.44) at which they were allotted CDEL shares in 2015.

Notwithstanding the CDEL IPO's dismal listing, VGS was ranked 1605th on the 2015 Forbes billionaires list with a reported net worth of $1.15 billion (around ₹7377 crore). This was the only year in which he featured in the Forbes billionaires list. With the CDEL share price heading south in the subsequent years, VGS no longer featured in the billionaires list.

The pressure on CDEL was mounting. The conglomerate faced the onerous task of generating profits, moderating its debt and ensuring that the IPO investors, the market value of whose holdings had depreciated on listing day, earned a decent return.

Chapter 5

The Meltdown

There was an explicit acknowledgement of weak financial performance in CDEL's IPO prospectus. The company identified generating post-tax losses in four of the preceding six years and its indebtedness as key risk factors. Of the ₹1150 crore ($179 million) IPO proceeds, CDEL proposed to use ₹633 crore ($99 million or 55 per cent of IPO proceeds) for loan repayment, 25 per cent for expansion, and the balance 20 per cent for general corporate purposes.

Did the company keep up its commitment to deleverage (repay debt) using the IPO proceeds? Did CDEL and its multiple constituent businesses turn profitable after listing? These issues are key to understand what motivated VGS to undertake that fateful drive to the Netravati on 28 July 2019.

CDEL repaid ₹959 crore ($148 million) debt, 50 per cent more than the target stated in its IPO prospectus. In fact, FY2016 is the only year during the decade ending March 2019 that the company achieved a debt reduction. However, CDEL's reported debt, which had declined after its IPO to ₹3703 crore ($570 million) as of end-March 2016, almost doubled in the subsequent three years to ₹7269 crore ($1 billion).

Why was CDEL unable to rein in its debt?

CDEL continued to incur sizeable capital expenditures, financed entirely through debt. The company incurred ₹2974 crore

(\$445 million) capital expenditures during the four years between FY2016–FY2019. This accounted for 83 per cent of the ₹3566 crore (\$485 million) incremental debt CDEL availed of during the same period. However, profits did not increase in tandem with higher investments. This did not deter VGS from continuing his expansionary spree.

CDEL has, since FY2014, reported the performance of its six businesses—Coffee Day Global, SICAL Logistics, Way2Wealth (financial services), Tanglin Developments (leasing of commercial space), The Serai (hospitality) and Coffee Day Trading (private equity investments). The coffee vertical, Coffee Day Global, is CDEL's largest business, accounting for about half its consolidated revenues and a third of its operating profits. The financial services and hospitality businesses started generating operating profits consistently from FY2015 and FY2016 respectively.

High operating costs and interest expenses depressed CDEL's profitability. Bala Naidu, who was part of the Goldman Sachs team that financed CDEL said, 'VGS was keen to ensure Café Coffee Day became the largest café chain in India. He entered into long term leases of seven to ten years in prime localities when lessors were willing to contract two- to three-year leases. This strategy worked to his disadvantage when commercial rents started declining.'[1] In FY2017, the first year after listing, CDEL reported a modest post-tax profit of ₹82 crore (\$12 million).

Yet, VGS was unable to heave a sigh of relief.

Raid

On 3 August 2017, a Firstpost column quipped, 'When poachers do not succeed, send in the raiders.'[2] The columnist, T.S. Sudhir, was commenting on the raids initiated by the IT department at various properties owned by Shivakumar, VGS's friend and Karnataka's energy minister, who was one of the most affluent politicians in the state at the time. How did these raids on a prominent politician work to VGS's detriment?

The Congress party Member of Parliament (MP) from Gujarat, Ahmed Patel, was standing for re-election to the Rajya Sabha, also known as the Council of States or the Upper House of Indian parliament. It is members of the (state) legislative assembly (MLAs) who elect Rajya Sabha MPs.

The Congress party was concerned that the BJP, which was in power in Gujarat, may coerce its forty-two MLAs to vote in favour of the BJP candidate, Balwantsinh Rajput. The Congress high command, keen to ensure legislators voted along party lines, resorted to a strategy that is probably unique to India known as 'resort politics'. Indian politicians are a rather fragmented bunch, divided by innumerable issues such as party affiliations, the state or region they hail from, religion, caste and language. However, the single-minded pursuit of power and the practice of 'resort politics' unites them.

In 'resort politics', politicians belonging to a certain party are shepherded to a resort, usually located at the outskirts of a city, to prevent them from being poached by the opposition ahead of an election or confidence motion in the state legislature or the Parliament and cause a power upset. These politicians acquiesce to being cloistered in a resort, surrender their mobile phones and submit themselves to the supervision of a party strongman ahead of a vote.

However, sometimes, there is a black sheep among the dissidents, who dares to resort to rebellion. To take a historic sidestep from our story, in 1982, the then Indian National Lok Dal (INLD) chief, Devi Lal, closeted forty-eight MLAs from the INLD and BJP in a hotel in New Delhi.[3] One legislator, however, escaped by scaling down the hotel's water pipe. When the state governor asked Devi Lal to prove his majority, the legislator who got away voted for Bhajan Lal, the opposition candidate who was affiliated to the Congress party. Bhajan Lal thus secured a majority and was sworn in as the chief minister of Haryana.

In 2017, the wheels of history turned full circle. It was the Congress party's turn to confine its MLAs in a resort. Unwilling to risk the safeguarding of its MLAs in Gujarat, a state under BJP rule, the Congress high command dispatched the MLAs and Ahmed Patel to Karnataka, where a Congress government was in power. Shivakumar, who was tasked with safeguarding the MLAs, arranged for the 42 MLAs, Ahmed Patel and himself to be accommodated at the Eagleton Golf Resort, on the outskirts of Bengaluru.

This was when the Department of Income Taxes, under the jurisdiction of the Centre ruled by BJP's Modi government, raided Shivakumar's thirty-nine properties in Bengaluru, Bidadi (a town in Karnataka) and Delhi, as well as the room he occupied at the Eagleton Golf Resort. The Congress alleged that the raid was politically motivated. The IT department countered that 'events involving certain MLAs of another state being brought to Karnataka were unforeseen and unpredictable. The search team were not concerned with the MLAs and there had been no contact with the MLAs. The income tax search was only on one Karnataka minister'.[4]

Notwithstanding the IT raid, Shivakumar successfully safeguarded the Congress legislators and Ahmed Patel was re-elected to the Rajya Sabha. However, the IT department unearthed ₹300 crore ($46 million) of Shivakumar's previously undisclosed income and an incriminating paper trail of transactions between him and VGS.

Within two months of the raid on Shivakumar, the IT department, on 21 September 2017, raided twenty properties that belonged to VGS in Bengaluru, Chikkamagaluru, Chennai and Mumbai. S.M. Krishna quitting the Congress and joining the BJP in March 2017 did not deter the IT department, which unearthed ₹650 crore ($100 million) as undisclosed income. The incremental tax liabilities and penalties weighed down VGS, who was already overwhelmed by CDEL's excessive indebtedness, the company's inability to pay dividends since listing, and lacklustre stock performance.

Pledging the Family Silver

Companies whose growth is financed by diverse funding sources—profits, debt and equity—are most likely to flourish in the long run. CDEL's growth after its IPO was predominantly financed through debt. A structural weakness of Indian capital markets is the absence of a vibrant bond market through which corporates may raise unsecured debt without pledging the company's assets. Naturally, the interest rate on unsecured bonds is higher than that on secured debt.

Indian corporates borrow money mostly through secured bank loans, wherein companies' assets are pledged to banks as collateral. An accumulation of non-performing loans and RBI's stricter oversight since Raghuram Rajan assumed charge as the central bank's governor in 2013 resulted in a slowdown in bank loan disbursements. Controlling shareholders of cash-strapped businesses, including CDEL, the Anil Dhirubhai Ambani Group (ADAG) and Yes Bank, pledged their holdings with mutual funds and NBFCs to raise debt for their companies. CDEL's share price mostly declined since its IPO while the broader market denoted by the BSE Sensex was mostly rising. VGS was forced to offer more shares as collateral to mutual fund and NBFC lenders.

Figure 1: CDEL Share Price Versus the Sensex

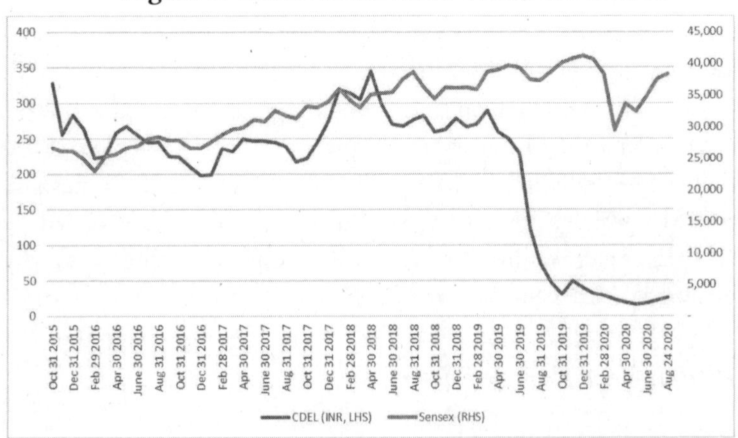

Source: Bloomberg

VGS, Malavika Hegde, his parents and entities owned by them (collectively referred to as promoters) together held 53 to 54 per cent stake in CDEL since its 2015 IPO. However, as VGS pledged more and more of the promoters' shares to raise debt, promoters' effective stake (stake held minus stake pledged) more than halved to 23 per cent by end-March 2018 from 53 per cent as of end-March 2016. VGS had also borrowed from NBFCs and mutual funds by offering as collateral promoters' stakes in the group's unlisted companies, Coffee Day Global, Tanglin Developments and VGS's crown jewel, Mindtree Limited.

However, one man not only remained invested in CDEL but also had more than doubled his holding to 5.68 million shares by 31 March 2019 from 2.07 million shares after the May 2010 bonus issue. It was Nandan Nilekani. His investment in CDEL was a loss-making one, but this gesture of friendship ensured that VGS effectively controlled CDEL notwithstanding his declining personal stake.

VGS's propensity to raise gargantuan quantum of debt (relative to CDEL's profits) hit a speed breaker when one of India's premier infrastructure financing institutions—Infrastructure Leasing & Financial Services (IL&FS)—defaulted on its debt repayments in August 2018.

Pandemonium

IL&FS, one of India's most high-profile infrastructure financing companies that RBI had designated as a systemically important NBFC, was founded in 1987. The unlisted NBFC had an impressive line-up of shareholders led by India's largest life insurer, state-owned Life Insurance Corporation of India (LIC), which held a 25.34 per cent stake. Other shareholders were Japan's ORIX Corporation (23.54 per cent), Abu Dhabi Investment Authority (12.56 per cent), IL&FS Employees Welfare Trust (12 per cent), HDFC Limited (9.02 per cent), Central Bank of

India (7.67 per cent) and India's largest bank, the State Bank of India (6.42 per cent).

IL&FS had executed projects in several sectors including roads, water, power, ports, and social and environmental infrastructure. It was the primary financier of India's longest tunnel, the 9.28-kilometre-long Dr Syama Prasad Mookerjee tunnel in Jammu & Kashmir.

IL&FS and HDFC Bank share interesting similarities. First, both institutions were the brainchildren of Deepak Parekh, who was then the chairman of HDFC Limited. Second, it was Parekh who hand-picked Aditya Puri and Ravi Parthasarathy as the first CEOs of HDFC Bank and IL&FS respectively. Both Puri and Parthasarathy held high-profile positions in Citibank, which they quit to helm HDFC Bank and IL&FS. But that's where the similarity ends.

Whereas HDFC Bank was renowned for its performance and governance, IL&FS was an unlisted, secretive organization. Parekh and Parthasarathy grew apart and the former went on to establish yet another infrastructure financing entity in India—the Infrastructure Development Finance Company Limited (IDFC)—a decade later in January 1997.

IL&FS was the fiefdom of Parthasarathy—an alumnus of India's premier business school, the Indian Institute of Management (IIM), Ahmedabad—till he resigned in July 2018 citing poor health. Power was concentrated in the hands of a small group of senior IL&FS employees who were loyal to Ravi Parthasarathy, reportedly a politically connected person.

It appeared to be routine business when three domestic CRAs—CARE Ratings, ICRA and India Ratings—affirmed the highest credit rating that they had assigned to IL&FS between March to May 2018. The highest rating on the credit rating scale, AAA, indicates minimal probability of default. CARE Ratings is a listed CRA in which LIC and CRISIL, a listed subsidiary of Standard & Poor's, hold 9.85 per cent and 8.90 per cent stakes respectively. Moody's Investor Services holds close to 52 per cent stake in the listed ICRA Limited. India Ratings is a wholly owned subsidiary of Fitch Ratings.

The CRAs assigned 'AAA' on the domestic rating scale to IL&FS notwithstanding multiple red flags.

First, Mauritius-based AIDQUA Holdings, which held a 27.89 per cent stake in one of IL&FS's projects—New Tirupur Area Development Corporation—had been sharing multiple concerns including misgovernance and accounting jugglery for a decade with the RBI, Company Law Board, MCA, the Madras High Court, and the Supreme Court. None of these government institutions initiated an enquiry into IL&FS.[5] Second, IL&FS's debt increased by 87 per cent to a staggering ₹91,091 crore ($13 billion) between FY2014 to FY2018. A combination of poor lending decisions and fraud led to a sustained and steep deterioration in profit after tax from a negligible ₹398 crore ($65 million) in FY2014 to a loss of ₹2395 crore ($350 million) in FY2018. Third, IL&FS's dividend payout ratio (dividends paid expressed as a percentage of profits) increased from 54 per cent in FY2014 to 97 per cent in FY2015.

In FY2016 and FY2017, the NBFC paid dividends in excess of profits. This practice continued in FY2018, when IL&FS had reported a loss! For three consecutive years—FY2016 to FY2018—IL&FS paid dividends out of reserves. This is not just a sign of poor financial management but also an indication of a wilful lapse of judgement on part of IL&FS's knowledgeable institutional shareholders. Fourth, for IL&FS's sterling performance, the institutional shareholders awarded ₹35 crore ($5 million) remuneration, a 43 per cent hike over FY2017 to its three senior-most personnel: chairman Ravi Parthasarathy, vice chairman and managing director Hari Sankaran and joint managing director and CEO Arun K. Saha.

This was in addition to the aforesaid key management personnel (KMP) unlawfully profiting from two trusts—IL&FS's

Employee Welfare Trust (EWT) and IL&FS Group Employees Trust (IGET)—of which they were the largest beneficiaries. IGET had aggregated all shares held by the above-mentioned KMPs and sold it to LIC at ₹1,100 ($16.08 in 2008) per share. EWT had distributed these shares to the employees at ₹84 to ₹132 ($1.23 to $1.93) per share, resulting in the beneficiaries reaping windfall gains of around ten times. Further, EWT has itself purchased the unlisted IL&FS shares for a miniscule ₹2 ($0.03). Moreover, the KMPs had not secured prior board approval to set up IGET.[6] It is no wonder that the late Anil Dharker, a veteran journalist, called IL&FS 'Internal Looting & Fraud Syndicate'.[7]

Notwithstanding IL&FS's weakening financials, Piramal Enterprises Limited (PEL) had offered to acquire IL&FS at ₹860 ($13.41) per share in 2015, which was 10.0 per cent higher than its reported book value of ₹784.30 ($12.23 per share). Ramesh Bawa, the erstwhile CEO of one of IL&FS's subsidiaries—IL&FS Financial Services—informed investigators in 2019 that LIC rejected the deal as it opined that PEL ought to pay at least ₹1100 ($17.15 in 2015) per share.[8] This was the price at which LIC had bought IL&FS shares from IGET in 2008. This was a decision that LIC would regret as it had lost the opportunity to cut its losses and would see the value of its stake in IL&FS reduced to naught by 2018.

Ravi Parthasarathy resigned in July 2018 citing 'health grounds'. Between July and September 2018, news of subsidiaries of IL&FS defaulting on their debt repayments began to emerge. IL&FS and its subsidiaries failed to repay ₹450 crore ($66 million) of inter-corporate deposits to state-owned Small Industries Development Bank of India (SIDBI), ₹52.4 crore ($8 million) of short-term deposits to other lenders and ₹104 crore ($15 million) term deposits.[9]

It was only after IL&FS's defaults became public did the three CRAs take rating action. By September 2018, all three CRAs had progressively downgraded IL&FS by 20 notches from the highest

'AAA' rating to the lowest 'D' rating. The RBI asked IL&FS's shareholders to arrest defaults. In October 2018, IL&FS floated a ₹4500 crore ($658 million) rights issue, from which it raised a paltry ₹5.47 lakh ($8000).[10] The institutional shareholders, who had no compunction in collecting dividends in excess of IL&FS's profits for three consecutive years, abstained from investing.

Why had the CRAs assigned the highest ratings to IL&FS notwithstanding its dismal performance?

CRAs assign two types of credit ratings to an entity—standalone and supported. The standalone rating reflects an entity's debt servicing ability, which in turn is determined by its performance, management quality and prospects. A supported rating, which is usually higher than the standalone rating, is assigned to entities who by virtue of having the government or strong institutions as shareholders are likely to receive financing during crisis to avert a default.

Notwithstanding IL&FS's dismal performance, the CRAs had expected its institutional shareholders to inject the necessary financing to avoid a default. Their fault lies in reporting IL&FS's supported rating and not disclosing IL&FS's standalone rating. Disclosing standalone and supported ratings is a practice that has been long followed by the big three international CRAs—S&P, Moody's, and Fitch. Yet, ICRA and India Ratings, which are subsidiaries of Moody's and Fitch respectively, did not adopt this approach. Further, the credit rating methodologies of global and domestic CRAs is available on their websites free of cost. Hence, CARE Ratings too had no excuse for not reporting standalone and supported credit ratings.

Distinguishing between standalone and supported credit ratings may have forced IL&FS's institutional shareholders to exercise better oversight, approve a dividend policy that did not debilitate IL&FS, and inject adequate equity in a timely manner to forestall default.

IL&FS defaulting resulted in all hell breaking loose in Indian capital markets.

Figure 2: IL& FS—Select Financial Metrics (Consolidated)

₹ Crore	FY2014	FY2015	FY2016	FY2017	FY2018
Post-tax Profit	347	373	57	286	-2,396
Dividends	188	363	361	437	258
Dividend payout ratio	54%	97%	638%	153%	n.a.
Debt	48,671	63,114	70,374	80,018	91,091
Renumeration of Ravi Parthasarathy, Hari Sankaran & Arun Saha	22.86	18.17	27.05	24.61	35.21

Source: IL&FS annual reports

The default had a contagion effect. Banks were unwilling to renew their existing lines of credit and increase their credit limits to NBFCs. This resulted in a liquidity crunch for NBFCs, most of which are not, by law, permitted to accept public deposits. The still nascent bond markets in India and the excessive dependence on banks for financing worked to the detriment of NBFCs. As banks were unwilling to lend to NBFCs, they in turn had to curtail their lending.

By 1 October 2018, the GoI's ministry of corporate affairs replaced IL&FS's board of directors with a six-member board headed by Kotak Mahindra Bank's managing director, Uday Kotak. Former Tech Mahindra CEO Vineet Nayyar, former SEBI chief G.N. Bajpai, former ICICI Bank chairman G.C. Chaturvedi and former IAS officers Malini Shankar and Nanda Kishore were the other five members of the MCA-appointed board. The new board appointed Grant Thornton to conduct a forensic audit.[11]

Between April 2019 and June 2019, the Serious Fraud Investigation Office (SFIO) and the Enforcement Directorate (ED) arrested IL&FS's erstwhile senior management personnel—Ramesh Bawa, Hari Sankaran, Arun Saha and Karunakaran Ramchand.[12] Ravi Parthasarathy relocated to London citing health grounds just before IL&FS defaulted on its debt obligations. He lived in London till the uproar regarding IL&FS's collapse had died down. Based on a complaint filed in 2020 by the Mumbai-based 63 Moons alleging that IL&FS Transportation Networks had failed to repay investors ₹200 crore ($27 million), the Economic Offences Wing (EOW) arrested Ravi Parthasarathy in June 2021 at his hometown, Chennai. Previously, the Madras High Court had rejected his anticipatory bail application filed in relation to the 63 Moons complaint.[13] The seventy-year-old Ravi Parthasarathy, who was suffering from cancer, passed away on 27 April 2022 at his Mumbai home.[14] Senior management personnel at ICRA, CARE and Fitch Ratings lost their jobs.

Ripple Effect

Of CDEL's ₹5082 crore ($771 million) consolidated debt outstanding as of 31 March 2018, NBFCs had lent ₹1984 crore (39 per cent of consolidated debt) and mutual funds had lent ₹833 crore (16 per cent). In the aftermath of IL&FS's default, the NBFCs were either unwilling to or unable to refinance CDEL's debt and/or lend more money to the company. From May 2018 onward, CDEL's share price started declining. VGS had no option but to pledge more of promoter holdings in CDEL and his stakes in other companies like Coffee Day Global, Tanglin Developments and Mindtree to maintain and avail more credit from mutual funds.

The promoters' effective stake in CDEL declined to 14 per cent by March 2019 from 23 per cent as of March 2018. While the promoters continued to hold 119.93 million shares or a 54 per cent stake in CDEL, they had pledged three-fourths of their stake in FY2019. This was to meet CDEL's ₹892 crore ($130 million) capital expenditure in FY2019 and a mysterious and ill-timed ₹789 crore ($115 million) loan to a related company, Mysore Amalgamated Coffee Estates Limited.

CDEL's consolidated debt had increased in one year by 43 per cent to ₹7269 crore ($1.0 billion) as of end-March 2019. VGS was under tremendous pressure to avert a default.

Chapter 6

The Jewel in the Crown

'It was the best of times, it was the worst of times, it was the age of wisdom, it was the age of foolishness, it was the epoch of belief, it was the epoch of incredulity, it was the season of Light, it was the season of Darkness, it was the spring of hope, it was the winter of despair . . . ' So begins Charles Dickens' classic, *The Tale of Two Cities*, which is set in the years leading up to the French Revolution. Like most words of wisdom, these too hold true in several contexts including business cycles and, particularly, the period of the dotcom boom, 1995 to 2001.

It was during such heady times that nine friends from Wipro, Cambridge Technology Partners and Lucent Technologies joined hands to incorporate an IT firm, Mindtree.[1] These nine men were Ashok Soota (then vice chairman of Wipro's IT services division), Subroto Bagchi, Krishnakumar Natarajan, Parthasarathy N.S., Scott Staples, Anjan Lahiri, Kalyankumar Banerjee, Kamran Ozair and Rostow Ravanan.

Soota talked about his intention to co-found an IT firm to his friend, VGS, who became the new firm's first investor. In February 1999, Soota shared his decision to leave Wipro with his boss and Wipro's chairman, Azim Premji. VGS and the venture capital firm, Walden Capital, invested $8 million while the founders put in $1.4 million.

The co-founders appointed Soota as chairman and managing director of their firm, which they named Mindtree. On the morning of 19 August 1999, the launch of Mindtree was announced at a press conference in Bengaluru. That evening, the founding team organized a get-together at Taj Residency, which was attended by around 100 guests, including Premji and Nilekani. The tenth founder, S. Janakiraman, who was Wipro's global head of research and development, joined the company in October 1999.

Kohinoor

Mindtree raised ₹40 crore ($9.4 million) in 1999. Its ten promoters held the majority stake of 75 per cent, while VGS and Walden Capital, which exited in 2012, held the balance 25 per cent stake. In 2001, Mindtree undertook another round of financing, in which the Capital Group and Franklin Templeton infused equity of ₹47 crore ($10 million) and ₹21 crore ($4.4 million) respectively.

Mindtree launched its IPO eight years after its incorporation, between 9–14 February 2007.[2] The IT company targeted to raise ₹238 crore ($58 million) by selling 5.59 million equity shares in the price range of ₹365–₹425 ($8.83–$10.28) per share. These equity shares represented a 15 per cent stake in the company, thereby valuing the company at ₹1585 crore ($383 million). Mindtree's valuation during its 2007 IPO was nine times the ₹172 crore ($40 million) valuation at inception, a testimony to its founders' vision and diligence.

Mindtree's performance justified the exponential growth in valuation. The company's revenues had grown more than five-fold from ₹78 crore in FY2002 ($17 million) to ₹455 crore ($103 million) in FY2006,[3] a time when India's two largest listed IT firms, Tata Consultancy Services (TCS) and Infosys, were generating revenues of ₹13,386 crore ($3 billion) and ₹9521 crore ($2 billion) respectively. Mindtree had started to generate post-tax profits from FY2003. It was practically debt free with its ₹13.5 crore ($3 million) net debt as of March 2006 at just 0.16 times its

₹82 crore ($19 million) earnings before interest, tax, depreciation and amortization (EBITDA).

In November 2006, like CDEL, Mindtree too had a bonus issue ahead of its listing. The terms were less generous, though. Mindtree's shareholders approved a 4:1 bonus issue, which means shareholders were awarded one share free of cost for every four shares they owned. Prior to the listing, the promoters held a 42.23 per cent stake in Mindtree, investors held 49.45 per cent and employees and others held 8.32 per cent. VGS held an 8.36 per cent stake through his private equity arm, Global Technology Ventures.

Of the ₹238 crore ($58 million) IPO proceeds, Mindtree proposed to deploy ₹121 crore ($29 million) to construct a new development centre in Chennai, ₹19 crore ($5 million) for debt repayment and the balance ₹98 crore ($24 million) for general corporate purposes.

Kotak Mahindra and JM Morgan Stanley, VGS's first employer, were appointed lead managers to the IPO, which was a resounding success. The IPO was oversubscribed by over 100 times. All investor categories—institutions, retail investors and employees—subscribed well in excess of their respective quotas. Mindtree's employees placed bids equivalent to 2.79 times the number of shares set aside for them. In comparison, CDEL's employees, in October 2015, subscribed to just 86 per cent of their quota.

On listing day, Mindtree's shares opened at ₹599 ($9.20), which was 41 per cent higher than the ₹425 ($6.53) IPO price. The share price continued to rise through the day and closed at ₹620.30 ($9.53); 46 per cent higher than the listing price on 7 March 2007.

It was not always smooth sailing. Nevertheless, Mindtree steered though the challenges posed by the 2008 global financial crisis and the failed move to manufacture mobile handsets after paying $8 million in 2009 to buy San Diego-headquartered Kyocera Mobile's R&D unit in India. In 2011, Soota resigned from the chairman's role and sold his 11.6 per cent stake to VGS, whose stake subsequently quadrupled due to Mindtree's 1:1 bonus issues in 2014 and 2016. VGS, in his individual capacity and through his investment vehicles, now owned 13.53 million shares—equivalent to a 19.95 per cent stake in Mindtree as of March 2018. This was more than five times the 2.65 million shares he owned at the time of Mindtree's IPO.

During the twelve-year period from April 2006 to March 2018, the estimated dividends VGS earned from his Mindtree holding amounted to about ₹125 crore ($19 million). The market value of his holding, which was ₹55 crore $12 million as of March 2007, had grown by 46 times to ₹2588 crore ($392 million) as of March 2018. VGS was also a non-executive director on the Mindtree board from the date of its 2007 IPO up to 9 March 2018, when he resigned due to 'preoccupation with his primary businesses'.[4]

Notwithstanding Mindtree's impressive performance, VGS could bolster neither CDEL's net worth nor his own through his Mindtree stake. He had started to pledge his Mindtree shares to raise debt to fund CDEL's ever-growing financing needs since FY2015.

Barbarians at the Gate

While TCS, Infosys, Wipro and HCL Technologies are tier-1 IT firms, Mindtree, by 2018, had consolidated its market position as a mid-tier IT firm, along with Mphasis, Tech Mahindra and Coforge (formerly known as NIIT). This was when Mindtree caught the eye of another mid-tier IT firm—L&T Infotech, a subsidiary of India's largest engineering conglomerate, L&T. Apart from L&T Infotech, L&T held majority stake of over 70 per cent in another listed IT firm—L&T Technology Services.

In FY2018, L&T Infotech earned ₹507 crore post-tax profits from ₹3941 crore revenues. Mindtree made ₹570 crore post-tax profits from ₹5653 crore revenues that year. While Mindtree was a larger revenue generator, L&T Infotech was more profitable. Its net profit margin (post-tax profits expressed as a percentage of revenues) was almost 13 per cent in FY2018 vis-à-vis Mindtree's 10 per cent. By March 2018, both L&T Infotech and Mindtree were in a net cash position; their cash holdings exceeded their outstanding debt.

Taking advantage of Mindtree's Achilles' heel—its dispersed shareholding with the promoters' holdings being just 13.37 per cent of the shares—and with L&T's backing, L&T Infotech boldly embarked on India's first hostile acquisition of a listed IT company. The parent, L&T, generates a significant chunk of its revenues from engineering, procurement and construction (EPC) contracts, which tend to be volatile and cyclical. The Mindtree acquisition made sense to L&T as it would enhance the share of the relatively stable and recurring cash flows from its IT business.

Two Danish engineers, Henning Holck-Larsen and Soren Kristian Toubro founded the company in 1938. L&T was listed on the BSE in 1965 and has been an independent, professionally managed company for most of its operating history. Manohar (alias Manu) Chhabria in 1987, Dhirubhai Ambani in 1989, and Kumar Mangalam Birla in 2001–02 attempted to acquire L&T, which fended off these bids with the support of the government and its institutional shareholders—General Insurance Corporation of India, Unit Trust of India and LIC—all state-owned entities.[4]

Ironically, after functioning as an independent, professionally managed conglomerate for over fifteen years, L&T, through its subsidiary L&T Infotech, set its sights on Mindtree, another stand-alone, professionally managed company. L&T Infotech's non-executive chairman, A.M. Naik, had reportedly met VGS in January 2019, followed by a team meeting between L&T Infotech and the Mindtree management.[5]

L&T Infotech's overtures coincided with VGS's troubles arising from CDEL's mounting debt and the September 2017 income tax raids at his properties. In fact, on 25 January 2019, the Income Tax department attached the Mindtree shares that VGS and CDEL owned for a period of six months.[6] These shares had already been pledged with banks, NBFCs and mutual funds to raise debt for CDEL.

At this juncture, VGS owned a 20.45 per cent stake in Mindtree, which exceeded the promoters' 13.37 per cent stake. Another significant shareholder in Mindtree was the Singapore-headquartered investment firm, Nalanda Capital, with a 10.63 per cent stake. Mindtree's top ten shareholders, including VGS and Nalanda Capital, held just 43.26 per cent of the shares. Therefore, for L&T Infotech to become a majority shareholder in Mindtree, it needed to acquire VGS's stake before announcing its open offer to purchase Mindtree shares owned by retail and institutional shareholders.

When Mindtree got wind of L&T Infotech's intention, the company mounted a defence. Nalanda Capital backed Mindtree's incumbent management. Understanding that VGS was in a liquidity crunch, the company negotiated with PE firms to buy his stake and launch its own open offer. It was essential for these PE firms to buy VGS's stake ahead of the open offer; this would enable the Mindtree senior management to control 44.45 per cent of the shares – their own 13.37 per cent, VGS's 20.45 per cent and Nalanda Capital's 10.63 per cent. Unfortunately for Mindtree's senior management, the PE player who backed them was unable to buy VGS's stake, already pledged with banks as collateral. PE players usually purchase unencumbered assets.

This situation worked in L&T Infotech's favour. Following IL&FS's collapse, lenders had tightened their underwriting and were unwilling to refinance and extend maturities of loans to weaker counterparties. Under pressure to raise money to repay debts, VGS landed straight into L&T Infotech's outstretched arms.

Standard Chartered Bank facilitated the Mindtree stake sale.[7] The bank arranged a ₹3000 crore ($426 million) non-convertible debenture (NCD) issue by CDEL. The issue had two escrow accounts.[8] The proceeds of the NCD issue were maintained in one escrow account to repay lenders (whose exposure was secured by a pledge of Mindtree shares) and revoke the pledge on Mindtree shares. The unencumbered Mindtree shares were to be sold to L&T Infotech, which deposited the purchase consideration into the second escrow account to repay the NCD holders.

On 18 March 2019, L&T Infotech entered into an agreement with VGS to purchase the latter's stake in Mindtree for ₹3269 crore ($464 million). The volatile situation was exacerbated by an anonymous complaint filed with SEBI in which the complainant alleged that VGS had engaged in insider trading when the Mindtree trading window was closed. Promoters, related entities and employees are forbidden by law to trade in their company shares during periods in which they have access to material non-public information, such as weeks or months preceding the announcement of results and transactions including mergers, acquisitions, spin-offs and listings. Trading window refers to periods when both third-party investors and promoters, related entities and employees may trade in an entity's shares.

Mindtree CEO Ravanan informed reporters, 'On the pledge disclosure issue, there was a disclosure that he made at certain point of time of all the pledge. At that point of time, there were some irregularities in his disclosures. Our board and audit committee evaluated it and handled it as per the rule(s) that were prevailing at that point of time.'[9]

By March 2019, it became clear that Mindtree could no longer count on VGS's stake. An agitated Krishnakumar Natarajan, Mindtree's executive chairman, called Subroto Bagchi, who was then the chairman of Odisha Skill Development Authority. Bagchi was living in Odisha's capital, Bhubaneswar.

'An imminent threat of hostile takeover of Mindtree has made me to resign from the government to be able to go, save the company. I must protect the Tree from people who have arrived with bulldozers & saw chains to cut it down so that in its place, they can build a shopping mall,' Bagchi tweeted on March 17.[10] Mindtree had branded itself as 'the Tree' over the years.

Minutes later he tweeted again, 'Mindtree has not been designed as an "asset" to be bought & sold. It is a national resource. It has a unique culture that humanizes the idea of business. It sets the standards of corporate governance. I need to be there in its time of difficulty. Hence the hard decision to return.'[11]

Mindtree announced that it was exploring the feasibility of a share buyback. As this very public battle between L&T Infotech and Mindtree played out, Mindtree's share price started rising. The share price rose by 4 per cent per month from ₹908.80 ($12.91) on 28 February 2019 to ₹944.50 ($13.41) on 31 March 2019 and further to ₹981.25 ($13.93) on 30 April. Investors sensed a profitable opportunity to sell their shares as both Mindtree and L&T Infotech were keen to purchase the free float. As L&T Infotech was a fundamentally sound company, retail and institutional investors were probably neutral to the outcome of Mindtree's ownership battle.

Capitulation

L&T Infotech also announced its intention on 18 March 2019 to launch an open offer to buy 31 per cent of Mindtree's shares at ₹980 ($13.92) per share. BloombergQuint estimated that a ₹980 offer price implied a price earnings (PE) ratio of 21.3 for Mindtree, making it the most expensive IT stock in India after TCS whose PE ratio was 24.1.[12]

SEBI rules require the acquirer to possess a minimum 25 per cent stake in its target before announcing an open offer. At Mindtree's insistence, SEBI started examining whether L&T Infotech had the requisite 25 per cent stake in Mindtree.[13] L&T Infotech had no option but to postpone its open offer launch from 14 May to 17 June. The company used this window of time to purchase an additional 2 per cent stake in the company by paying over ₹316 crore ($45 million).

L&T also required approval for this takeover from the Competition Commission of India (CCI) as the company had majority stakes in two IT firms, L&T Infotech and L&T Technology. On 6 April 2019, *Mint* quoted an anonymous source as saying, 'The CCI approval came in record time. Usually, CCI approvals take more than 21 days. This shows the confidence of the regulatory authorities in the deal.'[14]

This was the beginning of the end of David's battle against Goliath. L&T Infotech, backed by its parent, L&T, had the financial muscle to engage in a bidding war. Mindtree's senior management dropped its plans of a share buyback and formed a panel to evaluate L&T Infotech's open offer to purchase Mindtree shares.

Nalanda Capital appeared not to have given up, though. *CNBC-TV18* reported that Nalanda Capital was dissuading minority shareholders from selling their stakes to L&T Infotech and was nudging them to ask for a higher price.[15] This was despite a committee of independent directors opining that L&T Infotech's offer price was fair. Mindtree's shares were trading between ₹950 ($13.49) and ₹970 ($13.77) in April and May 2019 when SEBI sought an explanation from Nalanda Capital.

Yet, when L&T Infotech launched its open offer for a 31 per cent stake in Mindtree on 17 June, Nalanda Capital sold its entire 10.63 per cent stake at the ₹980 offer price. While some market watchers were of the opinion that the investor's capitulation was due to pressure from regulators, others thought the decision was entirely commercial.

L&T thus successfully acquired a 66 per cent stake in Mindtree for a cash consideration of around ₹10,800 crore ($1.53 billion). VGS had exited a company he helped incubate, in which he was the first investor and an independent director till a year before his stake sale. Bagchi was a trustee of Amber Valley School, the boarding school VGS had founded. It was curtains down for a symbiotically fruitful relationship in India Inc.

On 5 July 2019, Krishnakumar Natarajan, Mindtree's executive chairman, Parthasarathy N.S., executive vice chairman and COO, and Ravanan, CEO and managing director, resigned. The trio had been members of Mindtree's founding team. L&T veterans, A.M. Naik and S.N. Subrahmanyan, replaced them as Mindtree's chairman and vice-chairman respectively. Debashis Chatterjee, who was formerly Cognizant's executive vice president, assumed charge as Mindtree's CEO.

VGS, in his purported suicide note, mentioned that the Income Tax department attaching his Mindtree stake had resulted in a liquidity crunch. But was this the sole reason that drove him to take the extreme step?

Chapter 7

Collateral Damage

'VG Siddhartha made a profit of ₹2858 crore from his Mindtree stake sale to L&T,' proclaimed a *Business Today* article dated 20 March 2019. ₹2858 crore is around $406 million.

The next day, an article published by Moneycontrol optimistically stated, 'With Mindtree stake sale helping him clear debts, Siddhartha may perhaps don the role of an investor, again.'

These articles failed to mention that VGS did not personally profit by selling his Mindtree stake. The proceeds were used entirely to repay CDEL's debt. Nevertheless, paying down CDEL's debt, even partially, especially in 2019 when institutional lenders had tightened their purse strings in the aftermath of the IL&FS default, was no mean achievement.

So, what were the pressures VGS was up against, what were his strengths and weaknesses, and what challenges did he face? An analysis of these issues is necessary to understand the reasons for his final decision.

Co-location

Sucheta Dalal, one of India's most renowned business journalists and the person who uncovered the Harshad Mehta perpetrated securities scam in 1992, received an envelope from Singapore through snail mail. It contained a letter dated 14 January 2015 addressed to B.K. Gupta, a deputy general manager in SEBI's market regulation department, and was copied to Dalal. The writer of the letter, who wished to remain anonymous, contended that a set of traders had earned exponential and unfair profits by rigging the National Stock Exchange's (NSE) algorithmic trading (algo-trading) platform that engaged in high frequency trading (HFT) and the use of co-location servers.[1] The letter alleged that NSE insiders were involved in this front running—an illegal practice whereby a broker who possesses material non-public information that would affect the price of a stock, trades the stock before the news is disseminated to the public.[2]

Dalal informed SEBI and NSE and started covering this issue on MoneyLife, a business news portal she manages with her husband and author-journalist, Debashis Basu. SEBI, in turn, initiated investigations into NSE's co-location facility, which took four years to complete.

NSE had launched the co-location facility in 2010. It is customary for SEBI to put out a discussion paper to solicit market feedback and consult with its technical advisory committee (TAC) before permitting stock exchanges to launch new products. There is no evidence in the public domain that SEBI undertook either of these steps. SEBI's investigations revealed at least four damning findings.

First, NSE had, between 2010 and 2015, used the TCP-IP protocol to disseminate order book data to trading members in its co-location facility. The TCP-IP protocol disseminates data sequentially, benefitting trading members who are ahead in the queue. NSE had not specified a framework to determine queuing and had left it to its junior employees to decide the queuing of trading members. The NSE switched to the fairer multicast system only in 2015. While SEBI's investigations found that the TCP-IP protocol was open to manipulation, it did not find proof of trading members making undue gains.[3]

Second, it was possible for some trading members to switch their connections to NSE's backup servers, which were less crowded, to gain quicker data access. Though NSE warned the wrongdoers, it did not penalize them. SEBI found New Delhi-based OPG Securities to have earned unlawful gains of ₹15.57 crore ($2.21 million) through this route.[4]

Third, two brokers—Way2Wealth Brokers and GKN Securities—hired Sampark, which did not have a license from the Department of Telecom (DoT), to lay dark fibre connectivity to the NSE's co-location facilities for faster trade execution. NSE did not permit other brokers, who approached it with similar requests, to avail of Sampark's dark fibre connectivity. SEBI asked NSE to pay a fine of ₹62.58 crore ($8.89 million), Way2Wealth Brokers a sum of ₹15.34 crore ($2.19 million) and GKN Securities ₹4.90 crore ($0.70 million). Interestingly, in September 2015, the Anil Ambani-owned Reliance Communications, which possessed a DoT license to provide dark fibre services, acquired Sampark.[5]

SEBI's fourth finding was that NSE had shared data with related parties, violating the capital market regulator's Prohibition of Fraudulent and Unfair Trade Practices relating to Securities Markets (PFUTP) Regulations, 2003. One of SEBI's orders stated that Ajay Shah, a senior academic with the government think-tank National Institute of Public Finance and Policy, along with his wife and sister-in-law, had misused market data obtained from NSE for commercial gains. According to SEBI, NSE had mandated Infotech Financial Services Pvt Ltd to build a Liquidity Index (LIX). Sunita Thomas—Shah's sister-in-law and wife of an NSE assistant vice president, Suprabhat Lala—was a director in Infotech Financial Services. Further, Shah, who was on the board of National Securities Clearing Corp. Ltd, NSE's wholly-owned subsidiary, currently known as NSE Clearing Limited, failed to disclose this to NSE.[6]

SEBI concluded its investigations by penalizing NSE to the tune of ₹624.89 crore ($88.74 million) plus 12 per cent interest per annum for five years. NSE's chairman, Ravi Narain, and CEO, Chitra Ramkrishna, were ordered to disgorge 25 per cent of their salaries from the previous five years and were barred from associating with market institutions for five years. While Ramkrishna had quit NSE in 2016 citing personal reasons, Narain resigned in 2018 over the co-location investigations. SEBI barred Shah from associating with any market infrastructure institute, listed company or registered intermediary for a period of two years.[7] Chitra Ramakrishna was arrested in March 2022.[8]

The NSE-stockbroker-Sampark nexus that enabled both NSE and a group of twenty-two brokers, including OPG Securities, Way2Wealth Brokers and GKN Securities, would not have come to light if the whistleblower had not alerted SEBI and Dalal, who was sued unsuccessfully by NSE for defamation.

This incident highlights the need to set up a robust and remunerative whistleblowing mechanism that protects the identities of whistleblowers, along the lines of the whistleblowing mechanism in the US. It also illustrates the woefully inadequate disclosure requirements for listed entities in India. Listed entities are not required to report operating information. CDEL's financial services division, which included Way2Wealth Securities, appears to be small in relation to its coffee café division. The financial services division was loss-making in FY2014. Its EBITDA peaked to ₹75 crore ($11.57 million) in FY2016 (which was the last financial year NSE used the TCP-IP protocol) and progressively declined to ₹34 crore ($4.93 million) in FY2019. We do not know if the cessation of preferential access to NSE's co-location servers, or a bloated cost structure or both contributed to the deterioration in Way2Wealth Securities' performance.

VGS probably believed that he would be able to trade his way out of CDEL's debt woes. While the extent to which VGS profited in his individual capacity through algo-trading is not known, the SEBI investigations must have added to the stress he was facing due to CDEL's lacklustre performance, the income tax raids, and his inability to support Mindtree's management during L&T's hostile acquisition.

Missing Winning Ingredients

Most businesses that have a successful track record in generating stable and sustainable long-term returns for their shareholders and have discharged their contractual obligations including debt repayments in a timely manner share two common traits: one, their core businesses generate recurring operating cash flows, and two, the founder has a team of capable and trusted lieutenants to execute their vision.

VGS excelled at product delivery. CCD, The Serai and Global Technology Park are testimony to his execution skills. The inability to ensure his businesses generated sustainable cash flows was VGS's Achilles' heel. Instead, he kickstarted multiple ventures, most of which earned negligible profits or losses, and were financed by debt. A consultant to CDEL, who did not wish to be named, said that VGS's proclivity to micromanage every aspect of his business resulted in him neglecting the core tasks of a CEO– providing strategic direction to and ensuring financial stability of the conglomerate he founded.

Another factor that weakened VGS's empire-building aspiration was the absence of one or more strong deputies who could share the burden of execution and, more importantly, cross swords with him without fear or favour. Independent and strong-minded deputies like Manoj Modi, Mohandas Pai and Vineet Nayyar have played significant roles in the success of their bosses—Mukesh Ambani, Narayan Murthy and Shiv Nadar.

It was certainly not because VGS was intolerant to criticism from his peers and subordinates. His decision to buy back AIG's equity stake in 2003 when Nilekani had expressed his reservations, and giving his subordinates latitude to experiment with decisions such as setting up two CCD cafés in the same building support this view. So, did VGS consciously or unconsciously attract stakeholders who did not disagree with him? We can only speculate.

The Combustible Combination

A key issue that needs to be addressed is the role of politics in VGS's life. With due apologies to Jane Austen, it is a truth universally acknowledged that businesses seeking to evolve into empires must be in want of political backing. Or at least minimal political interference as the rise of FANG (Facebook, Amazon, Netflix and Google Alphabet) has demonstrated. Did VGS tap into India's political machinery to further his businesses, or did he seek to play a part in it?

On 26 May 2020, *Nikkei Asia* published a column that is probably the most extensive English language account of VGS's political dealings.[9] The views stated in the column were attributed to various anonymous sources. Most of those I interviewed to understand VGS's role in Karnataka politics either refused to speak on the subject or did not wish to be named.

One of VGS's close associates, who wished to remain anonymous, told the *Nikkei Asia* columnist, Henny Sender, 'He was a political junkie. He was a kingmaker in his own mind.' VGS bankrolled his father-in-law's 'political activities and was rewarded with proximity to the backroom politics in Karnataka and in Delhi.'

Nikkei Asia also quoted an unnamed political consultant as saying that the popular perception of Krishna facilitating VGS's growth was incorrect. It was actually the other way around. An anonymous CEO of a software company quipped, 'Every politician wanted him to bankroll them. Everyone expected his support.'

One of VGS's creditors informed *Nikkei Asia*, 'In Karnataka politics, money flows both ways.' VGS had reportedly assisted Congress politicians in Karnataka with fund-raising and took money from them when confronted with a liquidity trap. The 27 July 2019 letter stated that VGS had borrowed money from a friend to buy back shares from a PE investor.

The *Nikkei Asia* column also opined that VGS's proximity to Congress politicians had become a liability when the BJP-led National Democratic Alliance (NDA) won a landslide victory in the 2014 union elections. Krishna, who was rumoured to have been sidelined by the Congress and who joined the BJP in 2017, was apparently persuaded by VGS to do so. S.M. Krishna was not alone in moving from the Congress to BJP. Three other former chief ministers from the Congress shifted their allegiance to the BJP. N.D. Tiwari, Narayan Rane and Shankersinh Vaghela, former chief ministers of Uttar Pradesh, Maharashtra and Gujarat respectively, left the Congress to join the BJP. Former union minister for power, Jyotiraditya Scindia, was another high-profile politician who joined the BJP in 2020. The *Sunday Guardian* reported that 30 politicians had moved from the Congress to the BJP between 2013 to 2020.[10] The BJP, which came to power on an anti-corruption plank, did induct Congress politicians in its fold.

However, S.M. Krishna's one-time protégé, D.K. Shivakumar, remained with the Congress and was Karnataka's minister for energy at the time of the former joining the BJP. Shivakumar had his share of legal wrangles. In 2015, the Karnataka High Court had issued a notice against him, his family members and a few granite companies for allegedly engaging in illegal mining in his constituency, Kanakapura and Ramanagara. This was when he was the state minister for energy. In 2017, when the Income Tax department raided Shivakumar while he was safeguarding the Gujarat-based Congress MPs at Eagleton Resorts, it reportedly uncovered his dealings with VGS.[11]

In 2019, the ED questioned Shivakumar regarding a money laundering case, after which he spent almost two months at Tihar jail in New Delhi before being released on bail. In 2020, the CBI raided Shivakumar's premises. Shivakumar was one of the numerous Indian politicians who has had corruption charges slapped on them.[12] The politician reported assets of ₹840 crore ($123 million) while filing his nomination papers for the 2018 state elections. This was more than a three-fold jump from the

₹251 crore ($43 million) he had reported ahead of the 2013 state elections.[13]

A veteran Bengaluru-based journalist pointed out that the frequency of raids by several regulatory agencies on Shivakumar had intensified after the 2014 union elections. This was on account of Shivakumar's loyalty to the Congress. VGS was caught in the crossfire.

The Lure of Debt

A trait that VGS shares with the other protagonists of this narrative—Anil Ambani, Naresh Goyal and Vijay Mallya—is a high-risk appetite. These men chose to borrow monies far in excess of their enterprises' ability to repay. These borrowings financed their enterprises' expansion and further their personal agendas. Notwithstanding their knowledge of finance, each of them believed that he was different. All of them prioritized expansion, a favourite goal of empire-builders, over sustainability. The quartet, though by no means unique, were blind to the likelihood of a cyclical downturn or a black swan event leading to a credit crunch.

VGS was weighed down by the additional tax liability arising from his undisclosed income that the Income Tax department had uncovered, the insider trading allegation filed with SEBI and, reportedly, pressure from one of the PE partners to buy back the PE firm's shares. VGS's purported suicide note stated, 'I could not take any more pressure from one of the private equity partners forcing me to buy back shares, a transaction I had partially completed six months ago by borrowing a large sum of money from a friend.'

The PE firms, KKR and NSR, held close to 17 per cent stake in CDEL. PE investors earn profits by investing in unlisted companies and selling their investment when the investee company lists itself and the share price appreciates subsequent to the listing or the investee company buys back the PE investor's stake. CDEL's share price had declined by 30 per cent from its listing price of ₹328 in October 2015 to ₹229 on 30 June 2019, while the Sensex had appreciated by almost 50 per cent during this period. No dividends were paid since CDEL's October 2015 listing, while the Sensex's annual dividend yield during this period was around 5.25 per cent. In reality, the PE investors had earned neither capital gains nor dividends through their investment in CDEL. VGS's final letter did mention that he was pressurized by PE investors and that he had borrowed from a friend to pay the PE investors.

Standard Chartered Private Equity had sold its stake in CDEL in FY2016, within a year of the IPO. Marina III (Singapore) sold its 2.57 million CDEL shares in FY2019 and would have realized ₹60 crore ($8.71 million) to ₹90 crore ($13.06 million), had it sold these shares in the open market. The holdings of the three major PE investors – KKR Mauritius, NLS Mauritius, and Marina West (Singapore) remained unchanged at 45 million shares between 1 April 2017 (twenty-seven months before VGS's demise) to 31 March 2021 (twenty-one months after VGS's demise). It is not known if PE firms had invested in the unlisted businesses VGS owned.

What else could have triggered VGS to take his own life?

Figure 1: CDEL Shares Hels By PE Investors, Number in Millions

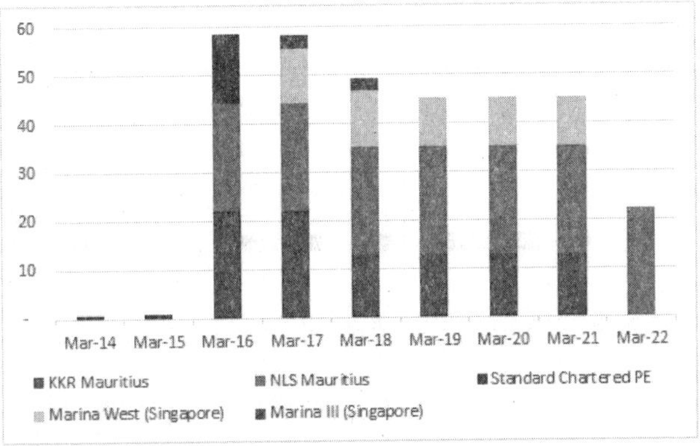

Source: CDEL Annual Reports

The Iceberg

The answer lies in the annual reports of CDEL's four holding companies that together held a 17.13 per cent stake in CDEL as of March 2019 and a related entity, Mysore Amalgamated Coffee Estates Limited (MACEL). The four holding companies are Coffeeday Consolidations Private Limited, Devadarshini Info Technologies Private Limited, Gonibedu Coffee Estates Private Limited and Sivan Securities Private Limited. As the four holding companies and MACEL are unlisted, their financials are neither available on CDEL Group's websites nor the stock exchanges (BSE and NSE).

In India and the rest of the world, unlisted companies are not required by law to make their financials available in the public domain. Disclosures of unlisted companies may be purchased from the ministry of corporate affairs website, www.mca.gov.in, for a modest fee of ₹100 ($1.36) per company per year. The annual reports of these holding companies and MACEL give us a more complete picture of VGS's financial obligations.

The four holding companies shared some interesting similarities (Figure 2).[14] First, all four companies had reported losses in FY2018 and FY2019. Second, the net worth of all four companies was negative in both years, implying that they had generated significant losses during the years preceding FY2018 that had eroded their share capital. Third, the debt outstanding with these companies as of March 2019 was ₹1,220 crore ($177 million).

Even more critical to VGS's financial jugglery was MACEL.

MACEL's annual reports from FY2017 to FY2019 filed with the MCA indicate that VGS's father, Gangaiah Hegde, was its majority shareholder with a 91.75 per cent stake in the company since at least FY2016. The remaining 8.25 per cent stake was held by around 70 individuals.

MACEL, like CDEL's holding companies, reported losses in FY2018 and FY2019. Its net worth was negative during both years, implying that the company had been generating losses even before FY2018. MACEL's main activity was extending loans and advances to 'related parties'. Outstanding loans and advances as of March 2019 were ₹3859 crore ($560 million) that had more than trebled from ₹1175 crore ($178 million) from March 2016. These loans and advances constituted 99.1 per cent of MACEL's ₹3895 crore ($565 million) assets as of March 2019.

The recipients of these loans and advances were over twenty corporates and individuals. The lion's share went to VGS, his wife Malavika and his parents, Gangaiah and Vasanthi. Outstanding advances extended by MACEL to VGS, Malavika and an unnamed partnership firm in which either or both of the couple were partner(s) stood at ₹3235 crore ($470 million) or 83 per cent of MACEL's assets as of March 2019. If the loans and advances extended to Gangaiah and Vasanthi are taken into account, the family's debt to MACEL inches up to ₹3239 crore ($470 million). The family's borrowings from MACEL as of March 2019 had grown almost five times the ₹693 crore ($107 million) as of March 2016.

MACEL was a loss-making entity whose net worth had eroded and turned negative. So how did it finance the loans it had on-lent? MACEL had availed of bank loans and intercorporate deposits from unnamed corporates to the tune of ₹5,333 crore ($774 million) by March 2019. The unlisted, loss-making holding companies and MACEL had borrowed almost as much as CDEL (Figure 3).

CDEL's consolidated debt as of March 2019 was ₹7269 crore ($1.0 billion). This information is available in the company's annual report. If the debt of CDEL's four holding companies and that of MACEL is added to CDEL's consolidated debt, Coffee Day Group's debt almost doubles to ₹13,822 crore ($2.0 billion).

Figure 2: Loans and Advances Given by MACEL

Pages 28 to 30 of MACEL's FY2019 Annual Accounts

iii) Balances with the related parties

Name of the Related party	Nature of Transaction	As on 31.03.2019	As on 31.03.2018
Sri S V Gangaiah Hegde	Loans/advances Given/(received)	2,31,42,061-00	62,42,061-00
Smt Vasanthi Hegde	Short term advances given	1,48,72,986-00	1,39,22,986-00
Gonibeedu Coffee Estates Private Limited	Advances received	171,58,86,935-00	187,23,34,770-00
Coffee Day Consolidations Private Limited	Long Term Advances given	36,42,20,118-00	36,28,75,781-00
Chethan Wood Processing Private Limited	Advances Given Advances Received	10,0019,407-00/ ---	--- 26,21,04,090-00
Devadarshini Info Technologies Private Limited	Long term advances given Long Term borrowings	- 91,81,58,509-00	25,57,13,607-00 -
Coffee day Natural Resources Private Ltd	Long term advances Received / given	77,68,00,975-00	35,45,55,061-00 ---

		-	23,00,89,807-00
Chandrapore Estate Private Ltd	Long term advances given Long Term Advances received	 120,86,21,492-00	 73,19,00,000-00
Dark forest Furniture Company Private Ltd	Advances given	58,49,12,983-00	16,53,69,937-00
Kurkenmutty Estates Private Ltd	Long term advances given	118,17,05,412-00	113,81,00,818-00
Sri V G Siddhartha, Smt Malavika Hegde & partnership firm in which he/she is a partner	Long Term Advances	3235,16,49,924-00	1878,59,45,680-00
Kathlekhan Estates Private Ltd	Long term advances given Long Term Advances received Amounts payable	115,35,71,388-00 93,40,00,000-00 63,84,000-00	96,58,37,249-00 93,40,00,000-00 63,84,000-00
		61,04,03,945-00	61,88,36,745-00

[illegible]		-	23,00,89,807-00
Chandrapore Estate Private Ltd	Long term advances given		
	Long Term Advances received	120,86,21,492-00	73,19,00,000-00
Dark forest Furniture Company Private Ltd	Advances given	58,49,12,983-00	16,53,69,937-00
Kurkenmutty Estates Private Ltd	Long term advances given	118,17,05,412-00	113,81,00,818-00
Sri V G Siddhartha, Smt Malavika Hegde & partnership firm in which he/she is a partner	Long Term Advances	3235,16,49,924-00	1878,59,45,680-00
Kathlekhan Estates Private Ltd	Long term advances given	115,35,71,388-00	96,58,37,249-00
	Long Term Advances received	93,40,00,000-00	93,40,00,000-00
	Amounts payable	63,84,000-00	63,84,000-00
		[illegible]	61,88,36,745-00
Tanglin Development Limited	Long Term Advances given	11,68,29,002-00	-
Coffeeday Barefoot Resorts Private Ltd	Long Term Advances given	-	10,02,41,303-00
	Long Term Advances received	64,97,48,997-00	-
Coffee Day Resorts (MSM) Private Limited	Short Term Borrowings	481,81,81,259-00	268,85,84,141-00
Coffee Day Global Ltd	Borrowings	64,81,80,161-00	3,46,15,175-00
Karnataka Wildlife Resorts Private Limited	Long Term Advances received	6,06,47,765-00	6,06,45,765-00
Wilderness Resorts Private Limited	Advances given	55,31,31,740-00	-

Source: MACEL FY2019 annual report downloaded from www.mca.gov.in

Coffee Day Group is non-exhaustively defined as CDEL, its four holding companies and MACEL.

The ratio of CDEL's on-balance sheet debt to EBITDA was a sizable 9.36 times as of March 2019. If the debt of CDEL's holding companies and MACEL were added to CDEL's on-balance sheet debt, the resultant debt to EBITDA ratio was a gargantuan 17.81 times. It was this debt that VGS found difficult to refinance in the credit crunch that ensued after IL&FS's default.

The Coffee Day Group borrowed primarily through bank and NBFC loans, intra-group loans and inter-corporate loans (also known as inter-corporate deposits). The disclosures by the four holding companies are inadequate to segregate the shares of bank and NBFC loans, intra-group loans and inter-corporate loans in the group's total outstanding debt. It is also not known if there exist any profitable entities within the Coffee Day Group, excluding CDEL, that have not resorted to borrowing and have lent their surplus monies to their related firms. If this were the case, the group's debt may be lower than ₹13,822 crore ($2.0 billion). The available disclosures are inadequate to make this assessment.

MACEL, however, reports the shares of bank loans and inter-corporate loans in its outstanding debt. The composition of MACEL's debt sheds light on the pressures VGS was subject to due to the colossal debt. Bank loans constituted 36 per cent or ₹1,902 crore ($276 million) of MACEL's ₹5333 crore ($774 million) debt as of March 2019. The balance 64 per cent, or ₹3432 crore ($498 million), were inter-corporate loans. The identities of the lenders of these inter-corporate loans are not divulged in MACEL's annual reports. It was the pressure of repaying this debt that prompted VGS to direct CDEL to extend a ₹789 crore ($115 million) loan to MACEL in FY2019. Was a private equity investor among those who extended inter-corporate loans to MACEL and consequently pressurized him to repay?

A government agency accessing MACEL's bank accounts and following the money trail is a legal way of finding out. In August 2019, CDEL had commissioned Ashok Kumar Malhotra, a retired deputy inspector general of the Central Bureau of Intelligence (CBI), to probe into the purported letter written by VGS before his death. The probe describes MACEL as an entity that handled VGS's personal businesses. Media reports of the probe's findings were published in July 2020.[15]

Figure 2: Select Financial Metrics of CDEL, the Holding Companies and MACEL

₹ Crore	Revenue		Post-tax Profit		Networth		Debt	
	FY2018	FY2019	FY2018	FY2019	FY2018	FY2019	FY2018	FY2019
CDEL (Listed Entity)	3,851	4,467	148	147	3,015	3,166	5,082	7,269
Holding Companies	22	19	-64	-109	-7	-135	1,227	1,220
MACEL	4	4	-33	-58	-166	-224	4,019	5,333
CDEL Group	**3,878**	**4,490**	**52**	**-19**	**2,843**	**2,808**	**10,328**	**13,822**

Source: Annual reports of CDEL, MACEL & the four holding companies—Coffeeday Consolidations Private Limited, Devadarshini Info Technologies Private Limited, Gonibedu Coffee Estates Private Limited and Sivan Securities Private Limited.

The probe reported that entities of the Coffee Day Group had lent MACEL ₹3535 crore ($513 million). Does this mean that the ₹3432 crore ($498 million) inter-corporate loans borrowed by MACEL according to its FY2019 annual accounts and the ₹3535 crore ($513 million) lent by Coffee Day Group entities to MACEL refer to the same transaction, albeit at different dates? MACEL's FY2019 annual accounts do not have sufficient information to ascertain this.

Unsurprisingly, the probe findings that were reported by the media made no reference to MACEL's ₹5333 crore ($774 million) debt and the fact that almost all of the debt was on-lent to related parties, predominantly VGS and his immediate family members.

A journalist observed that VGS, by virtue of his proximity to politicians, was collateral damage to the BJP–Congress rivalry in Karnataka. Another collateral damage is evident in the CDEL saga. The rigour of banks' credit underwriting and due diligence in India has become collateral damage to crony capitalism.

Part 2: High-Flyers

Chapter 8

Take Off

> 'No document has ever given me a greater thrill than the little blue and gold certificate delivered to me on 10 February 1929, by the Aero Club of India and Burma on behalf of the Federation Aeronautique Internationale (F.A.I.). The fact that it bore the Number I added to my pride in owning it, even though it meant nothing more than that I was the first one to have qualified in India . . . '[1]
>
> —*Jehangir Ratanji Dadabhoy Tata chairman, Tata Sons (1938–1991)*

Aviation is a high-risk industry. The capital-intensive nature of business, minimal barriers to entry, volatile aviation turbine fuel (ATF) prices and high reliance on debt have resulted in airline failures recurring globally.

Tongue-in-cheek remarks by high-profile CEOs aptly describe this industry's riskiness and performance. Warren Buffet quipped, 'If a far-sighted capitalist had been present at Kitty Hawk, he would have done his successors a huge favour by shooting Orville down.' Richard Branson, who once helmed Virgin Atlantic, prophetically remarked, 'If you want to be a millionaire, start with a billion dollars and launch a new airline.'

The Indian aviation industry is not an exception to the global norm. Since the industry was liberalized in the 1990s, most airlines—including India's flag carrier Air India, East West Airlines, Jet Airways, Kingfisher Airlines and SpiceJet—are struggling or have become defunct.

Airline failures in India are commonly attributed to the price-sensitive domestic market and ambitious entrepreneurs like Naresh Goyal and Vijay Mallya, who founded Jet Airways and Kingfisher Airlines respectively, undertaking debt-financed expansions far in excess of what their cash flows justified. However, as I delved deeper into this mercurial industry, I realized that there was a third factor that had contributed to the dismal performance of airlines in India: the intriguing policies of the Indian government. The government's actions since Independence lend credence to the memorable observation, 'Insanity is doing the same thing over and over and expecting different results.'

Airline founders and the government ought to have nurtured a promising industry to fulfil its potential, leverage on the nation's locational advantage to evolve into a global airline hub and generate employment opportunities for millions. This section of *Unfinished Business*—The High-Flyers—narrates how ambition and politics propelled an industry, which had and has great potential in India, into a mess.

Impeccable Antecedents

In January 1929, the Aero Club of India and Burma opened in Bombay. Barely twelve days later, on 3 February 1929, the twenty-five-year-old JRD Tata, after having undergone the requisite 3 hours and 45 minutes dual flying experience, qualified for the 'A' license and embarked on his first solo flight.

However, renting a plane from the Aero Club was expensive. So, in May 1929, JRD travelled to London and purchased a Gipsy Moth for £1,200; worth around ₹85,000 in 2019 without accounting for inflation. Around the same time, Imperial Airways,

Britain's commercial airline, planned to ferry passengers and mail from London to Australia in a flight that would halt at Karachi and Calcutta (now Kolkata).

This news piqued the interest of Nevill Vintcent, a World War I pilot and heavyweight boxing champion with the British Royal Air Force in the Middle East. This adventurous pilot, alongside Capt. J.S. Newall, flew to India in a De Havilland 9A in the late 1920s. Vintcent drew up a plan for a flight that would fly from Karachi to Colombo with stopovers at Bombay and a city in south India. Armed with an idea, but without the financial clout, the duo initially went around the country offering joy rides. Later, they also undertook aerial photography and survey work until they could locate a business partner.

Russa Mehta, son of Sir Homi Mehta, a textile magnate, was Vintcent's first port of call. The Mehtas did not evince much interest in Vintcent's proposal. Homi Mehta, however, directed Vintcent to approach the Tatas. Vintcent met JRD within a month of the latter getting his license. The two men hit it off instantly and India's aviation industry was on the verge of take-off.

When Vintcent and JRD decided to collaborate, their challenge was to get Sir Dorab Tata, the ageing chairman of Tata Sons, to approve the proposal. The Tatas were recovering from the downturn in the 1920s and had to shut down some of their enterprises. However, JRD's mentor, John Peterson, a retired Indian Civil Services (ICS) officer and director-in-charge at Tata Steel, interceded and persuaded Sir Dorab to invest 2,00,000 in the new enterprise. JRD was Peterson's understudy at the beginning of his career in Tata Steel.

Peterson also wrote to the GoI, on behalf of the Tatas, Vintcent and Newall, proposing a mail service between Karachi and Bombay, on 20 March 1929. After multiple missives and much to-and-fro, the government awarded Tatas a ten-year contract on 24 April 1932. JRD Tata went to England and purchased two Puss Moths for Tata Air Mail.

An important milestone in India's civil aviation history was achieved on 15 October 1932. It was the first day the twenty-eight-year-old JRD flew Tata Air Mail's brand-new Puss Moth from Karachi to Bombay, ferrying 63 pounds of mail. The Postmaster of Bombay was present to receive 55 pounds of mail as JRD had already dropped off 8 pounds in Ahmedabad. Within twenty minutes of JRD's landing, the mail was transferred to the second, waiting Puss Moth. Vintcent took off with 47 pounds of mail for Madras and 6 pounds for Bellary, which was a refuelling halt en route.

In January 1934, Vintcent announced that Tata Air Mail had made a profit of ₹10,000 despite receiving zero subsidies from the government. Further, the airline had achieved 100 per cent reliability while nine out of Imperial Airways' 52 flights were delayed. As Tata Airlines grew and the planes became slightly bigger, a solitary passenger was accommodated in an open seat behind the cockpit. The pilots took time to get accustomed to plying passengers. One pilot apparently munched on a leg of chicken and flung the bone out of the cockpit. The wind deposited the bone onto the lap of a rather astonished passenger.

Capt. K. Visvanath, who rose to become the director of operations in Air India and would accompany JRD on his thirtieth and golden jubilee anniversary flights, joined Tata Air Mail in 1936. In 1938, the British government introduced the 'All-Up Empire Airmail Scheme'. Both Tata Airlines and its competitor, Indian National Airways, received generous mail carriage payments for their respective routes. R.E. Grant Govan, a Delhi-based British industrialist, who co-founded Board of Control for Cricket in India (BCCI) and the Cricket Club of India (CCI), incorporated Indian National Airways in 1933. Tata Air Mail's profits grew almost ten-fold to ₹6,00,000 in 1938 from ₹66,000 in 1937. While passenger traffic, facilitated by bigger planes, had grown six-fold, mail volume grew four times. By October 1940, eight years since inception, Tata Airlines had covered 1.50 million miles. The Bombay–Delhi airfare was priced slightly lower than the prevailing first-class rail fare.

Air India

When World War II drew to a close in 1945, KLM and Air-France resumed their services to India. British Overseas Airways Corporation (BOAC), the precursor to today's British Airways, continued to fly to Karachi, New Delhi and Calcutta while TWA and Pan Am too started flying to India in 1947, thus intensifying the competitive landscape.

It was also the year when Pakistan was carved out of India and the two nations became independent. Both countries witnessed a migration of 14 million people, one of the largest forced migrations of the twentieth century. Tata Airlines, under the GoI's directive, flew Muslims from Delhi to Lahore (mostly) in Pakistan.

Against this bloody backdrop, Tata Airlines, now renamed Air India, submitted a proposal to the government to create a new international airline, Air India International. Under the terms of the proposal, Air India (the domestic carrier), the GoI and the public would subscribe to the capital of the new entity. Air India would provide the technical and management expertise and Air India International would initially operate services between India and the UK.

Air India International secured government approval—which had taken almost three years for Tata Air Mail—in a matter of weeks. Years later, JRD asked Jagjivan Ram, who served as a union minister for over three decades, about this volte-face. The latter replied, 'We did not know any better then!' Jagjivan Ram did not acknowledge that the GoI would have taken much longer to launch an international airline.

The government agreed to pick up a 49 per cent stake in Air India International, while the Tatas and the public would hold 25 per cent and 26 per cent respectively. JRD was willing to offer the government an incremental 2 per cent stake from Tata's share, if the government was desirous of holding a majority stake of 51 per cent. Air India International was to be the first joint venture between the government and the Tatas.

Maneck Dalal, a Cambridge graduate who had supervised the repatriation of Muslims to Lahore at Air India's Delhi office, was dispatched to London to oversee Air India International's launch from the London side. A shortage of office space near the old airport in north London resulted in Air India's traffic department having to work out of a caravan in the harsh winter of 1947. Air India rented a second caravan six months later. The airline arranged for the training of its pilots and other staff with an international airline.

Fortuitously, Air India received delivery of new planes six months ahead of schedule as another airline had cancelled its purchase. Air India International was incorporated on 8 March 1948 and its maiden flight from Bombay to London was scheduled exactly three months later. JRD, his wife Thelma Vicaji, the Jamsaheb of Nawanagar and industrialist Neville Wadia were among the first passengers who boarded a spanking new Constellation—a propeller-driven, four-engine airliner, christened Malabar Princess—at Bombay on Tuesday, 8 June 1948. The Indian high commissioner to the United Kingdom was present at London airport to receive the Malabar Princess.

Air India imbibed JRD's reverence for punctuality. Nari Dastur, who for over two decades worked in Air India's multiple offices in Europe and later took charge as the regional director, relates how in the 1950s, Air India flights used to arrive at Geneva at 11 a.m. He overheard one Swiss ask another, 'What's the exact time?' His companion looked out of the window and said, '11 o' clock.' 'How do you know? You haven't looked at your watch.' The other replied in a matter-of-fact way, 'Air India has just landed.'[2]

In 1949, Air India inaugurated its service to the African continent with flights to Nairobi, which had a sizeable Indian population. The airline's reach spanned from Japan and Fiji in the east to the US in the west. In fact, Air India International started flying to West Germany in the 1950s, even before Lufthansa launched its services in 1955.

Floodgates

Operations of Air India and Air India International were cruising along smoothly even when the operating environment for domestic airlines ran into rough weather in India. The reason was over-capacity. The government had, in 1943, accepted the Tymms plan for the post-war development of aviation. Sir Frederick Tymms, director of civil aviation in India, had drawn up a plan for the orderly development of the aviation sector with government oversight. This plan proposed the licensing of three to four airlines to ensure adequate route mileage for all and the opportunity to develop traffic along the allotted routes, while simultaneously ensuring the airline industry was competitive.

As Air India and Indian National Airways were already plying domestic routes, it would have sufficed if the government had awarded licenses to two additional players. However, the government awarded licenses to at least eight more players! These were Airways India, Air Services of India, Ambica Airlines, Bharat Airways, Deccan Airways, Himalayan Aviation, Jupiter Airlines and Kalinga Airlines.

At the end of World War II, the American Air Force left behind hundreds of airplanes, mostly Dakota DC3s. The government awarded the Tatas a contract to buy and sell these airplanes, which lay across several Indian aerodromes. Some of these airplanes had been sabotaged and had to be sold as scrap. The Americans had destroyed the in-flight instruments with pickaxes to render the airplanes unfit for sale. This was to ensure that the market for new airplanes manufactured in the US was protected. Also, refurbishing the DC3s was more expensive than buying new airplanes.

Indian businessmen ignorant of the dynamics of managing an airline and keen to enter the glamourous aviation industry rushed to avail of licenses the government was distributing freely. Ambica Airlines and Jupiter Airlines were driven to liquidation by 1948.

In February 1950, the government appointed a committee headed by Justice G.S. Rajadhyaksha to assess the condition of the civil aviation industry. The committee recommended that the government extend subsidies to domestic airlines and reduce the number of operators. However, the committee advised against immediate nationalization.

Expropriation

As other domestic airlines continued to struggle, the Planning Commission, in 1952, recommended that all licensed airlines may be merged into a single entity, in which the government would own the majority stake.

JRD submitted an alternate proposal under which the government could create two corporations, one each for domestic and international aviation, and hold majority stakes in both entities. This would insulate Air India International from being clubbed with other poorly performing airlines and the resultant reputation risks. He further recommended that the government pay the airlines compensation based on the market value of the fleet as opposed to acquisition cost minus depreciation, as the latter metric ignored refurbishment expenses.

The government disregarded this proposal and decided to proceed with nationalization in November 1952. Rather unfairly, it decided to compensate the airlines based on their fleets' acquisition cost minus depreciation. The compensation offered was ₹28 million (approximately $398,000 in 2019, excluding inflation) for Air India and ₹30 million ($426,000) to be divided among the eight domestic airlines, which were merged to form Indian Airlines (IA).

The government invited JRD to be the chairman of both the domestic and international airlines. However, realizing that it would be impossible for him to simultaneously discharge his duties as chairman of Tata Sons and the chairman of the two airlines, JRD accepted the position as chairman of Air India International, but declined to accept any compensation. The government then proceeded to appoint a bureaucrat as chairman of IA.

Though Air India was a smaller airline than market leaders then such as KLM, Pan Am and British Airways, it built its reputation by offering the best flight experience.

Operating a state-of-the art fleet was Air India's forte. The airline had acquired Boeing 747s, which were named after Indian emperors (Shahjahan, Ashoka, Rajaraja and Vikramaditya). The Constellations were named after princesses, the Super Constellations after the queens and the Boeing 707s after Himalayan peaks.

During Air India's twentieth anniversary celebrations in 1968, JRD observed, 'At one time I remember we were the thirteenth largest airline in IATA. Now we are the nineteenth. So, it is obvious, that six airlines have grown ahead of us. Some of them by mergers, many by getting deeply into debt by expanding too fast. Throughout this period, we have always made a profit for Government, and we paid them a dividend. For the last five years we have not asked Government for a single penny to finance our expansion.'[3]

JRD not only had the conviction and ability to incorporate and manage a world-class airline that generated profits, he possessed a rare third attribute—vision. Way back in 1971, he had proposed the listing of Air India and IA in correspondences with Karan Singh, the then union minister for civil aviation, and Mohan Kumaramangalam, union minister for steel and heavy engineering.

Credit: Gujarat Cooperative Milk Marketing Federation Ltd. (Amul)

In 1972, the Government of Singapore incorporated Mercury Singapore Airlines, which was later renamed as Singapore Airlines (SIA). The Singapore government consulted several leading airlines to adopt global best practices. Among the first airlines it tied up with for training and operations was Air India. While JRD's proposal for listing did not gain traction, SIA listed itself in 2000. Air India failed to participate in the first phase of disinvestment of public sector companies during Prime Minister Atal Bihari Vajpayee's tenure between 1998–2004.

The Pall of Politics

The seeds of Air India's downfall were sown during JRD's meeting with Morarji Desai in the mid-1950s, when the latter was the chief minister of the undivided state of Bombay, which comprised present-day Maharashtra and Gujarat. J.R.D. Tata and Homi Modi, then head of Tata Electric Company, had met Desai. JRD had rightly stated during the meeting that additional electricity generation capacity had to be built to avert a power shortage. Desai disagreed, resulting in JRD almost staging a walk out. While Desai dissuaded JRD, the latter's behaviour did not go down too well. The Bombay government accepted JRD's assessment and sanctioned additional capacity, resulting in JRD winning the battle. But Air India was to lose the war nearly two decades later.

The friction continued when Desai became the union minister of commerce and, later, minister of finance in the Congress cabinet. Until 1975, the two men locked horns on policy matters, but there was no major altercation. This changed in the aftermath of the Emergency (June 1975–March 1977), when the Janata Party swept into power in the 1977 union elections. Desai, who had shifted his allegiance to the Janata Party, was elected prime minister. One of the first acts of the new government was to reconstitute the Atomic Energy Commission (AEC). JRD, who had been an AEC member since its inception along with Dr Homi Bhabha, was removed.

On 1 February 1978, when the boards of Air India and IA came up for reconstitution, JRD was dropped. As he was the chairman of Air India, his exclusion from the board meant that he was dismissed. The Janata government, without even informing JRD of this decision, proceeded to announce the appointment of Air India's new chairman that very evening on All India Radio (AIR). The new chairman, Air Chief Marshal P.C. Lal, who was the chairman of IA and Indian Tube Company, a Tata firm, had to convey the news of the ouster to JRD.

Indira Gandhi, who was voted out of power in 1977, wrote to JRD expressing her regret for the ignominious turn of events and appreciation for his services to Indian civil aviation. Within a month of being voted back to power in 1980, Indira Gandhi reappointed JRD to the boards of Air India and IA. When the boards were reconstituted in 1982, all non-bureaucrats—including JRD and Field Marshal Sam Manekshaw—were dropped.

The lack of understanding of the importance of board appointments on GoI's part is evident in the short tenures they gave JRD (who was reappointed to the boards of Air India and IA from 1984–86) and that of his cousin and successor-chairman of Tata Sons Ratan Tata (1986–89). Their tenures were too short and their roles, probably ceremonial, for them to add any real value.

Nosedive

The government, in 1981, started Vayudoot as a regional airline in order to address the transport needs of North-east India and to expand India's domestic air transport network. Vayudoot, which means wind-borne messenger in Hindi, was a joint venture between the two state-owned monopolies, Air India and Indian Airlines. Vayudoot was designed to ferry passengers to IA's network at its hubs in state capitals and other cities. However, Vayudoot consistently lost money due to low occupancy; its operations were fully stopped in 1997.

The government's attempts to privatize Air India in 2000 failed. In 2007, the National Aviation Company of India Limited (NACIL) was formed by merging Air India and Indian Airlines. In 2010, NACIL was renamed Air India. This merger precipitated the fall of India's national carrier.

The airline reported twelve consecutive years of losses starting April 2006. By 31 March 2019, the airline had accumulated ₹66,190 crore ($9.61 billion) debt and financial liabilities. Its net worth (share capital plus accumulated profits less dividends) was completely wiped off and stood at negative ₹35,738 crore ($5.19 billion).[4] The GoI sold Air India back to the Tatas in October 2021 for ₹18,000 crore ($2.43 billion), comprising ₹2700 crore ($365 million) cash and ₹15,300 crore ($2.07 billion) takeover of the airline's debt. Air India's consolidated debt as of 31 August 2021 was ₹61,562 crore ($8.33 billion), of which the Tatas had assumed 25 per cent and GoI transferred the balance 75 per cent, or ₹46,262 crore ($6.26 billion), to a special purpose vehicle, Air India Assets Holding Limited.[5] Ironically, SIA—Tata Sons' joint venture partner in Vistara, which had availed of training and operational guidance from Air India in 1972—did not wish to be associated with the national carrier. SIA declined to partner Tata Sons in the Air India acquisition and furnished a no-objection certificate to enable Tata Sons to acquire another airline.[6]

Chapter 9

Open Skies

On 12 March 1990, a seven-seater aircraft carried World Bank President Barber Conable and his five colleagues from Dhaka to Delhi.

So, what was new? This was the first flight of the first privately-owned air taxi that the government had licensed to operate in India after the nationalization of the aviation industry in 1953. The aircraft's owner, India International Airways Pvt Ltd, was controlled by a then thirty-seven-year-old UK-based non-resident Indian (NRI), an entrepreneur named Surinder Singh Gill.[1]

Hardly a month later, the union minister for civil aviation in Prime Minster V.P. Singh's cabinet, Arif Mohammed Khan, announced a slew of policy changes that aimed at addressing the severe shortage of passenger and cargo flights in India.

The Pioneer's Fall

In March and April 1990, months when Indian garment exports peaked, the cargo backlog at New Delhi airport alone exceeded 22,000 tonnes. IA's dismal performance extended to its passenger business as well. Punctuality, JRD Tata's obsession, had by 1990 become a 'household joke', according to retired Air Marshal S.S. Ramdas, IA's former chairman and managing director. Only 70 per cent of IA flights ran on time. IA's strained employee relations were a contributory factor. The airline's engineers had adopted a go-slow policy demanding pay parity with Air India.

The crash of Airbus A320 at the Bangalore (now Bengaluru) airport on Valentine's Day, 1990, exacerbated the situation. This crash left ninety-two persons, including four crew, dead; there were fifty-four survivors, many of them injured.[2] The government grounded the remaining eighteen Airbus A320s and dithered to re-induct these aircrafts into IA's fleet for months.

In FY1991, IA's revenues halved from FY1990 levels. The airline had also incurred sizeable interest payments on the borrowings it had undertaken to purchase the Airbus A320s. IA declared an ₹83 crore ($44 million) loss in FY1991. The state-owned regional airline, Vayudoot, also declared losses of ₹125 crore ($67 million).[3] It became unviable for Vayudoot to operate as an independent entity, courtesy its consistently poor operating and financial performance. In April 1997, IA took over its flight operations while IA and Air India absorbed its employees.

The government was clearly unable to stem the deterioration in Air India's and IA's performance and rightly believed that competition was essential to improve India's connectivity. Khan announced the 'Open Sky' policy, which removed restrictions on the number of airports from which air taxis could operate, the number of landings they could make, and raised minimum seating capacity to ninety passengers, except for smaller aircrafts. This policy that ended the monopoly of the national carriers also permitted air taxis to charge lower fares than domestic carriers and extended incentives to domestic and foreign airlines to ferry cargo out of India. 'The policy was announced in a bit of a huff,' stated Harsh Vardhan, Vayudoot's managing director.[4] The measures constituted a partial, yet significant reversal of the 1953 nationalization of airlines.

In 1990, the government issued over twenty air taxi licenses. The recipients were a motley crew, including large corporates like Tata Steel, Dalmia Resorts, Lloyds Steel and Indian Metals & Ferro

Alloys, the controversial and politically connected god man- cum-yoga proponent, Dhirendra Brahmachari, and an airline ticketing company, East West Travel and Trade Links Private Limited.

Humble Beginnings

East West was founded in the 1970s by Nasiruddin Wahid, one of the eleven children of Haji Abdul Wahid Mussaliar, an Islamic scholar and a prominent local businessman of Odayam, a fishing village in the south-western state of Kerala. When the business started to flourish in the 1980s, Nasiruddin roped in his younger brother, Thakiyuddin Abdul Wahid, who was then working as a manager in a local department store in United Arab Emirates (UAE).

In 1983, East West acquired a travel agency accredited by International Air Transport Association (IATA). By 1985, it had four offices in Bombay and was expanding across India. East West became the largest ticketing agent in India for Air India, Gulf Air and several other airlines by 1986. The company also recruited thousands of Indians for firms in the Middle East, including Saudi Arabia's Bin Laden group.

This was when the first clash between East West and a small-time travel agency called Jet Air occurred. Gulf Air was looking to appoint an exclusive general sales agent (GSA) for India. Despite being Gulf Air's largest ticketing agent in India, the airline's representative reportedly asked Thakiyuddin for a ₹50 lakh ($397,000) 'personal fee' ahead of awarding the contract. Thakiyuddin scrambled to mobilize the amount and paid the Gulf Air representative in cash without even consulting Nasiruddin, who was then in Bahrain. However, Gulf Air awarded the GSA contract to the much- smaller Jet Air. Shortly thereafter, Kuwait Airways appointed Jet Air as its GSA.

Notwithstanding Jet Air's rise, East West continued to be a dominant force in the Indian air ticketing industry. By the late

1980s, East West had recruited over 75,000 Indians to work in the Persian Gulf and was issuing around 600 airline tickets daily.

Thakiyuddin was a student leader of the Congress party during his college days. Rajiv Gandhi's personal secretary, Vincent George, also hailed from Kerala. Thakiyuddin had befriended George, who introduced him to Rajiv Gandhi when he was the prime minister. Thakiyuddin claimed that it was Rajiv Gandhi, a former pilot of Air India, who urged him to launch an airline.

In 1990, during Prime Minister V.P. Singh's tenure, multiple entities—including East West—received licenses to operate air taxis. Faisal Wahid, Thakiyuddin's younger brother, avers that Rajiv Gandhi's assassination in May 1991 left Thakiyuddin heartbroken, but determined to start an airline as a tribute to India's youngest prime minister.

An entrepreneur from a modest family in Kerala, Thakiyuddin embarked on the mission of launching the first private airline in independent India. Weeks after Rajiv Gandhi's assassination, he started to hire pilots. The first was Rajiv Gandhi's former flight instructor from Indian Airlines, and the second, a nephew of Datta Samant, a trade union leader in Bombay who had led the city's textile workers' strike in 1982. East West's third pilot was Rajiv Gandhi's favourite and the one who used to fly the former prime minister's aircraft for Air India. By cultivating Gandhi, the prime minister and the Indian National Congress, India's dominant political party of the era, and hiring politically-connected professionals, Thakiyuddin demonstrated the strategic vision required to succeed in a regulated industry like civil aviation.

When three US carriers—Pan Am, Eastern Airlines and Midway Airlines—went bankrupt in 1991, their fleet of over 1000 Boeing 737s was left grounded. At that time, airlines could lease a fully functional Boeing 737 by paying a modest advance and monthly lease rental of \$100,000 to \$120,000 (₹22.69 lakhs to ₹27.23 lakhs). East West Airlines raised the requisite capital to take advantage of these bankruptcies and lease aircrafts at competitive rentals.

East West raised ₹35 crore ($15.50 million) capital comprising ₹15 crore ($6.60 million) from the state-owned Industrial Development Bank of India (IDBI), and ₹10 crore ($4.40 million) each from Nasiruddin Wahid and Fair Growth Financial Services, that played a role in the stock trader Harshad Mehta-perpetrated 1992 securities scam.[5]

East West also leased a Boeing 737 from Guinness Peat Aviation at a monthly rental of $110,000 (₹25 lakhs). The Wahids' travel agency, East West Travel and Trade Links, became the new airline's holding company. However, the Wahids' feverish run up to the launch of their airline hit a roadblock when they realized that import of aircrafts attracted a countervailing duty equivalent to 33 per cent of the aircraft's value.

They met then Prime Minister Narasimha Rao to lobby for a reduction in countervailing duty. Rao, though a veteran Congressman, was not favourably disposed towards the Nehru-Gandhi family and their acolytes. They subsequently met the finance minister, Dr Manmohan Singh, who expressed his inability to waive the duty. However, Dr Singh suggested that East West pay a part of the duty under protest whereby the airline could claim a refund when the leased aircraft was returned to Guinness Peat Aviation at the end of the lease term. East West's first aircraft landed in India in January 1992 after the airline paid a duty of ₹3 crore ($1.32 million) under protest.

On the morning of 28 February 1992, the Wahid brothers' invitees—including politicians, journalists and friends—along with forty fee-paying passengers, boarded independent India's first privately-operated aircraft. The Boeing 737 took off from Bombay and landed at Cochin (Kochi at present), the commercial capital of the Wahid brothers' home state, Kerala. The East West flight subsequently ferried passengers from Cochin back to Bombay.

Several politicians travelled as Thakiyuddin's guests on East West flights. He unabashedly lobbied with them for the rescindment of the countervailing duty. He collected the signatures of 125 Members of Parliament (MP) on a petition for the abolition of countervailing duty. Thanks to Thakiyuddin's efforts, Dr Singh progressively slashed the duty from 33 per cent to 18 per cent and then to 8 per cent and finally, zero.

In FY1992, East West's first year of operations, the airline reported an ₹8 crore ($3 million) profit on ₹130 crore ($50 million) revenues. That year, IA reported a ₹150 crore ($58 million) loss. East West's fares were, on an average, 20 per cent less expensive than Indian Airlines and its flights ran close to full capacity. East West created quite a splash in the hitherto staid domestic civil aviation scene. There were impromptu magic shows, ice cream festivals and live music performances on board the flights. Its pilots drew a monthly salary of ₹1.0 lakh ($3900), four times the ₹25,000 ($965) pay IA's pilots drew. By end-1992, Air India and IA pilots went on strike, demanding better pay and working conditions. The airlines' unions and the government undertook protracted negotiations which led nowhere. Madhavrao Scindia, a former royal, as union civil aviation minister, summoned the Wahid brothers to New Delhi for a discussion that included Prime Minister Rao. Scindia, in this meeting, reportedly asked East West to fly as many routes as possible to 'break the back of the striking pilots.'[6] He assured the Wahid brothers of all possible assistance from the government. A characteristically taciturn Rao reluctantly nodded in agreement.

Buoyed by Scindia's support, Thakiyuddin decided to more than double East West's fleet. Within hours of meeting with Scindia and Rao, he started calling aircraft leasing companies. By January 1993, East West's fleet more than doubled from five aircrafts to twelve.

Scindia did not stop with asking the Wahid brothers to expand East West's route coverage. The civil aviation minister also leased a few three-engine Tupolev-154s from Uzbek Airlines with pilots. On 9 January 1993, one of these aircrafts landed in New Delhi's fog-covered airport, hit its left wheel on the runway first, then skidded and flipped over and broke into three pieces as it went up in flames. Fortunately, the 163 passengers and crew on board escaped. The public, led by the striking IA pilots, was enraged. Scindia resigned and Rao severed all ties with the Wahids.

Meanwhile, the competition for Indian skies was heating up. IA's inefficiencies and the striking pilots left passengers stranded. Four privately-owned airlines entered the fray as air taxi operators between 1992 and 1993. These were Damania Airways, Air Sahara, ModiLuft and Jet Airways. Of these, ModiLuft had a technical partnership with the German flag carrier Lufthansa, and Damania Airways had a short run. Both ceased flying in 1996 and 1997 respectively. The Subrata Roy-helmed Sahara Group founded Air Sahara in 1991. Air Sahara, which commenced flying in 1993, did grow its market share but was unable to flourish in the intensely competitive environment. The airline was ultimately acquired by Jet Airways in 2007.

Jet Set Go(yal)

Naresh Goyal, who founded Jet Airways, the airline that would dominate the Indian skies for close to a decade, was born in a humble family in Sangur, Punjab. Naresh and his elder brother, Surinder Kumar, lost their father early in life. Goyal's maternal uncle supported the family and educated the Goyal siblings following their father's premature demise.

Goyal secured his undergraduate degree in commerce in 1967 and then joined his uncle's travel business as a cashier. Two years later, he joined Iraqi Airways and, over the next few years, gained extensive experience in all facets of civil aviation through his association with predominantly Middle Eastern airlines.

In 1974, Naresh Goyal borrowed money from his mother to start Jet Air, a travel agency, with his brother. Jet Air provided sales and marketing representation to foreign airlines in India. When the GoI announced the 'Open Skies' policy, Goyal incorporated Jet Airways in 1992.

Jet Airways got off to a rather bumpy start. Its maiden flight in 1993 landed at the wrong airfield in Coimbatore in Tamil Nadu.

Jet's fleet comprised Boeing 737-300s whose low-hanging engines increased the risk of accidents, unlike the safer Boeing 737-200s that were the mainstay of East West's fleet. So, Goyal started poaching East West's employees and replicating its business practices.

Underworld Connections

Troubles started brewing for East West on the legal front as well. The airline was subject to scrutiny by the Income Tax department, the Department of Revenue Intelligence and other agencies. The government and regulatory agencies appeared to be convinced that the Wahids had dealings with underworld don Dawood Ibrahim.

In Bombay, gangs led by Dawood Ibrahim and Arun Gawli clashed for supremacy of the underworld in the 1990s. On 12 September 1992, Shailesh Haldankar, a Gawli gang member, was imprisoned and admitted to Bombay's JJ Hospital. Six hitmen from Dawood's gang stole into the hospital in the night and conducted a shootout. This was in retaliation for Haldankar killing Dawood Ibrahim's brother-in-law, Ibrahim Parker. Haldankar was killed on the spot, while three police constables, a nurse, a patient and an attendant were injured in the shootout.

Investigations led the police to V.N. Rai, the nephew of Congress party leader and union minister Kalpnath Rai, and subsequently to Mohammed Farooq, a hawala operator (money launderer) with links to Dawood. Simultaneously, while raiding an apartment in New Delhi, the police unearthed an envelope addressed to Farooq that was meant to be delivered to Sabu Chacko, who was East West's head in New Delhi and the brother-in-law of Vincent George, Rajiv Gandhi's personal assistant.[7] These developments convinced the government and regulatory agencies that East West had dealings with Dawood. Years later, however, the Supreme Court cleared Chacko of all charges and he moved to the US.

The police also claimed at the time that Dawood's operatives, who had been apprehended in New Delhi, had stated that the gangster's agents had handed over large sums of money to East West, including ₹5 crore ($1.93 million) during the summer of 1992. The *Times of India* subsequently published a report claiming that East West's travel division (East West Travel and Trade Links Private Limited) had issued air tickets for Tiger Memon and his family to flee India after the 1993 Bombay blasts.[8] Memon was Dawood's accomplice and the mastermind behind these blasts. Later, it emerged that the tickets were issued by another travel agency bearing a similar name, East West Travel and Tours. East West Airlines put out advertisements in leading newspapers to dispel the misconception.

Notwithstanding the adverse publicity, it became clear subsequently that East West Airlines was not involved in the 1993 bombings. The government had no option but to grant a registered airline license to East West Airlines. In 1994, the airline became India's first private player to be granted scheduled routes. The progression from an air taxi operator to an officially registered airline was a significant milestone. East West Airlines could now advertise its routes and fares and undertake promotional efforts. Air taxis were prohibited by law to advertise routes and fares. This provided East West the impetus to launch an IPO in mid-1994. East West believed that it was possible to raise ₹250 crore ($80 million) through the IPO. Its bankers, however, advised the airline to consider a modest ₹50 crore ($16 million). The company acquiesced. The IPO was a resounding success; it was 23 times oversubscribed.

The IPO provided East West the funding to embark on the next phase of expansion. In late 1994, East West placed an order for three new Boeing 737-400s and introduced business class on domestic routes. As Malaysian Airlines had already placed an order for 737-400s with Boeing, East West planned to lease these aircrafts from Malaysian Airlines.

It was at this juncture that Goyal visited the Wahid brothers. According to Faisal, Goyal complained about Jet Airway's fleet of Boeing 737-300s and their low-hanging engines and announced his intention to emulate East West by acquiring 737-200s.

Thakiyuddin informed Goyal about the new 737-400s and their availability on short notice from Malaysian Airlines.

A few days later, the Directorate General of Civil Aviation (DGCA), India's aviation regulator, wrote to East West stating that it was not familiar with the new Boeing 737-400s and asked East West to submit three copies of the aircraft's manual that contain confidential intellectual property, including aircraft blueprints and drawings. Boeing termed the demand 'ridiculous' and refused to share the aircraft manuals. DGCA withheld approval for the purchase of the new 737-400s. The Wahid brothers' lobbying with the aviation ministry and the government at large was of no avail.

Malaysian Airlines, which had received one month's rental in advance and five months' deposit from East West, issued a termination notice. It intimated East West that if the airline failed to either lease or purchase the aircrafts within the stipulated deadline, the contract would be void. DGCA approval did not come through before this deadline and East West had to forfeit the advance payments made to Malaysian Airlines. A few weeks later, Jet Airways leased three Boeing 737-400s from Malaysian Airlines. When the tail paint of these new aircrafts started to peel off, passengers reported sighting the Easy West colours beneath.

To add insult to injury, Thakiyuddin received a call from Boeing. The Boeing representative requested him to depute an East West engineer to service a 737-400 in India that had developed structural problems. The 737-400 in question was part of the Jet Airways fleet. Thakiyuddin saw this as an opportunity for East West to service state-of-the-art aircrafts and deputed his engineer. East West subsequently launched an advertisement campaign highlighting its aircraft servicing capabilities. Jet Airways hit back with advertisements that stated that its competition was flying older aircrafts.

Destructive Competition

Josy Joseph in his *Feast of Vultures* narrates a chilling account of Goyal's wiliness following his appropriation of the Boeing

737-400s that Malaysian Airlines had earmarked for East West. In June 1995, Damodaran, one of Naresh Goyal's close confidants and Jet Airways' point person for marketing, visited Thakiyuddin. Damodaran, a Malayali from Kerala, expressed his disillusionment with Goyal and a desire to join East West Airlines. Notwithstanding stiff internal opposition, Thakiyuddin recruited Damodaran, who was tasked with spearheading East West's marketing strategies. He was also inducted into the airline's strategy team—which predominantly comprised the Wahid siblings—from day one. Four months later, Damodaran stopped coming to East West's office and was untraceable. Days later, Thakiyuddin received a phone call. The caller said, 'Taki, my man is back with me. Don't ever try that with me again!'[9] The caller was Naresh Goyal.

Goyal's guile appeared to have little impact on the East West juggernaut. Faisal described the last two quarters of 1995 as East West's 'golden period'. In October 1995, East West recorded its highest-ever monthly revenue. The Wahid family tied up with Marriott International to open its first hotel in India, in Kovalam. East West also started looking for a strategic partner to buy an equity stake in the airline. Emirates, the newly incorporated flag carrier of the UAE, evinced interest. Thakiyuddin flew to Dubai and signed a memorandum of understanding with Emirates.

Shortly thereafter, an Emirates official let it slip in the media that the airline had tied up with an Indian company. Although, the official did not name the company, it was evident that Emirates was partnering with East West, as Kuwait Airways and Gulf Air had invested in Jet. Within days of the leak, the Indian government prohibited foreign airlines from investing in domestic airlines. The government also required domestic airlines that had secured equity investments from foreign airlines to sever ties with their foreign investors.

Thakiyuddin had no time to mount a defence. On the evening of 13 November 1995, as he was being chauffeured back home in his brand-new blue Mercedes Benz, three armed men in a red Maruti van blocked his vehicle and shot at its occupants. Thakiyuddin tried to duck. The chauffeur, Barkatalai, froze initially, then recovered and rammed the Mercedes into the van. The assailants fled and Barkatalai rushed Thakiyuddin to the nearby Bhabha General Hospital. The forty-year-old Thakiyuddin Abdul Wahid was wheeled into the emergency ward at around 9.55 p.m. and declared dead.

Police investigations concluded that Rohit Verma, an aide of yet another Bombay gangster, Chhota Rajan, had led the Thakiyuddin shooting. In September 2000, Verma met his end while shielding Rajan from an attack by Dawood's hitmen.

In 2003, India's foreign intelligence agency, Research & Analysis Wing (RAW), intercepted a conversation. As a RAW officer informed Joseph, 'It was a conversation between Chhota Shakeel and one of his men in Mumbai. He was abusing [an airline big shot] and asked the aide to go and meet him, to tell him that he has not, after so many years, paid up the promised amount for killing Thakiyuddin.'[10] Chhota Shakeel was a high-ranking leader of Dawood's D-Company in Mumbai. The officer stated there were a few other conversations over the years along similar lines. 'It fell into a pattern. We had reliable evidence that Thakiyuddin was killed by a rival who had colluded with and commissioned the underworld,' the officer concluded.[11]

It is noteworthy that while the police concluded that Dawood's rival had shot at Thakiyuddin, RAW reportedly uncovered evidence of Dawood's gang member murdering East West's head honcho. Thakiyuddin, contrary to media speculation and police investigations, may have been Dawood's victim and not an accomplice.

Chapter 10

Simply Fly

The DGCA started publishing air transport statistics from FY1998. East West Airlines, India's first privately-owned airline since independence and the country's first listed airline, does not even find a mention in DGCA's maiden publication. The trailblazer, weighed down by investigations and financial difficulties, ceased flying in August 1996, barely nine months after Thakiyuddin's murder.

According to DGCA's domestic airline statistics, in FY1998 Indian Airlines operated half of India's domestic aircrafts, while Alliance Air—a wholly owned subsidiary of Indian Airlines founded in 1996—operated 15 per cent. Jet Airways and Sahara Airlines operated 24 per cent and 8 per cent of domestic aircrafts respectively, and Archana Airways operated a miniscule 3 per cent. However, the private airlines outdid state-owned carriers in terms of average daily revenue hours. Sahara led the pack with its aircrafts clocking an average 14.1 hours per day, followed by Jet (10.1), Alliance (8.4) and Indian Airlines (6.6). Archana Airways, as in the case of fleet strength, brought up the rear with its carriers flying an average 3.6 hours daily.[1] The death of its promoter, Dhirendra Brahmachari, in an air crash in 1994 and the absence of a strong management team lead to the airline ceasing operations by 2000.

The Wahid brothers, Nasiruddin and Faisal, attempted to revive East West Airlines after Thakiyuddin's murder. Fortunately for them, or so they believed, Chand Mahal Ibrahim was the union civil aviation minister in the short-lived cabinets of prime ministers H.D. Deve Gowda (June 1996–April 1997) and Inder Kumar Gujral (April 1997–March 1998). Ibrahim, though a Karnataka-based politician, was a Malayali Muslim like the Wahid brothers.

The siblings enlisted Ibrahim's support and reached out to Singapore Airlines, which was keen to enter the Indian market. The Tata Group had also initiated discussions with Singapore Airlines. Ratan Tata was also a pilot and zealous about re-entering the aviation industry. However, neither East West nor Tata Sons was able to secure government approval to operate a domestic airline as a joint venture with Singapore Airlines. It was only in 2013 that Tata Sons and Singapore Airlines formed a joint venture, Vistara, to operate a full-service carrier (FSC) in India. Ratan Tata stated in 2010 that, 'We approached three prime ministers. But an individual thwarted our efforts to form the airlines . . . I did not want to go to bed knowing well that I set up an airline by paying ₹15 crore (as bribe).'[2] In 2010, ₹15 crore was equivalent to $3.28 million. While Tata did not mention the name of the 'individual', fingers were pointed at Ibrahim. Allegations that Ibrahim was acting at the behest of Naresh Goyal surfaced.[3]

In June 1993, India's Foreign Investment Promotion Board (FIPB) permitted Gulf Air and Kuwait Airways to purchase equity stakes in Tail Winds, Jet Airways' holding company. Subsequent to this approval, Goyal held a 60 per cent stake in Tail Winds, while Gulf Air and Kuwait Airways each held a 20 per cent stake.

A few years later, the government changed its stance and prohibited non-Indian entities from holding equity stakes in domestic carriers. In April 1997, therefore, the ministry of civil aviation directed Jet Airways 'to take steps for disinvestment of Equity Shares held, directly or indirectly, by foreign airlines pursuant to the GoI's policy on foreign equity and NRI/OCB equity participation in the domestic air transport services sector.'[4] OCB stands for overseas corporate bodies. Goyal, by buying back the stakes of Gulf Air and Kuwait Airways, became the 99.99 per cent owner of Tail Winds. Had Goyal thwarted competition at significant personal expense or had the ownership of Tail Winds become more opaque?

In 2001, Ibrahim, who was then an MP in the opposition, accused the Vajpayee-led BJP government of trying to sell Air India to foreign airlines. The pro-reform disinvestment minister, Arun Shourie, shot back, 'I have been trying to find out one thing. Nobody is able to tell me who owns Jet Airways. Is it an Indian airline or a foreign airline? . . . What I have been able to discover through all agencies of government is that Jet Airways is owned by a company called Tail Winds, registered in the Isle of Man, a tax haven.' Ibrahim was quick to assert that Jet Airways was run by an Indian national with capital that was raised within India.[5]

It was the suspicion about Jet Airways' antecedents that led Shourie to scuttle the government's move to allow Jet Airways and Sahara Airlines to fly international routes in 2004, despite Prime Minister Atal Bihari Vajpayee and Deputy Prime Minister Lal Krishna Advani backing the proposal. Advani had affirmed in Parliament that enquiries conducted by the Intelligence Bureau and RAW did not uncover evidence to dispute Goyal's ownership of Jet Airways. Advani's equivocation left Shourie unconvinced, and Vajpayee adjourned the parliamentary discussion on allowing domestic airlines to fly international routes.[6]

Jet Takes Off

The lingering doubts about Jet Airways' ownership and the government withholding permission to the airline to fly overseas did not hamper the airline's emergence as the market leader among domestic carriers. While IA and Alliance Air combined continued to operate the largest fleet of sixty-two aircrafts as of March 2004, Jet operated forty-two aircrafts. Sahara was third with its fleet of twenty aircrafts. Yet, Jet had overtaken IA and Alliance Air, and secured a 44 per cent market share in passenger traffic. The market share of Alliance Air and IA, a monopoly until 1992, and which had enjoyed the first mover advantage for decades, had dwindled to 37 per cent. IA and Alliance Air continued to be market leaders in cargo traffic, with a market share of 47 per cent, but even here, Jet was not far behind. Its market share was 37 per cent, and Sahara had garnered a market share of 10 per cent.

That overstaffing was the Achilles' heel of IA and Alliance Air was evident in the two airlines employing almost thrice Jet Airway's staff strength of 6676. To put this in perspective, while Jet and Sahara employed 163 and 164 people per aircraft, IA and Alliance Air employed almost double the number—315 people per aircraft. Inefficient operations and a bloated salary bill led to IA and Alliance Air reporting post-tax profits of ₹45 crore ($10 million) in FY2004, which was less than a third of Jet Airways' post-tax profits of ₹163 crore ($35 million). Sahara had managed to break even, reporting a meagre profit of ₹96 lakhs ($208,000).

Enter David

FY2004 marked the debut of India's first low-cost carrier (LCC) or budget airline, Air Deccan. Its founder was the fifty-two-year-old retired captain of the Indian Army, Capt. Gorur Ramaswamy Iyengar Gopinath, who launched the airline with a modest fleet of four aircrafts and staff strength of 286 people.

Captain Gopinath, as he is popularly known, was born in November 1951 in the remote hamlet of Gorur in Karnataka. His father, Ramaswamy Iyengar, was a schoolteacher and a Kannada novelist. Gopinath attended the Sainik School in Bijapur and subsequently, the National Defence Academy

(NDA) in Khadakvasla, Pune. Sainik Schools are a network of schools managed by the ministry of defence that aim to train students across India to enter the NDA, regardless of their socio-economic background.

Gopinath was commissioned into the army as a second lieutenant and posted in the School of Artillery in Devlali, near Nasik in Maharashtra. He fought in the 1971 India–Pakistan war. He was a captain in the Indian Army by the time he was twenty-seven years old. A desire to explore new vocations prompted him to resign from the army, return to his village and pursue farming.

Gopinath's father, though initially taken aback by this decision, helped him to embark on a career as an agriculturist. The experience made Gopinath aware of the challenges of rural life, including the difficulty in securing loans and adopting best scientific practices and traditional techniques in farming. In 1979, Gopinath married Bhargavi. It was a match arranged by their families. After his marriage, he moved to Hassan with his wife so that their children had access to quality education. The couple have two daughters—Pallavi and Krithika.

Using the earnings from agriculture, Gopinath floated a slew of commercial enterprises: a motorcycle dealership, a hotel and an agricultural consultancy. He also frequently visited his village to supervise his agricultural holdings. Gopinath's innovative approach to farming led to Rotary International awarding him a scholarship to visit farms in the US in 1984. He visited Vermont and New Hampshire and learnt innovative farming practices over six weeks.

Sericulture was yet another area of interest. Gopinath won the Rolex Laureate Award in 1996 for reviving and improvising on the age-old environment-friendly technique of harvesting silkworm cocoons on paddy straw as opposed to the contemporary practice of using bamboo scaffolds that entails the felling of bamboo plants.

In 1992, the family relocated to Bengaluru. The move to the metropolis resulted in Gopinath renewing his acquaintance with army colleagues. Among them was a freelance pilot,

Capt. K.J. Samuel. Sam, as he was affectionately called, was toying with the idea of setting up a commercial helicopter service. It was an idea that found resonance with Gopinath. In 1995, Gopinath and Sam launched Deccan Aviation.

The venture was a success. Deccan Aviation became the preferred means of travel for most politicians. Its helicopters were ubiquitous during India's rambunctious election campaigns. Deccan Aviation was also involved in rescue missions in Sri Lanka, Nepal, Kabul and south India. Gopinath's intimate experience of living and working in rural, semi-urban and urban India made him aware of the growing purchasing power of the nation's sprawling middle class. Setting up an airline seemed to be a natural progression. Gopinath stated, 'I wanted every Indian to fly at least once in his/her lifetime.'[7]

Air Deccan, with the tagline 'Simplifly', was launched in 2003.[8] Air Deccan reported a profit of ₹56 lakhs ($121,000) during its first year of operations. However, Air Deccan would not enjoy its first mover advantage for long. Ajay Singh, an entrepreneur, purchased the defunct ModiLuft in 2004 and re-christened it SpiceJet. The airline operated its first flight in 2005. The Mumbai-headquartered Wadia Group, whose best-known companies include Bombay Dyeing and Britannia Industries, founded GoAir in 2005. Rahul Bhatia and Rakesh Gangwal launched IndiGo in 2006.

By end 2005, Air Deccan was operating 22 aircrafts and was the fourth-largest domestic airline by fleet size. The three largest domestic operators were Indian Airlines, which operated a fleet of sixty-eight aircrafts, followed by Jet Airways (fifty-one) and Air Sahara (twenty-six). Kingfisher, SpiceJet, GoAir and Paramount together operated fifteen aircrafts.

Innovative marketing strategies enabled Air Deccan to ensure that passenger traffic was commensurate with its fleet expansion. On 6 June 2005, Air Deccan announced that the airline would sell 1000 tickets priced at ₹1 plus ₹221 taxes ($5.03) for the period

7 June to 31 July 2005 across ten routes. The airline had also tied up with Hindustan Petroleum Corporation Limited (HPCL) to sell air tickets at its petrol pumps.[9] According to statista.com, internet penetration in India, which was a paltry 4 per cent in 2007, had almost doubled to a still abysmal 7.5 per cent in 2010. Thus, the decision to sell air tickets through HPCL petrol pumps was an instant hit.

In October 2005, Gopinath unveiled Air Deccan's brand ambassador that was immortal and iconic for decades before the airline's incorporation and one that has even outlived its creator. The brand ambassador for the no-frills budget airline was R.K. Laxman's 'Common Man'. Air Deccan's advertisement agency, Orchard Advertising, part of the Leo Burnett Group, had suggested that Bollywood stars like Amitabh Bachchan or one of the three Khans—Shahrukh, Aamir and Salman—or even Gopinath himself could be roped in as a brand ambassador. However, Gopinath rejected the idea. He rightly decided that signing up a Bollywood star as a brand ambassador would send Air Deccan's costs skyrocketing. Gopinath opined that his donning the role of a brand ambassador 'smacked of hubris and pomposity'.

Orchard Advertising informed Gopinath that their previous attempts to work with Laxman had failed. So, Gopinath directly called Laxman, a Tamilian born and raised in Karnataka, and spoke to him in Kannada. It turned out that Laxman's father was Gopinath's father's headmaster at the Government High School, Hassan. There was an instant rapport between the two men. Laxman permitted Air Deccan to use his Common Man as the airline's brand ambassador.

When Gopinath asked Laxman about the commercial terms, the master cartoonist's response—whatever pleases you—left the airline founder nonplussed.[10]

Jet had, by October 2005, emerged as the undisputed market leader of India's domestic civil aviation market, with a market share of 35 per cent. Indian Airlines' market share had slipped to

26 per cent despite operating the largest fleet among domestic airlines, while Air Sahara's market share was the third highest at 12 per cent. However, it was Air Deccan's performance that was most impressive. Within a period of three years, the airline had caught up with Air Sahara, clocking a market share of 11 per cent.

Achilles' Heel

Though the numerous airlines operating in India in the 2000s were characterized by varying degrees of operational efficiency, they were identical in one respect. They were deeply indebted.

As of March 2004, Jet Airways' ₹3210 crore ($694 million) debt was almost 15 times its ₹216 crore ($47 million) net worth. Air Deccan's debt was around ₹427 crore ($97 million), while its net worth had turned negative by September 2005.[11]

The extent of the state-owned carriers' indebtedness is evident in the first annual report of the NACIL, the entity formed by the government-directed merger of Air India and IA in 2007. NACIL was renamed Air India in 2010. In March 2008, NACIL's ₹18,413 crore ($4.39 billion) debt was more than double its ₹8039 crore ($1.92 billion) net worth.[12]

Though NACIL's outstanding debt was the highest in rupee terms, Jet had the highest balance sheet leverage, which is the ratio of an entity's borrowings to its net worth. This meant that debt, a riskier source of financing, formed a higher proportion of Jet's capital than NACIL's. Ironically, the government had invested more equity in the bleeding NACIL than Goyal had invested in the market leader—Jet Airways.

The Tale of Two IPOs

Jet being more profitable than IA and Alliance Air and emerging as the market leader in domestic passenger traffic went in its favour. Jet reported ₹149 crore ($32 million) profit in FY2004 after two consecutive years of losses. Jet's FY2004 profits were thrice the ₹46 crore ($10 million) combined profits reported by IA and Alliance Air.[13]

However, it was imperative for Jet to strengthen its capitalization and reduce its balance sheet leverage. In February 2005, Jet launched an IPO of 17.27 million shares, offering investors a 20 per cent stake in the company. Each share was priced at ₹1110 ($25), which was 126.50 times the ₹8.70 ($0.20) average price at which shares were allotted to pre-IPO investors. This meant IPO investors' share in Jet Airways' equity capital was 96.8 per cent in terms of value, for which they were given a 20 per cent stake.

Not many retail investors saw through this. After all, what was the probability of them poring over pages 22 and 23 of Jet Airways' 286-page IPO prospectus, to discover the disproportionate financial investment they were making for a modest ownership stake? Investors responded enthusiastically and the IPO was over-subscribed to the extent of 18.7 times and across all investor categories—retail, non-institutional and institutional. The private carrier raised ₹1899 crore ($431 million).[14]

Jet proposed to use these IPO proceeds to repay ₹792 crore ($180 million) debt and compulsory convertible redeemable preference shares (CCRPS), incur ₹461 crore ($105 million) of capital expenditures and deploy the balance ₹646 crore ($146 million) for general corporate purposes. The reduction in Jet's debt was temporary. By March 2009, its debt zoomed to ₹16,534 crore ($3.7 billion). Jet's debt four years after its IPO was more than five times its pre-IPO level.

By end-2005, Air Deccan's financial position was even more precarious. The rapid expansion in fleet size had taken a toll. The airline, which reported a modest profit in FY2003—its first year of operation—had reported losses in FY2004 and the first half of

FY2005. While it had accumulated ₹427 crore ($97 million) debt, 18 months of losses had completely eroded its net worth.

Almost sixteen months after Jet Airways' IPO, Air Deccan launched an IPO in May 2006 to raise ₹400 to ₹432 crore ($88 to $95 million). Air Deccan proposed to use ₹133 crore ($29 million) for debt repayment, ₹168 crore ($37 million) for setting up a training centre and a hangar facility at Chennai besides setting up infrastructure at airports and market development initiatives. The balance ₹99 crore ($22 million) were earmarked for general corporate purposes.

The public offer was priced at ₹150 to ₹175 ($3.31 to $3.86) per share, which was slightly over five times the ₹28.52 ($0.63) average price at which shares were allotted to pre-IPO investors. However, even after extending the IPO deadline by three days and reducing the lower limit of the price band to ₹147 ($3.24), the issue was subscribed just 1.23 times. On 12 June 2006, the first day of trading on the BSE, Air Deccan's share price crashed by 33 per cent below the IPO price and ended the day at ₹98 ($2.16).[15]

The poor share price performance on listing day was attributed to an adverse ruling by a consumer court in New Delhi. The court ruled that Air Deccan had to pay compensation to a business passenger for a delayed flight and poor in-flight service. As part of the court proceedings, Air Deccan admitted that it had 'many defective aircraft'. The court opined that the airline needed to improve its fleet maintenance.[16]

Analysts also attributed the IPO's lacklustre performance to choppy market conditions and the intensely competitive nature of the domestic civil aviation industry. The proliferation of budget airlines had dampened Air Deccan's share price performance but caught Goyal's attention.

Pyrrhic Victory

Jet Airways offered to acquire Air Sahara, India's third-largest domestic airline, for ₹2250 crore ($500 million) in January

2006. The transaction, if successful, would have added twenty-six aircrafts to Jet Airways' fifty-one-strong fleet. With a fleet of seventy-seven aircrafts, Jet would have supplanted IA, which operated sixty-eight aircrafts, as the largest domestic airline.

At the time of announcement of the acquisition, India had no mergers and acquisitions policy in place specifying the terms of transfer of airport infrastructure. Jet Airways' acquisition of Air Sahara was the first major airline consolidation in India. When NEPC Airlines acquired Damania in the mid-1990s, airport infrastructure was in surfeit. With the entry of LCCs in the 2000s, the domestic aviation market had become intensely competitive and airport infrastructure was inadequate.

The key attractions for Jet Airways in this transaction were Air Sahara's airline infrastructure and rights to fly on international routes, especially Singapore and London. However, the transaction did not go through; not in 2006. The reasons were three-fold.[17]

First, the home ministry's security clearance for Goyal's induction in Air Sahara's new board came on 21 June 2006—a day after the deadline for the share purchase agreement had expired. The government had approved four members to be inducted in the new Air Sahara board by 29 May and a new board could have been constituted with these four members. Naresh Goyal could have been inducted in the board after his approval came through. So, the timing of the home ministry's security clearance, while not a deal breaker, was a deterrent.

Second, Jet Airways claimed that further clarity was required regarding the transfer of facilities like hangars, check-in counters and passenger lounges as outlined in a government policy document of 4 May 2006. The ministry of civil aviation (MOCA) quoted one critical statement from the policy in rebuttal: ' . . . the user rights over such infrastructure that are given to an airline on non-payment basis e.g. parking bays, landing slots etc. may be allowed to be used by the airline that takes over the aircraft. For all other rights, the terms of lease/sale agreement between the airport operator and the airline may apply.' Thus, as per MOCA, policy,

Air Sahara's facilities were to be handed over to Jet Airways. When an *India Today* columnist raised the issue of Jet Airways seeking clarifications, an annoyed MOCA official retorted, 'Do they need to be taught the Queen's English to interpret these guidelines?'[18]

The third and most important reason why the takeover bid failed was the confusion regarding the transfer of Air Sahara's international routes to Jet Airways. In June 2005, Jet Airways Inc., a US-based airline company yet to begin operations, had filed a petition with the US Transport Department that if the Indian carrier were allowed to operate in the US 'then we will once again have the Al Qaeda flying and controlling aircraft over American cities'.[19] Jet Airways Inc. had filed the petition before Jet Airways had made an acquisition bid for Air Sahara. With the US transportation department looking into the matter, Jet Airways claimed that it had not received approval to operate Air Sahara's lucrative routes to Singapore and London. MOCA remained silent.

Goyal had long harboured ambitions of flying international routes. In 2004, the Congress-led United Progressive Alliance (UPA) was voted to power in the union elections. Sharad Pawar, who led one of UPA's key constituents—the Nationalist Congress Party (NCP)—was a friend of Goyal's. According to New Delhi's political grapevine, NCP's Praful Patel was appointed civil aviation minister on Pawar's insistence. Praful Patel was a businessman whose family had made its fortunes in tobacco.

In early 2004, MOCA had not permitted private airlines to fly overseas. Yet, Jet Airways started applying for (landing) slots at the London, Kuala Lumpur, Singapore and Bangkok airports. When this issue was raised in Parliament, Patel affirmed that Jet Airways was proceeding with its international foray at its own risk. What was left unsaid was that a committee appointed by the previous BJP-led National Democratic Alliance (NDA) government had submitted a detailed roadmap for the expansion and modernization of the aviation sector.

A key recommendation of this committee was to permit private airlines to operate international routes. The committee report was not made public; neither was Parliament appraised of it. However, in March 2004, Jet Airways began its international foray by flying from Chennai to Colombo.[20]

Jet Airways developed cold feet ahead of its proposed acquisition of Air Sahara in 2006 as the former was not certain of operating the latter's London and Singapore routes after the acquisition. Understandably, there was much rancour in the aftermath of the acquisition being called off. Goyal and Patel were made out to be the villains of this episode. However, Air Sahara, which was in a financially precarious position, continued to be on Goyal's radar.

In March 2007, Jet Airways once again agreed to buy out Air Sahara for ₹1450 crore ($351 million), which was 35 per cent lower than the June 2006 offer of ₹2250 crore ($500 million). Of the ₹1450 crore purchase consideration, ₹500 crore ($121 million) was paid ahead of the announcement and another ₹400 crore ($97 million) was paid by 30 April 2007. The balance ₹550 crore ($133 million) was payable in four interest-free annual equal instalments commencing 31 March 2008.

Jet Airways' acquisition of Air Sahara was the first major airline consolidation in India. Though analysts opined that Jet Airways had overpaid for the acquisition, purchasing Air Sahara at a significantly lower price than initially negotiated bears testimony to Goyal's political connections and deal-making prowess.

Notwithstanding the acquisition, Jet Airways' market share declined to 29 per cent in 2008 from 44 per cent in 2004: the recently-launched budget carriers were eating into Jet Airways' market share. Jet Airways reported consolidated losses of ₹961 crore ($201 million) in FY2009 and ₹420 crore ($88 million) in FY2010. Its ₹14,280 crore ($3.0 billion) consolidated debt as of March 2010 was almost 4.25 times its diminishing net worth of ₹3371 crore ($706 million).[21]

Despite all this, Jet continued to be a force to reckon with for almost a decade after the Air Sahara acquisition.

No chronicle of Indian aviation would be complete without an account of the nosedive of Kingfisher Airlines, the turbulence of SpiceJet, and the rise of IndiGo.

Chapter 11

Overbooked

The entry of private sector players into the Indian civil aviation industry occurred in three temporal phases.

The first was in pre-independent India with the entry of the Tata Group-promoted Air India in 1932 and subsequently Air India International. Several others followed the Tata Group's foray—Airways India, Air Services of India, Ambica Airlines, Bharat Airways, Deccan Airways, Himalayan Aviation, Jupiter Airlines, and Kalinga Airlines. The intensely competitive environment and deteriorating service standards led to the Indian government nationalizing the airlines and merging them into a domestic airline, Indian Airlines, and an international airline, Air India.

In doing so, the government ignored the 1950 recommendations of the Justice G.S. Rajadhyaksha Committee, and the father of Indian civil aviation, JRD Tata. The Rajadhyaksha Committee recommended that the industry players be consolidated, the government extend subsidies and not proceed with nationalization right away. JRD submitted an alternate proposal under which the government would create two corporations, one each for domestic and international aviation and hold majority stakes in both entities. This was to insulate Air India International from being clubbed with other poorly performing airlines and the resultant operation and reputation risks.

The second phase of private sector players entry into civil aviation, a result of the government's 'Open Sky' policy, occurred in 1992 and 1993. Half-a-dozen private sector airlines were launched during these eventful two years. While East West Airlines was founded in 1992, Archana Airways, Damania Airways, Jet Airways, ModiLuft and NEPC were all incorporated in 1993. NEPC acquired Damania in 1995 for around ₹108 crore ($33.3 million), but had to cease operations by 1997.[1] East West and ModiLuft wound up operations in 1996, and Archana Airways in 2000. A combination of factors—including a murder, cut-throat competition, an inability to navigate India's complex politics and bureaucracy, the high cost of aviation turbine fuel (ATF), limited access to funding, and financial and operational inefficiencies—resulted in the exodus.

Jet Airways was the sole survivor among the private airlines that started business in the early 1990s. The airline went on to overtake Indian Airlines and garner the highest market share among domestic airlines for a period. However, Jet Airways' financials were always shaky with the company reporting losses in two years (FY2002 and FY2003) during the five-year period between FY2000–FY2004 and for eight consecutive years thereafter.

However, Jet Airways' weak financials did not deter or probably emboldened the deluge of private sector companies foraying into civil aviation during the third and ongoing phase that began in 2000. Air Sahara (started flying in 2000), Air Deccan (2003), SpiceJet (2004), Kingfisher Airlines (2005), IndiGo (2005), GoAir (2005), Paramount Airways (2005), AirAsia India (2013), Vistara (2013), Air Costa (2013), Air Pegasus (2015) and Flybig (2021) entered the industry. Paramount Airways, Air Pegasus and Air Costa ceased flying by 2010, 2016 and 2017 respectively due to multiple factors, including antagonistic government policies, cut-throat competition, and management inefficiencies.

In July 2021, billionaire-investor, Rakesh Jhunjhunwala, and former Jet Airways CEO Vinay Dube announced the formation of an ultra-low-cost carrier (ULCC), Akasa Air, which started flying in August 2022.

Free for All

This third phase is different from the second phase in two respects. First, three of the airlines launched during this phase were backed by conglomerates with a track record of managing profitable businesses since before India became independent. The United Breweries (UB) Group promoted Kingfisher Airlines, the Wadia Group promoted GoAir and the Tata Group promoted AirAsia India and Vistara. These airlines had better access to financing and managerial expertise than stand-alone airlines. Second, this phase marked the entry of budget airlines—LCCs and ULCCs—in India, with Air Deccan followed by SpiceJet, IndiGo, GoAir, AirAsia India, the regional airline, Flybig, and Akasa Air.

Why is the entry of budget airlines a landmark event? The aviation industry is cyclical and capital intensive in nature. Passenger traffic is robust during upswings and muted during downswings. ATF—which constitutes around one-third of international airlines' expenses and a much higher proportion of airlines' expenses in India—and crude oil prices are closely correlated and volatile. Sizeable and recurring capital expenditures are required to purchase or lease aircrafts, maintain and service them and replace aircrafts as they age. This implies that airlines need ample debt and equity financing as their bottom line oscillates between meagre profits and significant losses.

A budget airline offers a 'no-frills' flying experience, optimizes the fleet's flying hours and passenger load factor, which is the percentage of available seats occupied by passengers. Hence, a budget airline's expenses are lower than those incurred by full service carriers (FSCs) and hybrid carriers. Well-managed budget airlines tend to generate more stable profits and cash flows than FSCs. A hybrid airline operates on a low-cost business model, but its services are at par with FSCs.

In India, Indian Airlines and Jet Airways began as FSCs and, with the entry of LCCs, evolved into hybrid airlines. Kingfisher Airlines started off as a hybrid airline and subsequently focused on the FSC business. Vistara is an FSC. Air Deccan, SpiceJet, IndiGo, AirAsia India and Flybig are LCCs. GoAir and Akasa Air are ULCCs.

Big Bang

In 2005, two conglomerates—the UB Group and the Wadia Group—launched their airlines. The Wadia Group's GoAir, which renamed itself Go First in 2021, has been an unlisted, budget airline since inception, According to DGCA statistics, GoAir's fleet size grew from six aircrafts as of March 2008 to 56 aircraft as of February 2021. Its market share, in terms of passengers flown, has inched up to 9.6 per cent in April 2021 from 4 per cent in FY2009.[2] GoAir's impressive 58 per cent revenue growth since FY2018 to ₹7258 crore ($1.0 billion) was accompanied by at least three years of losses and a build-up of sizeable liabilities—₹16,420 crore ($2.20 billion as of December 2020. The airline's net worth has been negative since at least FY2018 and was a negative ₹1962 crore ($265 million) as of December 2020.[3] In August 2021, GoAir received SEBI's approval to float a ₹3600 crore ($487 million) IPO, which, if successful, will enable the airline to bolster its net worth to about ₹1500 crore ($203 million).

The year 2005 was a milestone in Mallya's professional life, or so he may have thought at that time. On 20 March 2005, Mallya's UB bought liquor manufacturer Shaw Wallace at an exorbitant price of ₹1545 crore ($350 million). Barely two months later, on 9 May 2005, his hybrid airline, Kingfisher Airlines, flew its maiden flight from Mumbai to Delhi.

Mallya earned the dubious distinction of buying Shaw Wallace for the second time despite not selling the company after his first purchase. Shaw Wallace was a liquor company that sold several popular whisky brands, including Royal Challenge, Haywards,

Director's Special, Officer's Choice, Antiquity and Antiquity Blue. Mallya had purchased Shaw Wallace in 1985 for ₹55 crore ($44 million). Shaw Wallace was then a subsidiary of the Malaysian conglomerate Sime Darby, and Mallya was a resident Indian. Indian laws did not allow resident Indians to purchase assets from overseas sellers; non-resident Indians (NRIs) were permitted to do so. Mallya used an NRI businessman, Manohar Rajaram Chhabria, popularly known as Manu Chhabria, as a front and purchased Shaw Wallace through a Singapore-based special purpose vehicle (SPV). Manu Chhabria later claimed that he owned Shaw Wallace. Mallya was unable to seek legal recourse as it meant that he had contravened Indian laws. The two men were at loggerheads till Manu Chhabria's death in April 2002. In March 2005, Mallya bought Shaw Wallace off Chhabria's wife and daughters.

The logo of Mallya's new airline, a kingfisher in flight, was a replica of the logo of Kingfisher, India's best-selling beer. Kingfisher was manufactured and marketed by UB, a cash cow that Mallya inherited from his father, Vittal Mallya. A first-generation entrepreneur and an acclaimed empire builder, Vittal Mallya's UB Group encompassed India's largest liquor manufacturers, United Breweries and United Spirits, in addition to pharmaceutical, finance and petrochemical companies. When Vittal Mallya suffered a heart attack in 1977, he inducted his only son, Vijay, into the UB Board and sent him to the US to work at Hoechst, a pharma major. Vijay became the chairman of the UB Group following fifty-nine-year-old Vittal Mallya's death in 1983. He was then twenty-eight years old.

Father and son were diametrically opposite, in terms of character, personality and management style. The senior Mallya was an unobtrusive personality who was cautious with money to the point of being tight-fisted. He was also fastidious about delivering on commitments.

For instance, Vittal Mallya had personally interviewed and recruited to United Breweries, U.B. Bhat, an alumnus of IIM, Ahmedabad. An office car was part of Bhat's compensation package. During the license-permit raj that prevailed in India before the economy's liberalization in 1991, it took several months to obtain delivery of a new car after placing an order. When Vittal Mallya learnt that Bhat's new car would be delivered a week after he had started working for UB, he lent his own car to the new recruit for the intervening period.

Vittal Mallya was punctilious about checking hotel bills after every business trip. He used to cross-check the total bill amount by keying in every item of the bill into a calculator that was built into his watch. When asked if hotels were not to be trusted, the senior Mallya replied that he was a custodian of shareholders' wealth and, hence, had to be careful with their resources.[4]

Though Vijay Mallya was not as meticulous or frugal as his father, he did share similarities. Both men married more than once and had a penchant for empire building. In 1985, two years after his father's demise, Vijay Mallya set up Unitel Communications as a joint venture with Ericsson to manufacture telephones, EPABX (switchboards) and fax machines. In 1988, he acquired the 228-year-old Berger Paints. In the expansion blitzkrieg that followed, Mallya added pizzas, colas, engineering, aviation, healthcare, chemicals and fertilizers, hotels and resorts, media and even elevated light trains to the UB group stable.

Mallya differed from his father in one crucial respect, though. United Breweries and United Spirits evolved into market leaders that were consistently profitable under Vittal Mallya's stewardship. With the exception of Mangalore Chemicals & Fertilizers which turned profitable after being inducted in the UB fold, Mallya's acquisitions were not exactly a testimony to his managerial prowess. Shaw Wallace and Berger Paints were profitable entities even before the UB group acquired them. In the thirty-two-year- period ending 2015, Mallya had entered and exited as many businesses as thirty-two.

Mallya professes to be a devout Hindu and an ardent devotee of Lord Subramanya at Kurke and Lord Venkateswara at Tirupati, one of the world's most affluent religious organizations.

In November 1998, Mallya donated 32 kilograms of gold and 1900 kilograms of copper worth ₹18 crore ($4.36 million) to gold plate the sanctum of the renowned Sabarimala Ayyappan temple at Kerala. However, it was not Mallya but UB that donated this money to the temple, as disclosed in the company's annual report.

When an irate shareholder, who had read the fine print, questioned Mallya during the company's annual general meeting, Mallya's response was that 'liquor is a very tough business to be in and the donation had been done to seek divine blessings on behalf of all shareholders.'[5]

Mallya aspired to leave his mark in politics as well. In 2003, he relaunched the Subramanian Swamy-led Janata Party in Karnataka and contested in the state assembly elections that year. Not a single candidate of the party was elected to the 224-seat assembly, even as Mallya continued to be the party's national working president till 2010. He was elected to the Rajya Sabha as an independent MP in 2002 and then again in 2010. While the Janata Dal (Secular) [JD(S)] and Congress supported him in 2002, JD(S) and BJP supported him in 2010.

Kingfisher Airlines was not Mallya's first venture in civil aviation. In 1990, he founded a company called UB Air, which was to operate flights between Bengaluru and Mangaluru. He abandoned this venture, though, as he thought the market was nascent.[6]

In 2003, Mallya incorporated Kingfisher Airlines despite being dissuaded by A.K. Ravi Nedungadi, UB's former group CFO. Nedungadi's concerns were not unfounded. After all, Warren Buffet had opined, 'The worst sort of business is one that grows rapidly, requires significant capital to engender the growth, and then earns little or no money . . . Think airlines . . . Here a durable competitive advantage has proven elusive ever since the days of the Wright Brothers.'[7]

On Saturday, 7 May 2005, Mallya flagged off Kingfisher Airlines' inaugural flight from Mumbai to New Delhi with his characteristic fanfare and festivities. This was the first time a

Figure 1: The Vijay Mallya Roller Coaster

Entity	Current Status
United Communications Ltd	Set up in 1985; wound up in 2000
Pizza King	Set up in 1986; closed in 1989
Berger Paints	Acquired in 1988; sold in 1996 for $200 million profit
Best & Crompton	Acquired in 1989; referred to BIFR in 1995
Western India Erectors	Set up in 1970; dissolved in 1993
UB Mysore Electrochemicals Batteries Ltd	Inherited; sold in 1991
Vijay TV	Acquired in 1994; sold in 1999
Kissan Products Ltd	Inherited; sold in 1994
Carbonated Beverages Ltd	Set up in 1970s; closed in early 1990s
Asian Age Holdings Ltd & UB Publications Ltd	Set up in 1997; sold in 2005
Hindustan Polymers	Set up in 1961 sold in 1997
Mines Exploration Pvt Ltd & UB Mining Ltd	Set up in 1995; dissolved in 1999
UB Petrochemicals Ltd	Inherited; dissolved in 2001
UB Air	Started in 1990; dormant since 2012 board meeting
Shilton Hotels Pvt Ltd	Year of setting up not known; merged with UB Holdings
UB Hoppeckke Energy Products Ltd	Set up in 1989; dissolved in 2001
Face One Model Pvt Ltd	Year of setting up not known; closed in 2008
UB Pharmaceuticals Ltd, Dominion Chemical Industries Ltd, Carews Pharma & Optrex Ltd	Inherited; year of sale not known
Aventis Phrama & Bayer India	Majority stakes purchased in 1956 & sold in 2010
UB Transit Systems Pvt Ltd	Set up in 1994; scrapped in 2001
Blue Pearl Internet Group	Set up in 1993; dissolved in 2002
UNB Healthcare Ltd	Set up in early 1990s; sold in 2015
UB Resorts Limited	Year of setting up not known; wound up in 2001
City Properties Maintenance Company Bangalore	Set up in 2007; current status not known
Masonelian India Ltd	Acquired in 1993; sold in 1997
UB Electronics Instruments Ltd	Set up in 1985; dissolved in 2001
Kingfisher Sports Gear Pvt Ltd	Set up in 1999; dissolved in 2002
Sotiba Graments	Year of setting up & current status not known
United Spirits Ltd	Inherited; sold majority stake to Diageo in 2012
Krest Finance Ltd	Inherited; now in BIFR
Cardboard Industries Ltd	Set up in 1998; year of shut down not known
Mangalore Chemicals & Fertilisers	Acquired in 1990; sold majority stake in 2015

Source: The Flight and Fall of Vijay Mallya, India Today, 27 March 2016

private Indian carrier had taken delivery of a brand-new Airbus A320 to launch its operations. A sound-and-light show unveiled the new aircraft to the august audience. Kingfisher Airlines was Mallya's birthday gift to his son, Siddhartha, who was turning eighteen in May 2005.

Gracing the occasion were a galaxy of Bollywood stars, page three personalities and leading politicians including then Maharashtra governor S.M. Krishna, chief minister of Maharashtra Vilasrao Deshmukh, and cabinet ministers

Praful Patel (civil aviation) and Sharad Pawar (agriculture, food & civil supplies, consumer affairs and public distribution).

Speaking on the occasion, Mallya declared, 'This is the moment we have been waiting for. Our entire Kingfisher Airlines team has been working relentlessly to make this vision come true. We are finally set to conquer the Indian skies. I offer to you, Kingfisher Airlines. Come fly the good times with us.'[8]

If there was an airline in India that was poised to achieve the rare and often contradictory attributes of market dominance and financial stability, it was Kingfisher. The UB Group's flagship companies, United Breweries and United Spirits, were both profitable and liquid with a ninety-year track record of managing a portfolio of sound businesses, navigating India's complex political labyrinth and nurturing deep relationships with bankers and capital market participants. Further, Mallya, in his capacity as an MP, was even inducted in the parliamentary committee on civil aviation in 2012. While this appointment reeked of a conflict of interest, it could have endowed Kingfisher Airlines with a competitive edge.

Kingfisher, as a hybrid airline, charged fares at par with the LCCs, but offered an FSC's services. The first class and economy cabins of Kingfisher's A320 seated twenty and 114 passengers respectively. Other LCCs accommodated 150 passengers in a single economy class cabin on their A320s. Kingfisher's first-class seats offered a 126 degree recline. Both first and economy class cabins offered in-flight entertainment. Also included was an onboard ironing service for first class passengers![9]

Means to an End

In an industry where, in Captain Gopinath's words, 'cheques fly faster than aircrafts', Kingfisher's business model was clearly unsustainable. This did not deter Mallya from quadrupling the Kingfisher fleet from five aircrafts in 2005 to twenty in 2007. Passenger load factor (PLF), a metric that measures an airline's capacity utilization, was middling at slightly over 68 per cent in 2007. Well-managed airlines sustain PLFs at close to 80 per cent. Without waiting to stabilize Kingfisher's domestic business, Mallya set his sights on launching overseas routes. Here, he hit a roadblock.

Government regulations, known as the '5/20 rule', required airlines to operate a fleet of at least twenty aircraft and fly domestic routes for at least five years before embarking on overseas routes. Goyal is known to have lobbied for this policy to ensure Jet Airways had the first mover advantage among private airlines to operate international routes.[10]

Mallya was not deterred. He initially considered acquiring Air Sahara, but in an uncharacteristic display of caution, did not pursue the acquisition as he believed that the price was too high. In May 2007, Mallya announced that Kingfisher was interested in acquiring Air Deccan. As Air Deccan had started flying in 2003, the acquisition would enable Kingfisher to fly overseas routes by 2008. Captain Gopinath retorted, 'He may want to buy the moon, but the moon may not be available for sale.'[11] But Air Deccan was making losses; the airline did not have the wherewithal to continue functioning as an independent entity for long. Barely a month after the rebuttal, Captain Gopinath capitulated. Kingfisher acquired a 26 per cent stake in Air Deccan and made an open offer to purchase another 20 per cent. The open offer was successful and Kingfisher acquired a 46 per cent stake in Air Deccan by forking out almost ₹1000 crore ($242 million).

At the time of its acquisition, Air Deccan was a listed entity. In order to remain listed, Kingfisher's acquisition of Air Deccan was structured as a reverse merger, whereby Air Deccan acquired Kingfisher and was subsequently renamed as Kingfisher Airlines. Mallya became the chairman and CEO of the listed Kingfisher Airlines and Captain Gopinath, the vice chairman.

Air Deccan was rebranded as Kingfisher Red and continued to operate as an LCC, focused on connecting India's tier-II cities, while Kingfisher Airlines connected India's metros and prepared to fly international routes in 2008.

Prior to the acquisition, the market shares of Air Deccan and Kingfisher were 16.5 per cent and 12.4 per cent respectively. The combined entity's market share of 28.9 per cent was a shade lower than Jet Airways' and JetLite's (the erstwhile Air Sahara) combined market share of 29.4 per cent. Indian Airlines had, by then, dropped to third place, with a market share of 17.8 per cent.[12]

Prima facie, the acquisition appeared to be a sound business proposition that catapulted Kingfisher's market share to the second highest in the country, expanded its network to cover the entire nation and enabled the airline to fly overseas in a year. But the transaction was fundamentally flawed.

First, the deal was fraught with integration risks. The business models and organization cultures of the two airlines were drastically different. Second, in choosing to reverse merge the unlisted Kingfisher Airlines with the listed Air Deccan, Mallya lost the opportunity to float an IPO that would have diversified Kingfisher's investors and the proceeds, which could have been used to part-finance the acquisition and to repay debt. The ₹1000 crore ($242 million) acquisition being financed predominantly through borrowings added to the sizeable debt on both Kingfisher Airlines' and Air Deccan's balance sheets. Third, the problem of excessive indebtedness was exacerbated by both airlines consistently generating losses. The two airlines had reported aggregate losses of ₹580 crore ($131 million) in FY2006 and ₹996 crore ($225 million) in FY2007.

Damp Squib

Notwithstanding Kingfisher's mounting losses, Mallya's shopping spree continued through 2007 and 2008. In late 2007, Mallya purchased the ailing Spyker Formula1 (F1) team for around

₹509 crore ($123 million) and rebranded it Force India. United Spirits, in 2008, purchased the Indian Premier League (IPL) Bangalore cricket team for ₹486 crore ($111.60 million). Mallya named the team 'Royal Challengers Bangalore' (RCB). Mallya viewed the Air Deccan acquisition as strategically important. The Force India and RCB acquisitions entailed a cash outflow that almost equalled the Air Deccan purchase consideration and was superfluous, especially at a time when a global financial crisis eclipsed the world.

Mallya seemed to have believed that Air Deccan's incompatible acquisition was a small price to pay to achieve his larger goal of Kingfisher Airlines flying overseas routes. In August 2008, Kingfisher announced its international foray amidst the financial crisis. The airline planned to launch up to fifteen overseas routes by November 2008.

Kingfisher announced its intention to take delivery of five A320s and five A340-500s, both in two class configurations, with thirty and thirty-six 'Kingfisher First' seats respectively, plus 187 and 201 seats in economy, by October 2008. The A320s were to connect Heathrow to Bengaluru and Mumbai while the A340s were to fly between Bengaluru and San Francisco.

Kingfisher First featured lie-flat massager beds, custom built by B/E Aerospace, and a 17-inch Thales in-flight entertainment screen. Mallya was extremely proud of the staffed bar, surrounded by bar stools and two sofas, which he said was designed 'to put back style into travel that over the years has disappeared.'[13]

In addition to launching long-haul international operations, Kingfisher planned to redeploy its fifty-one Airbus A320s from domestic to short-haul international flights. The airline planned to start flying to UAE, Qatar, Kuwait, Thailand, Malaysia, Singapore, Sri Lanka, Bangladesh, Pakistan and the Maldives during the second half of 2008.[14]

On 3 September 2008, Union Minister for Civil Aviation Praful Patel flagged off the airline's maiden overseas non-stop flight from Bengaluru to London.[15] Nevertheless, Kingfisher's international foray did not turn out to be the trailblazing affair Mallya had envisaged. The global financial crisis achieved what Goyal and Indian regulation couldn't—bring the Mallya juggernaut to a grinding halt.

Credit: Gujarat Cooperative Milk Marketing Federation Ltd. (Amul)

In October 2008, barely five weeks after the maiden Bengaluru–London flight, the airline put its international expansion on hold. Kingfisher did not inaugurate the Mumbai–London flights in late October 2008, as it had initially planned. Passenger traffic on international routes was low due to the global macroeconomic slowdown, not just for Kingfisher, but for all airlines. Jet Airways too announced the temporary withdrawal of its Mumbai–Shanghai–San Francisco flights due to poor passenger response.

Air Deccan used to clock PLFs close to the optimum level of 80 per cent before its acquisition by Kingfisher. In FY2008, the combined PLF of Kingfisher and Air Deccan dipped to 68.2 per cent due to the ongoing recession and the integration challenges following the acquisition. So, Kingfisher returned eight aircraft previously owned by Air Deccan to the lessors and sold three of the five A340-500s it had purchased for international operations, to Nigeria's Arik Air. The airline also deferred taking deliveries of thirty-two aircraft from Airbus SAS.

Usually, airlines contract aircraft deliveries with manufacturers years ahead of the required delivery date. The contract terms do not permit airlines to cancel orders at short notice. The combined fleet of Kingfisher and Air Deccan, which stood at sixty-four aircraft as of March 2007 before the acquisition, had swelled to eighty-three aircraft by March 2009. Kingfisher was forced to dispose seventeen aircraft in FY2010, thereby reducing the fleet strength to sixty-six aircraft by March 2010. Notwithstanding the aircraft rationalization initiatives, Kingfisher incurred total capital expenditure of ₹6708 crore ($1.46 billion) in FY2009 and FY2010 to obtain deliveries of aircraft.

Even as airlines' declining passenger traffic resulted in lower revenues, expenditures increased due to a rise in ATF price, which was driven by the rise in crude oil prices internationally. For airlines across the world, it was a double whammy. ATF price is closely correlated with crude oil price, which skyrocketed by almost 51 per cent to $96.99/bbl in 2008 from $64.29/bbl in 2006. Fuel expenses of airlines in India, however, rose more sharply than those of their global peers. According to the business daily, *Mint,* ATF price in India was around 70 per cent more expensive than international prices in 2008, due to several taxes, including value added tax (VAT) up to 30 per cent, and excise duties levied on ATF.[16]

The Emperor's New Clothes

Kingfisher was in desperate need of funds, and it found a creative lender in IDBI Bank. It would be a loan that would come back to haunt the senior managements of IDBI Bank and Kingfisher.[17]

Airlines seldom own their aircraft; instead, they lease them, and leased aircraft cannot be offered as collateral for bank loans.

With most, if not all, of its other tangible assets already pledged with banks, Kingfisher offered its brand as a collateral to avail a loan from IDBI Bank. The airline mandated two firms to value its brand—Brand Finance and the multinational audit, tax and advisory firm, Grant Thornton.

While Brand Finance valued the Kingfisher brand at ₹1911 crore ($400 million), Grant Thornton's valuation was 78 per cent higher at ₹3406 crore ($714 million).[18] Differences in the valuation of assets are bound to occur when different agencies value an asset, but the sharp divergence in valuations, in this instance, was unusual.

Kingfisher reportedly did not disclose Brand Finance's valuation, pledged its brand, and availed of a ₹900 crore ($189 million) loan from IDBI Bank.[19] There were procedural lapses in IDBI Bank's sanctioning of this loan. No credit rating was assigned to Kingfisher before sanctioning the loan. The bank's senior management also overruled their subordinates' insistence that Mallya provide unencumbered shares as collateral.

Lifeline

Though Kingfisher's PLF had improved to 72.70 per cent by FY2010, other private airlines had overtaken Mallya's pet project. IndiGo had emerged the clear winner, clocking a PLF of 80 per cent. The other two LCCs, GoAir and SpiceJet, were not too far behind, clocking PLFs of 78 per cent and 76.6 per cent respectively. At 72.6 per cent, Jet Airways' PLF was marginally lower than Kingfisher's. The state-owned airlines—Indian Airlines, Alliance Air, Air India, and Air India Express—were together clocking an abysmal PLF of 65.1 per cent.

In the meantime, resentment was brewing within Kingfisher. It was clear to Captain Gopinath that Mallya had used the Air Deccan acquisition as a stepping stone for Kingfisher to fly international routes. It was evident that Kingfisher was focusing on the FSC arm of the business while the LCC side languished. Captain Gopinath, who held a 9 per cent stake in Kingfisher Airlines in June 2008, gradually sold his stake and exited Kingfisher. By September 2009, he held just a 0.32 per cent stake in the airline.[20]

On 24 March 2010, he and Captain K.J. Samuel resigned from Kingfisher's board of directors.[21] In an interview with news website The Quint, Captain Gopinath remarked, 'Vijay Mallya cheated me of my dream.'[22]

In FY2010, Kingfisher Airlines—which now included Air Deccan's business—generated a loss of ₹1609 crore ($360 million) and had accumulated ₹5666 crore ($1.27 billion) debt. In the two years following Kingfisher's acquisition of Air Deccan, there were no synergies and cost reductions. The combined entity was generating more losses than the two airlines operating independently.

This is when the bankers voluntarily or involuntarily swung into action for debt recovery. In November 2010, Kingfisher's consortium of bankers extended the tenure of loan repayment to nine years with a two-year moratorium, reduced interest rates and sanctioned a fresh loan. Importantly, the banks converted ₹1355 crore ($284 million)—or slightly more than one-fifth of the airline's debt—into equity at a 61.6 per cent premium to the airline's share price. This was despite the share price having consistently declined during the last three years! *Mint* reported that Mallya had also converted the ₹648 crore ($141 million) debt he had extended to equity.[23]

Courtesy the debt-to-equity swap, Kingfisher's equity was bolstered from ₹451 crore ($94 million) as of March 2010 to ₹2397 crore as of March 2011 ($522 million). Debt correspondingly moderated from ₹7923 crore ($1.66 billion) in March 2010 to ₹7057 crore ($1.54 billion) as of March 2011. This was the first and last time that Kingfisher's debt declined.

Kingfisher's November 2010 debt restructuring was unusual on three counts.

First, while banks extended additional loans to Kingfisher, they did not stipulate that Mallya infuse fresh capital into the airline. Instead, the banks permitted Mallya to convert the loans he had already extended to Kingfisher to equity, which entailed zero cash outflow for him.

Second, banks converted Kingfisher's debt into equity at a 61.6 per cent premium to the share price, which as of 29 October 2010 was ₹76.10—76 per cent lower than the ₹316.60 peak it had touched on 18 December 2007 following its reverse merger with Air Deccan. Why did the banks ascribe a hefty premium to the plummeting share price of a company that had generated losses since inception, had accumulated a mountain of debt and whose net worth was eroding? After the debt-to-equity swap, Mallya's and the banks' shareholdings stood at 58.61 per cent and 23.39 per cent respectively.[24]

Had the banks converted debt to equity at the prevailing market price, their shareholding would have been close to 38 per cent. Why did the banks, by opting for a lower stake, forego the opportunity to earn higher dividends and capital gains, if and when the airline turned around? Unnamed bankers informed the author and *Mint* columnist Tamal Bandyopadhyay that there was 'pressure from certain quarters to restructure the loan'.[25] Mallya was, after all, serving his second term as MP in 2010.

Third, Kingfisher must have submitted a detailed business plan as part of this debt restructuring exercise, which is not available in the public domain. Had Kingfisher committed to the bankers that it would migrate to an LCC model or continue as an FSC? In FY2010, the market share of the domestic LCCs—Alliance Air, JetLite, SpiceJet, GoAir and IndiGo—had increased to 47 per cent, a remarkable feat achieved within seven years of the founding of the nation's first LCC, Air Deccan.

The business plan Kingfisher submitted as part of the debt restructuring exercise is important in light of the strategic change the airline implemented during the latter half of 2011. Kingfisher announced its exit from the LCC segment: it shut down Kingfisher Red. By 2011, the airline's FSC arm was rebranded 'Kingfisher Class'. Mallya observed, 'We believe there are more than enough guests who prefer to travel the full-service Kingfisher Class. And that shows through in our own performance where load factors in Kingfisher Class are more than in Kingfisher Red.'[26]

With the benefit of hindsight, it is easy to criticize Kingfisher's counterintuitive decision to shut down its LCC arm, notwithstanding the sound operating performance of domestic LCCs. Focusing on the FSC business, especially against the backdrop of elevated ATF price, entailed higher risks. However, the decision was not entirely quixotic. The Chennai-based Paramount Airways had catered to business travellers and yet, operated profitably from 2005 to 2010. Legal issues between Paramount and the lessors of the Embraer aircraft unfortunately rung the death knell for this airline.

Kingfisher's decision to focus on the FSC business was approved by its bank lenders who were also shareholders. Financing such high-risk businesses falls within the purview of private equity and venture capital firms, not banks. Public deposits are a key source of financing for banks, which are regulated entities that ought to ideally lend only to stable and profitable borrowers. On the other hand, institutional investors and high net worth individuals finance private equity and venture capital firms, which in turn invest in high-risk ventures. Why did banks assume the role of private equity and venture capital firms in Kingfisher's case?

End of the Road?

During the 2011 annual general meeting, shareholders unanimously approved the airline's proposal to raise ₹2000 crore ($435 million) through a rights issue. The rights issue, like the global depository receipt (GDR) issue that the shareholders had previously approved, was a non-starter.

The debt restructuring and closure of Kingfisher Red did little to revive Kingfisher's fortunes. The airline's PLF did improve to 83.30 per cent in FY2011 and 79.2 per cent in FY2012. However, high fuel and interest expenses eroded Kingfisher's profitability. The airline continued to generate losses in FY2011 and FY2012.

Kingfisher's FY2012 PLF reflects regular capacity utilization till around February 2012, by which time rumblings of non-payment of salaries had started. By June 2012, more than 200 Kingfisher pilots, including captains, went on strike; the airline had not paid them salaries for at least four months. On 1 October 2012, Kingfisher suspended all operations after its engineers refused to certify the aircraft, a prerequisite for any aircraft to take to the skies. By then, the engineers had not been paid salaries for seven months. On 12 October, the DGCA suspended Kingfisher's license as the airline failed to satisfy the directorate that it had a 'safe, efficient and reliable service.'[27] The airline was forced to stop selling tickets immediately.

Around October 2012, 'What if we run out of fuel mid-flight?' jokes about Kingfisher Airlines started surfacing.[28] State-run oil firm, Indian Oil Corporation (IOC), stated in January 2013 that the airline had been buying fuel on a cash-and-carry basis for the last year. Even though the government had, in October 2008, allowed all airlines to pay their dues in six equal instalments, Kingfisher Airlines had been unable to meet its commitments.[29]

London-based Diageo, the maker of Johnnie Walker Scotch whisky and Smirnoff vodka, came to Mallya's rescue in November 2012. Diageo agreed to buy 19.3 per cent promoters' stake in United Spirits for around ₹4045 crore ($757 million). After this transaction, the United Breweries Holdings Limited (UBHL) stake declined to 14.9 per cent.

Diageo, the world's largest distiller by revenue, was keen to acquire a majority stake in the number two player, United Spirits. In April 2013, Diageo made an open offer for United Spirits shares at ₹1440 per share. As United Spirits' share price was 25 per cent higher than Diageo's offer price, investors understandably did not tender their shares.[30] In April 2014, Diageo made a second open offer of ₹3030 per share—more than double the first offer price. It mopped up 26 per cent of the outstanding shares from the public by paying out ₹11,420 crore ($1.87 billion). Mallya continued to be chairman of United Spirits.[31]

In FY2013, which was the last year its annual report was published, Kingfisher's losses hit a nadir of ₹4301 crore ($786 million). As of March 2013, Kingfisher's net worth was a negative ₹12,920 crore ($2.36 billion) and its debt was ₹9345 crore ($1.71 billion). Overdue interest in FY2013 amounted to ₹1231 crore ($225 million). Kingfisher also owed its 3000 employees ₹312 crore ($57 million).

In 2014, the United Bank of India (UBI) labelled Mallya a wilful defaulter, but he was successful in getting the court to dismiss the move. India's largest bank, the State Bank of India (SBI), followed in UBI's footsteps in 2015. On 25 April 2015, Mallya was forced to step down as chairman of United Spirits after an internal probe allegedly uncovered financial irregularities. He struck a sweetheart deal with Diageo, which agreed to drop all charges and pay a ₹516-crore ($75 million) severance package.[32]

Even Zuari Agro Chemicals, which purchased a majority stake in Mangalore Chemicals & Fertilizers, had uncovered irregularities in the ₹217 crore ($33 million) intra-group investments and loans and advances the company had extended when Mallya was chairman.

The Last Hurrah

These setbacks failed to dampen Mallya's irrepressible spirit. On 18 December 2015, he threw a lavish birthday party at his 'Kingfisher Villa' in Goa to celebrate his sixtieth birthday. High-profile guests were flown in from across India and the world for the party, at which singers Enrique Iglesias and Sonu Nigam performed.

Lionel Richie had performed at the same venue a decade ago for Mallya's fiftieth birthday.

The party drew opprobrium even from Raghuram Rajan, who was then the RBI governor. Rajan observed, 'If you flaunt your birthday bashes even while owing the system a lot of money, it does seem to suggest to the public that you don't care.'[33]

In February 2016, a socialite in New Delhi learnt from a government official that legal proceedings against Mallya were imminent and that he was likely to be arrested soon. She reportedly tipped off Mallya, who also learned that senior Supreme Court counsel, Dushyant Dave, had advised SBI to approach the courts to restrain him from leaving the country.

On 16 October 2015, the CBI had issued a lookout notice for Mallya to the Bureau of Immigration. This meant that he should be detained the moment he presented himself at any immigration counter in India. Interestingly, the CBI amended the notice on 25 November 2015, requiring immigration authorities to intimate CBI of Mallya's movements, not detain him as was the order in the original notification.

Flight

On the night of 1 March 2016, Mallya, accompanied by his partner, Pinky Lalwani, who used to be a cabin crew member with Kingfisher, boarded the London-bound Jet Airways flight 9W-122 from New Delhi. He reportedly carried seven pieces of luggage, which was equivalent to the luggage allowance of five passengers, and occupied seat 1-D in first class. Mallya held a permanent residency in the UK.[34]

'Mallya exited the airline business in 2012, a major part of his liquor business in 2016 and finally exited the country on March 2 (2016) for the UK, waving his diplomatic passport, one of his perks as a Rajya Sabha MP,' declared columnist Venkatesha Babu in an *India Today* cover story titled '*The flight and fall of Mallya*'.

On 4 March 2016, Kingfisher's consortium of 17 banks led by SBI moved the Karnataka High Court for arresting Mallya, impounding his passport and claiming the ₹516 crore ($75 million) severance package Diageo and United Spirits had jointly signed with him on 25 February 2016.[35]

Credit: Gujarat Cooperative Milk Marketing Federation Ltd. (Amul)

On 8 March 2016, the banks moved the Supreme Court. Attorney General Mukul Rohtagi sought an urgent hearing against the Karnataka High Court order. On 9 March 2016, the Supreme Court was informed that Mallya had left the country a week ago. Also, as per Diageo's filing with the London Stock Exchange, the company had paid Mallya ₹275 crore ($40 million), or 53 per cent of the severance package, on the very day the agreement was signed. The balance was payable over five years.[36] On 2 May 2016, Mallya resigned as MP, a day before the Ethics Committee of the Rajya Sabha was set to recommend his expulsion.

In January 2017, CBI arrested at least eight officials of IDBI Bank and Kingfisher Airlines.[37] Those implicated included the bank's former chairman, Yogesh Aggarwal, and the airline's CFO, A. Raghunathan. The arrests were related to IDBI Bank's infamous loan to Kingfisher based on the airline's inflated brand valuation. CBI and the ED further alleged that Mallya had siphoned more than ₹100 crore ($15 million) to 30–40 London- and

Singapore-based companies. The Supreme Court found Mallya guilty of contempt of court after he failed to comply with orders for disclosure of assets.

On 25 January 2017, SEBI passed an order restraining Mallya from holding the position of director or key managerial person of any listed company. The defiant liquor baron had to be persuaded to step down as chairman of United Breweries Limited, which he did in October 2017.[38]

The UK authorities, on India's extradition request, arrested Mallya on 18 April 2017. A London court released him on bail within hours.[39] The extradition proceedings against Mallya concluded in May 2020 after the UK High Court rejected his plea to approach the UK Supreme Court against the proposed extradition to India. In October 2020, the GoI informed its Supreme Court that Mallya's extradition was stalled by 'secret' proceedings that had commenced in the UK. Media reports suggested Mallya may be seeking asylum in the UK.[40]

Further, the Covid-19 outbreak has enabled Mallya to remain a free person in the UK. The pandemic delayed his extradition due to UK's Article 3 obligations under the European Convention on Human Rights relating to inhuman and degrading treatment or punishment. 'There is a question now that the UK could be in breach of Article 3 if it were to extradite a person to a country where they could be at risk of being detained in an environment where they are at risk of contracting coronavirus,' said barrister Toby Cadman, co-founder of Guernica 37 International Justice Chambers and an extradition specialist. Mallya is likely to appeal to the European Court of Human Rights in Strasbourg, France, seeking an interim order against his extradition. 'The issuance of interim orders barring extradition are quite rare and the threshold is relatively high,' Cadman opined.[41]

Breach of Trust

Of the ₹9345 crore ($1.59 billion) debt as of March 2013, the SBI-led bank consortium informed the Karnataka High Court that they had recovered around ₹3600 crore ($486 million) until October 2020. The pending amount, after taking into account interest on the overdue principal and interest, was ₹11,000 crore ($1.48 billion).[42]

Kingfisher is not, by a far stretch, the most indebted listed company in India. That distinction goes to the conglomerate headed by the protagonist of the next section of this book, Anil Ambani. Kingfisher Airline's debt was a mere 7.7 per cent of Reliance Anil Dhirubhai Ambani Group's (ADAG) debt of ₹1,13,544 crore ($20.75 billion) as of March 2013, which represents the end of the financial year for which Kingfisher last published its annual accounts.[43]

Mallya's troubles did not just stem from Kingfisher's inability to service its debt. His unbridled empire-building aspirations, obdurate refusal to defer expansion plans amidst a recession and flagrant disregard for the law were significant contributory factors. Kingfisher launching its international flights amidst the GFC and the back-to-back debt-funded purchases of Air Deccan, RCB and Force India were strategic blunders. Mallya's blatant disregard for the law is evident in his using Manu Chhabria as a front for buying Shaw Wallace, availing a loan against Kingfisher's inflated brand value and the financial irregularities at United Breweries and Mangalore Chemicals & Fertilizers.

The Congress-led UPA and the BJP-led NDA displayed (not uncommon) solidarity in directing banks to finance Kingfisher at rather liberal terms and enabling Mallya to flee the country ahead of his potential conviction. It was during the UPA's tenure that the loan secured by Kingfisher's brand was disbursed and banks converted the airline's debt to equity at a price that was almost 62 per cent higher than its prevailing share price. The CBI, too, played its part and diluted its lookout notice, enabling Mallya to fly to London using his diplomatic passport during the NDA's tenure.

Finally, banks reneged on their fiduciary duty to their depositors, lenders and shareholders on two counts. First, banks lent Kingfisher monies far in excess of its debt servicing capacity. Second, banks did not insist that Mallya provide sufficient and liquid collateral for the vast sums of money Kingfisher borrowed. Had the banks insisted Mallya pledge his stakes in UB Group's listed entities, Mallya would have found it difficult to gamble with other people's money.

Forbes' peak estimate of Mallya's net worth at over ₹6600 crore ($1.6 billion) in 2007 and 2010 was slightly over 70 per cent of Kingfisher's debt.[44]

Figure 2: Vijay Mallya's Stakes in Select Listed Companies

	FY2010			FY2020		
	Stake	**Value (INR Crore)**	**Value (USD Million)**	**Stake**	**Value (INR Crore)**	**Value (USD Million)**
United Breweries Limited	38.69%	409.78	85.84	11.20%	2,720.44	366.97
United Spirits Limited	29.16%	985.34	206.42	0.82%	13.33	1.80
Mangalore Chemicals & Fertilisers Limited	30.44%	82.80	17.34	0.00%	-	-
Total		**1,477.91**	**309.61**		**2,733.77**	**368.77**

Source: Company annual reports, Bloomberg & author calculations

Chapter 12

Holding Pattern

In stark contrast to Kingfisher's precipitous nosedive was Jet Airways' gradual downward glide. The airline, which was a market leader commanding a market share of 54 per cent in 1998, witnessed its market share more than halve to 24.6 per cent by 2013. Two factors contributed to Jet Airways' decline: the absence of a coherent strategy when budget airlines were eating into FSCs' market share, and financial mismanagement.

The budget airlines offered competitively priced tickets and no-frills service. Lower fares contributed to a surge in passenger volumes in the price-sensitive Indian market. Budget airlines, especially IndiGo, operated a single aircraft model, point-to-point routes, and no sales were extended on credit. Operating a single aircraft model meant budget airlines could optimize aircraft maintenance costs and hold lower inventories of aircraft spare parts. Refraining from credit sales and lower inventories underpinned budget airlines' efficient working capital management and enhanced their operating cash flows.

Jet's trajectory

Jet Airways, instead of rethinking its strategy and cost structure, chose to react to emerging market trends. Goyal resorted to price competition, which as an FSC was suicidal, and attempted to erect competitive barriers to entry to stymie the rise of budget airlines.

After forking out ₹1450 crore ($351 million) to acquire Air Sahara in March 2007, Jet Airways embarked on an aggressive international expansion. Analysts had opined that the purchase consideration Jet Airways had paid to acquire Air Sahara was excessive. Later, a former Jet Airways vice president divulged in a *Forbes* column, 'We had decided that it wasn't worth it and Goyal agreed that we shouldn't pursue the deal. Then he went to meet [Subrata] Roy and within half an hour called us to say that he had purchased Sahara. It was nothing, but his ego at play . . . In hindsight, it was the Sahara deal that was the beginning of the fall.'[1]

Like Mallya, Goyal did not wait to consolidate Air Sahara's operations with Jet Airways. The airline placed orders for twenty-two wide-bodied aircraft, including Boeing 777s and Airbus 330s, and began applying for route rights for many international destinations. The aforesaid vice president explained, 'When you get a route and don't use it within six months, it goes back to the pool . . . With Kingfisher on its toes, there was a need to begin operations soon. However, we didn't have the back-end infrastructure to deal with these aircraft. Pilots were not trained and maintenance was an issue. So, we had to hire expats for maintenance and flying . . . all that meant that the costs spiraled up.'

Jet Airways' international expansion was aggressive but haphazard. It inducted A320s while having an all-Boeing fleet. It partnered with Etihad but reallocated capacity to a competing airline alliance. The airline flew on routes to compete with Singapore Airlines and Emirates, but used a smaller aircraft type, which led to a vastly different product experience. Jet Airways, both on its domestic and international routes, was priced as a LCC while offering a full-service product.

Satyendra Pandey, a certified pilot and an aviation expert, astutely observed, 'In trying to be all things to all people, it ended up as just another airline, albeit with a much higher cost base.[2]

It was this higher cost base, exacerbated by the prohibitive ATF price in India, which resulted in Jet Airways reporting losses for at least seven consecutive years, from FY2009 to FY2015. During the five-year period of FY2009 to FY2013, the airline reported aggregate losses of ₹3667 crore ($768 million). Jet Airways was already severely indebted and unable to borrow further to finance its losses. In fact, the airline was contractually obliged to repay debt amidst recurring losses. Consolidated debt declined to ₹10,504 crore ($1.92 billion) as of March 2013 from ₹16,634 crore ($3.72 billion) in March 2009.

To finance its recurring losses and repay debt, Jet Airways delayed its payments to its vendors. Credit purchases of ATF constituted a significant proportion of the airline's payables. Jet Airways' payables, that were equivalent to forty-eight days of revenues in FY2009, grew to seventy-eight days by FY2013. The airline was substituting its financial liabilities with operational liabilities.

It became imperative for Jet Airways to raise equity. It was around this time that Mallya was attempting to rope in Etihad Airways as an equity investor in Kingfisher Airlines; nothing came of it. Etihad Airways responded to Goyal's overtures, and in April 2013 acquired a 24 per cent stake in Jet Airways for ₹2244 crore ($379 million) by paying a premium of 42 per cent over the market price. Retail and institutional investors held 25 per cent in Jet Airways. This partnership also gave Etihad Airways the right of first refusal should Goyal dilute his stake further.

Jet Airway's shareholding structure changed in the aftermath of Etihad Airways' acquisition of a minority stake. As of March 2013, which was prior to Etihad Airways' acquisition, the Isle of Man-incorporated Tail Winds Limited held an 80 per cent stake in Jet Airways. However, Goyal, in his individual capacity, became the controlling shareholder with a stake of 51 per cent as of March 2014. One cannot help but recollect Arun Shourie's comments.

While this deal enabled Jet Airways to pare down its debt to ₹9557 crore ($1.61 billion), it was controversial. The ministry of civil aviation had simultaneously approved a bilateral agreement with Abu Dhabi that resulted in a four-fold expansion of capacity between the two countries. This development was widely perceived as a quid pro quo for Etihad Airways purchasing a minority stake in Jet Airways. Aviation experts questioned the necessity of linking a bilateral pact with an investment in a private airline. 'Granting such a huge hike in capacity suggests a scam-like dimension to the deal,' suggested Jitender Bhargava, a former executive director of Air India.[3] A senior airline executive who wished to remain anonymous observed, 'It isn't just Goyal who's selling out; India's selling out.'[4]

Etihad Airways additionally acquired a 51 per cent majority stake in Jet Airways' frequent flyer program, Jet Privilege, for ₹888 crore ($150 million), and purchased Jet Airways' slots at Heathrow Airport for ₹414 crore ($70 million).[5]

However, what was most controversial about this deal was that the recipient of the ₹1302 crore ($220 million) cash that Etihad Airways paid for these assets was not the listed entity, Jet Airways (India) Limited. It is natural and legal for an entrepreneur to own assets besides his flagship enterprise. But not deploying the cash received from the sale of such assets in the heavily indebted and loss-making enterprises he has majority stakes in reflects lax if not non-existent corporate governance standards. Interestingly, Jet Airways' lenders did not insist that Goyal invest at least a fraction of the cash received in the listed entity, Jet Airways (India) Limited.

Dead End

Etihad Airways' investment was inadequate to reverse Jet Airways' losses. In FY2014, it touched a seven-year peak of ₹4130 crore ($698 million). The global decline in crude oil price, and hence ATF price, offered some reprieve in FY2015 with losses moderating to ₹2097 crore ($339 million). With fuel prices continuing to remain low, Jet Airways reported modest profits for the first time in almost a decade in FY2016 and FY2017. But the profits were inadequate to bolster the airline's net worth, which had turned negative in FY2013 and remained in the red till the airline ceased flying in April 2019.

Jet Airways' interest and lease rentals were too high for the airline to generate meaningful cash to repay debts. The airline's fleet of 86 aircraft in FY2009 had grown to 120 in FY2018. The recovery of crude oil and ATF prices in FY2018 spelt the death knell of the airline, which relapsed to losses. To make matters worse, in August 2018, Jet Airways' statutory auditor refused to sign off the results for the first quarter of FY2019 citing differences in the interpretation of accounting rules.

Goyal tried to rope in more equity investors. He reached out to the Tata Group and Etihad Airways. An anonymous source was quoted in a *Mint* article stating that the Tata Group's 'relations with Goyal had been thorny from the early days of private airlines in India. Nevertheless, they were willing to invest provided Goyal was willing to cede control . . . But Tatas, suspecting revenue leakage, also made it amply clear that all of Jet's existing vendor contracts including ground handling had to end.'[6] The Tata Group reportedly wanted Goyal to exit Jet Airways completely.

Though Etihad Airways had acquired a 24 per cent stake in Jet Airways in 2013, Jet Airways remained Naresh Goyal's fiefdom. Also, Jet Airways never really became the feeder airline from India that Etihad hoped it would for its global operations. A former Jet Airways senior executive informed *Mint* for the same article, 'There was no love lost between Goyal and Etihad . . . Like Tata, Etihad too wanted Goyal out, but alongside also wanted a waiver on the mandatory open offer post equity infusion . . . But the Securities and Exchange Board of India, which felt Etihad should have made an open offer back in 2013 since there was a change in management control in Jet Airways, said there could not be any waiver this time around'.

The Exit

Goyal was reportedly insistent about retaining control of Jet Airways. By January 2019, the airline had defaulted on loan repayments to lenders led by SBI. The airline had not paid pilots their salaries months ahead of its default. Jet Airways' FY2019 losses had deepened to ₹5536 crore ($803 million). In March 2019, the airline negotiated a debt restructuring package with its lenders, who agreed to provide additional funding of up to ₹1500 crore ($218 million). The restructuring plan gave the lenders a 50.1 per cent stake in the airline and led to Goyal stepping down as Jet Airways' chairman.[7]

The lenders released only ₹300 crore ($44 million) by April 2019. Jet Airways was compelled to suspend its operations. On 17 April 2019, the airline flew its last flight from Amritsar to Mumbai. Jet Airways' unpaid debt reportedly exceeded ₹8000 crore ($1.1 billion). It had around 20,000 employees on its rolls when it ceased flying.

On 25 May 2019, the air traffic control at Mumbai's Chhatrapati Shivaji Maharaj International Airport called back a Dubai-bound Emirates flight as it was taxiing to take off. This was done at the behest of immigration authorities. Seated among the first-class passengers of that flight were Goyal and his wife, Anita. The couple, who had cleared the immigration checks prior to boarding the flight, were asked to disembark. They were informed that they were barred from travelling abroad and were requested to return to their residence. The ministry of corporate affairs had issued a lookout circular for them.[8]

Jet Airways' lenders had referred the airline to the National Company Law Tribunal (NCLT), India's adjudicating authority for the insolvency resolution process of companies and limited liability partnerships. Goyal, backed by the Delaware-based Future Trend Capital, submitted a bid for Jet Airways when the ministry of corporate affairs auctioned the airline in August 2019. Goyal had to withdraw his bid when the consortium led by Etihad Airways and TPG Capital threatened to withdraw their expression of interest. This was despite SBI chairman Rajnish Kumar saying that 'nobody is barred from bidding or taking over the airline' as per the rules.[9]

Financial and operational creditors and employees had filed claims of ₹44,146 crore ($6 billion), of which the bankruptcy resolution professional admitted only around one-third—₹15,234 crore ($2 billion).[10] Of the admitted claims, the share of financial creditors' claims was 51 per cent or ₹7808 crore ($1.03 billion).

On 17 October 2020, eighteen months after Jet Airways shut down and sixteen months after it became the first airline in India to be admitted under the Insolvency and Bankruptcy Code, the lenders approved the resolution plan submitted by Kalrock Capital and Murari Lal Jalan. Kalrock Capital is part of the Fritsch Group, an investment group founded by serial real estate and tech entrepreneur Florian Fritsch. Murari Lal Jalan, a hitherto unknown figure in India, helms the MJ Group, which is engaged in property development in Uzbekistan.[11] Financial creditors have agreed to a 95 per cent haircut. The Kalrock–Jalan consortium will pay them ₹385 crore ($51 million) in cash and zero-coupon bonds over two years after the airline resumes flying.[12]

Jet Airways was scheduled to resume flying during the summer of 2021, but the Covid-19 pandemic has thrown a spanner in the works. The erstwhile market leader—Jet Airways—finally obtained an air operator certificate from the DGCA in May 2022 and started recruiting pilots in July 2022.

The crashlanding of Jet Airways coincided with the sustained nosedive of another airline to which Goyal's airline had dealt a mortal blow—Air India.

The Maharaja's Downfall

In India, the market shares of the state-owned Life Insurance Corporation of India (LIC) and the four non-life insurance companies—New India Assurance, Oriental Insurance, National Insurance, and United India Insurance—declined after the entry of private sector insurers. This is the case with public sector banks and Air India too.

Competition cannibalizing the incumbents' market share is natural. However, it was not just competition that impelled Air India's nosedive. Politics had a significant role to play as well.

Between 2001 to 2004, the BJP government led by Prime Minister Vajpayee successfully divested its stake in at least seventeen PSUs, raising ₹38,500 crore ($8.2 billion).[13] Air India and Indian Airlines had each reported profits for four of the preceding six years as of Mach 2004, while Alliance Air had reported profits for three years. Indian Airlines and Alliance Air combined were the market leaders among domestic airlines at this juncture. Not listing either or both Air India and Indian Airlines was a strategic error. It was not as if listed airlines were non-existent in Asia. Singapore Airlines had successfully completed its IPO in 2000. A listing would have enabled these airlines to raise equity, paydown debt, diversify their investor base and, most importantly, render them accountable to their investors.

In 2003, the government constituted the Naresh Chandra Committee to recommend solutions for the revitalization of India's civil aviation industry. Key recommendations of this committee included permitting foreign investors and airlines to acquire up to 49 per cent stake in airlines in India with the approval of the Foreign Investment Promotion Board (FIPB); the privatization of Air India and Indian Airlines; allowing airlines to purchase ATF from a supplier of their choice and setting up of an Aviation Economic Regulatory Authority (AERA).[14]

This was the third government-mandated committee, after the Tymms Committee of pre-independence India and the

Rajadhyaksha Committee of 1953, which recommended civil aviation be the domain of private sector airlines albeit with government oversight. However, the Naresh Chandra Committee's recommendations were also ignored.

When the UPA was elected to power at the Centre in 2004 (UPA-I), the civil aviation minister, Praful Patel, pushed for the modernization of Air India and Indian Airlines. The two state-owned airlines undertook a debt-funded purchase of 111 aircraft worth ₹70,000 crore ($15.5 billion), which the CAG subsequently described as a 'recipe for disaster'.[15]

Soon after this large-scale aircraft purchase, on 15 July 2007, the government merged Air India and Indian Airlines to form NACIL, which was subsequently renamed Air India. The government opined that the merger would result in a performance improvement arising from the synergy between the two airlines. The combined losses of Air India, Indian Airlines and Alliance Air that amounted to ₹143 crore ($31 million) in FY2003 grew almost fifty-fold in eight years to ₹7000 crore ($1.5 billion) in FY2011. The CAG criticized the government for not merging the two airlines ahead of the aircraft purchase.

In 2011, the UPA-II government announced a ₹48,212 crore ($10.3 billion) equity infusion into Air India over twenty years ending March 2032. However, even the equity infusion could not spur Air India's recovery. The airline continued bleeding as there was no effective cash inflow to alleviate its liquidity woes, at least during the five years ending March 2019. Air India's annual reports are available in the public domain only from FY2015.

The ₹21,826 crore ($3.5 billion) equity infusion by the government was inadequate even to meet Air India's interest expense, which amounted to ₹27,667 crore ($4.3 billion) during the five years ending March 2019. Air India had to fork out an additional ₹5841 crore ($832 million) in interest expenses. The government, which was enterprising enough to oversee Kingfisher Airlines' debt restructuring in 2010, failed to carry out an organizational restructuring of Air India along with the equity infusion.

Though Air India is a loss-making entity, it owns prime real estate across multiple Indian cities. The government had, in 2012, approved monetizing Air India's real estate assets worth ₹5000 crore ($936 million) over a ten-year period, with an annual target of ₹500 crore ($94 million) from FY2013 onwards.[16] Air India's asset sales during the six-year period FY2014 to FY2019 was ₹18,446 crore ($2.9 billion)—more than thrice the stipulated target. The cash raised from asset sales were used to finance Air India's inflated operating expenses, including salaries, interest expenditure and lease rentals. The sizeable asset sales were not used to repay the state-owned airline's debt, which rose from ₹51,616 crore ($8.7 billion) as of March 2014 to ₹57,484 crore ($8.3 billion) as of March 2019.

Even after selling the real estate assets, the government states Air India has surplus real estate to sell. Was the government's ₹5000 crore ($936 million) asset monetization target a tad too modest?

The CBI alleged that Air India, while purchasing aircraft on one hand, was simultaneously leasing aircraft without due consideration, a proper route study or a marketing-pricing strategy. The CAG estimated that Air India incurred ₹405.8 crore ($78 million) losses from leasing aircraft between March 2011 and May 2014.

The CAG further stated in a March 2017 report tabled in Parliament that Air India incurred a loss of more than ₹671 crore ($103 million) by selling five Boeing 777-200 long-range aircraft to Etihad below cost price. According to the CAG, two parties—Avitas and Ascent—had indicated a market price of $86.92 million per aircraft. Air India had, however, sold these aircraft to Etihad at $67.30 million per aircraft –almost 23 per cent lower than the market price.

The government has been trying to divest Air India since 2018. However, when it made the announcement, it also stated that it would retain a stake of 24 per cent in the airline, despite the government's policy think-tank Niti Aayog recommending that the entire stake in Air India be off-loaded. There were no takers.[17]

In 2020, the government announced that it would sell its entire stake in Air India. The winning bidder would be awarded a 100 per cent stake in the low-cost carrier, Air India Express, and 50 per cent stake in Air India SATS (AISATS), which provides ground handling and cargo services at major domestic airports. Air India, in FY2020, received ₹22,346 crore ($3.1 billion) from Air India Assets Holding Limited that enabled the airline to reduce its debt to ₹39,726 crore ($5.6 billion) ahead of its divestment.

Three entities—the Tata Group, SpiceJet's CEO Ajay Singh in his individual capacity, and an employee consortium submitted expressions of interest.[18] The GoI accepted Tata Group's offer, resulting in the Maharaja returning home after seventy years.

Credit: Gujarat Cooperative Milk Marketing Federation Ltd. (Amul)

SpiceJet's Turbulence

Operating a sustainable airline in India is more challenging than in most countries. Domestic airlines operate in a price sensitive market against the backdrop of high ATF prices, high borrowing costs and shallow capital markets that render raising equity and refinancing debt difficult. Politics and precarious financials complicate the performance of India's second-largest airline by market share as of 2020—SpiceJet.

SpiceJet traces its origins to one of the first private sector airlines set up in post-independent India—ModiLuft—which operated from 1993 to 1996. ModiLuft was the first private sector airline to fly a three-class configuration on domestic routes. Conflicts between ModiLuft's promoter, S.K. Modi, and his technical partner, Lufthansa, brought operations to a standstill.

In the early 2000s, UK-based businessman Bhupendra Kansagara purchased ModiLuft and renamed it Royal Airways. The airline never took off. In 2005, Kansagara joined hands with Ajay Singh, a politically connected New Delhi-based entrepreneur. Singh purchased a 20 per cent stake in the airline for ₹50 crore ($11.3 million) and renamed it SpiceJet.[19] In August 2008, investment vehicle(s) owned by the US-based distressed asset investor, Wilbur Ross, invested in SpiceJet.

The 1965-born Ajay Singh had completed his engineering degree from the Indian Institute of Technology (IIT), Delhi, and MBA, specializing in finance, from Cornell University. Singh's proximity to the BJP had resulted in his being inducted, in 1996, in the board of the Delhi Transport Corporation (DTC), the government-owned corporation that operates intra-city passenger buses. DTC was floundering; Singh is credited with its revamping and fleet expansion from a few hundred to 6000.

Singh caught the attention of BJP leader and union information and broadcasting minister, Pramod Mahajan, who posted him as an officer on special duty to rejuvenate the state-run television channel, Doordarshan. Two new TV channels—DD Sports and DD News—were launched under Singh's watch. When Mahajan became the telecom minister, Singh worked on assignments in the telecom ministry as well. He is credited with coining the hugely popular slogan 'Abki baar, Modi sarkar' (This time, it's the turn of the Modi government) ahead of the 2014 union elections.

Not much information is available on SpiceJet's performance between 2005 and 2009 in the public domain. According to the airline's FY2010 annual report, it had generated a profit of

₹61 crore ($9 million) on revenues of ₹2242 crore ($470 million). Its indebtedness, as measured by the ratio of net lease adjusted debt to EBITDAR, though on the higher side, was manageable at 4.43 times. SpiceJet's market share in March 2010, at 12.4 per cent, was the fifth largest in Indian civil aviation following Jet Airways at 25.5 per cent, Kingfisher's 23 per cent, Air India's 17.6 per cent and IndiGo's 14.3 per cent.

In June 2010, Kalanithi Maran, the media baron who founded Sun TV, a leading Tamil language TV channel, purchased the Kansagara family's and Wilbur Ross' combined 38.66 per cent stake in SpiceJet for ₹750 crore ($163 million) through his aviation company, KAL Airways. Kalanithi Maran and his politician-brother, Dayanidhi Maran, are grand-nephews of M. Karunanidhi, the five-time chief minister of Tamil Nadu.

The CBI had accused the Maran brothers of setting up a private telephone exchange of 764 telephone lines in Dayanidhi Maran's Chennai residence to facilitate the illegal uplink of Sun TV data when he was the union telecom minister from 2004 to 2006.[20] In March 2018, the Maran brothers were acquitted. Kalanithi Maran and his wife, Kavery Kalanithi have consistently ranked among the highest-paid Indian CEOs for several years. The couple's ₹175 crore ($23.6 million) aggregate salaries and bonuses exceeded the earnings of India's highest-paid executive, C.P. Gurnani, Tech Mahindra's CEO, who drew ₹165.6 crore ($22.3 million) in 2020 despite Tech Mahindra being a much larger and more profitable entity than *Sun TV*.[21]

Ajay Singh, whose stake in SpiceJet declined to 4.13 per cent, did not seek to be reappointed when his term as independent director ended in August 2010. In compliance with SEBI norms, KAL Airways purchased an additional 20 per cent stake in SpiceJet through an open offer for ₹479 crore ($104 million). Kalanithi Maran became SpiceJet's largest shareholder with a stake of 43.60 per cent as per SpiceJet's FY2011 annual report; he pared down his stake from 58.66 per cent after the public offer.

The year Maran acquired SpiceJet, FY2011, was the first and last year the airline was profitable under his watch. In a bid to maximize market share, SpiceJet doubled its fleet from twenty-three aircraft in FY2011 to forty-seven in FY2012. This aggression was accompanied by two strategic errors. First, SpiceJet, whose fleet till FY2011 comprised a single aircraft model, Boeing 737s, leased Bombardiers to connect with tier-II and tier-III towns. This led to higher operating expenses. Second, the airline focused on flying to multiple destinations instead of operating frequent flights to select high-traffic destinations. Singh cryptically commented in an interview with *Outlook*, 'The cost structure went wrong. Some of the contracts that were signed imposed a cost, which was not sustainable.'[22]

SpiceJet's revenues, which more than doubled between FY2010 and FY2015, were still inadequate to meet the skyrocketing operating expenses including fuel costs, interest and lease expenses, and employees' salaries. The airline reported recurring losses during the four-year period from FY2012 to FY2015. SpiceJet's purchases on credits were equivalent to sixty days of revenues in FY2014; in FY2010, they had been equivalent to twenty-five days of revenues.

Its net worth, which turned negative in FY2012, deteriorated to a negative ₹1265 crore ($205 million) by March 2015. This was despite Maran and KAL Airways investing ₹769 crore ($135 million) in SpiceJet's equity, share warrants and non-convertible preference shares (CRPS) between FY2012 and FY2015. The stake that Maran and KAL Airways held in SpiceJet had increased to 58.46 per cent after the equity infusion.

However, SpiceJet failed to achieve the goal for which it had embarked on this breakneck expansion—market leadership. Its market share had grown to 17.8 per cent in FY2014 from 12.4 per cent in FY2010. The airline that had capitalized on Air India's and Jet Airways' inefficiencies and Kingfisher's collapse was IndiGo, whose market share had more than doubled to 30.3 per cent in

FY2014 from 14.3 per cent in FY2010. IndiGo, an LCC like SpiceJet, had garnered the highest market share among domestic airlines while remaining profitable and keeping its indebtedness under check.

SpiceJet's financial position turned so precarious that the aviation ministry, in December 2014, had to request oil marketing companies that sold ATF to extend a fifteen-day credit to SpiceJet. The oil companies refused to comply with this request.[23] The DGCA also required SpiceJet to submit daily reports of flights operated and cancelled and adhere to the aircraft maintenance schedule. On 17 December 2014, SpiceJet was grounded due to non-payment of dues to the oil marketing companies.

Maran reached out to Singh and private equity partnerships to sell his stake and exit the beleaguered airline. On 29 January 2015, Singh executed an agreement with Maran to purchase the latter's and KAL Airways' majority stake in SpiceJet. Despite SpiceJet being a listed entity, the purchase consideration was not immediately reported. When it ultimately emerged that Singh had paid ₹2 ($0.03) to acquire 58.46 per cent stake in SpiceJet, all hell broke loose. As of March 2015, SpiceJet's ₹3871 crore ($626 million) liabilities exceeded its ₹2607 crore ($422 million) assets, resulting in a negative net worth of ₹1265 crore ($ 205 million). Recurring losses had eroded shareholders' equity investment.

This was not the first time that an entity with negative net worth was being acquired for free. In 1995, the Dutch bank, ING, bought the 1762-incorporated Barings Bank that collapsed on account of its trader Nick Leeson's unauthorized trades, for £1. Finablr Plc, the scandal-marred payments and foreign exchange solutions platform owned by UAE-based Indian entrepreneur, B.R. Shetty, was sold to a UAE-Israeli consortium for $1 in December 2020.

It was the secrecy surrounding the SpiceJet sale that led to the controversy. SEBI regulations require an acquirer purchasing a stake in excess of 25 per cent in a company to launch an open offer. SEBI waived this requirement for Singh, which certain market participants viewed as unprecedented.

R. Vaidyanathan, a professor of finance at IIM, Bangalore, stated, 'In the Form B and D filings, both Maran and Singh have put the face value of shares and not the actual transaction price.'[24] Whether a less politically connected entrepreneur could have obtained such dispensations to purchase a floundering airline is open to conjecture. But the saga did not end here.

In FY2014 and FY2015, Maran and KAL Airways had invested ₹264 crore ($43 million) as advance for the issue of convertible warrants and ₹120 crore ($20 million) as advance for the issue of non-convertible cumulative preference shares (CRPS). A share warrant is a financial instrument that gives the holder (in this case Maran) the right but not the obligation to purchase the shares of a company (SpiceJet)—at a specific price on a specific date.

Had SpiceJet issued these warrants and Maran had exercised his right to purchase the shares, he would have acquired a 24 per cent stake in the company subsequent to Singh acquiring a majority stake in SpiceJet. A 24 per cent stake in SpiceJet was worth ₹312 crore ($51 million) as of March 2015 and ₹920 crore ($142 million) as of March 2016, as the airline's share price had appreciated after Singh's acquisition. Had Maran converted the warrants in March 2016, he would have earned a profit of ₹656 crore ($100 million), which is the difference between the ₹920 crore ($142 million) market value of a 24 per cent stake in SpiceJet, less ₹264 crore ($43 million) advance paid for the issue of convertible warrants.

In 2016, Maran filed a suit against SpiceJet in the Delhi High Court claiming ₹1323 crore ($197 million) damages for not issuing convertible warrants and CRPS to him and KAL Airways. The Delhi High Court created an arbitration tribunal comprising three judges. The proceedings started in 2016 and concluded in April 2018.

The tribunal unanimously rejected Maran's ₹1323 crore ($197 million) damage claim but awarded him a ₹579 crore

(\$85 million) refund, which represents the advances he had paid towards the allotment of convertible warrants and CRPS plus 12 per cent interest for 30 months. The tribunal allowed SpiceJet to furnish a bank guarantee for ₹329 crore (\$48 million) and pay cash for the balance ₹250 crore (\$37 million). The tribunal stated that SpiceJet had not breached its contractual obligation by not allotting the convertible warrants and CRPS to Maran and KAL Airways as SEBI had not approved the allotment.[25] Maran continued legal proceedings against SpiceJet as the airline had not paid the dues of ₹243 crore (\$36 million).[26] In September 2022, the Supreme Court appointed its former judge, P. V. Reddi, to mediate the dispute between Singh and Maran.

Singh was fortunate to have acquired SpiceJet when crude oil and consequently ATF prices had declined. The airline reported profits from FY2016 to FY2018. SpiceJet did reduce its payables from a peak of sixty days in FY2014 to less than a week since FY2015. Indebtedness, as measured by the ratio of net lease adjusted debt to EBITDAR, had also substantially declined to 3.73 times by March 2018 from 26.19 times as of March 2014. SpiceJet achieved this feat despite expanding its fleet from thirty-two aircraft in FY2015 to sixty-two aircraft in FY2018. Its market share, however, declined from 17.8 per cent in FY2014 to 12.7 per cent in FY2018. SpiceJet's focus on performance instead of market share is a testimony to Singh's temporary prudence.

SpiceJet's financial performance started deteriorating again in FY2019 and FY2020 when the airline once again aggressively expanded its fleet to 105 aircraft by March 2020. The resultant increase in fuel, employee and interest costs led to SpiceJet reporting losses. The Covid-19 outbreak exacerbated the situation. The airline reported losses for three consecutive years ending FY2021, while debt has grown 10-fold to ₹9831 crore (\$1.33 billion) as of March 2021. This, however, did deter Singh from throwing his hat in the ring to acquire Air India. Fortunately for SpiceJet's lenders and investors and Air India, GoI decided to sell the flag carrier to the Tata Group.

SpiceJet's credibility was dented when a 2021 DGCA investigation revealed that that the airline was delaying payments to suppliers and vendors, which resulted in a shortage of spare parts. Safety concerns arose as SpiceJet aircraft were involved in nearly ten incidents ranging from mechanical issues to smoke filling an airborne flight between 10 June to 5 July 2022. On 30 July 2022 the DGCA ordered SpiceJet to cut its schedule in half up to 30 September 2022.[27, 28] In August 2022 the DGCA ordered the deregistering of four SpiceJet aircraft at the request of lessors due to delay or non-payment of lease rentals. The struggling airline is yet again on the lookout for a financial lifeline through a stake sale or other means; this time for ₹2000 crore ($250 million).[29]

The SpiceJet saga thus far highlights the still nascent investor activism and awareness in India. Though SpiceJet was profitable from FY2016 to FY2018, the profits were inadequate to offset the airline's negative net worth. SpiceJet's net worth, which turned negative in FY2012, has remained in the red for nine consecutive years now. As of March 2022, the airline's negative net worth touched an eleven-year trough of ₹4340 crore ($581 million). Had SpiceJet's shareholders bothered to peruse the company's financials during the last decade, they would have realized that the book value of their shares was zero, at best. In this scenario, rational shareholders would have sold their shares. SpiceJet would have been reduced to a penny stock.

The reality is quite different, though. SpiceJet's share price surged 124 per cent in 2017, becoming the best performing stock on the Bloomberg Intelligence Index of airline stocks that year![30] SpiceJet's share price surge between FY2016 to FY2018 may be attributed to the airline's profitability during this period.

Singh's managerial prowess and proximity to the BJP underpin SpiceJet's attractiveness as an investment proposition. Singh and his family members have held close to 60 per cent stake in the airline since January 2015. But Singh has continuously pledged his stake in SpiceJet ever since he acquired the airline from Maran. His effective stake, which is the difference between his gross stake and the shares pledged to lenders, has declined from 40.95 per cent in March 2015 to 33.55 per cent in March 2020. This information is, again, available in SpiceJet's annual reports. Yet shareholders appear to be unperturbed by Singh's declining skin in the game and his attempt to purchase Air India.

Beacon of Hope

Thomas Carlyle, a Scottish essayist, called economics a dismal science. This was supposedly a reaction to Thomas Malthus's prediction that, as population growth outstripped food production, the world would face inevitable famine and a subsistence standard of living. After reading the chronicles of Air India, Jet Airways, Air Deccan, Kingfisher and SpiceJet, it is not irrational to view civil aviation as a dismal industry. Fortunately, one airline—IndiGo—offers hope.

In 2006, Rakesh Bhatia and Rahul Gangwal founded IndiGo, an LCC. The airline is of the same vintage as SpiceJet. Bhatia holds an engineering degree from the University of Waterloo in Ontario, Canada. Prior to the founding of IndiGo, Bhatia was and continues to be the managing director of InterGlobe Enterprises (IGE), an unlisted conglomerate with interests in hotel, airline and travel technology. IGE's clientele had included Air Deccan. The servers used for Air Deccan's centralized reservation system were located at IGE's premises. This and IGE's potential foray into civil aviation were listed as risk factors in Air Deccan's 2006 IPO prospectus.[31]

Gangwal, born in the early 1950s, holds an engineering degree from IIT, Kanpur and an MBA from Wharton. *Forbes* columnist Cuckoo Paul remarks, 'In the US, Gangwal is remembered for bailing out of US Airways in 2002 with retirement benefits of $15 million, leaving the airline deep in the red in the aftermath of September 11. To be fair to him, old timers in the US airline industry say the airline had problems that preceded him and continued well after his departure. He left to join the private equity business and is currently [in 2010] advisor at Teachers' Private Capital . . .'[32]

Bhatia and Gangwal reportedly bumped into each other in the corridors of the United Airlines headquarters in Chicago in 1985, while Bhatia was doing IT work for the airline. The acquaintance grew into friendship over the next fifteen years, before IndiGo was launched.

Bhatia informed *Forbes*, 'The idea for us was to set up a certain kind of an airline . . . the kind that is on time, clean and delivery is well executed.' IndiGo's advantage was the knowhow and skill brought in by Gangwal. Bharat Bhise, CEO and founder of Bravia Capital, a New York-based transportation advisory and investment company, told Paul, 'Gangwal brings in the global networking and the expertise that comes from running global airlines. He has made the mistakes and knows how to avoid them.'

The founders conceived an airline best-suited for the price-sensitive Indian market—an LCC—and executed its business model to perfection. Economies of scale apply to aircraft fleet acquisition just as they do to the purchase of other goods and services. The founders used most of the ₹100 crore ($22 million) capital they invested in IndiGo as advance for 100 Airbus A320 aircraft. An *Economic Times* column estimated that aircraft manufacturers give airlines a discount of around 42 per cent when such bulk orders are placed. Besides, the single aircraft model fleet optimized repairs and maintenance expense and required IndiGo to hold lower inventories of spare parts.[33] IndiGo, by adhering to a single model fleet, emulated the US-based LCC Southwest Airlines, the only airline in the world to have been consistently profitable during the forty-seven years ended December 2019. After reporting a

Covid-19 induced loss of $3 billion in 2020, Southwest Airlines recovered to report a $977 million profit in 2021.

Sale and leaseback transactions form the cornerstone of IndiGo's fleet acquisition strategy. Under this arrangement, IndiGo sells its aircraft to an aircraft leasing company at a profit and then leases the same aircraft back from the lessor usually for five-and-a-half years.

Airlines need to place orders for new aircraft around three years in advance and are required to pay just 5 per cent of the aircraft's price as advance while placing the order. Airlines pay the aircraft manufacturer the balance 95 per cent purchase consideration in instalments. The sale proceeds IndiGo receives from the lessor is used to pay the aircraft manufacturer.

Purchasing brand new aircraft and leasing them for around five-and-a-half years (after selling the aircraft to the lessor) entails another benefit for IndiGo. Maintenance expenses are lower for new aircraft. IndiGo returns its aircraft to the lessor at the end of the lease period. Every six years, an aircraft is dismantled and re-assembled as part of a D-Check. This comprehensive test takes three to six weeks to complete and costs millions of dollars. By returning the aircraft to the lessor before the D-Check, IndiGo saves on costs. A sale and leaseback transaction is attractive to the leasing company as it earns lease rentals from a creditworthy lessee without having to buy the aircraft.

IndiGo combined this perfectly legal financial engineering with a high level of operating efficiency to achieve two metrics that airlines in India hitherto found elusive: consistent profits and low indebtedness. IndiGo's PLF was at or above the optimal level of 80 per cent during nine of the eleven years ended March 2020. Its PLF fell just short of 80 per cent at 77.2 per cent in FY2014 and 79.8 per cent in FY2015. The liquidity afforded by the sale and leaseback transactions enabled IndiGo to keep its borrowings under check and pay its operating creditors, including oil companies, promptly. The ratio of net lease adjusted debt to EBITDAR ranged from a minimum of 0.80 times in FY2011 to a maximum of 2.03 times in FY2014, and stood at 1.54 times in FY2020. The airline's payables period has ranged from eleven to eighteen days of revenues during the eleven years ended March 2020.

There are instances when a company's share price appreciates to stratospheric levels notwithstanding its weak underlying performance. Why allow performance to mar an engaging investment hypothesis? Tesla is a case in point. The electric vehicle manufacturer reported a meagre profit of $721 million, equivalent to 2.3 per cent of $31.55 billion sales for the first time in thirteen years in 2020. Yet, its share price consistently appreciated over the years by 185 times to $742 in February 2021 from $3.99 in July 2010; this translates to an annualized return of 61 per cent!

IndiGo's fundamentals, however, justify its share performance. The LCC has, aided by its robust business and financial strategy, achieved yet another milestone no other listed airline in India has thus far. The airline has paid dividends in eight of the eleven years ended March 2020. During the six months ended November 2020, Interglobe Aviation, IndiGo's parent company, was the world's best performing aviation stock. Needless to mention, Interglobe Aviation's shares have consistently outperformed those of Jet Airways and SpiceJet.

Figure 1: IndiGo's Shares Outperform Domestic and Global Peers

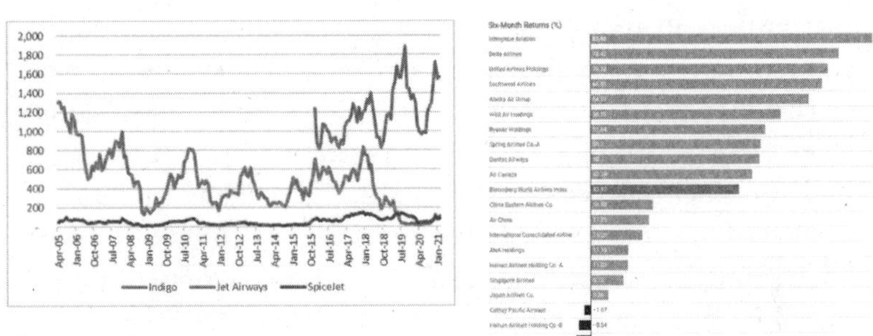

Source: Bloomberg

However, there are kinks in IndiGo's armour.

In July 2019, Gangwal wrote to SEBI, alleging corporate governance lapses on the part of Bhatia and IGE. These, according to Gangwal, included Interglobe Aviation's related party transactions with IGE without the audit committee's approval, lapses in the appointment of independent directors, powers exercised by the nomination and remuneration committee and misrepresentations in Interglobe Aviation's October 2015 IPO prospectus.[34]

This letter took everyone by surprise as Interglobe Aviation's chairman was Meleveetil Damodaran, the former chairman of SEBI. M. Damodaran was also an independent director on Interglobe Aviation's board. Gangwal rather belatedly objected to a clause in Interglobe Aviation's articles of association, which stated, 'The Chairman of the Board shall be appointed on the nomination of the IGE Group . . .'. Gangwal did clarify in his letter, 'While we aren't questioning the independence of the current Chairman in his decision making, we are questioning the designation of such an individual as "independent". . . .'[35] Interestingly, Dr Venkataramani Sumantran was appointed as IndiGo's independent non-executive chairman in May 2022, while M. Damodaran was appointed as non-independent non-executive director in July 2022.

In December 2020, Interglobe Aviation proposed to settle the proceedings SEBI had initiated against it. Under SEBI's consent mechanism, an entity is allowed to settle charges without admission or denial of guilt. Interglobe Aviation settled the charges by paying a ₹2.1 crore ($290,000) penalty.

This did not resolve the conflict between the warring promoters, who approached the London Court of International Arbitration (LCIA) to settle their differences. The LCIA's final award in September 2021 decreed that the right of first refusal (ROFR) both promoters held may be scrapped. Gangwal and Bhatia convened an extraordinary general meeting in December 2021 in which shareholders voted in favour of scrapping the ROFR. Going forward, both Bhatia and Gangwal are not required to offer their shares for sale to the other before proceeding to sell their stake, partially or completely, in the open market. However, market watchers opine that neither promoter is likely to dilute his stake in IndiGo.[36, 37] Interglobe Aviation's share price was mostly rising during this four-year saga; yet another sign of shareholder ignorance.

IndiGo's dividend payout, which is the percentage of profits a company pays as dividends, has historically been high. Between FY2010 and FY2020, the airline has paid 72 per cent of its profits as dividends. This was not a concern till FY2018 as the airline was profitable. However, IndiGo undertook an aggressive expansion of its fleet from 159 aircraft in FY2018 to 217 in FY2019 and 262 in FY2020.

The increase in operating expenses on account of the fleet expansion outstripped revenue growth. For the first time in a decade, IndiGo reported a loss before tax in FY2019. The Indian financial year ends on 31 March; hence, COVID-19 had not yet impacted businesses. A sizeable deferred tax credit enabled the airline to report a ₹157 crore ($22.8 million) post-tax profit in FY2019, which was 93 per cent lower than the FY2018 profit. In FY2020, IndiGo reported a ₹234 crore ($31.5 million) post-tax loss, both on account of elevated costs and the COVID-19 outbreak. The airline had never reported a post-tax loss until FY2020.

IndiGo paid dividends, albeit lower than the ₹1480 crore ($224.5 million) in FY2018, despite its weak performance in FY2019 and FY2020. IndiGo's dividends were ₹278 crore ($40.4 million) in FY2019 and ₹232 crore ($31.3 million) in FY2020.

Bhatia and Associates hold a 38.3 per cent stake in Interglobe Aviation, while Gangwal and associates hold 36.64 per cent. The two founders jointly hold almost 75 per cent stake in the airline. In February 2021, Rahul Bhatia and his father, Kapil Bhatia, were together ranked 30th on the Forbes billionaires list with a net worth of $5.1 billion. Gangwal was ranked 359th with a net worth of $3.8 billion. Their dividends from IndiGo in FY2019 and FY2020 were around $54 million—less than 1 per cent of their combined net worth. Yet, the two founders were unwilling to forego dividends.

The COVID-19 pandemic continued to rage through FY2021, resulting in most, if not all, airlines around the globe reporting losses. IndiGo too reported a ₹5806 crore ($787 million) loss. Fortunately, no dividends were paid out.

Subscriptions to IndiGo's hugely successful October 2015 IPO were over six times the number of shares on offer. The ₹765 ($11.92) IPO price was 74 times the ₹10.34 ($0.16) average share price at which pre-IPO investors were allotted shares. The IPO investors' share of financial investment in IndiGo's equity share capital was 89.7 per cent, for which they were allotted a 10.6 per cent equity stake! The steep premium which the IPO investors had paid for a modest stake in IndiGo and the large dividend payouts—the major recipients of which are Bhatia and Gangwal as the duo holds close to 75 per cent stake in IndiGo—even during years of weak financial performance points to the promoters' tendency to enrich themselves at the expense of shareholders and lenders and raises corporate governance concerns.

Shifting Sands

In the two decades ending 2020, the baton of market leadership has passed from Air India to Jet Airways to Kingfisher, albeit briefly, and finally to IndiGo, which has emerged as the undisputed market leader since 2013.

However, this market structure is unlikely to remain the status quo. With the Tatas, who are already operating AirAsia India and Vistara, acquiring Air India, the entry of Akasa Air, and Jet Airlines likely to resume operations soon, India's civil aviation industry has become even more competitive.

Indian skies have progressively become crowded since the liberalization of civil aviation in 1990. Fourteen airlines have failed in India over a twenty-five-year period (1996 to 2021).

Figure 2: The Fluid Domination of the Indian Skies

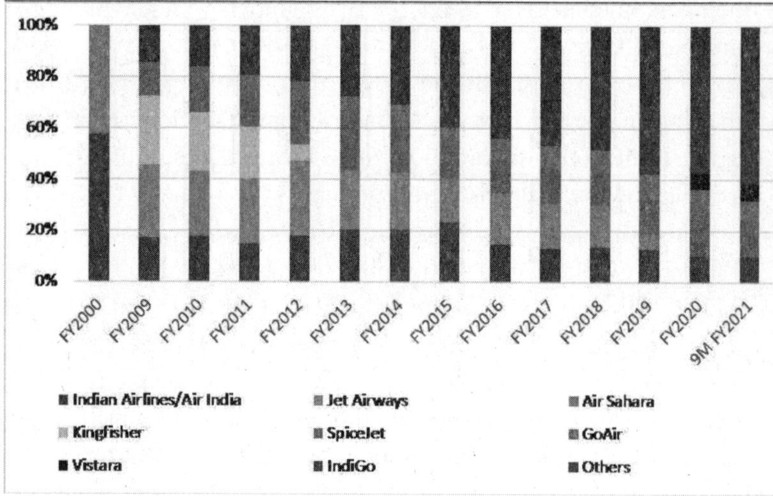

Source: DGCA

Figure 3: Airlines Acquired or Shutdown in India Since 1996

Source: Deep Blues, V. Keshavdev, Outlook Business, 29 May 2019

Yet, the experience of the failed airlines has not deterred new entrants. As of the first quarter of 2021, eleven airlines ply Indian skies—Air India, Air India Express and Alliance Air, Air Asia, Air Heritage, Flybig, Go Air, IndiGo, SpiceJet, Star Air and Vistara.

This overcrowding in a price-sensitive market does not bode well for Indian civil aviation. The Covid-19 outbreak has exacerbated the already fragile environment of the civil aviation industry. Thousands of people employed with the failed airlines have lost their jobs. Lenders and equity investors suffered major capital losses, which a developing country like India can ill-afford.

Can the livelihood and financial losses incurred in the past be averted going forward?

Chapter 13

Air Pockets

The key takeaways from the narrative thus far are that a combination of unbridled ambition and inept management resulted in numerous failures of airlines in India. This situation has been exacerbated and probably encouraged by government policies, the government's stubborn refusal to implement the perfectly sensible recommendations of the successive committees it constituted, and politics.

A peer comparison would facilitate the understanding of the performance gap between airlines in India and their global counterparts and the best practices for airlines that the government may adopt.

To drive home these issues, I have chosen three airlines not domiciled in crude oil-producing countries, whose performance track record has been relatively stable, until the outbreak of Covid-19, in the notoriously precarious airline industry as benchmarks. These airlines are the Sydney-headquartered Qantas, Hong Kong headquartered Cathay Pacific and Singapore Airlines (SIA). One operating parameter, passenger load factor (PLF), and two financial parameters, profitability and indebtedness, form the basis of this peer comparison.

Passengers, Profit and Debt

Cathay Pacific, Qantas and SIA have sustained passenger load factors (PLF) of around 80 per cent for at least a decade preceding the Covid-19 outbreak. This supports the airlines' ability to generate profits during most years. In India, barring IndiGo, which demonstrated such consistency, other airlines including the LCC SpiceJet operated at 80 per cent PLF only from FY2015. Air India's PLF was an abysmal 65.1 per cent in FY2010. The erstwhile state-owned carrier took a decade to gradually improve its PLF to a 79 per cent in FY2019 (Figure 1).

Operating at lower-than-optimal load factors depresses revenues, especially in an emerging market like India, where airlines have to price tickets competitively. Domestic airline profitability, defined as profit after tax expressed as a percentage of revenues, clearly lags global peers (Figure 2). The FSCs—Air India, Jet Airways and Kingfisher—struggled more than the LCCs to recoup costs. With the exception of IndiGo, the profit track record of domestic airlines is lacklustre. International airlines, too, generate low and volatile profits and occasionally, losses against the backdrop of cyclical passenger traffic and ATF prices.

Companies typically use a part of their profits to pay dividends and plough back the rest to finance capital expenditure and repay debt. Most domestic airlines are loss-making or barely profitable, compelling them to borrow to meet not just capital expenditure but also operating expenses! So, domestic airlines' indebtedness defined as debt plus leases minus cash (net lease adjusted debt) expressed as a proportion of earnings before interest, taxes, depreciation, amortization and lease rentals (EBITDAR) is significantly higher than for global peers (Figure 3). Dividend payments for domestic airlines, except for IndiGo, is a mirage.

High ATF and Interest Costs Depress Employee Remuneration

The losses, depressed profits and high indebtedness of airlines in India are not merely a reflection of sub-optimal PLFs and a price-sensitive market. The levels and trends of the three key operating expenses incurred by airlines—employee expenses, fuel costs and

Figure 1: Passenger Load Factors

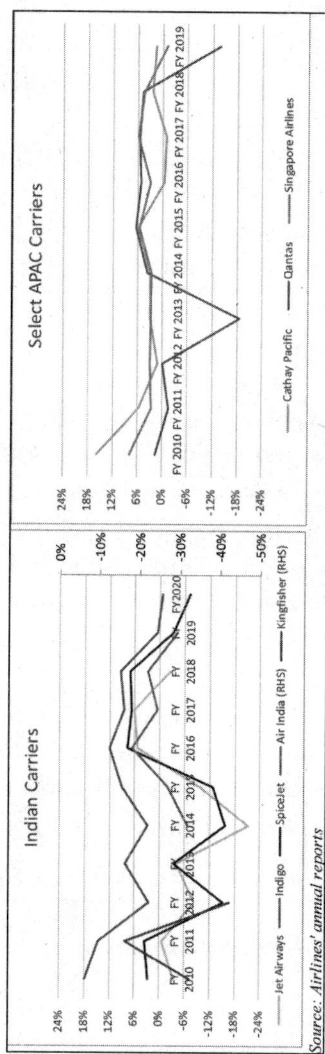

Source: Airlines' annual reports

Figure 2: Profit After Tax / Revenues (%)

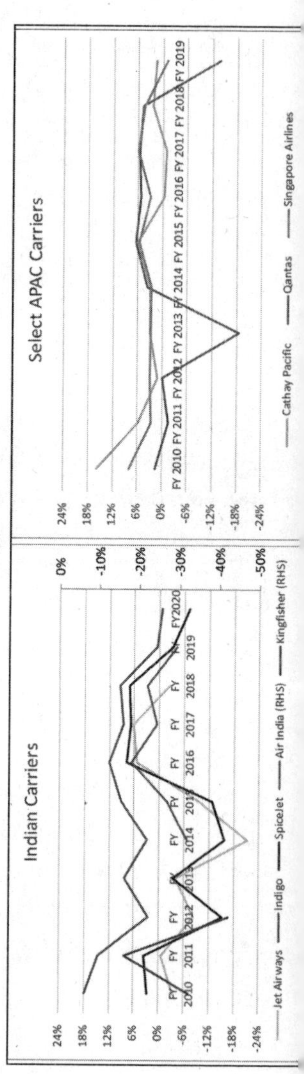

Figure 3: Net Lease Adjusted Debt/EBITDAR

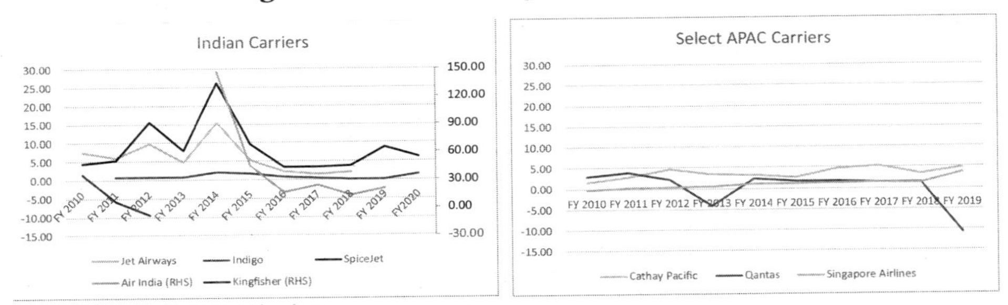

Source: Airlines' annual reports & Bloomberg

Figure 4: Employee Expenses/Revenues (per cent)

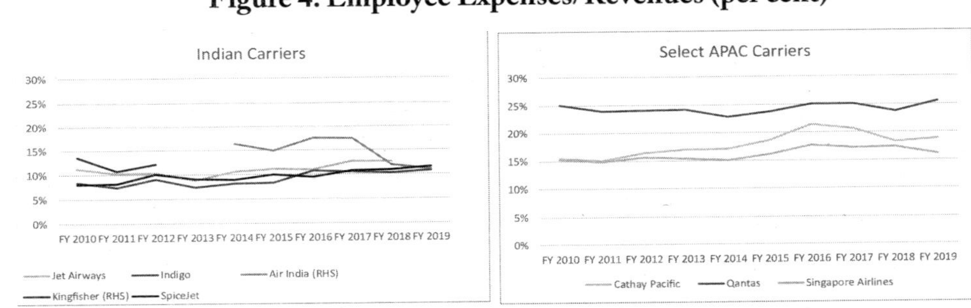

Source: Airlines annual reports

Figure 5: Fuel Expenses/Revenues (per cent)

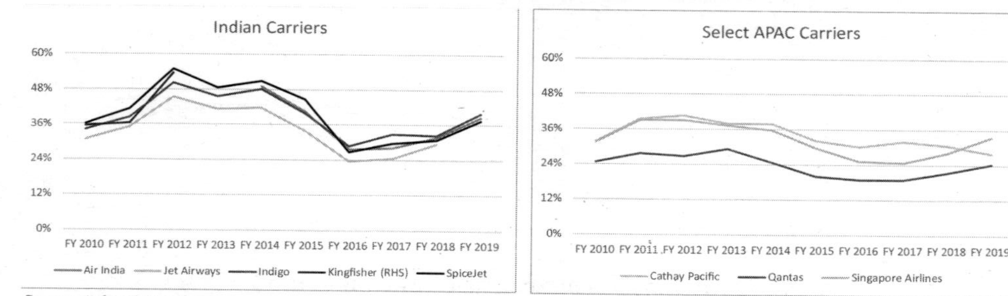

Source: Airlines' annual reports

Figure 6: Interest Expenses + Lease Rentals/Revenues (per cent)

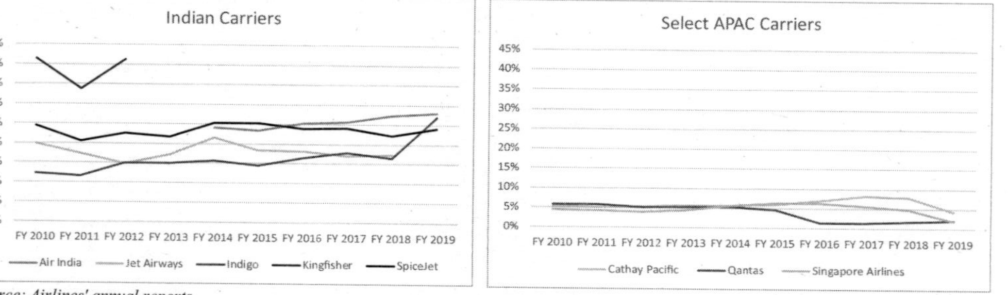

Source: Airlines' annual reports

financing costs comprising interest and lease expenses—offer useful insights.

Guess which domestic airline incurred the highest employee expense, as a percentage of its revenues, till FY2017? It was Air India, which paid between 15 per cent and 18 per cent of its revenues as employee expenses between FY2014 and FY2017. This was on par with the percentage of revenues Singapore Airlines' pays as salaries. With Air India completing additional payouts to its employees as per the seventh pay commission recommendations in FY2017 and PLF improving, employee expenses moderated to 11.9 per cent of revenues in FY2018 and 11 per cent in FY2019. Indian carriers typically pay between 8–12 per cent of their revenues as salaries. This is significantly lower than the 15–25 per cent of revenues paid by global peers. Domestic carriers economize on salaries due to the high fuel and financing expenses they incur.

India's annual ATF consumption was 7.99 million metric tonnes in FY2020. In 2017, India was ranked the ninth largest ATF consumer globally. It may come as a surprise to many that the country is the sixth largest ATF producer globally, with an annual production of 15.24 million metric tonnes in FY2020. With such large manufacturing capabilities, domestic airlines should be able to purchase competitively priced ATF. Sadly, ATF is a heavily taxed commodity in India. The fuel is subject to a 5 per cent basic customs duty, 11 per cent additional customs duty, and another 11 per cent basic excise duty as of August 2022. Besides, states levy a value added tax (VAT) ranging from 1.0 per cent to 30.0 per cent. Airlines purchasing ATF for aircraft plying under the government's regional connectivity scheme are subject to a lower additional customs duty of 2 per cent.[1] Despite the government cutting the excise duty on ATF from 14 per cent to 11 per cent in October 2018, fuel expenses of domestic carriers are significantly higher than those of their global peers.[2] In FY2019, domestic carriers' ATF expenses were equivalent to 37.5–40 per cent of their revenues. The ATF expenses of Cathay Pacific, Qantas and SIA ranged between 24.3 per cent and 33.5 per cent of revenues during the same year.

Qantas' ATF expenses, expressed as a percentage of its revenues, has ranged from a minimum of 18.9 per cent to a maximum of 29.3 per cent during the decade ended 2019, and has consistently been the lowest among the eight airlines covered in this chapter. The Australian airline, through effective hedging of volatile ATF prices, has managed to rein in its fuel expenses. Qantas' fuel purchase strategy is a model worthy of emulation.

On 30 August 2022, *The Economic Times* reported that India's civil aviation ministry is in the process of rationalising ATF pricing by linking the fuel's price to a global benchmark index like the MOPAG (Mean of Platts Arab Gulf) and engaging with the states to reduce VAT to the range of 1.0 per cent to 4.0 per cent. International airlines that purchase ATF in India are currently charged on the basis of MOPAG. Airline executives informed *The Economic Times* that domestic airlines may save at least 15.0 per cent in fuel costs by purchasing ATF at MOPAG-linked prices.[3] This long overdue reform is a step in the right direction.

Analysts and media have repeatedly raised the issue of domestic carriers having to, rather unfairly, pay a lot more for ATF than their global counterparts. There is one more expense, which is exorbitant for airlines in India and rather modest for their well-managed overseas peers. This is the financing expense, which is the sum of interest expense and lease rentals.

Cathay Pacific, Qantas and SIA have paid less than 10 per cent of their annual revenues as interest expense and lease rentals over the past decade. Financing expenses for domestic carriers have typically ranged from 15 to 30 per cent during the decade ending FY2019. This reflects the high levels of indebtedness prevalent among domestic airlines, their mostly non-investment grade credit ratings and, consequently, high borrowing costs.

This disturbing phenomenon is also an outcome of the absence of dedicated aircraft financing desks at Indian banks, an investment grade credit guarantee institution, and the shallow corporate bond market in India. Specialized aircraft financing desks extend and arrange debt, equity and hybrid securities, such as preference shares and convertible bonds, thus enabling airlines to optimize their financing costs and risks. Investment grade credit guarantee institutions guarantee debt for a fee and thus enable airlines to reduce borrowing costs.

In the absence of these facilities, bank loans constitute the dominant mode of financing for Indian corporates. Corporate bonds, as a percentage of GDP, is among the lowest in Asia at 17.16 per cent in June 2018. Singapore (34.02 per cent), Malaysia (44.50 per cent) and South Korea (74.30 per cent) have much larger corporate bond markets. Corporate bond penetration in Japan (14.57 per cent) and China (18.86 per cent) is quite low too.[4]

The appetite in India's nascent corporate bond markets for airline issuances is quite low. Whereas principal repayments for bank loans are made on a monthly or quarterly basis, bonds are usually repaid at the end of their tenor, either as a lump sum or in instalments. Domestic carriers are unable to diversify their borrowings and manage their cash flows by issuing bonds.

UDAN—a Necessity or Nice to Have?

Adding to the woes of India's over-crowded, intensely competitive civil aviation industry is the central government-sponsored regional connectivity scheme called UDAN. As an acronym, its tagline in Hindi—*Ude desh ka aam nagrik*, meaning 'may the country's common citizen fly'—represents the aspiration of the Indian government.

In June 2016, the BJP government launched UDAN, which is intended to make air travel to India's tier-II and tier-III cities affordable for the common citizen. In 2017, five airlines—SpiceJet, Alliance Air, Trujet, Deccan Charters, and Air Odisha—were awarded 128 UDAN routes. IndiGo joined UDAN a year later. Trujet is a Hyderabad-headquartered regional airline founded by Ram Charan, a leading man in Telugu films and the son of Telugu actor-politician, Chiranjeevi. Deccan Charters, headquartered in Bengaluru, was founded by Captain Gopinath. Bhubaneshwar-headquartered Air Odisha was started by the government of Odisha.

At its launch, UDAN listed 398 unserved and sixteen underserved airports or airstrips across India in the first round of bidding. State governments could develop new airports under the scheme. Airfare caps were introduced depending on distance, ranging from ₹1420 ($22) for the shortest flight to ₹3500 ($54) for the longest.

UDAN gave a host of incentives to airlines—significant reduction in central and state taxes on ATF, waiver on parking and landing charges, a 58 per cent discount on route navigation and facilitation charges, and exclusive rights on networks for three years.

Airlines were to be compensated for capped airfares through a system called viability-gap funding (VGF), which was to be paid out of a corpus named Regional Connectivity Fund (RCF). Half the seats on a flight have capped fares and the rest are sold at market rates. Airlines were expected to sell the subsidized seats first and operate at least three flights a week from an airport.

The Airports Authority of India (AAI) was to collect money for RCF and disburse it to airlines as compensation for cost differentials. The government told Parliament in 2016 that the RCF was built with a levy of ₹7500 ($115) to ₹8500 ($131) on all departing domestic flights in the country. As much as 80 per cent of the levy so collected would pay for the dues of airlines and the rest of the funding would come from state governments. In other words, the RCF would not depend on the Union government for funding.

Business Standard reported in 2020 that a rough calculation, based on 900,000 flight departures on an average over the past three years, showed that AAI would have collected upwards of ₹700 crore ($94 million) a year from the RCS levy.

Four rounds of bidding and the awarding of routes under UDAN were completed by 2020. The scheme, though well-meaning, was ill-conceived. The total number of airports designated as underserved and unserved had halved to 209 in the fourth round, from 414 in the first round, 328 in the second, and 271 in the third round. Of the 414 airports and airstrips identified in 2016, only 50, including five heliports, were operationalized by October 2020 as the AAI, the agency responsible for developing airports, faces a funding shortage.

The shortlisting of airlines was haphazard. In the aftermath of the UDAN announcement, a new breed of airlines, namely regional airlines, proliferated in India. Close to a dozen newly-incorporated airlines were shortlisted to fly UDAN routes. These regional airlines included Trujet, Zoom Air, Skyone, Pinnacle Air, Maritime Energy Heli Air Services, Heligo, AAA Aviation, Heritage Aviation, Aviation Connectivity and Infrastructure Developers, Zexus Aviation and Flybig. Air Odisha, which operates a fleet of only two aircraft, was awarded the maximum number of routes—fifty. The state-owned airline's mandate was to operate certain routes designated as key under UDAN and connect Odisha's capital, Bhubaneswar, to the smaller cities in the state. The airline was unable to entirely fulfil its mandate and there were frequent cancellations on some of the routes Air Odisha managed to fly. The airline was eventually debarred for not operating at least 70 per cent of scheduled flights on UDAN routes.

Deccan Charters, founded by Captain Gopinath, was meant to connect Kolkata to smaller towns like Cooch Behar, Burnpur, Jamshedpur and Rourkela as well as Mumbai to Sholapur, Kolhapur and Jalgaon. Operations by this airline were supposed to improve the connectivity of India's northeastern states. Failure to execute these mandates resulted in the airline's contract being cancelled and its routes being reallocated to Alliance Air and Trujet.

Not all routes identified by the government garnered sufficient traffic and were, hence, commercially unviable even after taking into account the VGF. Trujet's PLF for its Chennai–Cuddapah–Chennai flights in FY2019 was a mere 50 per cent. Between end April to October 2018, Zoom Air had flown 4327 passengers with just about 10 passengers on every flight on the Kolkata–Tezpur route. Low traffic prompted SpiceJet to back out of routes like Chennai–Hubli, Kolkata–Jharsuguda and Guwahati–Lilabari. In a country where airlines struggle to remain profitable despite achieving an optimal PLF of 80 per cent, flying such low-traffic routes is a guaranteed ticket to bankruptcy.

UDAN increased the burden on the already busy metro airports such as Mumbai, Delhi, Bengaluru and Chennai. While pan-India airlines like IndiGo and SpiceJet found slots at the high-traffic airports, regional airlines struggled. A former official of a defunct airline informed *Business Standard*, 'To give you a hypothetical example, if I have to operate two flights a day from Mumbai to Nashik and back, I can't time my first flight at 2.00 p.m. and a return flight at midnight to Mumbai. People would want to fly out in the morning and be back by late evening. It's virtually impossible to get slots during these times at Mumbai and other airports. It further reduces the scope of any regional airline's business. UDAN is all about connecting a big airport to a small airport. Unless such problems are taken care of at bigger airports, regional connectivity will suffer.'[5] Mumbai International Airport's CEO, R.K. Jain, observed in 2018 that the smaller planes used for UDAN were taking runway time and reducing capacity to handle more lucrative flights.[6]

Jet Airways had bid for and was granted routes during UDAN's second phase in 2017. The airline's collapse in 2018 further dampened UDAN's performance. As of July 2022, only 425—or just 62 per cent of the 688 routes announced—are operational, as per official data.[7]

Within two years of UDAN's launch, the government announced an international UDAN, which aimed to connect India's smaller cities to key neighbouring countries. This move, the government hoped, would promote tourism and commerce. To encourage airlines to participate in international UDAN, the government offered a subsidy in the form of a pre-decided payout per seat. Airlines were required to bid on the number of passenger seats per flight for which such support was required.[8]

Unlike the domestic UDAN, the already fiscally strained state governments were to bear the entire burden of the subsidy. International UDAN did not elicit much interest from the airlines.

UDAN is not an unmitigated disaster. The Kannur airport in Kerala was operationalized in December 2018 and IndiGo was awarded most routes connecting it; these routes have witnessed a healthy traffic. Mumbai–Kandla was SpiceJet's best performing UDAN route in 2020, with the airline ferrying 70 passengers daily. Civil Aviation Minister Hardeep Singh Puri stated, 'UDAN has turned into a game-changer for a few airports, namely Darbhanga, Jharsuguda, Kadapa, Nasik, Belagavi, Hubbali, Kishangarh, etc. by triggering the air connectivity and regional growth.'[9]

While most of the eleven stand-alone regional carriers are struggling, IndiGo and SpiceJet have used the UDAN routes as spokes to ferry passengers to their hubs, from where they operate their non-subsidized domestic and international flights. This has resulted in an increase in passenger volumes. Passenger footfalls are robust at UDAN routes in south and west India, and industrial and tourist centres.

The lessons from the UDAN initiative are clear and unsurprising. Civil aviation is the domain of airlines with sound managements, deep pockets and scale. VGF is inadequate to sustain regional carriers plying routes with inadequate traffic. A large number of players operating on routes with varying traffic and limited flexibility in pricing tickets is not commercially viable.

The Indian government refuses to learn from past experience. Time and again, it has permitted and, in some cases, facilitated, the proliferation of airlines in a price-sensitive market. In this overcrowding lie the seeds of airline bankruptcies and the loss of scarce capital and livelihoods that a developing country like India can ill-afford.

UDAN's turbulent performance highlights the inadequate planning and research conducted ahead of the scheme's launch.

It was irrational for the government to identify and award routes from 414 underserved and unserved airports during UDAN's first round, when hardly a tenth of them were fully developed. Was an assessment of the traffic at these locations conducted before awarding the routes? Why did the government not conduct a pilot ahead of a full-blown launch of UDAN? Creating a sandbox with existing pan-India airlines like Alliance Air, IndiGo and SpiceJet flying from locations with airports and sufficient traffic to assess UDAN's viability would have been more prudent.

India does possess the fourth longest rail network in the world, following the US, China and Russia. In 2018, Indian Railways ferried 8.4 billion passengers and was second only to Japan, whose passenger traffic was around 9.4 billion. Numerous state-owned and private sector entities operate intra-state and inter-state buses. Most of the country is reasonably well-connected. Regional airlines are a nice-to-have service, but not a crying need.

Whither an Independent Aviation Regulator?

The Directorate General of Civil Aviation (DGCA), which is attached to the ministry of civil aviation, is the regulatory body that primarily deals with safety issues. It is responsible for the regulation of air transport services to, from and within India as well as for the enforcement of civil air regulations, air safety and air worthiness standards.[10] However, there are four more tasks that need to be carried out on an ongoing basis to ensure the sustainability of airlines in India: the assessment of the viability of policies proposed by the government; ATF price rationalization; facilitation of airlines' access to competitive financing, and periodic screening of incumbents and potential entrants to ensure they possess the integrity, financial muscle and operational expertise to run viable airlines.

It is neither the DGCA's mandate nor does it have the in-house expertise to carry out the four aforesaid functions. The government must perform its long overdue duty of constituting an independent aviation regulator to discharge these functions effectively.

Part 3: The Financial Whiz

Chapter 14

The Patriarch's Demise

On Saturday, 6 July 2002, twelve days after he was hospitalized, Dhirajlal Hirachand Ambani departed his earthly abode.

Politicians cutting across party lines, industrialists and film stars joined the six-kilometre-long funeral procession from Sea Wind, Dhirubhai Ambani's residence in the posh Cuffe Parade enclave of Mumbai, to Chandanwadi crematorium. This was the first time in India that thousands had thronged an industrialist's last journey.

As Mukesh and Anil Ambani carried their father's mortal remains into the crematorium, the assembled crowds chanted, '*Dhirubhai Ambani amar rahe*' ('May Dhirubhai Ambani remain immortal', in Hindi). The two sons together lit the funeral pyre at 6.30 p.m. After performing the last rites, the siblings stepped out of the crematorium. Mukesh Ambani addressed the congregation, 'I thank you for your prayers and your good wishes for my family. Dhirubhai had a dream when he came to Mumbai in 1959 with only ₹500 in his pocket. Today, with his own efforts, he has created a ₹75,000 crore empire. And this is a record for one person's lifetime. He also wanted that there should be hundreds of Dhirubhais like him'. Anil Ambani stood silently beside him with folded hands.[1]

Den of Thieves to Aden

Dhirubhai, born on 28 December 1932 at Chorwad ('settlement of thieves', in Gujarati) in Gujarat, was one of the six children born to Hirachand Ambani, a village schoolmaster. Dhirubhai went to high school at Bahadur Kanji School in Junagadh, a British protectorate till 1947, which lay 74 kilometres north of Chorwad.

It was customary for boys born in Gujarat's Bania community to head to Arabian trading ports and market towns of East Africa to gain business experience and capital to launch their own ventures. When sixteen-year-old Dhirubhai completed high school, he headed to Aden—a trading port, military bastion and British colony—located in Yemen at the eastern approach to the Red Sea. His elder brother, Ramniklal aka Ramnikbhai was there already, working for A. Besse & Co, a large trading outfit that sold cars, cameras, electrical goods, pharmaceuticals, crude oil products to British and French territories in Arabia, the Horn of Africa and Ethiopia. Ramnikbhai, who worked in Besse & Co's automotive division, arranged a job for Dhirubhai in the firm's division that sold Shell products. Dhirubhai, upon learning the ropes of the trade, was sent to market Shell and Burmah lubricants at various locations where Besse & Co's offices were located—French Somaliland, Berbera, Hargeysa, Assem, Asmara, Mogadishu and Ethiopia. It was an experience that would stand him in good stead when Reliance Industries ventured into what would become its flagship business—petrochemicals.

It was also the time Dhirubhai's proclivity to work within and around legal parameters became evident. Though Besse & Co's employees were forbidden to trade on their personal account, Dhirubhai unfailingly headed to the Aden souk after office, which closed at 4.30 p.m., initially to observe the Arab, Indian and Jewish traders transact. He subsequently began taking positions in commodities, especially rice and sugar, much to the disapproval of Ramnikbhai. While certain transactions did generate profits, others nearly wiped out his capital. Dhirubhai was forced to borrow from his colleagues to settle his debts in the souk. When this matter came to the notice of Besse & Co, his friend and relative—Jamnadas Sakerchand Depala—took responsibility for the trading and resigned. This was to enable Dhirubhai to complete seven years' service and secure the right of residence in Aden. Dhirubhai never forgot the incident. When, in 1958, Depala returned to India impoverished, after trading in the souk following Dhirubhai's strategies and losing heavily, Dhirubhai made him oversee a shop selling textiles and continued paying him a salary till his death in 1987. This was despite Depala more often than not failing to turn up at the textile shop.[2]

More famously, the officials in Yemen's treasury noticed that the country's main unit of currency—a solid silver coin called rial—was disappearing from circulation. Enquiries led them to Aden's souk, where Dhirubhai had placed orders to buy as many rials as were available. He had realized that the rial's intrinsic worth—the value of its silver content—exceeded its exchange rate vis-à-vis the British pound and other foreign currencies. So, Dhirubhai started buying the rials, melting and converting the coins to silver ingots, which were sold to bullion traders in London. Though the margin on these transactions were low, the large volumes enabled him to earn a few lakhs in three months. This arbitrage transaction had to be stopped after three months as it had caught the regulators' attention. Reminiscing about this incident decades later, Dhirubhai remarked, 'I don't believe in not taking opportunities.'[3]

Following his father's demise in 1951, Dhirubhai's mother arranged his marriage with Kokila Patel, the daughter of a postmaster in Jamnagar, in 1954. The couple's first son, Mukesh, was born in Aden in 1957. The stable job at Besse & Co and the adrenaline rush that trading at the souk offered did not satisfy Dhirubhai. After obtaining his right to residence in Aden in 1958, a fallback option, the born entrepreneur returned to India that very year. It was a propitious move. Barely a decade later, Gamal Abdel Nasser's message of Arab nationalism had captivated the Arab population. With south Yemen attaining independence in 1967 and Britain withdrawing from Aden, Besse & Co was among the companies expropriated by the new regime.

When returning to India, Kokilaben was pregnant for the second time. Anil was born in 1959, and the couple's two daughters—Dipti and Nina—were born in 1961 and 1962 respectively.

Masjid Bunder

On returning to India, Dhirubhai tried to zero in both on a location and business to kickstart his entrepreneurial career. Among the options he considered was an automobile spare parts shop at Rajkot in Gujarat. A friend pointed out that spare part shops were not doing too well. It was then that Dhirubhai met his friend, Chambaklal Damani whose father was willing to invest ₹1 lakh ($21,008) to start a trading business in Bombay.

The duo set up Reliance Commercial Corporation in a 350-square-feet rented room in the congested Narsinathan Street at Masjid Bunder with just two employees. This firm had adequate seating for just three. Reliance Commercial Corporation initially traded betel nut and spices with Aden, and cotton, nylon and viscose with Ethiopia, Somalia and Kenya.

The decision to start a trading business in Bombay was a sound one. The city was the capital of India's commodity trading business with over sixty commodity markets, most of which were the stronghold of Gujaratis. The partners soon realized that trading synthetic yarns was a profitable business. They may have been following in the footsteps of Rasikbhai Meswani—Dhirubhai's older sister's son—who had started trading in yarns a couple of years earlier.

Two factors contributed to the profits of a seemingly innocuous commodity like synthetic yarn. By the 1950s, there was a change in Indians' sartorial preferences in favour of nylon, viscose and polyester clothes over those made of natural fibres like cotton and silk. The former scored in terms of price, durability and physical properties—quick-drying and crease-proof—and it could replicate the finish of natural fibres. With the government supposedly focusing on the construction of infrastructure like power plants and steel mills and private sector's production capabilities curtailed by the license permit raj, Indian textile mills relied on imported and, sometimes, smuggled synthetic yarns. The Birlas owned India's sole viscose factory, and there existed a government-owned nylon plant.

At the Masjid Bunder office, Dhirubhai put together a team that remained with him as his trusted lieutenants for the rest of his life—Meswani, elder brother Ramnikbhai, younger brother Nathwarlal aka Nathubhai, an old acquaintance from Aden—Liladhar Gokaldas Sheth, and two former schoolmates—Rathibhai Muchhala and Narottambhai Doshi.

Within a decade of Reliance Commercial Corporation opening shop, the partners developed irreconcilable differences. It was only to be expected, as Damani's limited risk appetite and preference for conservative trading practices were at odds with Dhirubhai's dare devilry and risk-seeking behaviour. By 1965, the two parted ways, reportedly amicably, with Dhirubhai and his brothers paying Damani around ₹6 lakhs ($126,000) for his stake.[4]

Reliance Commercial Corporation must have been a profitable venture. Soon after buying off Damani's share, the company moved from Masjid Bunder to the more spacious Court House building at Dhobi Talao.

Polyester Wars

In 1966, Reliance Commercial Corporation ventured into textile manufacturing. Dhirubhai decided to locate the textile factory in Gujarat because real estate was cheaper in the neighbouring state; he also decided that Ramnikbhai would oversee the factory construction and operations. The brothers set off to Ahmedabad—Gujarat's commercial capital—and drove around the industrial areas in search of a suitable property. They zeroed in on a 100,000-square-metre plot at a state government-developed industrial estate at Naroda, around 13 kilometres to the northeast of Ahmedabad. Fortunately for him, farmers who collectively owned another 100,000-square-metre adjacent to Reliance Commercial Corporation's plot were looking to sell. Dhirubhai purchased the agricultural land parcel too.

With south Yemen attaining independence in 1967 and Besse & Co expropriated, Indians working in Aden started returning. Dhirubhai recruited the ready and grateful pool of trained manpower. However, none of them knew much about textiles and were learning on the job.

The textile brand was named 'Vimal' after one of Ramnikbhai's sons. Initially, sales were muted, but the team, infected by Dhirubhai's entrepreneurial spirit and enthusiasm, started marketing Vimal fabrics and sarees to Gujarat's retailers after completing their nine-to-five shift at the factory. The result was steady growth in sales and profits for Reliance Commercial Corporation. In 1967, the first full year of production at Naroda, the company's sales and profits stood at ₹90 lakh ($1.2 million) and ₹13 lakh ($173,000) respectively. In 1968, Dhirubhai moved his residence from a chawl[5] to a posh apartment overlooking the Arabian Sea at Altamount Road.

Author-journalist Hamish McDonald observes in *The Polyester Prince* that Reliance Commercial Corporation paid nil dividends during the early years and ploughed back profits to purchase more machines. By FY1980—in a period of thirteen years—Reliance Commercial Corporation, renamed as Reliance Textiles reported a 235 times' growth in revenues to ₹212 crore ($270 million) and an 86 times growth in profits to ₹11.21crore ($14 million).

In 1981, Dhirubhai decided to construct a nylon plant at Patalganga, an industrial township 550 kilometres to the west of Mumbai, developed by the state-owned Maharashtra Industrial Development Corporation (MIDC). The area derived its name from the eponymous river flowing in the vicinity. The responsibility of overseeing the construction of the factory was given to the twenty-four-year-old Mukesh Ambani, who had secured a degree in chemical engineering from the Institute of Chemical Technology, Mumbai and was pursuing an MBA at Stanford University. Mukesh dropped out of the MBA course and headed to Patalganga, where the new plant was constructed in eighteen months. Du Point's then international director, Richard Chinman, observed that such a plant would have taken twenty-six months to build in the US. Dhirubhai, the proud father and astute businessman, made sure that the comment was widely publicized in India.

On 23 November 1985, the cover story of Bombay's weekly tabloid, *Blitz*, pronounced, 'BIG 3 IN MAHA POLYESTER WAR . . . It's a Mahabharata War, or rather Mahapolyester War in Indian big business style . . . There are only Kauravas, no Pandavas and no Lord Krishna. The reason is that none is without blemish. The fight is neither for inheriting the earth nor the heaven, but for one of the most lucrative industrial markets—that is, polyester filament yarn, where profits soar around Rs. 80 to Rs. 100 per kg.'[6]

The three adversaries who aspired to achieve the pole position in the polyester feedstock industry were Orkay Mills' Kapal Mehra, Bombay Dyeing's Nusli Wadia, and Dhirubhai. Of the three, Mehra dropped out of the race early after two mishaps. In 1985, his son was abducted near Orkay Mills' Patalganga plant, beaten up and dumped in a drainage ditch some miles away. Mehra himself was imprisoned on charges of evading excise and customs duties a few days before Diwali and had to spend fifteen days in prison.

Wadia and Dhirubhai belonged to vastly different social milieu. The Wadias, like the Tatas and the Godrejs, were Parsis and among the first families of Indian business. Wadia's father, Nevill, married Dina, the daughter of Pakistan's founder, Muhammad Ali Jinnah. The Wadia Group was founded in 1736, when the British East India Company contracted the company to build ships and docks in Bombay. The Wadia ships were part of and formed the backdrop to significant historical events. Their ships were part of the British fleet during the Opium War, Crimean War and World

War II. The lyrics of the 'Star Spangled Banner' were written aboard a Wadia ship, HMS *Minden*. The treaty of Nanking ceding Hong Kong to England was signed on HMS *Cornwallis*. The oldest surviving English ship—HMS *Trincomalee*—was from the Wadia wharf. In the ensuing decades, the Wadias set up and acquired multiple businesses, which include Bombay Dyeing, Bombay Burmah Trading Corporation, Britannia Industries and National Peroxide. The 1944-born Nusli Wadia was eleven years younger than Dhirubhai and had a PhD in chemical engineering from the University of Florida.

Purified terephthalic acid (PTA) and dimethyl terephthalate (DMT) are both feedstocks in the production of polyester. These substitutes are usually made from the chemical paraxylene, which is produced by cracking the flammable liquid hydrocarbon naphtha found in natural gas and petroleum liquids. Both products have their advantages and disadvantages, and most polyester fibre plants can shift from one feedstock to another by making minor adjustments to their plants that take a few months to implement.

In 1978, Bombay Dyeing applied for a license to set up a DMT plant at Patalganga and received preliminary approval to set up a plant with 60,000 metric tonnes (MT) installed capacity within six months. Bombay Dyeing would have emerged as a market leader had the government issued the license promptly; Reliance Textiles was then applying for a license to manufacture polyester yarn using DMT as feedstock. However, the fall of the Janata Party government and Indira Gandhi's return to power worked against Bombay Dyeing. Wadia met Indira Gandhi and her son, Sanjay Gandhi, twice—in 1979 and 1980—to lobby for a license. The Gandhis expected Wadia to make political contributions, an act that was prohibited by an amendment to the Companies Act in 1969. When Wadia pointed out that the Wadia Group and the Tatas do not act in a manner that violates law, Sanjay Gandhi retorted that the Tatas had made a contribution. It later emerged that Russi Mody, the powerful managing director of Tata Steel, had indeed made a contribution. After Sanjay Gandhi's death in an air crash in 1980, Wadia lobbied his case again to a sympathetic Rajiv Gandhi, who had quit his pilot's job with Indian Airlines and become his mother's personal secretary.[7]

Bombay Dyeing received its license in 1981. It had purchased a second-hand DMT plant from a US-based company—Hercofna—dismantled the plant, and arranged for it to be shipped to Bombay in two consignments. Though the consignments reached Bombay by end 1981, Bombay Dyeing was unable to obtain delivery of the consignments for almost a month. The customs department undertook a rather unusual 100 per cent inspection of the consignments' contents, as directed by its commissioner, S. Srinivasan, who was retained by RIL as an advisor after retirement.

Bombay Dyeing took more than three years after obtaining delivery of the dismantled plant to complete the construction of its DMT facility, which began production only in April 1985. Notwithstanding the cost escalation arising from the licensing delay and the time taken to build the plant, Bombay Dyeing was well-poised to capitalize on the sizeable demand of 1,60,000 tonnes of feedstock (DMT or PTA) that was required to manufacture 1,50,000 tonnes of polyester in India. Bombay Dyeing's competitors were two state-owned companies—Indian Petrochemicals Corporation Ltd (IPCL) and Bongaigaon Refinery & Petrochemicals—with a combined capacity of 75,000 tonnes.

However, Bombay Dyeing encountered sustained negative coverage of DMT as an inferior product when compared to PTA by a group of journalists who, were reportedly referred to as RIL's 'Dirty Dozen'.[8] RIL's attempts to hamper Bombay Dyeing's DMT production were not surprising. The company, supported by Congress politicians, Pranab Mukherjee (who went on to become president of the country) and R.K. Dhawan, had obtained preliminary approvals for multiple plants including a 75,000-tonne

PTA plant in Patalganga. The Calcutta-based *Sunday* magazine quipped, 'Pranab Mukherjee's Slogan: Only Vimal', a play on the advertising slogan of that company. RIL was establishing itself as a rival feedstock provider to Bombay Dyeing and its Patalganga yarn plant had switched to PTA as feedstock during the first quarter of 1984.

Negative press coverage of Bombay Dyeing's DMT plant and the Wadias continued. The news agency UNI put out a story quoting official sources alleging that Wadia and his wife were involved in a fraudulent deal to sell land belonging to a Parsi trust, of which they were trustees.[9]

Despite the tariff and quota protection given to domestic DMT producers, Bombay Dyeing was forced to close down its plant for a few months due to a PTA glut Dhirubhai had engineered. Bombay Dyeing resumed DMT production and ran the unit as a profitable venture through the 1990s, but the market dominance it had aspired for and was poised to achieve failed to materialize. In an August 1989 interview with *India Today*, Wadia remarked, 'We have several plans, but none is likely to be approved. The DMT plant expansion is pending for 18 months. Everything we propose to the Government is neither approved nor refused.'[10] The upstart Reliance Commercial Corporation founded in 1958 had overtaken the then 250-year-old Wadia Group in size and profits.

It is common for industry watchers to divide India's post-independence business evolution into BD and AD—before Dhirubhai and after Dhirubhai. Till Dhirubhai's entry, large cap private sector companies were predominantly family owned. Not only did he set up a hugely successful enterprise by thwarting Nusli Wadia's plans, but the scale RIL achieved dwarfed enterprises that had been in business for decades. In addition to ingenuity and ruthlessness, Dhirubhai's ability to influence politicians to his benefit and financial dexterity contributed to his unprecedented success.

Minister(s) of Reliance

As a rookie, Dhirubhai frequently visited New Delhi with fellow yarn trader and a junior Congress party member, Murli Deora, to liaise with bureaucrats and politicians for the speedy approval of licenses to import synthetic yarn. Murli Deora would go on to become the mayor of Bombay, a Member of Parliament in the Lok Sabha and Rajya Sabha and, fortunately for RIL, the union minister for petroleum and natural gas between 2006 and 2011. The duo had befriended Indira Gandhi's powerful private secretary, Yashpal Kapur, and his successor and nephew, R.K. Dhawan, who was retained as Rajiv Gandhi's personal secretary after Indira Gandhi's assassination. Dhirubhai's practice of gifting polyester suit lengths or sarees manufactured by Reliance Textiles to mandarins made him very popular in New Delhi. Relationships cultivated across all echelons of power helped him even when faced with adversarial politicians like V.P. Singh.

Dhirubhai's political clout became evident when he hosted a party in New Delhi to commemorate India's Gandhi's victory in the 1980 union elections after the collapse of the short-lived Janata government (1977–1999) with Morarji Desai as prime minister. Indira Gandhi attending this party received wide media coverage.

Yet another Congress politician whom Dhirubhai had cultivated was Pranab Mukherjee. In 1983, *Business Standard* reported that eleven companies that had invested in Reliance Textile's shares and partially convertible debentures (PCDs), ostensibly promoted by NRIs and accounting for 98 per cent of investments made by NRIs that year under a new scheme, were owned by Dhirubhai himself.[11] Two of these companies were called Crocodile Ltd and Fiasco Overseas Ltd. As a minister of finance, Mukherjee faced considerable grilling in Parliament and censure from press, especially publications in his home state, West Bengal. *Telegraph*'s headline enquired 'Pranab Mukherjee: Minister of Finance or Reliance?'[12]

However, Dhirubhai ran into rough weather with V.P. Singh, a Congress politician. V.P. Singh became the union minister of finance when Rajiv Gandhi was sworn in as prime minister in October 1984, following Indira Gandhi's assassination. V.P. Singh was keen to outdo Rajiv Gandhi, who was known as 'Mr Clean' when he assumed office as prime minister. At that time, while PTA could be imported under open general license, DMT was on the limited permissible list. This meant that DMT imports required prior government permission. A customs duty of 100 per cent and an auxiliary duty of 40 per cent was levied on both chemicals. Bombay Dyeing had petitioned that both commodities be moved to the limited permissible list and levies be increased to 150 per cent. While the government moved PTA to the limited permissible list, it left the levies unchanged. Dhirubhai was tipped off by one of his contacts in Delhi. A day before PTA's move to the limited permissible list became effective, he obtained letters of credit to import one year's worth of PTA, thereby nullifying the government's rationalization.

In February 1986, V.P. Singh presented the 'carrot and stick' budget. The introduction of the modified value added tax that allowed manufacturers to obtain instant and complete reimbursement of the excise duty paid on the components and raw materials was the carrot. Empowering the ED and announcing crackdowns on smugglers, black marketeers, and tax evaders constituted the stick. Income tax raids were conducted at properties owned by Dhirubhai, Rahul Bajaj and S.L. Kirloskar. The eminent constitutional law expert, Nani Palkhivala, took up the cause of the industrialists, following which Rajiv Gandhi moved V.P. Singh to the defence ministry. As union minister of defence, V.P. Singh uncovered the Bofors scam, which led to the Congress party losing the 1989 union elections; Rajiv Gandhi had met with his Waterloo.

Between 1987 and 1989, RIL was Larsen & Toubro's (L&T) single largest shareholder with a stake of 18.5 per cent. Dhirubhai had purchased L&T shares from the open market to stave off a takeover attempt by Manu Chhabria at the behest of L&T's chairman, M.N. Desai. It was not just altruism that propelled Dhirubhai to acquire a stake in L&T. The project execution capabilities of the engineering major were valuable to RIL. As the single largest shareholder, Dhirubhai replaced Desai as L&T's chairman and Mukesh and Anil secured board seats.

In 1989, V.P. Singh succeeded Rajiv Gandhi as prime minister, helming Janata Dal, the party he founded. At the government's direction, domestic financial institutions that held a significant stake in L&T thwarted RIL's attempts to increase its stake and also pressurized Dhirubhai to resign as chairman and Mukesh and Anil to relinquish their board seats. The Ambanis complied and remained passive investors in L&T for a decade before selling their stake to Grasim Industries. This setback did not hamper RIL's progress. V.P. Singh's tenure as prime minister, however, barely lasted eleven months, after which he was succeeded by his Janata Dal colleague Chandra Shekhar, with Congress extending support from outside.

Vyaj Ketlu Chhe?

Reliance Industries Limited (RIL), as Reliance Textiles was renamed in FY1985, owes much of its meteoric rise to Dhirubhai's financial ingenuity. The former chairman of Lazard plc, Udayan Bose—knowingly or unknowingly, intentionally or unintentionally but certainly inaccurately—stated, 'He hated debt.' Bose informed *India Today* that Dhirubhai's aversion for debt was evident even when he was scanning other companies' balance sheets; he would enquire anxiously, '*Vyaj ketlu chhe* (How much is the debt, in Gujarati)?'[13]

However, Dhirubhai's financial decisions support the view that it was not debt, per se, that he was averse to, but the negative perceptions indebted companies attract. An unnamed broker succinctly articulated the patriarch's guiding principle to

McDonald, 'They (Reliance) do not distinguish between revenue and capital . . . They only operate on a cash flow.' In other words, Dhirubhai did not subscribe to the conventional view of raising debt and equity to finance expansion, which would result in higher profits, which in turn would be used to repay debt and pay dividends to shareholders. Instead, he sought to profit from RIL's core business and the issue of debt and equity.

Reliance Textiles/RIL's issue of ₹942 crore ($788 million) in seven tranches of PCDs between 1979 and 1986 illustrate how the company profited from fund raising. PCDs are debt instruments, a fraction of which may be converted to equity, and the issuer/borrower repays the balance like in the case of a loan or bond. The proportion of PCDs that may be converted to equity and the conversion price are stipulated at the time of issue.

After issuing the PCDs, Dhirubhai succeeded in securing regulatory approval for what is not permissible by law—converting entire tranches of PCDs into equity! By doing so, Reliance Industries did not have to repay the PCD investors, who were delighted to receive shares of a company helmed by Dhirubhai and that was growing in leaps and bounds. Reliance Industries also achieved considerable reductions in interest expense. According to the September 1984 issue of the magazine *Economic Scene*, RIL converted ₹73.5 crore ($72.5 million) PCDs into equity in 1983, resulting in the company paying incremental dividends of just ₹3.60 crore ($3.55 million), which was almost 63 per cent lower than the PCDs' annual interest of ₹9.65 crore ($9.52 million).[14] Of course, both Dhirubhai and the PCD investors were optimistic that RIL's share price appreciation would make the conversion of PCDs into equity shares worthwhile, despite dividends being lower than interest.

Between FY1980 and FY1988, RIL's net worth had risen by ₹990 crore ($712 million), of which retained earnings (profit after tax minus dividends) contributed to just ₹288 crore ($207 million), or 29 per cent. The balance ₹703 ($505 million) crore or

71 per cent of net worth increase was due to conversion of PCDs into equity. During this period, debt had also risen by ₹842 crore ($605 million).[15] Had the PCDs not been converted to equity, debt would have risen by a whopping ₹1544 crore ($1.10 billion)!

Yet another technique Dhirubhai employed to maximize RIL's cash flow was to minimize corporate tax payments. Between FY1972 and FY1996, RIL paid practically zero corporate income tax. This was despite RIL's profit before tax increasing almost 2300-fold from ₹57 lakh in FY1972 to ₹1305 crore in FY1996. RIL was not alone, though. Tata Engineering and Locomotive Company (TELCO, now renamed Tata Motors), Associated Cement, Ashok Leyland and J.K. Synthetics were the other profitable, listed private sector companies that paid nil corporate income taxes during certain years in the 1980s.

Companies adopting tax minimization techniques in the 1970s and 1980s was understandable. On the one hand, corporate income tax in India ranged between 45 to 65 per cent for domestic companies and touched 70 per cent for certain categories of foreign companies. On the other hand, the government was generous with tax incentives to encourage industrial growth—25 per cent of new investment on plant and machinery was exempt from tax, new units enjoyed partial tax holiday for a specified number of years, units set up in backward areas enjoyed an additional 20 per cent tax benefit, 50 per cent extra depreciation was tax deductible in a unit's first year of operations, and there were deductions for investment in research and development and export market development.

In a 1983 interview with *India Today*, Dhirubhai pointed out that while the government may be losing corporate taxes, it collected more excise duties as companies grew rapidly and increased production. The unflappable Dhirubhai concluded, 'The Government should be concerned with the total revenue earned.'[16] The government started levying a Minimum Alternate Tax of 15 per cent on book profits from FY1989. RIL started paying corporate taxes from FY1997.

Politicians and businessmen share an interesting similarity. While it is important for the former to appear upright, portraying an image of helming profitable enterprises is critical to the latter. To achieve this end, RIL lengthened its financial year to fifteen months each in FY1976 and FY1978, to eighteen months in FY1988, and shortened the following reporting period—FY1988—to six months. The multiple changes in the duration of reporting periods were done to ensure that a track record of consistent profitability was maintained. RIL has never reported a loss for fifty consecutive years (FY1972 to FY2022).

Neither did RIL consistently generate robust cash flows nor was it moderately leveraged even as it pursued an aggressive growth strategy. Dhirubhai realized performance and perception were equally important. By creating a perception of a growing yet moderately leveraged and cash accretive company and raising vast sums capital through PCDs, IPO and rights issues from the hitherto ignored category of retail investors, he ensured that the appreciation in RIL's share price and exponential growth in profits went hand in hand.

Between 1980 and 1985, the number of Indians owning shares of companies increased from less than one million to four million. The number of RIL shareholders rose to more than one million by end 1985. Dhirajlal Hirachand Ambani is the undisputed guru of India's equity cult.

Southern Storm

Dhirubhai did have to face the consequences of exploiting India's political and legal ecosystems to his benefit and impeding his competitors' expansion plans. Wadia was a close friend of Ramnath Goenka, the founder of The *Indian Express* newspaper. Under the 1904-born Goenka's stewardship, The *Indian Express*—which he founded in 1932—had, by 1985, grown to become India's largest newspaper by circulation with sales of 670,000 from twelve editions. He was also the chairman of the Press Trust of India (PTI).

Wadia's wife, Maureen, informed Goenka of the roadblocks posed by Dhirubhai to Bombay Dyeing's DMT business during one of the couple's monthly lunch meetings with the media baron. Goenka invited both Dhirubhai and Wadia to his residence and brokered a reconciliation, which was short-lived. He then chose an unlikely candidate who would go on to investigate and write a series of exposés on RIL in The *Indian Express.* This person, who Goenka held in high regard and implicitly trusted, was neither a journalist nor a resident of Bombay. It was Swaminathan Gurumurthy, a chartered accountant living in Madras (subsequently renamed Chennai), whose firm Guru & Varadan provided audit services to The *Indian Express.* The Ramon Magsaysay award-winning economist and journalist Arun Shourie, who would later become a minister in Prime Minister Vajpayee's cabinet, co-authored Gurumurthy's columns.

Wadia assisted Gurumurthy in recruiting overseas investigators to investigate Dhirubhai Ambani / RIL's overseas dealings. In a series of explosive articles published in The *Indian Express* from September 1985, Gurumurthy systematically brought to light the ruthless business and financial practices that the Dhirubhai-helmed RIL had employed to achieve exponential growth in scale, profits and clout, hitherto not witnessed in Indian business. These columns contended, with evidence, that RIL had indirectly raised ₹100 crore ($81 million) in bank loans to invest in its own PCDs, converted entire tranches of PCDs into equity, stashed away foreign exchange in overseas tax havens and used a part of these funds to purchase its own shares, smuggled polyester filament yarn plants into India, built and operated a PTA plant whose capacity was 50 per cent in excess of the licensed capacity, and corrupted 'virtually India's entire bureaucracy and intelligentsia'.[17]

The government had no option but to direct its investigative agencies and regulators to probe RIL. The findings were damning. On 10 June 1986, the ministry of finance banned the conversion of PCDs into equity; six days after officials of the ministry had approved the conversion of RIL's Series E and F of PCDs into equity. With this ban, RIL lost the opportunity to convert ₹770 crore ($615 million) PCDs into equity. Union finance minister V.P. Singh presided over an open house hearing about the ₹15,000 ($1586) per tonne anti-dumping duty that had been slapped on polyester yarn imports in November 1982. The very next day, V.P. Singh abolished the anti-dumping duty, resulting in a 20 per cent drop in domestic yarn prices. Yarn manufacturing was a key business for RIL. The same month, a ₹3000 per tonne extra duty was levied on PTA imports, a move that dented RIL's profits and benefitted DMT manufacturers including Bombay Dyeing.

Meanwhile, the RBI probed the loans that domestic banks had extended to entities indirectly owned by RIL and/or domiciled in RIL offices to purchase RIL's PCDs. The central bank confirmed that the banks had indeed conducted a 'loan mela' (loan festival) during which due diligence was lax. The RBI also found that its directive of extending loans for productive purposes was violated, though banks had complied with RBI norms of transferring the title to shares offered as collateral for loans exceeding ₹50,000 ($4,042) to the banks and restricting the tenor of loans against shares to thirty months. The borrowing entities, all of which were RIL associates, were shell companies with negligible capital not exceeding ₹10,000 ($808). The borrowers had stated that the loans were to be used for working capital or purchase of shares. RIL had deposited ₹91.90 crore ($74 million) with nine banks, which had extended ₹60 crore ($48 million) loans against RIL shares in 1985 alone. Despite lending to shell companies, the banks had not deemed it necessary to create a pledge on RIL's deposits.

The RBI committee, helmed by one of its deputy governors, C. Rangarajan, reported that RIL's shell entities had repaid high-cost loans availed to purchase RIL shares using the low-cost loans they borrowed from banks by pledging RIL shares. However, the report stated that the proceeds from the 'loan mela' were not used to subscribe to RIL PCDs.

An inspection of RIL's PTA unit revealed that the company was operating twelve lines, 50 per cent more than the licensed eight lines. Further, Bombay Customs, the very authority that delayed Bombay Dyeing from taking delivery of its consignments by a month, handed a show cause notice to RIL, alleging that the company had imported spinning machines and industrial capacity worth ₹114.50 crore ($91 million), estimating duties evaded by RIL at ₹119.60 crore ($95 million), and asking why these duties ought not be levied.

Waging polyester wars, dealing with income tax raids and *The Indian Express* exposés took their toll on Dhirubhai, who suffered a stroke that paralyzed his right hand in February 1986. Mukesh and Anil assumed more responsibilities in overseeing RIL; the indomitable Dhirubhai recovered and provided strategic direction. An unnamed source informed McDonald that Dhirubhai spent ₹500 crore ($397 million) in 1986 alone, to counter The *Indian Express*' offensive. RIL's profit after tax declined by 80 per cent from ₹71.34 crore ($63 million) in FY1985 to ₹14.17 crore ($11.50 million) in FY1986. RIL extended the next financial year by six months to report a ₹80.77 crore ($62 million) profit after tax in FY1988, a reporting period that comprised eighteen months.

Wadia and Gurumurthy did face backlash after crossing swords with RIL. The CBI charged Wadia, a UK passport-holder who resided in India, with falsely declaring that he was an Indian national while signing in hotel registers between 1985 and 1987. In 1990, a Bombay court charged an RIL employee unrelated to Dhirubhai's family, Kirti Ambani, of attempting to murder Wadia between 1988 and 1989. Kirti directly reported to Mukesh Ambani, who stated that he came to know of Kirti Ambani's act only after the latter's arrest. Gurumurthy himself was imprisoned for ten days in 1987 and subsequently released on bail for his alleged role in a case involving the US-based detective group Fairfax and the Official Secrets Act.[18]

This, by no means, is an exhaustive account of the controversies RIL was involved in during Dhirubhai's lifetime. Omitted from this narrative, in the interest of brevity, are at least three incidents. First, the attack on Jamnadas Moorjani, who was the president of the All India Crimpers Association, an organization that was protesting the imposition of the anti-dumping duty on polyester yarn that benefitted RIL and squeezed the crimpers' margins. Second, RIL collaborating with state-owned Bank of Baroda's subsidiary, BoB Fiscal, to increase its stake in L&T. Third, the suppliers credit L&T had extended to RIL after the latter had emerged as its largest shareholder.[19]

The Resurgence

Nevertheless, by FY1990 RIL was back on track again, expanding its business using other people's money and reporting sizeable profits in the process. While recovery from the backlash following *The Indian Express*'s exposés could not have been easy, the political churn at the Centre helped. The Bofors scandal that came to light in April 1987 put the spotlight on corruption in Indian politics during the latter half of Rajiv Gandhi's tenure (October 1984–December 1989). The short and turbulent tenures of the two prime ministers who succeeded Rajiv Gandhi—V.P. Singh (December 1989– November 1990) and Chandra Shekhar (November 1990–June 1991)—enabled RIL to recover from the setbacks it faced in the late 1980s with few distractions.

RIL acquiring a 26 per cent stake in the state-owned Indian Petrochemicals Corporation Ltd (IPCL) for ₹1,491 crore ($307 million) in March 2002, barely three months before Dhirubhai's demise, was a sure-shot sign that the company had recouped its financial muscle and was regarded as a partner to the political establishment again. It was ironical that Dhirubhai's erstwhile detractor, Arun Shourie, as union minister for disinvestment, secured the cabinet's approval for this deal, and announced it.

When Dhirajlal Hirachand Ambani—industrialist, trader, financial juggler and éminence grise all rolled into one—passed away on 6 July 2002, there was much discussion on RIL's trajectory going forward and the roadblocks it might face. After all, the conglomerate's tagline is 'Growth is Life'. *India Today,* in its profile of Dhirubhai published a fortnight before his demise, aptly observed, ' . . . the Ambani generational drama looks to run its true course: the heirs will grab a crisis by its horns, bow a little in respect and then slam it against the nearest wall.'[20]

Chapter 15

Ashwamedha Yagna

At the sidelines of a conference in early November 2004, a television reporter asked Mukesh Ambani about the future of Reliance. His response was that Reliance was a professionally managed company that was stronger than any individual. He then uncharacteristically acknowledged that there were some 'ownership issues', but these were in the 'private' domain. After divulging this tantalizing teaser, Mukesh flew out of the country. The television channel helpfully telecast this tête-à-tête two days after its occurrence.[1]

Mukesh later claimed that his 'off the cuff' remark about 'ownership issues' were 'torn out of context'.[2] Anil then shared his side of the story with the media.

Tug of War

RIL's board meeting on 27 July 2004 was supposed to be a routine affair. However, as the meeting drew to a close, Mukesh introduced a supplementary agenda with an innocuous title: the formation of a health, safety and environment committee. Item number 17 in the annexure of the supplementary agenda proposed to redefine the powers of the chairman, managing directors, executive directors and various committees of directors. It effectively gave Mukesh, as the chairman, overriding powers in deciding financial and investment matters.

While the other directors received the minutes of the board meeting a few hours after the meeting concluded, Anil was provided with it two days later, after making multiple requests. The draft minutes stated that the board members had discussed and unanimously approved the resolution; a statement with which Anil vehemently disagreed.

Despite Anil and Mukesh residing with their families in the same residential building, Sea Wind, Anil, during the next three months, repeatedly e-mailed Mukesh and the company secretary's office asking them not to finalize the meeting minutes without his approval. Mukesh reportedly, did not reply to his e-mails. Anil was finally informed 'on the CMD's [Mukesh Ambani] behalf that the matter is final and cannot be altered'.[3]

On 25 October 2004, Anil's e-mail response read, 'This is contrary to all past practice, whereby supplementary agenda items have always been pre-circulated, pre-discussed and pre-agreed between the two managing directors before any board meeting.' He further declared that he had been 'legally advised that the proposed redefinition of powers of the managing directors is not in accordance with law'.[4]

Within a few hours of Anil dispatching this missive, RIL's board met and approved the minutes of the 27 July meeting. Mukesh had gained control of the group's flagship entity and cash cow, Reliance Industries Limited. Anil had been sidelined.[5]

A rift between the heirs to a hugely successful enterprise after the demise of the founding parent is neither unheard of nor unexpected. Yet, there were numerous media accounts of the brothers' back-slapping camaraderie and their shared vision for the Reliance Group. So, what exactly caused the rift?

The most contentious and complex issue was RIL's ownership. Dhirubhai Ambani died intestate, and how RIL and his private assets were apportioned among his legal heirs (Kokilaben, Mukesh, Anil and his married daughters—Nina Kothari and Deepti Salgaocar) was not known. Promoter shareholding in RIL was always opaque. According to RIL's FY2003 annual report, promoter shareholding was 35 per cent. The FY2004 annual report states that promoters and persons acting in concert held a 46.67 per cent stake. We do not know if the Ambani family bought additional stake in RIL during FY2004 or if the persons acting in concert were not included in the FY2003 annual report.

In an article dated 14 January 2005, *Frontline* reported that the Ambani family directly held a 5.13 per cent stake in RIL; the Petroleum Trust held 7.5 per cent and a maze of investment companies, collectively referred to as 'persons acting in concert', held 34 per cent. Media estimates of the number of investment companies that collectively held the 34 per cent stake in RIL ranged from 300 to 500. Neither the stock exchanges nor SEBI had asked RIL to clarify its ownership structure.

Mukesh subsequently affirmed, 'There are no ownership issues in RIL.'[6] Did this imply that Mukesh controlled the 34 per cent stake held by 'investment companies' by virtue of being RIL's chairman, or did he actually own these shares? *Outlook India* reported that the Ambani family had informed SEBI, the income tax department and the department of company affairs during the investigations relating to the switching of shares in the 1990s[7] that it had no links with these investment firms. Regulatory and tax authorities would have initiated fresh investigations if it were established that the Ambani family indeed owned these investment firms.

A second reason for the conflict was the brothers inheriting their father's proclivity for mammoth projects. While Mukesh's dream venture was the group's telecom arm, started in July 2004, Anil was keen to showcase his project execution skills by setting up an ₹11,000 crore ($ 2.43 billion) gas-based power project at Dadri, Uttar Pradesh. India's first deep-water gas field, RIL's KG-D6 (Krishna Godavari Dhirubhai 6)—was to supply the natural gas for this project.

RIL's telecom business was conducted through two entities: Reliance Infocomm and Reliance Communications. By March

2004, RIL had invested close to ₹10,500 crore ($2.32 billion) in its two telecom ventures in the form of equity and cumulative redeemable and optionally convertible preference shares paying 10 per cent dividends. More than 80 per cent of RIL's investment in the telecom venture was as preference shares, because it is legal to pay a fixed dividend for preference shares but not equity shares.

In FY2004, RIL entered into an arrangement with Reliance Infocomm to buy and sell mobile handsets, maintain accounts, bill subscribers and collect the money due to Reliance Infocomm, activities completely unrelated to its core oil and petrochemicals business. This arrangement resulted in RIL accumulating around ₹3500 crore ($772 million) receivables, on account of which Anil refused to sign the RIL balance sheet. RIL subsequently transferred these receivables to Smart Entrepreneur Solutions Pvt Ltd, a Reliance Communications Infrastructure Ltd (RCIL) subsidiary. RCIL was also Reliance Infocomm's holding company. RCIL gave a ₹3426 crore ($756 million) loan to Smart Entrepreneur Solutions to purchase the receivables.

Anil alleged that Reliance Infocomm had paid RIL a paltry dividend of ₹16 crore ($3.53 million) on the preference shares, implying just 0.2 per cent return.[8] This was possible, notwithstanding the 10 per cent dividend rate, as Reliance Infocomm had the option to skip dividends during certain years and pay them cumulatively in subsequent years.

Anil made a more damning allegation of his elder brother acquiring a 12 per cent stake in Reliance Infocomm valued at ₹7000 crore ($1.54 billion) for ₹50 crore ($11 million) as sweat equity. He further stated that Mukesh and persons acting in concert held a 27.5 per cent stake in Reliance Infocomm, while RIL, despite making the bulk of investments, held only a 7.5 per cent stake.[9] This implied that Mukesh would reap the upside of RIL's investment if Reliance Infocomm's share price appreciated and the company paid dividends. Anil further alleged that SEBI and the stock exchanges were not informed about this transaction. RIL, on 23 December 2004, ahead of its 27 December board meeting, announced that Mukesh was foregoing his sweat equity in Reliance Infocomm.[10]

In addition to the ₹11,000 crore ($2.43 billion) investment for the Dadri power project, Anil wanted RIL to invest ₹2000 crore ($441 million) in Reliance Capital to transform the NBFC into a one-stop financial shop. Mukesh was reluctant to finance the Dadri power project and Reliance Capital.

In FY2004, RIL had generated operating cash flows, after paying interest and taxes, of over ₹10,000 crore ($2.16 billion) from ₹52,576 crore ($11.36 billion) revenues. The conglomerate reported ₹21,017 crore ($4.54 billion) consolidated debt, which was still moderate at twice its EBITDA. However, the telecom venture still required substantial investments. While RIL could support either the telecom venture or the Dadri power project, it did not have the capacity to finance both projects.

One of Mukesh's senior aides informed *Outlook India* that the elder brother was never in favour of the Dadri power project and felt that 'the group should own energy distribution channels, rather than be in the business of producing power'.[11] RIL announced that the natural gas from the KG-D6 basin would be available only from 2008 and not from 2006, as initially envisaged. This implied that Anil would have to either source natural gas for the Dadri project from a third party or defer the project by two years.

The third source of strife was Anil's foray into politics, which reportedly irked Mukesh. The younger brother was elected as an independent MP of the Rajya Sabha from Uttar Pradesh in 2004, supported by his close friend Amar Singh—the general secretary of the Samajwadi Party. Dhirubhai, renowned for his political acumen, had participated in the Congress' victory celebrations after Indira Gandhi was voted to power in the 1980 general elections. However, with the emergence of regional parties and the stranglehold of the Congress loosening on Indian politics since the late 1980s, the Reliance Group engaged with multiple political parties. By securing a Rajya Sabha seat with the Samajwadi Party's support, Anil had aligned himself with a political party and had thus flouted the group's unwritten policy of simultaneous engagement with significant political parties.

Further, rumours of Anil's friendship with film stars made the family uncomfortable. The family had reportedly opposed his marriage to Hindi film star, Tina Munim, and had acquiesced only after he threatened to leave the family home. Anil and Tina were married in 1991 and, by 2004, the couple had two sons—Jai Anmol and Jai Anshul. Media reported that Mukesh's wife, Nita, and Tina did not get along.

RIL's refusal to finance the Dadri power plant and Reliance Capital while making and committing to sizeable investments in telecom, and Mukesh manoeuvring to emerge as RIL's numero uno, understandably enraged Anil.

The Matriarch Intercedes

Kokilaben Ambani had not acquiesced to Anil's request that she succeed Dhirubhai as RIL's chairperson and that the brothers be appointed joint managing directors. The matriarch had supported Mukesh's appointment as chairman and managing director. She was, however, keen to ensure that the group's assets were distributed equitably between her offspring and to bring an end to the very public fracas, which had been raging for over seven months.

Kokilaben enlisted the support of family friend and ICICI Bank CEO and managing director (MD) K.V. Kamath, deputy MD Kalpana Morparia, law firm Amarchand Mangaldas' star lawyer Cyril Shroff, and RIL's erstwhile detractor and RSS ideologue, S. Gurumurthy, who, by then, had emerged as a preeminent mediator of conflicts among family-owned businesses, to propose a scheme for the division of assets. J.M. Morgan Stanley's CEO Nimesh Kampani was entrusted with the task of valuing the Reliance Group's assets. On 18 June 2005, invoking the blessings of Srinathji, the presiding deity of the Nathdwara temple in Rajasthan and the Ambani's family deity, Kokilaben announced the settlement through a terse media release.[12]

Figure 1: Kokilaben Ambani's Media Release Announcing RIL's Division

Kokilaben D. Ambani

18th June, 2005, Mumbai

With the blessings of Srinathji, I have today amicably resolved the issues between my two sons, Mukesh and Anil, keeping in mind the proud legacy of my husband, Dhirubhai Ambani.

I am confident that both Mukesh and Anil, will resolutely uphold the values of their father and work towards protecting and enhancing value for over 3 million shareholders of the Reliance Group, which has been the foundational principle on which my husband built India's largest private sector enterprise.

Mukesh will have responsibility for Reliance Industries and IPCL while Anil will have responsibility for Reliance Infocomm, Reliance Energy and Reliance Capital.

My husband's foresight and vision and the values he stood for combined with my blessings will guide them to scale new heights".

Kokila D. Ambani

KOKILABEN D. AMBANI

Source: Reliance Empire Divided, Financial Express, 18 June 2005

Credit: Gujarat Cooperative Milk Marketing Federation Ltd. (Amul)

The *Business Standard* reported that Kamath had suggested that the Ambani family divide its holdings in RIL in the ratio 30:30:40, under which the two brothers received 30 per cent each of the family's holding in RIL. Kokilaben would receive 40 per cent, of which she would retain 30 per cent while 10 per cent would be bequeathed to the two daughters.[13]

The Reliance Group was split into two with RIL's core businesses—crude oil refining, petrochemicals and IPCL, oil and gas exploration—remaining with Mukesh. Anil was to manage Reliance Energy, Reliance Infocomm, Reliance Capital and Reliance Natural Resources. The enterprises he managed were collectively referred to as the Anil Dhirubhai Ambani Group (ADAG). The media highlighted that Anil's businesses were new economy industries and hence, poised for accelerated growth.

The financials of Mukesh's RIL and Anil's ADAG in FY2007 highlight the disparity in scale and profits of the enterprises the siblings helmed going forward. ADAG's FY2007 revenues and profits were 24 per cent and 37 per cent of RIL's respectively. Yet ADAG's balance sheet bore a disproportionate quantum of debt equivalent to 78 per cent of RIL's. This was on account of the capital-intensive nature of ADAG's nascent businesses. While Mukesh had inherited the seasoned cash cow, Anil's bequest comprised a bunch of leveraged businesses in their growth phase.

Figure 2: RIL versus ADAG, FY2007

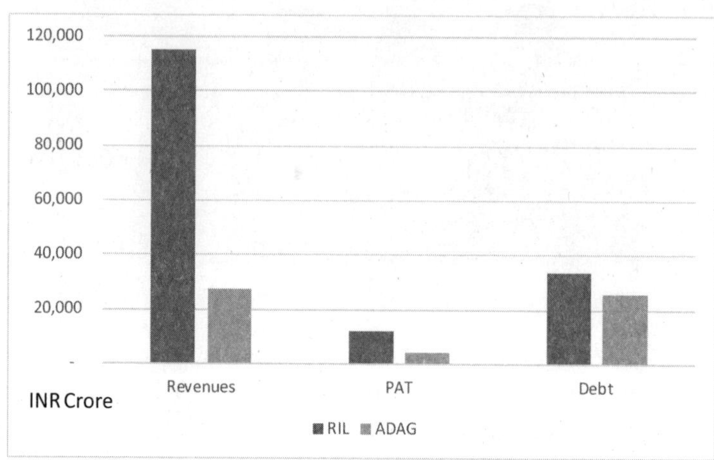

Source: RIL, Rcom, RInfra & Reliance Capital FY2007 annual reports

The market capitalization of Mukesh's companies was estimated to be slightly lower than 80 per cent of the undivided Reliance Group. Hence, Mukesh had to make a sizeable cash payout to Anil to offset the wide chasm in the scale and value of their businesses. Media estimates of the payout varied wildly from ₹4500 crore ($1.0 billion) to ₹15,750 crore ($3.5 billion), while RIL's disclosures mentioned nothing.[14,15]

RIL and the ADAG signed a natural gas supply agreement and a non-competition agreement with the right of first refusal (ROFR). The ROFR meant that should Mukesh or Anil intend to sell a company in his stable, he would have a contractual duty to first offer to sell it to his brother, who had the option, but not the contractual obligation, to purchase the company.

Anil, as RIL's vice-chairman and MD, resigned from the board and abstained from the meeting that was convened to kickstart the settlement process. RIL's board of directors put out a statement that they had 'decided to consider a proposal to reorganize the businesses as per Ms Kokilaben Ambani's principle of ensuring the highest shareholder value'.[16] No further information was officially provided about the reorganization plan.

The Divorce

On 19 June, Mukesh and Anil sent warm farewell e-mails to the employees of Reliance Infocomm and RIL respectively.[17] Mukesh, in the e-mail to Reliance Infocomm's 40,000 employees, stated, 'My younger brother Anil is taking over the stewardship of Reliance Infocomm. He has enormous energy and drive, and we share a common commitment to take forward the legacy of our father late Dhirubhai Ambani.'[18] Anil's e-mail to RIL employees complimented Mukesh for his 'outstanding leadership'.[19]

A striking aspect of RIL's FY2006 annual report was that, while details of the demerger were delineated, the entity to which the four new companies were transferred—ADAG—was not mentioned. The customary acknowledgement and appreciation for services rendered by the outgoing vice-chairman—Anil Ambani—were absent. Anil's name was not mentioned even once in RIL's FY2006 annual report.

Anil's Unveiling

Two days after Kokilaben announced the settlement, Anil convened a press conference on Sunday, 20 June 2005. Here, he unveiled his ₹80,000 crore ($18 billion) plan in power generation. He also announced ADAG's proposed ₹2000 crore ($454 million) investment in Reliance Capital, ₹1000 crore ($227 million) investment in Reliance Energy, and the group's foray into greenfield infrastructure projects. Anil announced that ADAG would also bid for the airport projects in New Delhi and Mumbai.[20]

Ten days after convening the press conference, Reliance Capital announced the acquisition of a 51 per cent stake in Adlabs Films for ₹100 crore ($23 million) and invested an additional ₹260 crore

($59 million) in purchase of Adlabs' preference shares. Adlabs, which was engaged in film production, distribution, exhibition and operating multiplexes, had reported ₹22 crore ($5 million) profits on ₹100 crore ($23 million) revenues. The stock markets, as usual, seemed to have got a whiff of the deal. Adlabs share prices zoomed on BSE to a fifty-two-week high of ₹240 ($5.44) on 30 June from ₹166 ($3.76) on 20 June. Equally telling was the more than 10-fold rise in traded volumes of Adlabs' shares to 700,000 from 68,000 during the ten-day period. While the Ambani family was known to hobnob with Bollywood A-listers, this was probably their first foray into the business of films.

Mukesh made no announcements after Kokilaben announced the settlement plan. Within hours of the press release, he left for Goa, accompanied by his wife, to attend close aide Anand Jain's daughter's wedding.

The Bombay High Court approved the Reliance Group demerger plan on 20 December 2005 and designated 25 January 2006 as the effective demerger or record date. Four new listed companies—Reliance Communication Ventures Ltd (RCom), Reliance Natural Resources Ltd (RNRL), Reliance Capital Ventures Ltd (Reliance Capital), and Reliance Energy Ventures Ltd (Reliance Energy)—were carved out of RIL. The undivided RIL had around 2.3 million shareholders when the Bombay High Court approved the demerger. Share certificates of the four new companies were dispatched to RIL's shareholders. RIL shareholders received, for every RIL share owned, one share each of RCom, RNRL, Reliance Capital, and Reliance Energy.

Sandip Tandon, the chairman of the four new companies that were to be helmed by Anil, announced, 'It was a mammoth exercise considering the fact that nearly 90 lakh [9 million] allotments were required for all the four new companies and the entire process was completed within a week of the record date . . . It was an unprecedented feat in the history of Indian stock market.'[21]

Indomitable RIL

The flagship RIL appeared to be unaffected by the demerger. Accounting policies enabled the entity to pull off this feat. Companies around the world typically report their assets at historical values. Accounting regimes permit companies to periodically revalue their assets at prevalent market values. This revaluation results in a simultaneous increase in the value of assets and revaluation reserve, which is a component of a company's net worth. Revaluations do not result in an increase in revenues, profits or tax liabilities, except when asset sales are synchronized with revaluation.

The revaluation of RIL's assets resulted in a ₹22,497 crore ($5 billion) increase in the value of undivided RIL's gross assets to ₹84,970 crore ($19 billion) as of March 2006. Of this, ₹19,119 crore ($4.31 billion) assets were transferred to ADAG. RIL's ₹2912 crore ($656 million) investments made prior to the demerger in the four new companies were transferred to ADAG. After taking into account new asset purchases, fresh investments and depreciation expenses, RIL's consolidated assets increased by 19 per cent to ₹96,871 crore ($22 billion) in March 2006, notwithstanding the demerger.

Soaring Personal Fortunes

There was some disparity in the siblings' personal wealth too. *Forbes* had estimated the Ambani family wealth in 2002, the year of Dhirubhai Ambani's demise, to be $2.90 billion. Between July 2002 and December 2005, the Sensex had trebled to 8770 points, while the RIL share price had almost quadrupled to ₹138 ($3.12). Consequently, Mukesh and Anil Ambani's combined net worth had more than doubled to $7.0 billion by 2005. In 2006, the year of the demerger, Mukesh Ambani was ranked 56th in the *Forbes* global billionaires list with a net worth of $8.50 billion, while Anil Ambani was ranked 104th with a net worth of $5.7 billion.

Their wealth was buoyed by the robust and sustained rise in RIL's share price and the BSE Sensex.

In ancient India, kings conducted a ritual called Ashvamedha Yagna (horse sacrifice, in Sanskrit) to prove their imperial sovereignty. A horse accompanied by the king's force would wander across the country for a period of one year. An opponent could challenge the king's authority by combating with the force accompanying the horse. If no adversary captured or killed the horse within a year, it would be led back to the capital. The horse would then be sacrificed, and the king will be declared an undisputed sovereign. After the demerger, the brothers embarked on their respective Ashwamedha Yagnas.

The RIL Juggernaut

In FY2006, RIL set up a refinery with a processing capacity of 5,80,000 barrels per day at Jamnagar, catering to advanced markets in the US and Europe. On a stand-alone basis, this was to be the sixth largest refinery in the world. In conjunction with RIL's existing refinery, Jamnagar was to become the single largest location of refinery assets in the world. The launch of RIL's pan-India multi-format retail stores was also announced in FY2006.

In September 2007, IPCL, the erstwhile state-owned company, was amalgamated with RIL. Shareholders of IPCL, were issued one RIL share for every five IPCL shares they owned. This transaction involved no cash outgo for RIL. Reliance Petroleum Limited (RPL), RIL's subsidiary, completed an ₹8100 crore ($1.86 billion) IPO of equity shares in April 2006. The RPL IPO was the world's 13th largest in 2006 and oversubscribed by over 50 times.[22]

In FY2007, RIL commissioned the world's largest polyester expansion project, bringing on steam 550 kilo tonnes per annum (KTA) polyester production within a tight timeline of eighteen months. On completion of this project, RIL accounted for 4 per cent of global polyester capacity and 6 per cent of global production.

Reliance Retail entered the organized retail market in India with the launch of its convenience store format, under the brand name of 'Reliance Fresh', in November 2006 in Hyderabad. The network had expanded to 96 stores by end FY 2007, covering locations like Jaipur, Chennai, New Delhi, Guntur, Vijayawada and Visakhapatnam.

In its FY2008 annual report, RIL announced that its ₹1631 crore ($389 million) dividend payout was the highest ever among India's private sector companies till then. The promoter stake in RIL as of March 2008 was 51.37 per cent, which meant the promoters received ₹838 crore ($200 million) dividends. The company also announced nine petroleum discoveries in the various exploration blocks in India and confirmed that 'creditable progress' was being made in the KG-D6 project. Mukesh, in his annual letter to shareholders, described the KG-D6 project as 'one of the largest and most complex deep water gas projects in the world'.

That year, RIL also took over the operations of Gulf Africa Petroleum Corporation and started shipping products to East Africa. RIL entered into an agreement to acquire Hualon Malaysia's assets, thereby increasing its share in global polyester production to 7 per cent. Reliance Retail continued its expansion spree and, by end FY2008, operated 590 stores in fifty-seven Indian cities, spanning thirteen states, and over 3.5 million square feet of trading space.

The New Kid on the Block

Anil's agenda was more daunting than his brother's at the time of the demerger. He was expected to scale up his businesses to evolve into market leaders. Anil also aspired to ensure that ADAG's market cap was at least comparable to RIL's, and his wealth was at par with Mukesh.

Anil bridged the gap between his and Mukesh's personal net worth at a lightning pace, or so it appeared, in 2007 and 2008. The world billionaires list ranked him eighteenth in 2007 with a $18.2 billion personal net worth; four places behind Mukesh who was ranked fourteenth with a $20.1 billion net worth. In 2008, the net worth of the brothers more than doubled and they were catapulted among the top ten on the list. Anil was ranked sixth, with a $42 billion net worth, which was just a billion short of the fifth most affluent man in the world—Mukesh.[23]

How did Anil Ambani achieve this feat?

Veritas Explains

According to RCom's FY2007 annual report, 2.04 billion shares of RCom were 'allotted as fully paid up, without payment being received in cash'. Of these, Anil was the recipient of 1.36 billion shares, or a 63 per cent stake. RIL's shareholders, who were allotted one RCom share for every RIL share they owned, received the balance.[24] RCom shares were listed on 6 March 2006 at ₹307 ($6.78). On listing day, RCom promoters' stake was worth ₹41,900 crore ($9.25 billion). The Canadian research firm, Veritas Investment Research, in its 18 July 2011 report assessed the loss incurred by non-promoter shareholders on account of RCom's management receiving free shares, to be ₹25,204 crore ($5.56 billion) at the listing price of ₹307 ($6.78).[25]

Veritas stated that, between the time RCom was demerged from RIL on 31 August 2005 and listed six months later, 'the ownership of promoters ballooned from 38.27 per cent to 63 per cent in RCom, under the guise of improving shareholder value'. Veritas estimated that RIL shareholders had invested ₹13,675 crore ($3 billion) in RCom, while the management had invested a meagre ₹186 crore ($41 million).

The investment research firm further alleged that RCom had inflated its profits between 2007 and 2010, accounting standards were subverted, governance was lax, and the directors had failed in their fiduciary duty towards non-promoter shareholders.

While the RCom listing facilitated Anil's ascent in the global billionaire's list, the Reliance Power (R-Power) IPO propelled him to the top ten on that list.

India's Fourth Largest IPO To Date

At the time of its January 2008 IPO, R-Power was developing twelve power projects, which included six coal-fired projects, four hydroelectric projects and two gas-fired projects in India. With an installed capacity of 24,200 megawatts (MW) once these projects were completed, R-Power was poised to become one of India's largest power generators. The gas-fired projects included Anil's dream project—the 7480 MW Dadri project, which was touted to be the largest gas-fired power project at a single location in the world.

At the time of its IPO, R-Power reported modest revenues and profits. It had generated ₹1.27 crore ($287,000) profits on ₹2.25 crore ($0.51 million) revenues in FY2007. R-Power's consolidated assets as of September 2007 were not an insignificant ₹2008 crore ($453 million), most of which was financed by its ₹2000 crore ($451 million) share capital.

On 15 January 2008, R-Power launched, with much fanfare, its ₹11,563 crore ($3 billion) IPO—India's fourth largest to date following Life Insurance Corporation of India's ₹21,008 crore ($2.70 billion) and Paytm's ₹18,300 crore ($2.48 billion) in 2021 and Coal India's ₹15,200 crore ($3.32 billion) in 2010.[26] R-Power shares were offered at an issue price of ₹450 ($10.34) per share for non-retail investors, and ₹430 ($9.88) for retail investors.[27] The IPO resulted in an instantaneous and more than five-fold growth in R-Power's assets.

It was a spectacular success and fully subscribed within a minute of its launch, and two-and-a-half times oversubscribed within twenty-five minutes. When the IPO closed on 18 January 2008, it was oversubscribed 72 times. R-Power's shares were listed on 11 February 2008. The share price surged 19 per cent to ₹538 within four minutes of the stock market opening.

Then the unthinkable happened. R-Power's share price nosedived to ₹355 ($8.16) and closed at ₹372.50 ($8.56), which was around 15 per cent lower than the offer price. Analysts attributed the share price crash to the ongoing global financial crisis. R-Power's share price performance on listing day was a rude shock for Anil.

As a face-saving measure, R-Power announced a bonus share issue, awarding retail and institutional shareholders three shares for every five shares they held. This reduced the cost of R-Power shares to ₹269 ($6.18) for retail investors and ₹281 ($6.46) for institutional investors, enabling them to earn listing day profits of 38 per cent and 33 per cent respectively.

Promoters were not awarded bonus shares, notwithstanding which the market value of their stake had appreciated considerably. Between January 1995 and September 2007, promoters had invested ₹2032 crore ($442 million), for which they allotted themselves 10.16 billion shares at a price of ₹2 per share (4 cents per share). Despite R-Power's share price declining to ₹372.50 (US$8.56), the market value of the promoters' investment had appreciated 18,600 per cent to ₹3,77,952 crore ($87 billion)!

That R-Power's IPO terms were to the detriment of non-promoter shareholders is evident in the lopsided distribution of ownership stakes and financial investment. The promoters' share of equity investment in monetary terms was 15 per cent; yet, they held a 90 per cent stake in R-Power. Non-promoters' share of equity investment in monetary terms was 85 per cent, for which they were allotted a 10 per cent stake.

R-Power's management was guilty of yet another wilful lapse. The Dadri and Shahpur power plants, which were to account for 42 per cent of R-Power's installed capacity when its twelve power plants began commercial operations, were solely dependent on RIL for natural gas supplies. The 335-page IPO prospectus, which included a long-winded disclosure of sixty risk factors that ran to nineteen pages, failed to mention this. Was Anil sagacious in embarking, perhaps prematurely, on an Ashwamedha Yagna, when he was still dependent on Mukesh?

Chapter 16

Kurukshetra

Anil was in a good place in March 2008, following the R-Power IPO. The market capitalization of his conglomerate, ADAG, comprising four listed companies—Reliance Capital, RCom, RInfra and R-Power—was ₹2,36,731 crore (short of $57 billion). This was 72 per cent of RIL's ₹3,29,368 crore ($79 billion) market cap. ADAG's profits in FY2008 were ₹9030 crore (over $2 billion), or 27 per cent of its ₹65,801 crore (US$16 billion) revenues and 6.6 per cent of its ₹1,37,008 crore ($33 billion) assets. Indebtedness was moderate with a debt-to-equity ratio of 0.64 times. The conglomerate's liquidity was also comfortable. with a ₹2477 crore ($591 million) cash balance.

Yet, there were concerns.

ADAG was excessively dependent on RCom, which contributed to 56 per cent of the conglomerate's revenues and 75 per cent of profits. At 17.68 per cent, RCom's market share, in terms of the number of mobile subscribers, was the second highest among Indian mobile phone operators. Bharti Airtel was the market leader with a market share of nearly 25 per cent, while Vodafone was close on RCom's heels with a 17.56 per cent market share. However, this flattering statistic and the fact that RCom's subscribers had more than doubled from nearly 31 million in December 2006 to 61.34 million by December 2008 camouflaged a worrisome trend.

RCom's market share had actually declined from 20 per cent in December 2006, following Vodafone's entry in 2007 and Bharti Airtel's aggressive expansion. Further, RCom had adopted the CDMA (code division multiple access) technology, which worked well with 2G and 3G networks. Vodafone and Airtel had adopted the GSM (global system for mobile communications) technology, which was better suited for the emerging 4G and 5G networks. This meant that RCom had to invest substantially to adopt GSM. This dilemma was not unique to RCom. India's fourth and fifth largest mobile operators—the state-owned BSNL and Tata Teleservices with market shares of 13 per cent and 9 per cent respectively—shared this predicament.

Worse, RCom's lax financial management was evident even in early 2008. By end 2007, Airtel's subscribers were slightly over 55 million, while RCom's were close to 40 million. However, Airtel's ₹6495 crore ($1.55 billion) profit in FY2008 was more than six times RCom's ₹1010 crore ($241 million). Also, Bharti Airtel's ₹19,769 crore ($4.72 billion) debt was 23 per cent lower than RCom's at ₹25,822 crore ($6.17 billion).

RCom was Mukesh's idea; the telecom venture was close to his heart. RCom had been conceived of as a division of RIL before Dhirubhai's demise. Even before RCom came into ADAG's fold, it had slashed tariffs in its bid to boost its market share. RCom's weak profits in FY2008 was both a reflection of its aggressive pricing strategy and the interest costs arising from high debt. Growing RCom's subscriber base and maximizing market share were Anil Ambani's goals too.

An opportunity arose, even amidst the ongoing global financial crisis. Merger discussions between the South African telecom company, MTN Group, and Airtel had come to naught. On 26 May 2008, MTN Group and RCom initiated merger discussions. The deal, if successful, would have created a telecom monolith straddling two major growth markets—India and South Africa—with an estimated market value of $70–80 billion.

However, RIL threw a spanner in the works. It initiated arbitration proceedings against RCom, invoking the right of first refusal (ROFR) clause in the 2006 agreements RIL and ADAG had signed. The merger deal between RCom and MTN Group fell through. Both companies attributed their inability to conclude the transaction to 'legal and regulatory issues'.[1]

The ROFR was not the sole bone of contention between the siblings. They competed against each other to secure the Mumbai Trans Harbour Link contract, the project cost of which was over $1 billion. Neither was awarded the contract. In 2007, when RIL proposed to set up power projects in special economic zones (SEZs) in Haryana, Gujarat and Maharashtra, Anil wrote to the Maharashtra chief minister remonstrating that this move violated the non-compete clause and that power projects were in ADAG's domain.[2]

All these conflicts paled in comparison to the 'gas wars' the Ambani brothers engaged in. The nation watched in rapt attention as the war unfolded in the courts of law, the floor of Parliament and in the media.

Price of Power

The 2006 terms of settlement agreement between the brothers resulted in RIL retaining natural gas exploration and extraction from the KG-D6 gas fields located on India's western coastline, while the ADAG company, R-Power's core business, was to develop, construct and operate power projects. In 2008, R-Power's twelve power plants, including two gas-fired power plants at Dadri and Shahpur, were at various stages of development. The 2006 settlement included an agreement that delineated the terms and conditions for RIL supplying natural gas to ADAG's gas-fired plants at Dadri and Shahpur. As mentioned earlier, R-Power was solely dependent on RIL for natural gas supplies.

The dispute this time was over the price at which RIL ought to supply natural gas to the ADAG company, Reliance Natural Resources Limited (RNRL), whose core business was sourcing, supplying and transporting gas, coal and liquid fuels. RNRL opined that the applicable price was $2.34 per mmBtu (million metric British thermal unit), which, according to Anil, was the price approved by 'RIL's board of directors nearly five years ago, and has been duly recorded in the commercial agreements signed by RIL'.[3] This was also the price at which RIL had offered to sell gas to the government-owned National Thermal Power Corporation (NTPC) years ago, a deal that was subject to long-drawn litigation and never implemented.

RIL countered that the applicable price was stipulated in the production sharing contract (PSC) it had signed with the government and was 80 per cent higher at $4.21 per mmBtu.

In November 2006, RNRL filed a case against RIL in the Bombay High Court. The high-decibel litigation raged for seven months. On 15 June 2009, the Bombay High Court ruled that RIL's board was fully aware of the settlement agreement, which was binding on both RIL and RNRL. RIL had earlier contended that the settlement agreement related to the Ambani family and had no place in the corporate domain. Further, RIL was contractually obliged to supply ADAG 28 mscmd (million standard cubic meters per day) natural gas plus the allocation to NTPC, should RIL's contract with NTPC not materialize or was cancelled.

The verdict stated that RIL's natural gas allocation to ADAG was independent of the PSC it had executed with the government, and that RIL would have to bear the cost of supplying natural gas to ADAG. Most damagingly, the judgement stated that 'there is no specific provision under the PSC to prevent the contractor

(RIL) from selling the gas at a price lower than the price fixed by the government for valuation of gas to the extent of its share'.[4] The court directed RIL and RNRL to enter into a gas supply agreement within a month.

Anil had won the first battle, but RIL announced its intention to appeal to the Supreme Court against the verdict.

Ad Blitzkrieg

Anil then launched a media offensive. A series of five advertisements were 'issued in the public and national interest on behalf of eight million shareholders of Reliance Anil Dhirubhai Ambani Group, the largest shareholder family in the world'.[5] These advertisements were published in major Indian newspapers.

The first advertisement questioned why NTPC must purchase natural gas from RIL at a price that was 80 per cent more than what was offered by RIL to NTPC. The second advertisement alleged that the petroleum ministry had approved the four-fold hike in RIL's project cost, resulting in a ₹30,000-crore ($6.20 billion) loss to the exchequer. The third advertisement questioned why RIL was allowed to hike its natural gas price by 20 per cent during a year when international natural gas prices had crashed by 80 per cent. The penultimate advertisement alleged that RIL was operating at less than 40 per cent of its natural gas capacity and the petroleum ministry was abetting RIL by proclaiming a scarcity, thereby enabling RIL to earn windfall gains at the expense of the government. The final advertisement accused the petroleum ministry of intervening in a commercial dispute over gas supplies between two corporates, and of supporting RIL.

All these advertisements ended with the question 'Is this in public or national interest?'

Figure 1: The Advertisements ADAG Published in 'National Interest'

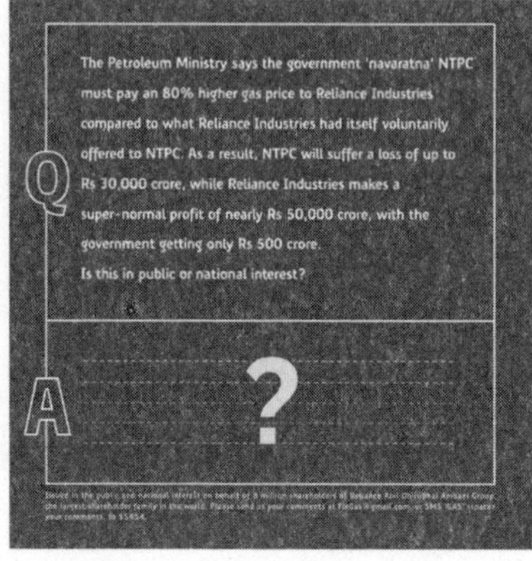

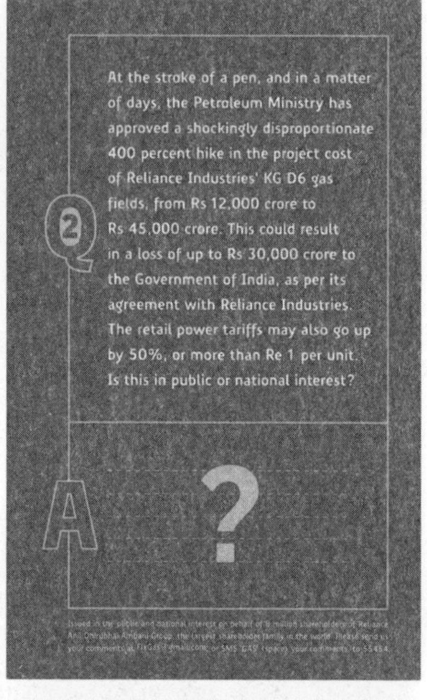

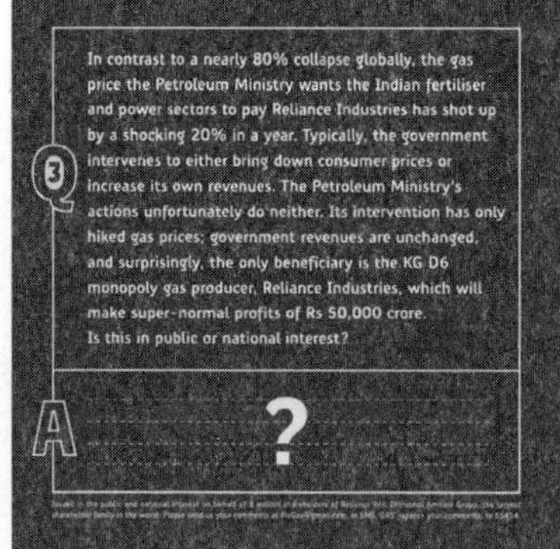

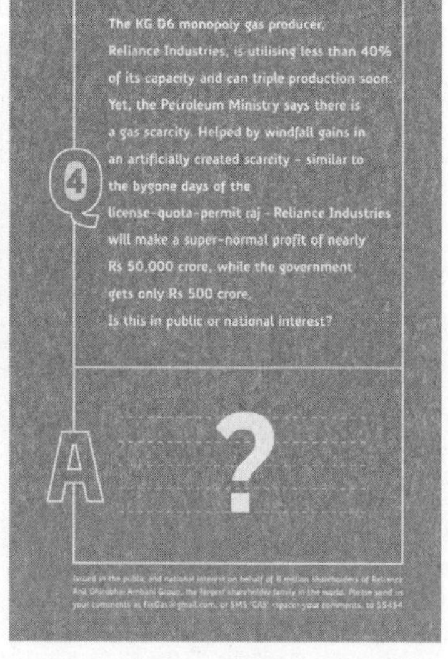

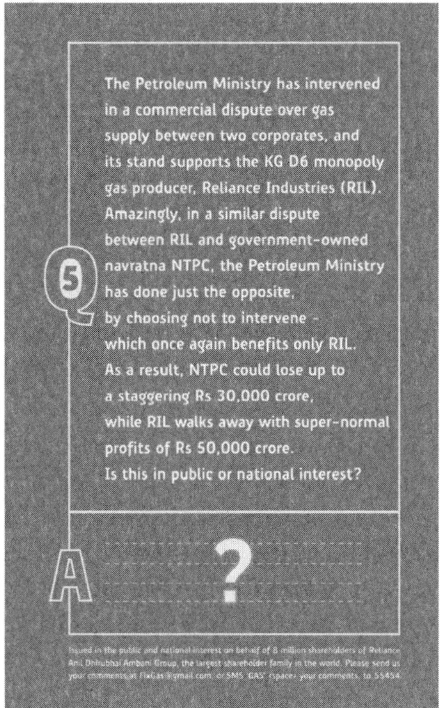

The government too stepped into the fray by observing that natural gas was a national resource, the transaction terms of which could not be determined by a private agreement.

Meanwhile, Anil, after undertaking a pilgrimage to temples in the Himalayas, performed a volte-face and expressed his fervent desire to end the deadlock. RIL, while welcoming the move, stated that the matter was subjudice and hoped 'any overtures for rapprochement are in no way related to the ongoing hearing of the case'.[6]

Supreme Court Verdict

A three-member bench of the apex court, including the then chief justice of India (CJI), K.G. Balakrishnan, began hearing the case on 20 October 2009. On 4 November 2009, one of the judges withdrew, citing potential conflict of interest as his daughter worked at a firm that was a consultant to RIL. On 5 November 2009, a new three-member bench that included the CJI resumed hearing arguments from scratch.

RIL argued that a private deal between the Ambani brothers cannot take precedence over government policy, which determines gas purchasers and the price. The applicable price according to the PSC at this juncture was $4.21 per mmBtu. ADAG claimed that the government would not suffer a loss even if RIL supplied gas to RNRL at $2.34 per mmBtu. The government stressed that it neither favoured RIL nor ADAG.[7]

On 7 May 2010, the Supreme Court ruled in favour of Mukesh and asked the brothers to renegotiate the gas contract within six weeks and approach a companies' court within eight weeks.

A fortnight after the Supreme Court verdict, on 24 May 2010, the brothers scrapped the non-compete agreement (NCA) that RIL and ADAG had signed in January 2006.[8] This meant that Anil was free to forge strategic alliances in telecom and insurance, while Mukesh could foray into telecom and financial services. The two conglomerates signed a simpler NCA that restrained RIL from setting up natural gas-based power projects until 2022. This was to be ADAG's domain.

The two conglomerates released a statement that they were 'hopeful and confident that all these steps will create an overall environment of harmony, co-operation and collaboration between the two groups, thereby further enhancing overall shareholder value for shareholders of both groups'.

S.P. Tulsian, an independent investment adviser, presciently remarked, 'This is more positive for Reliance Industries than ADAG, because this gives Reliance (RIL) an opportunity to look into expansion in other areas. You can't rule out the possibility of Reliance entering in sectors such as telecom.'

Credit: Gujarat Cooperative Milk Marketing Federation Ltd. (Amul)

The renegotiation of natural gas prices did not happen, though. But Anil did not lose hope.

Elusive Gas

It was almost two years after the Supreme Court verdict that R-Power alluded to the fact that the Dadri project was facing bottlenecks. In its FY2012 annual report, the company reported that it had written off ₹27.78 crore ($5.74 million) incidental expenses 'as a matter of prudence' on account of litigation relating to land acquisition for the Dadri project. R-Power had first reported the land acquisition-related litigation in its FY2010 annual report. The company had, however, stated that the project would commence 'as soon as the gas supply is firmed up and on settlement of land issues'.

In its FY2013 annual report, R-Power wrote off an additional ₹9.01 crore ($1.65 million) incidental expenses, again 'as a matter of prudence' due to the land acquisition-related litigation. The company again reiterated its intention to kickstart the power plant 'as soon as the gas supply is firmed up and on settlement of land issues'.

The 'land issues' mentioned was a reference to the legal dispute over the agricultural land that the Uttar Pradesh government had sold to R-Power. In 2004, the state of Uttar Pradesh had acquired 2100 acres of agricultural land and conveyed the same to R-Power in 2005 for construction of the Dadri power plant. The Samajwadi Party, led by Chief Minister Mulayam Singh Yadav, was in power then. Around 1000 farmers challenged the state's land acquisition in the Allahabad High Court on two grounds. First, they objected to the state government acquiring the land ostensibly for a public purpose and then conveying the same to a private company. Second, the farmers objected to the state government using an emergency clause, which waives the necessity of obtaining a no-objection certificate from the seller, to acquire land.

In December 2009, the Allahabad High Court quashed the state government's emergency notification. Both R-Power and the state government had contested the Allahabad High Court's ruling in the Supreme Court. In January 2015, the Supreme Court set aside the land acquisition and ordered R-Power to return 956 acres of land to the Uttar Pradesh government. In effect, the Supreme Court had upheld the Allahabad High Court's decision and required the state government to return the land to the farmers.[9]

Landmine

In its FY2015 annual report, R-Power reported its intent to return the land to the state government and claim reimbursement of land acquisition costs and other incidental expenses. Assets relating to the Dadri power project, valued at ₹91.33 crore ($14.78 million), were categorized as 'assets held for sale' and 'advance recoverable towards land.'

R-Power, in its FY2016 annual report, stated that it had 'realized' ₹25.22 crore ($3.89 million) from the Uttar Pradesh government and expected to recover the balance amount in the future. The Uttar Pradesh government did not settle its dues with

R-Power in FY2017. However, based on correspondence received from the government regarding land compensation and interest thereon, R-Power 'accrued', but did not receive, a ₹75 crore ($11.25 million) interest income in its FY2017 annual report.

The state government did not reimburse land acquisition costs and incidental expenses that R-Power had incurred even in FY2019, four years after the Supreme Court verdict. This did not deter R-Power from 'recognizing' a ₹4.81 crore ($0.79 million) interest income in FY2018 and ₹4.13 crore ($0.60 million) in FY2019.

In its FY2019 annual report—almost nine years after the Supreme Court had ruled in favour of RIL on natural gas pricing and four years after it upheld the Allahabad High Court's verdict quashing the land acquisition—R-Power classified the Dadri power project as 'discontinued operations'. Nevertheless, in the annual report, the company expressed confidence in recovering its dues from the state government. R-Power, 'out of prudence . . . fully provided for' ₹150.05 crore ($21.03 million) receivables relating to the Dadri project'.[10]

These figures pale in comparison to the ₹11,000 crore ($2.43 billion) investment Anil Ambani had announced in the Dadri power project in early 2004. R-Power's disclosures make it difficult, if not impossible, to ascertain the exact quantum the company invested in the project and the cash reimbursements received from the state government.

Interestingly, R-Power had never intended to use a part of its mammoth ₹11,563 crore ($3 billion) 2008 IPO proceeds to finance the Dadri project. According to the IPO prospectus, R-Power planned to invest ₹6148 crore ($1.5 billion), or 53 per cent of the IPO proceeds, in Rosa phases I and II, Butibori, Sasan, Shahapur Coal and Urthing Sobla power plants. R-Power had planned to use the balance 47 per cent for general corporate purposes and towards IPO issue expenses.[11] 'General corporate purpose' means that a company may use the funds in the manner it deems fit. Of course, it was entirely legal for R-Power to use the funds earmarked for general corporate purposes in the Dadri project later.

Was R-Power wary of divulging its proposed investment in the Dadri power plant in 2008, when the Supreme Court was hearing its appeal against the Allahabad High Court verdict favouring the farmers?

This incident and Tata Motors relocating its plant to manufacture its compact car, Nano, from Singur in West Bengal to Sanand in Gujarat in 2008 due to farmer protests against land acquisition, highlight the complexities of industrial land acquisition in India and the potential pitfalls of partnering with governments in commercial ventures.

Thus Spake RIL

The performance of RIL's oil and gas division following the Supreme Court's May 2010 verdict in its favour is illuminating. When RIL announced the discovery of natural gas in KG-D6 in 2003, it was touted as one of India's most promising natural gas reserves. The GoI's Petroleum Planning & Analysis Cell (PPAC) began publishing India's natural gas production, consumption and import statistics in FY2012. Net production of natural gas in FY2012 was 46,453 mmscm (million metric standard cubic meters), of which state-owned ONGC and OIL's share was 54 per cent, while that of the private sector and joint venture companies was 46 per cent or 21,460 mmscm. RIL and BP (formerly British Petroleum), who had formed a 70:30 venture to develop and operate the KG-D6 fields, were the largest among the private sector and joint venture (JV) entities engaged in natural gas production in India. Within a relatively short period of six years, RIL's natural gas output was second only to that of state-owned ONGC and OIL combined. The company's claim regarding KG-D6's potential appeared vindicated.

ONGC and OIL's combined natural gas output stagnated at around 25,000 mmscm between FY2007 and FY2020. However, the

Figure 2: India's Rising Reliance on Natural Gas Imports (mmscm)

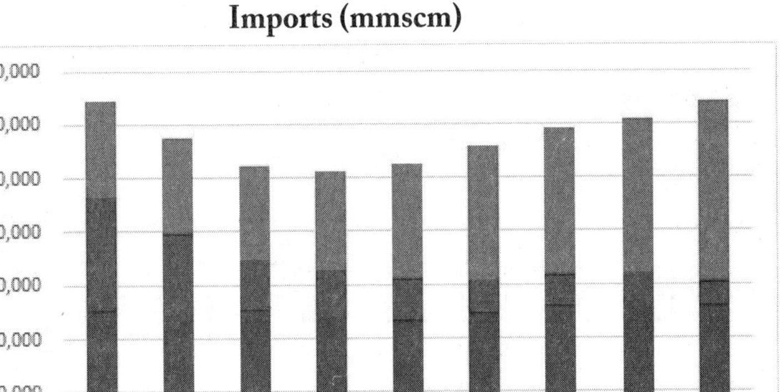

Source: Petroleum Planning & Analysis Cell, GoI

share of natural gas produced by private entities and JVs precipitously dropped from 33.3 per cent in FY2012 to 7.1 per cent in FY2020. This resulted in India's imports of natural gas rising from 27.9 per cent of total consumption in FY2012 to 52.8 per cent in FY2020.

From 2011 onwards, RIL's natural gas output started declining. The natural gas reserves at the KG-D6 gas fields were revised downwards from 10 tcf (trillion cubic feet) to the 3–5 tcf range. By May 2014, KG-D6 was producing around 14 mmscm per day, which was less than a fifth of its peak production of 80 mmscm per day. Mukesh, in his letter to shareholders in RIL's FY2012 annual report, stated, 'Production from the KG-D6 block has been adversely impacted mainly due to unforeseen reservoir complexities and water ingress in the producing fields.'

Why did the natural gas output at the KG-D6 fields plummet?

CAG's Censure

In 2011, India's CAG published a preliminary version of its performance audit report on hydrocarbon production sharing contracts (PSCs). While the CAG report covered RIL, Cairn India and BG (formerly British Gas) among others, it was RIL on which the report mostly focused. The report alleged 'large amounts of revenue had potentially been lost to the exchequer due to ad hoc extensions and policy relaxations granted by the upstream regulator to exploration companies'.

The report stated that the petroleum ministry and oil sector regulator, Directorate General of Hydrocarbons (DGH), facilitated flouting of contractual stipulations by RIL in discovery areas. 'The undue benefit granted to the contractor (RIL) is huge, but cannot be quantified,' the report observed.

The CAG focused on RIL more than trebling the development costs at the KG-D6 fields from $2.4 billion in 2004 to $8.80 billion in 2006, without the company offering a single comprehensive development plan, as required under the contract.[12] According to the report, RIL had declined to share information that would have enabled the CAG to ascertain if the cost escalation was justified. The CAG questioned RIL's practice of awarding multiple contracts without competitive bidding.[13]

The government-stipulated gas pricing formula was due for review on 1 April 2014. Following the CAG report, the GoI appointed a committee headed by former RBI governor, Dr C. Rangarajan, to review the upstream fiscal regime and the system of gas pricing, and to make recommendations for reform. In December 2012, the Rangarajan Committee published its recommendations, which were approved by the government in June 2013.

The Contentious Committee

Two recommendations by the Rangarajan Committee were potent. First, the committee clarified that the CAG possessed the incontrovertible authority to audit the gas fields and recommended that it perform the review within two years of the fiscal year under audit. Second, it recommended that the revenue sharing model replace the cost recovery model. Under the cost recovery model, the contractor shares a percentage of net revenue with the government. Net revenue is revenues minus all costs including capital expenditure. This model gave contractors the incentive to upfront capital expenditures—a practice known as 'gold-plating'. The CAG's allegation of high development costs in RIL's KG-D6 fields is a possible instance of gold-plating. On the other hand, the revenue sharing formula required contractors to share their revenues with the government, with this share to be determined through competitive bidding.

Two more of the committee's recommendations were aimed at attracting private sector players into the high risk, capital intensive and cyclical natural gas exploration and production industry. It suggested the extension of tax holiday from seven to ten years for blocks engaged in drilling offshore oil fields at a depth of more than 1500 metres. It also proposed the extension of the timeframe for exploration of frontier, deep-water, and ultra-deep-water oilfields from eight years to ten years.

The Rangarajan Committee simplified the natural gas pricing mechanism in India. Prior to the constitution of the committee, multiple natural gas price regimes prevailed in India: the administered pricing mechanism, the discovered fields regime, the New Exploration Licensing Policy (NELP) regime, LNG spot and LNG long-term contracts. The price paid per mmBtu of natural gas under these multiple regimes ranged from \$3.50 to \$17.44. The committee recommended a natural gas pricing formula that was predicated on an arm's length pricing principle and incorporated the opportunity cost of importing fuel by including the price of natural gas at major trading markets. The arm's length pricing principle meant that both buyers and sellers had equal access to information and acted independently in their own self-interest without colluding with one another.

The Rangarajan Committee also recommended that the price of domestically produced natural gas, coal bed methane (CBM) and shale gas should be the twelve-month trailing average of two sets of prices. The first was the volume weighted average of netback prices to producers at the exporting country wellhead for all Indian LNG imports. The wellhead price is the wholesale price of natural gas at its point of production. The major suppliers of natural gas to India in 2020 were Qatar, UAE, Nigeria, the US, and Angola.[14] The second was the volume weighted average prices of gas traded in three major markets: US Henry Hub, UK National Balancing Point and the netback price of Japan Customs-cleared Crude (JCC).

Had the Rangarajan Committee formula become applicable on 1 April 2014, natural gas price would have doubled from $4.20 to $8.40 per mmBtu.[15] The committee's natural gas pricing formula eliminated the multiple pricing regimes and was more transparent. However, it was not without detractors.

Surya P. Sethi, GoI's former principal adviser for power and energy and Dr Rangarajan's student, led the charge. In a hard-hitting column in *The Hindu* titled 'Making a mockery of domestic gas pricing', Sethi pointed out that the committee 'did not have a single member with any notable knowledge or understanding of the complex global gas markets'.[16] Further, the committee report did not make a distinction between dry and wet natural gas. Dry gas contains at least 85 per cent methane. Wet gas contains, in addition to methane, liquids such as ethane, propane and butane. Dry gas is most amenable for the production of compressed natural gas (CNG) and LNG, and is used for electricity generation and in homes and businesses for heating, cooling and cooking. The natural gas liquids in wet gas are used in petrochemical plants to manufacture plastics and are blended into petrol. The KG-D6 fields have dry gas deposits.

The most damaging of Sethi's critique was that the price formula was based on natural gas prices in foreign markets and did not reflect the supply, demand and cost of production of natural gas in India. Most Indian natural gas producers were, in 2013, guaranteed a wellhead price of at least $4.2 to $5.25/mmBtu.

The column stated that the Rangarajan Committee report had opined that this price was not sufficiently remunerative to encourage domestic natural gas production but failed to provide any evidence to support such a conclusion. Sethi questioned, 'Can the Committee identify any significant independent conventional gas field in the world that receives or has received this high a wellhead price for dry natural gas year after year on an arms-length basis?'

The PPAC has been publishing the natural gas price in India derived from the modified Rangarajan Committee formula and the price ceiling for gas produced from deep-water, ultra-deep water and high pressure-high temperature fields since April 2015. Though the data is available only from two years after the Rangarajan Committee report, a comparison of these prices with natural gas prices in Europe and US offers interesting insights.

Figure 3: Natural Gas Prices in India, US and Europe ($/mmBtu)

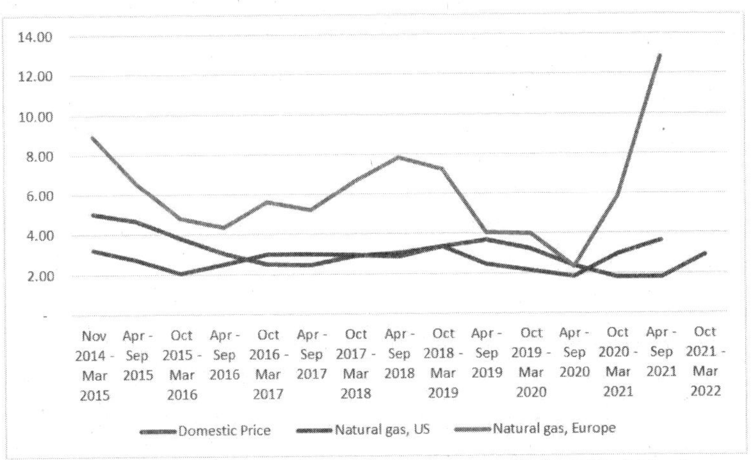

Source: Petroleum Planning & Analysis Cell, Government of India & World Bank Commodity Markets

Despite natural gas being a commodity, there is considerable variation between natural gas prices in the US and Europe, with natural gas in Europe being more expensive than in the US. The difference in price reflects the difference in demand, supply and cost of production in these two geographies.

From November 2014 to September 2021, the domestic price of natural gas has been at least equal to the US price for 53 of the 83 months, or 64 per cent of the time. The domestic price of natural gas has been lower than the prices in both US and Europe for thirty months, or 36 per cent of the time. This does not imply that the natural gas price is manipulated, as the formula and its inputs are transparent. But it does seem unlikely that the cost of producing natural gas in India—where costs are lower than in the US—is higher than in that part of the world. Sethi's views appear vindicated.

As the implementation date of the Rangarajan Committee's gas pricing formula coincided with the April 2014 general elections, the Election Commission directed the government to postpone the implementation of the natural gas pricing reform until after the polls. The NDA government led by the BJP that was elected to power and assumed office in June 2014 postponed the reforms by three months. Finally, on 18 October 2014, the government approved a modified version of the Rangarajan Committee formula.

Sethi's critique went unheeded. Two price benchmarks were removed from the Rangarajan Committee formula—the volume weighted average of netback prices to producers at the exporting country wellhead (for Indian LNG imports), and the volume weighted average producers' netback price of gas in Japan. Two new components replaced the benchmarks that were deleted—the Alberta (gas) Reference price weighted by the volume of Canadian gas consumption, and the Russian domestic gas price weighted by the total annual volume of natural gas consumed in Russia.

The government also stipulated that the new gas price will not apply to RIL's KG-D6 output till its arbitration with the government was completed. In June 2017, RIL and its partner, BP, withdrew from the arbitrations over the price of natural gas and GoI's 2013 order to relinquish 80 per cent of the KG-D6 block.[17]

Two months into FY2011—in May 2010—the Supreme Court verdict required RIL and R-Power to renegotiate the gas contract. In the following fiscal year, FY2012, RIL reported the decline in the natural gas output in its KG-D6 fields. The profits from RIL's oil and gas division peaked in FY2011 and started declining thereafter, a reflection of the reported decline in natural gas output.

Seven months into FY2015—in October 2014—GoI published the revised gas pricing formula. This was accompanied by the revenue sharing model replacing the cost recovery model, which had allowed contractors to deduct capital expenditures from revenues and share a percentage of net revenues with the government.

Of Fact and Fiction

RIL's oil and gas division started reporting losses from FY2017. These losses coincided with RIL selling most of its oil and gas exploration blocks outside India in 2017. In February 2021, RIL sold its entire stake in the Marcellus shale gas asset in Pennsylvania for $250 million. In November 2021, RIL exited the shale gas business in the US after divesting its interest in certain upstream assets in the Eagleford shale business in Texas 'at a consideration higher than the current carrying value of the assets'.[18] RIL did not report the sale proceeds from its November 2021 transaction. The conglomerate also ceased reporting business-wise profit after tax in its FY2021 annual report. These divestments, according to RIL, were meant to enable the conglomerate to achieve net zero carbon emissions by 2035.[19]

In December 2020, RIL and BP announced the commencement of production in the R-Cluster, an ultra-deep-water gas field in the KG-D6 fields. The R-Cluster is reportedly Asia's deepest offshore gas field, with water depth exceeding 2,000 metres. In June 2017, RIL and BP had announced a ₹40,000 crore ($6 billion) investment in three sets of gas discoveries—R-Cluster, Satellite Cluster and MJ Field—to reverse the flagging production in the KG-D6 fields. The R-Cluster was the first to come on stream; RIL announced that the three clusters were expected to meet 15 per cent of India's natural gas demand by 2023.[20]

While RIL's oil and gas division has been loss making since FY2017, the profits made in the decade preceding FY2017 more than offset the losses. Also, this division's losses have helped reduce the conglomerate's tax expense since FY2017. One does hope that the mammoth investment announced by RIL and BP leads to commensurate rise in the oil and gas division's profits and the interests of all stakeholders are protected. The performance of RIL's oil and gas division lends credence to Aldous Huxley's observation, 'The trouble with fiction . . . is that it makes too much sense. Reality never makes sense.'

Figure 4: RIL's Oil and Gas Business—Revenues and Profits (₹ crore)

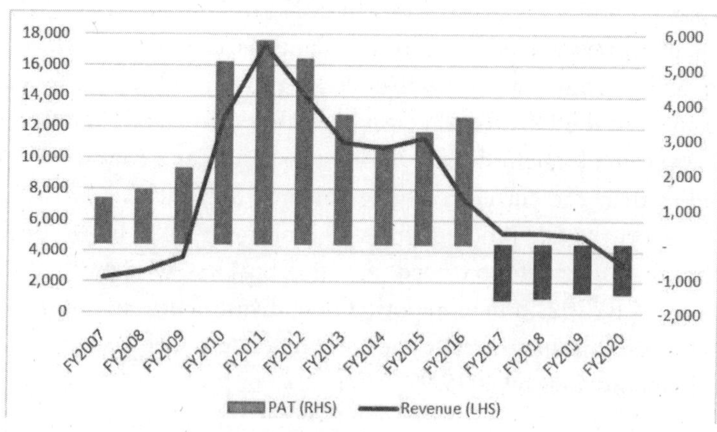

Source: RIL Annual Reports, FY2007 to FY2020

In March 2018, the CAG released the final performance audit report on hydrocarbon PSCs. The petroleum ministry and DGH received considerable flak for allowing RIL to retain the entire area of the KG-D6 fields without phase-wise relinquishment and for lack of oversight. The CAG's preliminary report questioned the exponential increase in the KG-D6 development costs and contended that RIL may have engaged in gold-plating. The final report did not dwell on these allegations.[21]

On 4 January 2019, the Standing Committee on Energy, chaired by Dr Kambhampati Haribabu, submitted its report on 'Stressed/Non-Performing Assets in Gas based Power Plants'. The report stated that, of the 24.9 megawatt (MW) installed capacity of gas-based power plants in India, 57 per cent or 14.30 GW, spread across 31 power plants, was stranded. All these power plants were planned based on the expectation of an increase in domestic gas production, particularly from the KG-D6 fields. Investments of ₹65,000 crore ($9.4 billion) were made in these 31 gas-based power plants, of which the share of bank loans was 77 per cent, or ₹50,000 crore ($7.3 billion).[22]

'Winners' and 'Losers'

Two groups of cousins—the Pandavas and the Kauravas—locked horns in the Kurukshetra War, the climactic confrontation of the Indian epic, the Mahabharata. The Kauravas fielded 2.4 million warriors while the Pandavas forces were 1.53 million strong. At the end of the thirteen-day war, only eleven warriors from both sides survived. All the hundred Kaurava brothers lost their lives. Although the five Pandava brothers survived the war, all their sons died on the battlefield. The Pandava dynasty was sustained by Abhimanyu's son, who was in his mother's womb at the time. There were no victors in this epic internecine war.

The Kurukshetra War is an apt analogy for the gas wars that unfolded in India during the first decade of the twenty-first century. The nation—with a population of over a billion—was the loser. The lower-than-announced natural gas output at the KG-D6 fields resulted in the country continuing to rely on a more polluting energy source—coal. Billions of dollars of investments, most of which were bank loans, made in gas-based power plants turned sour. Thirty-one power plants were stranded, of which one was owned by the central government, six by state governments and twenty-four by private companies (including R-Power). The loss of livelihoods, especially in private sector power plants, was yet another casualty. Anil Ambani's inability to secure natural gas supplies for the Dadri and Shahpur power plants was a fatal blow that considerably weakened ADAG.

Like the Pandavas' dynasty, RIL's franchise appears not to be dented by the reported decline in the conglomerate's natural gas output. In 2020, amidst the COVID-19 pandemic, RIL's multiple businesses raised over ₹2.60 lakh crore ($28.70 billion) from marque investors, including Facebook, Google and BP, and reduced its net debt substantially.

Chapter 17

Lakshagriha

The term 'banker' conjures images of energetic wheeler-dealers who execute multi-billion-dollar mergers, acquisitions and IPOs. In India, Hemendra Kothari, Nimesh Kampani and Udayan Bose exemplify frontline transaction closers. Hidden from the public eye is yet another category of rather unobtrusive bankers. They track the economy, industries and companies; they crunch spreadsheets and write reports. These bankers provide their more visible counterparts the intelligence required to close deals. They are known as analysts.

Analysts work hand-in-glove with frontline relationship managers and investment bankers to close deals. They are also the media's port of first call for insights on the economy, industry and specific companies. But seldom do analysts attain the renown that the above-mentioned investment bankers or bank CEOs like Aditya Puri, Naina Lal Kidwai and Uday Kotak have.

The analytical team at Credit Suisse, comprising Ashish Gupta, Kush Shah and Prashant Kumar, are an exception. They published a series of three reports titled 'House of Debt' in August 2012, August 2013 and October 2015. These reports, rightly, received wide coverage and acclaim. India's former chief economic adviser, Arvind Subramanian, hailed Ashish Gupta as 'one of the few heroes in India's sordid banking saga' in his book, *Of Counsel: The Challenges of the Modi–Jaitley Economy*.[1]

What did these reports portend?

India's Most Indebted

The August 2012 report highlighted that the robust 20 per cent growth Indian banks had registered in the preceding five years (FY2007–FY2012) was driven by a five-fold growth in loans extended to ten conglomerates. Outstanding debt at these ten corporate groups was equal to 13 per cent of bank loans and 98 per cent of the banking system's net worth.

"Will you stop saying 'the sky is the limit', please?"

Cartoon: Ravikanth Nandula. This cartoon was originally published in The Hindu BusinessLine. *Reproduced with permission.*

These groups operated in the cyclical and capital-intensive power and metals sector. Against the backdrop of India's slowing GDP growth, their gargantuan projects were stressed, leading to a deterioration in their financials. The ten conglomerates identified in the August 2012 report were, in alphabetical order, Adani, Essar, GMR, GVK, Jaypee, JSW, Lanco, (Reliance) ADAG, Vedanta and Videocon.

The Credit Suisse report dated August 2012 stated, 'Given the high leverage [debt], poor profitability and pressure from lenders, most of these debt heavy groups have initiated plans to divest some of their assets (cement plants / power / road projects). However, given that most domestic infra developers are already over geared, demand for these assets may be limited. Therefore, even as wholesale rates are showing signs of moderation, we remain cautious on corporate asset quality outlook for the banking sector . . . ' This report set the tone for the August 2013 and October 2015 reports.

The August 2013 'House of Debt' edition highlighted that the outstanding debt of these ten conglomerates had risen by 15 per cent in FY2013, even as their profitability was under pressure. Further, these corporates' borrowings for the year had exceeded their capital expenditure. In other words, they were borrowing to finance their operating expenditure. The situation was exacerbated as 40 to 70 per cent of these conglomerates' loans were denominated in foreign currencies and the depreciating rupee added to their debt burden. The Credit Suisse analysts had identified Reliance Communications, Reliance Infra and Reliance Power as vulnerable entities within ADAG.

Credit Suisse's October 2015 edition reported that the deleveraging initiatives of these ten conglomerates had not yielded results, and all of them were under financial stress. The credit rating agencies had downgraded 35 to 65 per cent of the debt of four conglomerates—Essar, GMR, Jaypee and Lanco groups—to default grade. Yet, banks continued to categorize loans to these entities as 'standard' loans.

This last edition of the 'House of Debt' report classified the quantum of debt under low, moderate and high stress for each of the ten conglomerates. Lanco Group was in the most precarious condition, with 95 per cent of its debt in the high stress category and the balance 5 per cent in moderate stress. The Vedanta Group appeared to be safest among the ten, with its entire debt falling in the moderate stress bucket. ADAG was still the third safest among the ten groups, with around 25 per cent of its debt in the low stress category, 52 per cent in moderate stress, and 23 per cent in high stress.[2]

The rationale for this categorization becomes clear when risk classification of loans is juxtaposed with these conglomerates' debt-to-EBITDA ratios. The debt of those conglomerates with lower debt-to-EBITDA ratios was deemed safer. The outliers were Videocon and GVK. Videocon's debt was assessed to be safer than Lanco, Jaypee and GMR despite the group reporting negative EBITDA. Similarly, the debt issued by GVK, whose debt-to-EBITDA ratio was the highest among the nine groups (excluding Videocon), was ranked safer than Lanco, Jaypee, GMR

Figure 1: Riskiness of the Debt Issued by India's Most Indebted Conglomerates, FY2015

	Low Risk Debt (%)	Moderate Risk (%)	High Risk (%)	Debt / EBITDA (Times)
Lanco		5.0	95.0	23.1
Jaypee		17.5	82.5	11.9
GMR	32.5		67.5	16.8
Videocon	25.0	10.0	65.0	Negative EBITDA
GVK	35.0		65.0	32
Essar	37.5		62.5	8.5
Adani	39.0	28.5	32.5	6.5
ADAG	25.0	52.5	22.5	6.8
JSW	15.0	85.0		4.2
Vedanta		100.0		2.3

Source: Credit Suisse's House of Debt, October 21 2015

and Videocon. Vedanta's debt to EBITDA ratio was a moderate 2.3 times. ADAG's debt-to-EBITDA ratio, though the fourth lowest among the ten conglomerates, was still high at 6.8 times.

The outstanding debt of six conglomerates—Lanco, Jaypee, GMR, Videocon, GVK and Essar—was even more excessive than ADAG in relation to their respective EBITDAs. However, ADAG had the highest outstanding debt among the ten conglomerates. ADAG was thus billed as India's most indebted company by the media.

According to Credit Suisse's 2012 report, ADAG's outstanding debt as of March 2012 was the third highest at around ₹86,700 crore ($18 billion). As per my calculations however, ADAG's debt was around 6 per cent higher at ₹91,497 crore ($19 billion), and the group was the most indebted in FY2012 itself. As ADAG's borrowing spree continued, the group performed a hat trick: it emerged as the most indebted among the ten conglomerates in FY2013, FY2014 and FY2015. Its debt had increased by 14 per cent to ₹1,24,956 crore ($20 billion) by FY2015. ADAG took umbrage at being labelled as India's most leveraged corporate. The group managing director, Amitabh Jhunjhunwala, asserted that the ADAG 'group companies have strong capitalisation, and have created assets of much larger magnitude than their peer groups across various infrastructure sectors'. He pointed out that the Tata Group, whose gross debt was more than twice ADAG's at around ₹3,00,000 crore ($49 billion), was, in fact the most indebted conglomerate in India.

Mint reported that Credit Suisse had not included the Tata Group, as the pace of growth of its debt was lower and its 'leverage and cash generation profile' was far better than the 'House of Debt' conglomerates.[3] In my opinion, this line of reasoning is flawed. The size of an entity's debt relative to its cash earnings is a key determinant of financial risk; the rate of growth of debt is secondary. Tata Group's cash rich software arm, Tata Consultancy Services, moderated the risk of the conglomerate. The aggregate debt of the Tata Group entities whose financials are in the public domain was ₹2,92,193 crore ($47.27 billion) as of 31 March 2015, according to Bloomberg data. However robust earnings resulted in a moderate debt-to-EBITDA ratio of 3.0 times and sizeable cash holdings translated to a lower net-debt-to-EBITDA-ratio of 2.10 times.

So, where was ADAG deploying all its borrowings?

Almost a decade had passed since Mukesh and Anil Ambani had divided the Reliance empire in 2006. By March 2015, ADAG's debt had grown more than five-fold to ₹1,24,952 crore ($20.2 billion). Its revenues too had grown almost ten times to ₹57,081 crore ($9.2 billion). However, its profits had more than halved from ₹90,351 crore ($2.2 billion) in FY2008 to ₹44,627 crore ($722 million) in FY2015. All of ADAG's businesses, except Reliance Capital, were performing poorly.

RCom, despite making sizeable investments to obtain a dual license (GSM in addition to CDMA) in October 2007, was unable to hold on to its market share, which had dropped from around 20 per cent in December 2006 to 10 per cent by December 2015. The halving of market share had resulted in a 90 per cent drop in post-tax profits from the FY2008 peak of ₹6794 crore ($1.62 billion) to ₹660 crore ($102 million) in FY2016. Bharti Airtel had retained market leadership with a 24 per cent share of subscribers, while Vodafone was not far behind with a 19 per cent share.

Though R-Power generated ₹896 crore ($138 million) profits from ₹10,622 crore ($1.64 billion) revenues in FY2016, the company was not functioning at maximum potential. Its inability to source natural gas from RIL had resulted in 42 per cent of its power plants, in terms of installed capacity, not coming onstream.

The performance of Reliance Energy, which was renamed as Reliance Infrastructure (RInfra), was lackadaisical. RInfra, which had started as a power utility, diversified into an infrastructure company engaged in the construction of roads, metro rail and airports and cement manufacturing. A defensive business, whose cash flows were relatively unaffected by business cycles, had become a capital intensive and cyclical business. The company's project portfolio was impressive: it had aggressively bid and won tenders for the construction of eleven roads traversing six states and the Mumbai and Delhi metro rail projects. Return on average assets had plummeted, though, from 4.85 per cent in FY2007 to less than 1 per cent in FY2016.

ADAG's finance arm, Reliance Capital, was the only entity whose post-tax profits more than doubled to ₹1265 crore ($195 million) since the demerger and had an unbroken track record of paying dividends for eleven consecutive years since the demerger. Reliance Capital had replaced RCom as ADAG's flagship company, with interests in asset management, broking, general and life insurance and lending.

The 2G Spectrum Allocation Case

ADAG's weakening financials were not the only cause for concern. RCom and Anil himself were embroiled in the 2G spectrum allocation case, which was dubbed as the biggest scam in post-independent India and ranked by *Time* magazine as the world's second biggest abuse of executive power following the Watergate scandal.

In May 2007, the DMK Member of Parliament, Andimuthu Raja, succeeded Dayanidhi Maran as the union telecom minister. On 25 September 2007, four months after Raja assumed office, the Department of Telecommunications (DoT) announced on its website that the application deadline for the 122 new second generation (2G) unified access service (UAS) licenses was 1 October 2007. The DoT received 575 applications from 46 companies. On 1 November, the Prime Minister's Office (PMO) wrote to Raja, directing him to ensure that the 2G spectrum allocation was conducted in a fair and transparent manner and to revise the spectrum fee. The finance ministry wrote to the telecom minister highlighting procedural concerns regarding the spectrum allocation process and demanded a review. Raja ignored these epistles.

On 10 January 2008, the DoT announced that it had narrowed the deadline to between 3.30 p.m. and 4.30 p.m. of 25 September 2007, and that companies who had applied within this window would be granted licenses on a first come, first serve basis. The DoT sold these licenses for ₹9200 crore ($2.11 billion) to eight applicants—Unitech, Sistema Shyam, Loop Telecom, Videocon, Etisalat DB Telecom (Swan Telecom), Idea Cellular-Spice, S Tel, and Tata Teleservices.

In September 2008, Etisalat, which was the second largest telecom company by market cap in the Middle East, announced the acquisition of a 49 per cent stake in Swan Telecom for ₹4113 crore ($900 million). Japan's leading telecom player, NTT DoCoMo, purchased a 26 per cent stake in Tata Teleservices for around ₹11,750 crore ($2.7 billion) in November 2008. By May 2009, Telenor, in which the Government of Norway held a 54 per cent share, acquired a 67.25 per cent stake in Unitech for ₹6,120 crore ($1.26 billion).

In 2008, Swan Telecom and Unitech had not started operations. TTSL was India's sixth largest telecom operator with a market share of 9.16 per cent. The rich valuations that TTSL, which was a middling player, and the new telecoms—Swan and Unitech—commanded was both a reflection of the Indian telecom industry's potential and the attractively priced licenses, which would enable the telecom companies to break-even faster.

In May 2009, two complaints were filed with the Central Vigilance Commission (CVC) alleging irregularities in the spectrum allocation to Loop Telecom and Swan Telecom. The CVC directed the CBI to investigate irregularities in the 2G spectrum allocation. The CBI investigated a wiretapped conversation by corporate lobbyist, Nira Radia, to uncover the involvement of middlemen in the award of licenses to telecoms. In March 2010, the Supreme Court upheld the Delhi High Court verdict that the advancement of the deadline by the DoT was illegal.

The Centre for Public Interest Litigation (CPIL), in May 2010, petitioned the Delhi High Court asking for a special investigation of the case. While the Delhi High Court dismissed the petition, the Supreme Court in September asked the government and

A. Raja to reply within ten days to three petitions filed by the CPIL and others alleging a ₹70,000 crore ($9.8 billion) scam in granting 2G telecom licenses.

The CAG, in November 2010, valued these licenses at ₹1.76 lakh crore ($40.5 billion), which was more than 19 times the ₹9200 crore ($2.11 billion) paid by the eight licensees. The CAG further alleged that Swan Telecom had served as a front for RCom to secure licenses in several circles.[4] Though the DoT filed a Supreme Court affidavit that the CAG lacked the authority to question the spectrum allocation, Raja resigned on 14 November 2010. Kapil Sibal replaced him as the union telecom minister. In January 2011, Sibal claimed that there was 'zero loss' on account of the government granting licenses to the eight companies in 2008.[5]

In February 2011, RCom clarified that its 9.9 per cent stake in Swan Telecom was within the legal ceiling of 10 per cent at the time of applying for 2G licenses and that information was in the public domain.[6] Subramaniam Swamy, who was then president of the Janata Party, petitioned the Supreme Court in January 2011 for the cancellation of the 2G licenses. The Supreme Court, in turn, notified the UPA government of Swamy's petition and issued notices to the 2G licensees who allegedly had not fulfilled the roll-out obligations or were ineligible. The apex court also challenged the government's decision to regularize the licenses of companies that had not met the criteria at the time of award.

Twenty months after the first complaint was filed with the CVC, heads started to roll. Raja, his former personal secretary, R. K. Chandolia, and former telecom secretary Siddharth Behura were arrested in February 2011. Raja was accused to have received a ₹3000 crore ($725 million) bribe through accounts in Seychelles and Mauritius held under his wife's name. Kanimozhi, the daughter of the DMK party supremo, M. Karunanidhi, and an MP, was arrested in May 2011 under charges of conspiring with Raja and another accused and diverting ₹200 crore ($48 million) to the DMK Party organ, *Kalaignar TV*. The eighteen accused and arrested in this case included ADAG's Group managing director, Gautam Doshi, and two senior vice-presidents, Hari Nair and Surendra Pipara.

In February 2012, the Supreme Court cancelled the 2G licenses issued to the eight companies. In August 2012, the Empowered Group of Ministers (EGoM) set the reserve price for the 2G spectrum auction at ₹14,000 crore ($2 billion), thereby validating the CAG's valuation of the 2G spectrum and disproving Sibal's 'zero loss' claim. A reserve price is the minimum or base price acceptable to the seller of a good or service in an auction. The Telecom Regulatory Authority of India (TRAI) had recommended a reserve price of ₹18,000 crore ($2,57 billion), which was 29 per cent higher than the price the EGoM had set.

Meanwhile, the CBI had inducted Anil Ambani as a witness. The court designated him as the prosecution witness. 'The understanding was that he could assist in the prosecution case against his own executives, who are accused in the 2G case of creating a web of shell companies within the ADAG Group that allegedly aided in transferring money to companies run by Karunanidhi's family members,' The Wire reported.[7]

Anil was, however, of little help. 'The picture it [Anil Ambani's testimony] paints is one of almost total memory loss on his part, at least as far as matters relating to 2G-related issues were concerned. As per his sworn testimony before the special CBI court, Anil Ambani remembers nothing of the companies he owns, the meetings chaired by him and, incredibly enough, whether he is even a promoter in some of the companies he runs.'[8] Wife, Tina Ambani, followed suit and testified that she was 'ordinarily a housewife' and had no recollection of the events relating to the 2G spectrum allocation.[9]

In December 2017, all eighteen accused in the 2G scam, including Raja, Kanimozhi and the three ADAG employees, were acquitted. Special CBI judge O.P. Saini declared in a packed courtroom, 'I have absolutely no hesitation in holding that prosecution has miserably failed to prove any of the charges against any of the accused.' The ED had lodged another case under the money laundering law arising out of the 2G spectrum allocation against Raja and Kanimozhi. The duo was acquitted in this case too.[10] The CBI and ED filed appeals against the verdict in the Delhi High Court in March 2018.

From FY2015, ADAG's profits started declining, even while the conglomerate's borrowing continued unabated. Reliance Capital's reported stable performance was inadequate to offset the declining profits and losses generated by RCom, RInfra, R-Power and Reliance Naval and Engineering (RNEL).

Like the Pandavas in the Mahabharata who were trapped in the Lakshagriha, or the house of lac, Anil was mired in political controversy and the deteriorating performance of his multiple businesses. Just as the Pandavas, aided by their uncle Vidura, engineered their escape from the Lakshagriha, did Anil Ambani have an escape route at this juncture?

Chapter 18

Chausar

Companies operating in the defence sector, though capital intensive, are protected by high barriers to entry in terms of government approvals and technology. They have a captive clientele—governments—whose contracts provide recurring and stable cash flows. Defence companies, on successfully navigating through their start-up phase and building a robust order book, tend to be profitable. ADAG's deteriorating financials did not deter, or probably impelled, Anil to acquire India's largest listed defence shipyard—Pipavav Defence and Offshore Engineering.

In FY2015, Pipavav Defence had reported a loss of ₹399 crore ($64 million) on revenues of ₹943 crore ($153 million). Pipavav Defence, like ADAG, was heavily indebted. The company's ₹6718 crore ($1 billion) debt was more than thrice its ₹1943 crore ($314 million) net worth. Creditors led by IDBI Bank were pressurizing Pipavav Defence's founder-chairman, Nikhil Gandhi, to either opt for corporate debt restructuring (CDR) or infuse equity in the firm. Nikhil Gandhi, who was unable to mobilize the equity stipulated by the lenders, began looking to divest his stake in Pipavav Defence.

The Defence Foray

There were potential suitors aplenty—ADAG, Mahindra & Mahindra, Hero MotoCorp and the French naval defence company,

DCNS SA. Pipavav Defence had also sent out feelers to L&T. Anil emerged victorious. Three factors went in his favour. *Mint* quoted an unnamed source as saying, 'Both the Munjals [Hero MotoCorp] and Mahindras were keen on doing extensive due diligence . . . But the Pipavav promoters were not willing to wait . . . [Anil] Ambani was willing to take a quick decision.'[1] Anil Ambani was also ready to pay cash immediately for Pipavav Defence's promoters' stake and follow this with an open offer to purchase a 26 per cent stake from retail and institutional shareholders. That ADAG offered to pay 10 per cent more than its rivals for Pipavav Defence's promoter stake did not hurt its prospects.

On 5 March 2015, RInfra announced its acquisition of an 18 per cent stake in Pipavav Defence for ₹819 crore ($128 million). RInfra had acquired the shares at ₹63 ($0.98) per share, which was 17.6 per cent lower than Pipavav Defence's prevailing share price. In the open offer, RInfra purchased shares from the public at ₹66 ($1.03 per share). It spent ₹1239 crore ($193 million) on the public offer and thus incurred a total cost of ₹2058 crore ($321 million) on the acquisition. The company was subsequently renamed Reliance Naval and Engineering Limited (RNEL).

Why was Anil Ambani in such a rush?

On 17 February 2015, the union government's cabinet committee on security had approved a ₹1,00,000 crore ($16 billion) outlay to build six nuclear-powered submarines and seven stealth warships. The Indian Navy was then assessing the capabilities of ABG Shipyard, L&T and Pipavav Defence to build the submarines through technology transfer from an overseas collaborator in a deal estimated at ₹50,000 crore ($8 billion). The last time there had been such a sizeable order was more than a decade ago, in 2002.

Anil believed that acquiring Pipavav Defence would facilitate its timely entry into the potentially booming defence sector. *Mint* quoted an unnamed source as saying, 'Amongst manufacturing defence equipment like guns or tanks or jets, naval is the quickest thing to do. Because it doesn't need much, you can yourself design from the open market and tech is minimal. All it needs is execution.'[2]

In 2015, the Indian defence industry was perceived as a sunrise sector. The country was projected to incur around $620 billion aggregate defence spending between 2014 and 2022, with capital expenditure accounting for half the outlay. In August 2014, the newly-elected BJP government had raised the FDI cap on defence manufacturing from 26 per cent to 49 per cent in the hope of transforming the nation from a leading buyer of expensive arms into an arms supplier to rich nations.

On 12 March 2015, The *Financial Express* reported that the union government had shortlisted L&T and Pipavav Defence for a ₹60,000 crore ($9.4 billion) contract to build six conventional submarines under its Project 75i.[3] The tender was to 'buy and make (in India)', which involved technological tie-ups with foreign collaborators and substantial manufacturing in India.

The Rafale Saga

Barely a month after Anil made his foray into defence, he was part of Prime Minister Modi's delegation on a state visit to France. The Indian prime minister made an unexpected announcement in Paris on 10 April 2015. He offered to buy thirty-six Rafale fighter jets manufactured by France's Dassault Aviation in a government-to-government (G2G) deal. *India Today* reported that even President Hollande was taken aback by the offer of a G2G deal. A senior Dassault official informed *India Today*, 'France never does G2G deals and does not have a Foreign Military Sales route like the US has.' It took France three months to set up a team headed by an air marshal from the Directorate General of Armaments (DGA), the government body that procures armaments for France's military.[4]

The proposal to purchase Rafale fighter jets was not new. On 31 January 2012, India's ministry of defence announced that

Dassault Aviation had won the tender to supply 126 medium multi-role combat aircraft (MMRCA) to the Indian Air Force, with an option to supply sixty-three more. Under the 2012 contract, Dassault Aviation would supply the first eighteen in a fly-away condition and would license the technology to state-owned Hindustan Aeronautics Limited (HAL) for the remaining 108 MMRCAs to be built in India. The UPA government announced that it had negotiated a price of ₹526 crore ($99 million) per aircraft. After protracted discussion regarding warranties and pricing, the deal fell through.

The deal announced by Prime Minister Modi in 2015 entailed the purchase of thirty-six Rafale MMRCAs, all in fly-away condition. India and France signed the memorandum of understanding in January 2016 and the inter-governmental agreement in September 2016. The NDA government stated that the new Dassault contract was negotiated at a price of ₹670 crore ($100 million) per aircraft. The minister of state for defence, Subash Bhamre, informed the Lok Sabha on 18 November 2016 that the newly-negotiated price did not include 'associated equipment, weapons, India-specific enhancements, maintenance support and services'. The Congress countered that the deal it had negotiated in 2012 was almost 22 per cent cheaper and included India-specific enhancements, maintenance support and services.

The Press Trust of India (PTI) filed a Right to Information (RTI) application to ascertain the price of the Rafale aircraft. The Indian Air Force (IAF) replied in February 2017 that 'the information sought is also held in fiduciary capacity and no larger public interest is served by disclosure of such information. Hence, the same is denied'.[5]

Unfortunately for the NDA government and IAF, the contract value disclosed by Dassault Aviation in its 2016 annual report suggested a much higher price that what the NDA government had declared on the floor of the Lok Sabha. Page 53 of Dassault Aviation's 228-page annual report of 2016 stated, 'The backlog as of December 31, 2016 was €20,323 million, compared to €14,175 million as of December 31, 2015. The increase is explained by the RAFALE India order in 2016.' This implied that the value of the contract to deliver thirty-six Rafale aircrafts to India was €6.15 billion (₹45,705 crore, $6.80 billion) and the price per aircraft was €171 million or ₹1270 crore.

The basis for the media reporting a price of ₹1639 crore ($255 million, €220 million) per Rafale jet is not known but pandemonium broke out in Parliament and the media. Rahul Gandhi called the government a '*suit-boot ki sarkar*' or a government that pandered to corporate interests.

The opposition parties vehemently opposed the deal and cried foul for two reasons. First, the cost per Rafale MMRCA negotiated by the NDA government appeared to be more than thrice the cost negotiated by the UPA. Second, the opposition parties alleged that the NDA government had favoured ADAG, which had no prior experience in defence manufacturing, and had sidelined state-owned HAL, India's sole aerospace and defence company.

Estimates of ADAG's share in the offset contracts varied widely from ₹900 crore ($132 million) by The *Economic Times*,[6] ₹3000 crore ($439 million) by Dassault itself,[7] and ₹21,000 crore ($3.1 billion) by *The Hindu BusinessLine*.[8] But they were all lower than the ₹30,000 crore ($4.50 billion) worth offset contracts, which ADAG declared it would accrue from its JV with Dassault Aviation.[9]

Key features of the offset contract were drowned in the cacophony around the deal. The offset clause was meant to strengthen India's defence manufacturing capabilities. The ₹30,000 crore ($4.50 billion) offsets were to be made in seven years (by 2023) by four companies—Dassault Aviation, Safran (the engine builder), Thales (the radar manufacturer) and MBDA (the missile maker). As the manufacturer of Rafale jets, Dassault Aviation's share in the offsets was highest at 50 per cent (₹15,000 crore, $2.25 billion), followed by Thales (22 per cent), Safran (18 per cent), and MBDA (10 per cent). The four companies had entered into agreements with seventy-two Indian firms, including ADAG, Bharat Forge, Godrej & Boyce, HAL, the Kalyani Group, Lakshmi Machine Works, L&T, Mahindra Aerostructure, Tata Advanced Systems, HCL, IBM India, L&T Infotech, Tata Consulting Services and Wipro.[10] ADAG held 51 per cent stakes in the JVs it had forged with Dassault (Dassault Reliance Aerospace Limited) and Thales (Thales Reliance Defence Systems). The foreign partners held 49 per cent stakes.

The deal NDA had swung suffered from other drawbacks too, as exposed by The Wire in a panel discussion whose participants were its founding editor, M.K. Venu, academic and columnist Happymon Jacob, and a retired colonel of the Indian Army and journalist, Ajai Shukla. In this panel discussion titled 'Rafale Deal: Understanding the Controversy', Ajai Shukla opined, 'It [Rafale] is a new deal with none of the benefits of the old deal and all the liabilities of the old deal. It is the worst of both worlds ... The offsets in the new deal have nothing to do with defence manufacturing. This [buying 36 Rafale jets vis-à-vis 126] is a serious blow to the defence of this country. From 2000 onwards, defence procurement has been mishandled by the first BJP government, two Congress governments, and now the second BJP government . . . The 126 aircrafts were meant to replace the single engine MIG21s and MIG27s the IAF was in the process of retiring. Quantity, as Stalin said, has a quality all of its own. Replacing an order for 126 Rafale jets to fill six squadrons with a 36 aircraft deal to fill two squadrons is a serious blow to defence preparedness. India has missed an opportunity to strengthen its manufacturing capabilities and defence ecosystem by not purchasing 126 aircraft with associated offsets.'[11]

The panellists pointed out that the IAF had approved both Rafale and Eurofighter jets. Dassault Aviation was awarded the contract to supply Rafale jets as it had quoted the lowest price among the bidders in 2012. However, certain contentious terms in the contract resulted in both the UPA government that was in power till 2014 and its successor, the NDA government, not being able to close the deal. It was these contentious terms that prompted NDA to scrap the old contract and enter into a new one in 2015. However, no tender was floated and Eurofighter's offer to reduce its price by 20 per cent was ignored.

M.K. Venu pointed out that Anil Ambani was already embroiled in the investigation and hearings of the 2G spectrum allocation case, which were underway from 2009 to 2018. In 2013, ADAG had backed out of the Delhi Airport Metro Express, touted as the fastest metro in India and the first one to be commissioned as a public-private partnership (PPP), citing lower-than-anticipated traffic. Yet, Anil was part of the delegation that accompanied Modi to meet the French President Francois Hollande in 2015, notwithstanding governance concerns and the conglomerate's debt overhang. These concerns heightened when it emerged that ADAG, through Reliance Entertainment, had thrown a ₹12 crore (€1.6 million) lifeline in 2017 to complete the production of actor-producer and Hollande's partner, Julie Gayet's film, *Tout là-haut*. Emmanuel Macron had succeeded Hollande as president of France in 2017. However, Reliance Entertainment's financing of Gayet's film was perceived as a quid pro quo. GoI had no qualms in blessing the JVs ADAG forged with Dassault Aviation and Thale.

In March 2018, a public interest litigation was filed in the Supreme Court seeking an independent probe into the union government's decision to procure thirty-six Rafale jets and the disclosure of their cost in Parliament. On 21 September 2018, Hollande informed a French publication, *Mediapart*, that it was the GoI that had recommended RNEL as the offset partner for Dassault Aviation. Hollande's statement contradicted what the then defence minister, Nirmala Sitharaman, had informed the media just three days earlier: 'I've not put his [Anil Ambani's] name or anyone in the Inter-Governmental Agreement nor can I tell a commercial firm to enter into an agreement.'[12]

In October 2018, the Supreme Court directed the union government to furnish, in a 'sealed cover', details regarding the agreements to procure the Rafale jets and the decision-making process. That very month, former BJP union ministers Arun Shourie and Yashwant Sinha, along with activist lawyer Prashant Bhushan, sought registration of a first information report (FIR) into the Rafale fighter jet deal. Following this, the Supreme Court gave the union government ten days' time to submit the 'sealed covers'. In November 2018, the union government provided 'sealed covers' with the pricing and information relating to the acquisition of the Rafale jets.

On 14 December 2018, a Supreme Court bench headed by CJI Ranjan Gogoi dismissed all petitions stating that it had studied the matter extensively and was 'satisfied that there is no occasion to doubt the process [of signing the Rafale deal]'. In its judgement, the apex court also noted that the pricing details had been shared with CAG, and the report of the CAG had been examined by Parliament's Public Accounts Committee (PAC). However, Congress leader Mallikarjun Kharge, who chaired the PAC, observed that no such report had come to him. On 15 December 2018, the union government filed an application in the Supreme Court seeking correction in a paragraph in its judgement in which references were made to the CAG report and PAC.[13]

On 2 January 2019, Arun Shourie, Yashwant Sinha and Prashant Bhushan moved the apex court seeking a review of the verdict and a fortnight later, the Aam Aadmi Party MP Sanjay Singh also filed a review petition in the Supreme Court. In February 2019, Prashant Bhushan sought hearing on the plea seeking perjury prosecution of some officials for misleading the Supreme Court. By end February, the Supreme Court announced that it would hear the plea seeking review of the Rafale verdict in open court.

An element of drama arose when the government informed the apex court that documents relating to the Rafale deal were stolen from the defence ministry. The union government alleged that the exposé by India's national newspaper, *The Hindu*, was based on these stolen documents and that it would pursue action against the newspaper under the Official Secrets Act. In March

2019, Attorney General K.K. Venugopal performed a volte face and stated that what he meant in his submission was that *The Hindu* used 'photocopies of the original' papers, deemed secret by the government.[14] In April 2019, the Supreme Court allowed the leaked documents, dismissing the government's plea that these papers would jeopardize national security.[15]

On 14 November 2019, the Supreme Court dismissed the pleas seeking reviews of its 2018 verdict stating, 'We find the review petitions are without any merit'. The unanimous judgement in effect gave the NDA a clean chit for the second time. However, Justice K.M. Joseph, a member of the apex court's bench, penned a dissent note, which held that the judgment would 'not stand in the way' if the CBI, after securing government approval, were to register an FIR on the basis of the complaint raised by the petitioners.[16]

The CAG report that the apex court's verdict referred to was quite critical of the union government, though. The process of acquisition of air assets starts with the formulation of user requirements known as the Air Staff Qualitative Requirements (ASQR). The CAG observed that the ASQR was repeatedly changed while purchasing Rafale jets. A Contract Negotiation Committee (CNC) is constituted to evaluate the price bid and negotiate the final contract. Before opening the price bid, the CNC is required to estimate the benchmark price, which is used to assess the various bids. The CAG noted that in eight cases, the benchmark price was significantly different from the bid price. It observed that repeated off-the mark pricing reveals an inability to estimate the market price. The government auditor recommended a simplification of the complex and multi-level approval process, which led to delays in the acquisition of air assets.[17]

Contrary to the defence ministry's claim that the 2016 contracted price of the thirty-six basic fly-away Rafale jets was 9 per cent cheaper than the 2007 price, the CAG observed that the 2016 price was 2.86 per cent cheaper. However, Dassault Aviation had provided financial and performance guarantees that constituted a quarter of the contract value as part of the 2007 contract. There was no guarantee or warranty in the 2016 contract and Dassault Aviation had not shared the resultant savings with the GoI. The CAG report stated that the 2007 contract included transfer of technology or license to HAL for the production of 108 Rafale jets. But no such transfer of technology was provided under the 2016 contract.[18]

Notwithstanding the high decibel campaign mounted by the opposition, accusing the NDA and Prime Minister Modi of corruption and crony capitalism, the Rafale deal did not dent the prime minister's franchise. Unlike Anil, Modi emerged stronger from the controversy. This was a major issue in the run-up to the 2019 union elections. The NDA won 353 seats in the Lok Sabha with a combined vote share of 45.43 per cent in the 2019 general elections; a significant improvement over its 336 seats and 38.5 per cent vote share in the 2014 elections. But the defence foray and Rafale controversy only added to Anil Ambani's woes.

High Stakes

What started as a deceptively cordial game of dice or chausar between the Pandavas and the Kauravas led to Yudhishtir, the eldest Pandava brother, pledging and losing his kingdom, his four brothers and himself, and their wife, Draupadi. It was evident that Mukesh was keen to transform the domestic market leader—RIL—to an international titan. His decisions, sometimes to the detriment of ADAG, facilitated RIL's evolution into one of the world's largest corporates. Anil, too, did not shy from crossing swords with Mukesh. His quest for supremacy and ambition to match, if not surpass RIL, may have propelled Anil's gambit to enter defence. But, in doing so, he committed the same error as Goyal and Mallya, who were unable to successfully integrate the Air Sahara and Air Deccan acquisitions, which were made at high cost and by incurring sizeable debt with their businesses.

Anil did not ensure that RNEL snapped out of its loss-making track record and pay down its debts before forging JVs with Dassault Aviation and Thale to manufacture fighter jet components. Opposition politicians never tired of highlighting his lack of experience in the sector and the mountain of debt ADAG had accumulated. RNEL's and RInfra's lacklustre performance, when juxtaposed with RCom and R-Power fiascos, cast serious doubts on the one attribute that Anil was keen to showcase—execution.

Chapter 19

Agyatvasa?

In June 2010, the GoI auctioned a part of its telecom spectrum. There were not many takers as the incumbent telecom companies did not find the bandwidth particularly attractive. An inconspicuous internet service provider (ISP) registered at Ambavadi in Ahmedabad, Gujarat, Infotel Broadband Services Private Limited (IBSPL), won the auction by placing the winning bid of ₹12,847.77 crore ($2.81 billion). Hours after the auction, RIL acquired a 95 per cent stake in IBSPL for ₹4800 crore ($1.05 billion). RIL's acquisition of IBSPL occurred during the very month the Ambani brothers had scrapped their non-compete agreement. An executive from an incumbent telco admitted, 'We would have entered the bidding if we had known Mukesh was going to end up owning this bandwidth . . . (By emerging from) behind this unknown company, he managed to get the spectrum at a far cheaper price.'[1]

Regulatory Capture?

The terms of RIL's license did not allow it to launch voice services. In 2013, TRAI, at GoI's behest, fortuitously permitted licensees to transmit both voice and data calls. RIL paid a ₹1660 crore ($283 million) 'migration fee' to become a full-fledged telecom player.

Initially, this move attracted the CAG's censure. In a 2014 draft report, the CAG opined, 'the DoT [department of telecom] failed to recognize the tell-tale sign of rigging of the auction right from beginning of the auction' in which IBSPL, ranked 150th in the list of ISPs, won the license for pan-India broadband spectrum by paying 5000 times its net worth. The CAG also stated that IBSPL, a small ISP, had submitted an earnest money deposit of ₹252.50 crore ($43 million) 'through the covert and overt assistance of third party/private bank . . . Due to inclusion of inadequate eligibility criterion for participation in the auction, the promoters of the IBSPL enriched themselves and made unfair gain. The IMC (inter-ministerial committee) did not satisfy itself as to how IBSPL, a company with a net worth of Rs 2.5 crore ($0.55 million), would be able to pay the bid amount of Rs 12,847.77 crore ($2.81 billion) within 10 days.' The CAG quantified the resultant loss to the GoI to be ₹22,842 crore ($5 billion). The government auditor recommended that the licenses be cancelled and the spectrum be auctioned again.

IBSPL, which was subsequently renamed Reliance Jio, responded, 'There is no final CAG report that we are aware of. That said, we outrightly reject any suggestion whereby spectrum was acquired in any manner other than through a transparent bidding process duly supervised by Government of India.'[2]

The CAG's final report in 2015 pared down its estimate of the loss incurred by GoI by almost 85 per cent to ₹3370 crore ($575 million) and did not mention the cancelling of licenses. When reporters questioned Suman Saxena, the deputy CAG, about the stark discrepancies between the draft and final reports, he responded, 'A draft is a draft.'[3]

Jio then circumvented the requirement to obtain TRAI's approval for its pricing plan by distributing millions of free SIM cards to subscribers during the trial period ahead of its formal launch in September 2016. In an August 2016 letter to GoI, the Cellular Operators Association of India (COAI) complained about the behaviour of its newest member. 'This is no test . . . This is the provisioning of full-blown and full-fledged services, masquerading as tests, which bypass regulations and can potentially game policy features.'[4]

Jio's entry strategy was identical to RCom's when the latter launched its telecom services fourteen years ago in December 2002. It resorted to price undercutting. Reliance Jio gave away voice calls for free and data for a pittance. Competitors accused Jio of predatory pricing and violating TRAI's guidelines by offering six months of giveaways. In 2002, TRAI had warned companies not to issue promotional offers for more than ninety days. Bharti Airtel lodged a complaint with the Competition Commission of India (CCI) in 2017. However, Jio's competitors' grievances did not get traction with the CCI or TRAI. Instead, the CCI ruled that Jio could not undermine the competition as it was not the market's dominant player. To make matters worse, TRAI ruled in 2015 that the three biggest telecom players—Bharti Airtel, Vodafone and Idea—were deliberately dropping calls made by Jio's subscribers and imposed a ₹1 fine per dropped call. The Supreme Court overturned this ruling the very next year.

Jio, in turn, complained in 2016 that over 75 per cent of calls on its network were failing as the three largest telecom companies did not release a sufficient number of points of interconnection. TRAI imposed a penalty of ₹1050 crore ($156 million) each on Bharti Airtel and Vodafone and a ₹950 crore ($141 million) penalty on Idea. The three incumbents protested that they did not have enough time to respond to Jio's expansion. But the Digital Communications Commission upheld TRAI's decision.

Thanks to Jio offering unlimited free voice calls to its subscribers, they were making eight times as many calls as they were receiving. This meant Jio had to pay its competitors a ₹0.14 interconnect usage charge (IUC) every time its user called a subscriber of another network. This pushed up Jio's costs. In July 2018, Jio submitted to TRAI that the IUC be abolished to encourage competitors to emulate Jio's cost-effectiveness by using 4G mobile technology to carry voice calls. Jio's competitors lobbied hard against this suggestion, highlighting that Jio would benefit by ₹5000 crore ($731 million) at the expense of the other incumbents. Nevertheless, two months later, TRAI obligingly slashed the IUC by 57 per cent and abolished this charge altogether by January 2020.

Jio's blitzkrieg entry and competitiveness resulted in Vodafone and Idea merging in 2018 and Bharti Airtel and Tata Teleservices' mobile arm merging in 2019. Jio effectively lobbied for a 43 per cent reduction in call termination charges for incoming international calls paid to Indian telcos by their foreign counterparts from ₹0.53 to ₹0.30 per minute. The resultant losses to Jio's competitors were estimated to be ₹2000 crore ($292 million). Jio's revenues, too, were adversely impacted. However, the company, in single-minded pursuit of market leadership, was willing to forego revenues.

Rajan Mathews, director-general of the COAI, quipped, 'In 40 years I did not see a single instance where a regulator was accused of bias. But now there is clear partisanship in favour of Jio.' Rohit Chordia, an analyst at Kotak Institutional Equities, observed, 'They're (Jio) giving up on future revenues for the sake of hurting the incumbents now.'[5]

The incumbent most hurt by Jio's relentless lobbying and competitive pricing was RCom. By end December 2016, within four months of its formal launch, Jio had acquired 72.16 million subscribers with a 6.40 per cent market share. RCom lost 14.35 million consumers during the calendar year 2016 and its market share dipped from 9.98 per cent in December 2015 to 7.68 per cent in December 2016. In 2017 and 2018, RCom lost 53.37 million and 33.15 million subscribers respectively. By December 2018, RCom had merely 22,000 subscribers and its market share were practically zero. The company filed for bankruptcy in February 2019.

Strategic Errors

The seeds of RCom's downfall from being India's largest mobile operator with a 10.15 million subscriber base and a 21 per cent market share as of December 2004 were in part sown in a genuine error in judgement that occurred before the Ambani brothers split. RCom, along with Tata Teleservices, Sistema Shyam Teleservices and BSNL, had adopted the CDMA technology, which worked well with 2G and 3G networks. The rival GSM technology adopted by Bharti Airtel and Vodafone was, however, better suited for the newer 4G and 5G networks. The incremental investments RCom made to adopt GSM technology in a fundamentally capital-intensive industry beset with high levies and taxes undermined its viability. This predicament was not unique to RCom. GoI continues to support the loss-making BSNL, while CDMA users like Tata Teleservices and Sistema Shyam merged with Bharti Airtel and RCom respectively.

The migration from CDMA to GSM was not the sole cause for RCom's failure. Bharti Airtel's fortuitously correct choice of technology and the vision of its chairperson, Sunil Mittal, enabled it to emerge as the market leader. In the rapidly growing Indian telecom market, RCom's subscribers grew ten-fold to 101 million subscribers from 10.15 million in December 2004; yet its market share declined to 10 per cent in December 2015. During this eleven-year period, Bharti Airtel's subscribers grew 24-fold to 243 million, with a market share of 24 per cent. Bharti Airtel's customers increased to 263 million in 2016, the year Reliance Jio entered the market. While RCom's subscriber base shrunk to 87 million, Jio garnered 72 million users and a market share of 6.4 per cent in the very first year of operations. RCom's and Tata Teleservices' customers moved to Jio, whose price plans had rendered voice and data affordable to users who had hitherto not used mobile phones. By FY2017, RCom had started generating losses and its ₹45,733 crore debt ($6.86 billion) exceeded its net worth by almost 58 per cent.

Lenders Support

Like the struggling enterprises run by VGS, Goyal, Mallya and other well-connected tycoons, the Anil Ambani-promoted RCom continued to enjoy lenders' support. In June 2017, RCom and its creditors negotiated an out-of-court restructuring, which entailed the company to merge with its rival carrier, Aircel and sell its cellular towers to Canada's Brookfield Infrastructure Group; the lenders also graciously agreed to swap some of RCom's debt to equity without requiring Anil to inject additional equity. However, Aircel's attempted merger with RCom and, subsequently, Bharti Airtel, did not go through. Neither did Brookfield's proposed purchase of RCom's towers fructify. Fortunately, unlike in the Kingfisher Airlines' debt-to-equity swap, lenders realized that RCom's share price, which listed at ₹300 in March 2006 and had hit a peak of ₹772 in October 2007, had consistently trended downwards for almost a decade, with minimal prospects of recovery after Jio's big bang entry. The debt-to-equity swap, which was negotiated when RCom's price was trading at ₹21.50 on 1 June 2017, did not go through.

By November 2017, RCom was unable to pay even a modest interest of around ₹65 crore ($9.75 million) on its $300 million foreign currency bonds. Lenders rallied around RCom again and brokered a deal for the beleaguered carrier to sell its spectrum, towers, fibre and media convergence nodes to Jio. This time around, the sale of telecom assets to Jio and commercial development of RCom's Mumbai property was expected to result in bondholders recovering three-fourths of the principal or $225 million.[6]

Storm Clouds

Meanwhile, by September 2017, the Swedish telecom group Ericsson initiated legal action against RCom. In January 2013, RCom and Ericsson had signed a managed service agreement (MSA) that mandated the latter to manage RCom's wireline and wireless network covering more than 100,000 kilometres of fibre and mobile infrastructure in eleven telecom circles, across the north and west of India, including Delhi and Mumbai. From 2016,

RCom had started delaying payments to Ericsson. In September 2017, Ericsson issued RCom a notice for the termination of the MSA, alleging non-payment of dues. The same month, Ericsson petitioned the NCLT to recover ₹1100 crore ($158 million) dues from RCom.[7]

Other creditors joined the fray. Between October and December 2017, Tech Mahindra and China Development Bank (CDB) filed an insolvency case against the ADAG carrier with the Mumbai bench of NCLT under the 2016 Insolvency and Bankruptcy Code. It became evident that RCom was not paying its operational and financial creditors. Operational creditors are firms like Ericsson and Tech Mahindra that provide goods and services on credit to their clients while financial creditors are lenders including banks, bondholders and lessors of equipment.

RCom attempted to address the situation through a debt resolution proposal in October 2017, under which the sale of telecom assets to Jio, ₹17,000 crore ($2.62 billion) worth asset monetization, and ₹10,000 crore ($1.5 billion) through sale and development of real estate would pare down its ₹45,733 crore ($7 billion) debt. RCom stated that it was aiming for a 'Zero Loan Write-off Plan', which would result in lenders recovering their dues in full.[8]

RCom's precarious financial state did not inspire trust. NCLT accepted Ericsson's petition and initiated insolvency proceedings against RCom, which at this juncture was still trying to sell its telecom assets to Jio. On 29 May 2018, RCom offered an upfront settlement of ₹550 crore ($79 million), which was half of Ericsson's claim, on the condition that Ericsson withdraw the insolvency petition. On 3 August 2018, the Supreme Court ordered RCom to pay the upfront settlement by 30 September. RCom failed to comply with the apex court's directive and sought a sixty-day extension from Ericsson, which refused and filed a contempt of court petition against Anil Ambani. When RCom moved the apex court for a deadline extension, its plea was initially dismissed. The apex court, however, did grant an additional sixty-day extension through its 23 October 2018 order. RCom failed to meet the second deadline and, in February 2019, filed a contempt of court petition against DoT for failing to furnish a no-objection certificate clearing Jio's acquisition of RCom's telecom assets. Jio's unwillingness to assume RCom's spectrum liabilities was the stumbling block.

This move did not go down well with the apex court. On 19 February 2019, the Supreme Court found RCom, Anil and two other group firms guilty of contempt of court and accused the defendants of adopting a 'cavalier attitude' despite the apex court lending a 'helping hand' to enable the beleaguered carrier to settle its dues to Ericsson. The bench ordered RCom to settle its dues within four weeks, failing which Anil and two senior RCom executives—Satish Seth and Chaya Virani—would be imprisoned for three months each. The apex court also imposed a ₹1 crore ($142,000) fine each on three ADAG companies—RCom, Reliance Telecom and Reliance Infratel.[9]

RCom did not pay Ericsson's dues during the intervening four weeks. The telecom company ultimately settled the dues on the last cut-off date stipulated by the Supreme Court—18 March 2019.

Sibling Support?

In RCom's filing with the stock exchanges, Anil Ambani thanked his brother and sister-in-law for supporting him. The media frenzy this announcement attracted overshadowed Ericsson winning the case against RCom and recovering its dues.

The wording of RCom's media release and the coverage that followed perpetuated the impression that Asia's richest man had extended financial assistance to avert his brother's imprisonment in the nick of time. It then emerged that the funds from a commercial transaction between Jio and RCom had enabled the ADAG company to settle Ericsson's dues. According to RCom's FY2019

Figure 1: RCom's Filing with the Bombay Stock Exchange

RELIANCE Media Release

Mumbai, 18th March, 2019:

A RCOM spokesperson stated:

The requisite payment of Rs. 550 crore and interest thereon to Ericsson has been completed today in compliance of the judgment of the Hon'ble Supreme Court.

Mr. Anil D. Ambani, Chairman, RCOM, said "My sincere and heartfelt thanks to my respected elder brother, Mukesh, and Nita, for standing by me during these trying times, and demonstrating the importance of staying true to our strong family values by extending this timely support. I and my family are grateful we have moved beyond the past, and are deeply grateful and touched with this gesture."

For details, please contact:

Rajeev Narayan
Reliance Communications
Mobile: +91 9310414119
E-Mail: rajeev.narayan@relianceada.com

Source: Reliance Communications

annual report, the company raised ₹974 crore ($141 million) from the sale of its assets. Both RIL and RCom did not disclose the nature of the transaction.

Delayed Downgrade

RCom had barely managed to settle Ericsson's dues when, in 2019, two more crises cropped up. On 20 September 2019, CARE Ratings downgraded what appeared to be the sole relatively stable ADAG company, Reliance Capital, by eight notches to the lowest rating of D, implying default. Two months later, a trio of Chinese banks—Industrial and Commercial Bank of China (ICBC), CDB and Export-Import Bank of China (Exim China)—initiated legal proceedings against the company and Anil at a London court.

Reliance Capital was a conglomerate within a conglomerate—a financial conglomerate ADAG controlled. As a non-banking finance company (NBFC) with an asset base of ₹83,973 crore ($12 billion) as of March 2019, Reliance Capital was larger than several Indian private sector banks including RBL Bank, Karnataka Bank and Karur Vysya Bank. Reliance Nippon Asset Management Company (RNAMC), Reliance Nippon Life Insurance, Reliance General Insurance, Reliance Health Insurance, Reliance Home Finance, Reliance Securities, Reliance Commercial Finance and Reliance Asset Reconstruction were all constituents of Reliance Capital. The Japanese insurance major, Nippon Life, held a 49 per cent stake in Reliance Nippon Life Insurance and close to 43 per cent stake in RNAMC, which was India's fifth largest mutual fund in 2019.

RBI had designated Reliance Capital as a systemically important core investment company (CIC) with effect from 31 August 2018. RBI defines a systemically important CIC as an NBFC with assets in excess of ₹100 crore ($ 14.5 million) that has invested at least 90 per cent of its net assets in the equity, debt and hybrids of its group companies. Net assets are a CIC's total assets less cash and bank balances, investments in money market instruments and mutual funds, advance payments of taxes and deferred tax payments. Simply put, a systemically important entity is a large entity whose collapse would threaten the stability of the financial sector.

CARE Ratings had assigned the highest credit rating 'AAA' to Reliance Capital from November 2008 to March 2017, when it was downgraded by one notch to 'AA+'. In October 2018, CARE downgraded it by another notch to 'AA' and placed it on 'rating watch to developing implications'. CARE attributed the credit rating downgrade to the delay in ADAG selling its assets and paring down debt. The rationale for placing the rating 'on watch with developing implications' was the continued exposure to RCom, which CARE had rated D. Reliance Capital's second downgrade in as many years occurred a month after IL&FS' first default came to light. In March 2019, CARE downgraded Reliance Capital by two notches to 'A+', while maintaining the 'rating watch to developing implications'. In addition to the reasons attributed to the previous downgrades, CARE stated the 'higher proportion of promoters shares being pledged' resulting in 'moderation in financial flexibility'. This was followed by a series of back-to-back negative rating actions. CARE downgraded Reliance Capital by one more notch to 'A' in April, by three notches to 'BBB' in May, by three notches to 'BB' in August and finally by eight notches to 'D' in September 2019. The CRA had also changed the rating watch to one with 'negative implications' from 'developing implications' in July 2019.[10]

After maintaining Reliance Capital's credit rating at the highest 'AAA' in the eight-year and four-month period ended March 2017, CARE downgraded the NBFC's rating by nineteen notches to the lowest 'D' in the ensuing two years and four months. At least five factors support the hypothesis that CARE Ratings' assessment of Reliance Capital's debt servicing ability was a tad too optimistic and the CRA had delayed communicating key risks to investors.

First, by 2012, ADAG was among India's most indebted conglomerates. ADAG was included in all three editions of Credit Suisse's 'House of Debt' report published between August 2012 and October 2015. Yet, CARE failed to report the extent of Reliance Capital's exposure to the highly leveraged ADAG constituents and its impact on the NBFC's debt servicing ability in its rating rationales during this period. Reliance Capital was assigned 'AAA' till March 2017, even as ADAG's elevated debt continued to spiral out of control.

Second, Reliance Capital's struggle to refinance its debt heightened, like most other NBFCs in India, after IL&FS's default in September 2018. Though CARE progressively downgraded Reliance Capital's rating from 'AAA' in March 2017 to 'BBB' in May 2019, these are essentially investment-grade ratings. Prudent debt levels and felicity in refinancing debt characterize entities rated investment grade. It was only in August 2019 that Reliance Capital's rating was downgraded to the non-investment grade 'BB'.

Third, a regulatorily mandated change in accounting regime to Indian Accounting Standards (Ind AS) occurred with effect from FY2019 from the Indian Generally Accepted Accounting Principles (GAAP). The restated FY2018 financials indicated that Reliance Capital had reported a ₹4556 crore ($691 million) loss under Ind AS vis-à-vis the ₹1309 crore ($199 million) profit under Indian GAAP. In FY2019, the NBFC again reported a loss, although the loss had narrowed to ₹1454 crore ($211 million). Reliance Capital, notwithstanding the loss, paid ₹412 crore dividends ($60 million), a 43 per cent increase over the ₹289 crore ($44 million) paid in FY2018. While Reliance Capital paying dividends in FY2018 was understandable as the NBFC had reported profits under Indian GAAP, paying higher dividends in FY2019 out of its reserves debilitated its financial profile and raised corporate governance concerns.

Fourth, Reliance Capital's statutory auditors, Pathak H.D. & Associates, had issued a qualified Independent Auditors Report in FY2019. The audit firm had highlighted the need for Reliance Capital to strengthen its loan-processing documentation and observed that the internal financial control systems of Reliance Commercial Finance and Reliance Home Finance were not operating effectively. Further, the audit firm reported that Reliance General Insurance's valuation of investments did not consider rating downgrades of certain investee companies. CARE failed to share both its views on the impact of Reliance Capital paying dividends out of reserves and the operational weaknesses highlighted by the auditors.

Fifth, promoters of the ADAG companies led by Anil had started pledging their stakes since FY2015. The need to provide additional collateral both on account of declining share prices and the conglomerate's escalating borrowing resulted in a significant increase in the percentage of promoters' shares pledged in FY2017. However, CARE highlighted the pledging of promoter stake as a risk only in March 2019. CARE's overdue rating downgrade was ill-timed. In the aftermath of the IL&FS collapse and the credit rating downgrade, Reliance Capital's funding sources dried up.

Anil's woes were compounded by the troika of Chinese banks initiating legal action against RCom and Anil at the Commercial Division of the High Court of England and Wales in London.

Chinese Aggression

ICBC, CDB and Exim China had extended $925.2 million (₹4475 crore) loans to RCom in 2012. These lenders alleged that RCom, which had been defaulting since 2018, owed the three banks around $717 million (₹3468 crore), and that Anil Ambani had not honoured the personal guarantee he had provided. Further, the banks asserted that a personal guarantee was part of the transaction, making Anil personally liable for the debt under English law. Anil denied that he had provided a personal guarantee. A personal guarantee is an individual's legal promise to repay the debt borrowed by the business they helm.

A senior RCom executive had been dispatched to Hong Kong to execute the loan documentation in 2012. The *Financial Times* reported that Anil Ambani 'had no knowledge when he gave his lieutenant power of attorney to sign on his behalf, it would be used for anything more than a non-binding "comfort letter" assuring the banks that the debt would be repaid'. Justice Waksman was sceptical, observing that had RCom executives furnished a personal guarantee without due authorization, it would amount to 'serious dishonesty and deception without obvious motive'. The judge said in its December 2019 ruling, 'I consider that Mr Ambani's evidence is inexplicably incomplete, implausible and highly unlikely.' The judge also said in February 2020 that Anil Ambani had been 'caught out on a lie' for suggesting he would not give a personal guarantee of such nature, after it was revealed in court filings that he had already done so to the State Bank of India.[11]

Figure 2: Gross and Pledged Stake of ADAG Promoters led by Anil Ambani

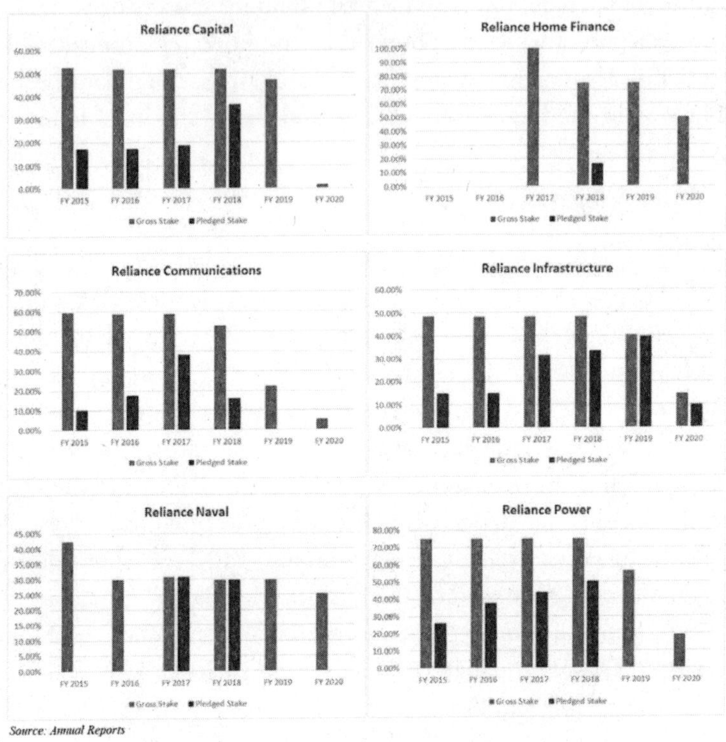

Source: Annual Reports

By September 2020, the Chinese banks had obtained an asset disclosure order requiring Anil to disclose the assets he owned worldwide in excess of $100,000 (₹75 lakh). Anil's lawyers informed the High Court in London that RCom's holding company, Reliance Innoventures, had a negative net worth of $412 million (₹2900 crore) by end 2019. Anil further averred that, contrary to the popular perception of a lavish lifestyle, 'My needs are not vast and my lifestyle is very disciplined.' An RCom spokesperson stated, 'Mr Anil Ambani has always been a simple man of simple tastes, contrary to exaggerated perceptions of his flamboyance and lavish lifestyle . . . He is devoted to his family and company, an avid marathon runner and deeply spiritual. He is also a lifelong vegetarian, teetotaler and non-smoker who would much rather watch a movie at home with his kids than go out on the town. Reports that suggest otherwise are completely misleading.'[12]

These depositions did not find much traction with the London High Court. Judge Waksman had earlier opined, 'Mr Ambani has, and continues to have, a very lavish lifestyle . . . I just do not accept that his own available assets are as limited or as negative as he says . . . He clearly has more assets and / or income than he is letting on.'[13] In May 2020, the London court ruled that the personal guarantee was binding on Anil Ambani and directed him to pay $717 million to the three Chinese banks within three weeks.

Justice Waksman's incredulity was probably not misplaced. According to the Pandora Papers released in October 2021, Anil and his associates set up eighteen offshore companies in Jersey, British Virgin Islands and Cyprus between 2007 and 2010 that borrowed and invested at least $1.3 billion.

Although Anil had lost the case at the UK court, him facing detractors head on did garner attention. But this did not mean he was immune to the Yes Bank collapse, in which ADAG had a role to play.

Hardik Rajgor

I have respect for Anil Ambani. While other businessmen took Indian money and fled to the UK, he took money from Chinese banks in the UK and is failing to pay it back whilst living in India. Go vocal for local.

Twitter Web App

Yes Bank Saga

September 2018 would go down in the annals of India Inc as one of its most eventful months. It was during this month that troubles brewing at IL&FS and Yes Bank came to light. IL&FS's first default coincided with RBI's refusal to extend the term of Yes Bank's CEO, Rana Kapoor, in September 2018. Rana Kapoor, whom industry watchers had dubbed as the lender of last resort, had a penchant for lending to high-risk borrowers including ADAG, Jet Airways, Kingfisher Airlines and CDEL. Yes Bank used to charge hefty upfront fees while extending loans to shore up its profits.

The slowdown in India's macroeconomy had worsened the debt servicing ability of Yes Bank's highly leveraged borrowers and resulted in an accumulation of non-performing loans (NPLs). While Yes Bank managed to recover its dues from Kingfisher Airlines and CDEL, ADAG was its largest non-performing borrower with outstanding dues of ₹12,800 crore ($1.80 billion) as of March 2020. The NPLs on account of Jet Airways had amounted to ₹1100 crore ($154 million).

The accumulation of NPLs resulted in RBI writing down the ₹8415 crore ($1.24 billion) additional tier-1 (AT1) bonds issued by Yes Bank by 100 per cent. The misleadingly named AT1 bonds are hybrid securities that incorporate the features of debt and equity with no maturity date. But the bank issuing these bonds has the option or flexibility to call or repay these bonds usually five years from the issue date. While AT1 bonds—like debt—carry a coupon or interest, the issuer has the option to skip coupon payments during years of low profits or losses. In this respect, AT1 bonds are akin to equity. Further, the AT1 bonds are subordinated to plain vanilla debt such as deposits, bonds and loans raised by banks. This implies that lenders will be prioritized over AT1 bondholders for interest payment and principal repayment. Hence, the coupon on AT1 bonds is higher than that on conventional debt to compensate AT1 bond investors for the higher risk.

Ahead of SBI acquiring a 49 per cent stake in Yes Bank, RBI directed that the AT1 bonds be written down by 100 per cent. This meant their ₹1,000 investment in the bond was worth zero or investors would not recover their principal. The terms and conditions of AT1 bonds allow the investment to be written down in a crisis situation. The worst hit were retail investors, especially senior citizens, as certain branches of Yes Bank had misrepresented these AT1 bonds to their depositors as instruments akin to fixed deposits carrying a higher interest. Several retirees had liquidated their fixed deposits and invested the proceeds in AT1 bonds. SEBI fined Yes Bank and three of its executives ₹25 crore ($3.5 million) for misrepresenting AT1 bonds to retail investors and facilitating their sale in the secondary market.

In March 2020, SBI led a consortium comprising LIC, HDFC Bank, ICICI Bank, Axis Bank and Kotak Mahindra Bank to acquire a 49 per cent stake in Yes Bank for ₹11,000 crore ($1.5 billion) and also deputed SBI's Prashant Kumar to assume charge as CEO.

The ED charged Rana Kapoor with engaging in money laundering in connivance with Kapil Wadhawan, the CEO of the embattled Dewan Housing Finance Limited (DHFL). The ED contended that, of the ₹3700 crore ($541 million) short-term debentures issued by DHFL that Yes Bank had subscribed to in 2018, ₹600 crore ($88 million) was diverted to private investment vehicles owned by Rana Kapoor and his family. The ED arrested Rana Kapoor on 9 March 2020 and on that very day restrained his daughter, Roshni Kapoor, from boarding an international flight at Mumbai. Roshni Kapoor was later arrested as were DHFL promoters, Kapil and Dheeraj Wadhawan.

Anil Ambani, the chairman of ADAG, Yes Bank's largest NPL, was summoned by the ED and questioned for hours at a stretch.

He maintained that ADAG's borrowings from Yes Bank were all backed by property as collateral and that he had no dealings with Rana Kapoor's investment vehicles.

Contrary to Anil Ambani's statements to ED, *Mint* reported that a Grant Thornton forensic audit revealed two ADAG entities had financed Rana Kapoor's investment vehicles. Reliance Home Finance had reportedly extended a ₹60 crore ($8.8 million) loan in August 2018 to Bliss House Pvt Ltd, a 100 per cent subsidiary of RAB Enterprises, to enable the latter repay a loan. Imagine Estate Pvt Ltd, yet another RAB Enterprises subsidiary, borrowed ₹125 crore ($18.3 million) in April 2018 to enable its parent to repay a loan. Rana Kapoor's wife, Bindu Kapoor, owned RAB Enterprises.

Retail investors were not the only ones who lost their monies by investing in Yes Bank's AT1 bonds. Reliance Capital had invested ₹244 crore ($33 million) in the AT1 bonds, ₹105 crore ($14 million) in DHFL's secured debentures and ₹48 crore ($6.5 million) in IL&FS's unsecured commercial papers.[14] The losses generated by these investments pale in comparison to the risks posed by Reliance Capital's investments in ADAG. However, these investments do provide a glimpse of Reliance Capital's lax underwriting and the incestuous nature of institutional investing in India.

Yes Bank turned around after Rana Kapoor's ouster. SBI's stake in Yes Bank declined to 30 per cent after its ₹1255 crore ($169 million) follow-on public offering in July 2020. That very month, Yes Bank took possession of two Mumbai properties of ADAG located at Veer Nariman Road and the conglomerate's headquarters spread across 21,432 square metres in Santa Cruz, for non-payment of ₹2892 crore ($390 million) loans.[15]

Selling Spree

By FY2018, three ADAG entities—RCom, Reliance Capital and Reliance Naval—were loss-making, while RInfra and R-Power were barely profitable. Both the 'House of Debt' and CARE

Ratings' reports had stated that ADAG was in the process of selling its assets to pay down its debts. As the debt-financed assets were generating inadequate cash, selling the assets to pay interest and repay principal was a logical corollary.

ADAG reported multiple asset divestments. The largest among these was Reliance Infrastructure's sale of its Mumbai city power distribution unit to Adani Transmission for ₹18,800 crore ($2.75 billion) in August 2018. Reliance Capital sold a 42.88 per cent stake in its mutual fund arm, Reliance Nippon Asset Management, to its JV partner Nippon Life Insurance for ₹6000 crore ($852 million) in September 2019. Reliance Mutual Fund was subsequently renamed as Nippon India Mutual Fund. Other divestments included the sale of Reliance Media Works' multiplexes to Carnival Cinemas in December 2014, and the sale of its radio and TV businesses to the Zee Group in November 2016 that reportedly achieved a ₹700 crore ($115 million) and ₹1900 crore ($283 million) debt reduction respectively.

Notwithstanding these big bang announcements, the debt reduction ADAG achieved between FY2018 to FY2020 was modest at ₹23,783 crore ($5.2 billion). ADAG's creditors had to devise their own means to realize funds. The conglomerate's precarious financial position and declining share price prompted L&T Finance, Edelweiss and STCI Finance—three NBFCs who had lent against the collateral of promoter shares—to sell their stakes in ADAG companies in the open market during the first week of February 2019. These bulk deals triggered a sharp decline in the ADAG companies' share prices and market capitalization. An understandably unhappy Reliance Capital accused the NBFCs of causing a ₹13,000 crore ($1.85 billion) erosion in the conglomerate's market capitalization within a period of four days by selling shares worth ₹400 crore ($57 million).[16]

The sale of RCom's telecom assets to Jio, though initiated in 2017, did not go through. Following this, RCom was referred to the NCLT in June 2019 for debt resolution under India's

IBC 2016. RCom's committee of creditors, led by SBI, in January 2020 approved RCom's insolvency resolution plan, by which UV Asset Reconstruction Company (UVARC) would purchase ₹14,700 crore ($2.0 billion) of RCom's assets, while Jio would purchase RCom's tower and fibre assets valued at ₹4700 crore ($634 million). Including the asset sales to UVARC and Jio, the resolution plan arrived at a ₹23,000 crore ($3.2 billion) recovery amount, or 70 per cent of the ₹33,000 crore ($4.6 billion) secured debt adjudicated by the NCLT. However, RCom's consolidated debt, including unsecured debt, was more than double the recovery amount at ₹45,548 crore ($6.4 billion) by March 2020.

The IBC 2016 was touted to be a game changer that would lead to quick and efficient resolution of bankruptcies. RCom, which initiated the asset divestment process in 2017, had not been able to realize cash as of end 2021. This illustrates the disconnect between IBC's intent and implementation. Outstanding debt of ADAG's listed entities as of March 2020 was ₹1,41,804 crore ($19.9 billion). Given ADAG's complex and opaque organizational structure that includes multiple unlisted holding companies and businesses like Reliance Entertainment, ADAG's overall debt including that of the unlisted entities is likely to be higher.

ADAG's excessive borrowing and lapses in execution, i.e., the inability to nurture its multiple constituents into market leading and sustainable entities, is key, but not the sole reason for its faltering. Strategic errors, extraneous events and personality traits contributed to the conglomerate's fall.

The division of businesses between the Ambani brothers in 2005 was skewed to begin with. Contrary to the popular view that Anil inherited new-age industries and was, hence, poised to scale great heights, it was Mukesh who retained the cash cow—RIL—that enabled him to pip his younger sibling to the post by a wide margin. However, there was no way RIL's flagship oil and gas business could have been divided between the two brothers.

Figure 3: Outstanding Debt of ADAG's Listed Entities

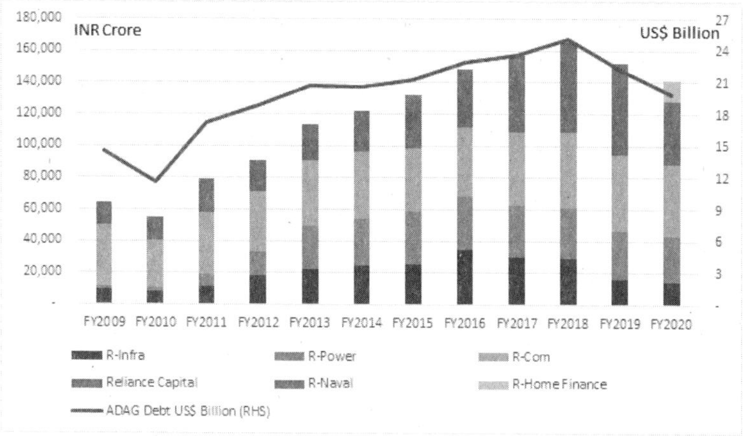

Source: ADAG Annual Reports

The desire to catch up with RIL prompted Anil to set up numerous, large-scale and capital-intensive businesses simultaneously. This empire building aspiration, which he shares with VGS, Goyal and Mallya, proved to be his undoing.

It is difficult to gauge how much flexibility Anil had in scrapping the non-compete agreement (NCA) between RIL and ADAG in 2010. RCom, an enterprise that was founded and nurtured by Mukesh, was reportedly close to his heart. The scrapping of the NCA paved the way for Mukesh's second foray into telecom, to the detriment of the incumbents, especially RCom.

Offshore Escapades

The propensity to get embroiled in controversy is yet another trait Anil shares with the other protagonists of this narrative. Besides the 2G spectrum allocation case and the Rafale deal, Anil was also embroiled in the 'Pluri Case' in 2017. At the heart of the Pluri Case were participatory notes, or P-Notes, issued by investment banks including Barclays and Societe Generale. P-Notes are overseas derivative instruments (ODI) issued by foreign institutional investors (FII) registered with SEBI to investors domiciled in countries other than India. Shares of Indian companies are the underlying assets of P-Notes. Overseas investors may purchase P-Notes from FIIs without having to register with SEBI. FIIs transfer the dividends and capital gains of the underlying P-Notes to the investors, who may anonymously invest in Indian capital markets.

Barclays and Societe Generale (SG) had issued P-Notes with RCom shares as the underlying asset to Hythe Securities, an overseas investor, which had sold down these ODIs to Pluri, an unregulated entity. *BusinessLine* reported that Barclays failed to report to SEBI that Hythe Securities had sold down the P-Notes to Pluri. SG too reportedly made incorrect disclosures regarding the ultimate investor in these P-Notes.[17]

While SEBI restricted its investigations to India, UK's Financial Services Authority (FSA) uncovered that Pluri Cell E was created by ADAG through the Swiss bank, UBS. ADAG was propping up RCom share price by investing in P-Notes. ADAG settled the Pluri case with SEBI through a consent order that resulted in a penalty of ₹50 crore ($ 7.7 million) and the banning of Reliance Natural Resources, RInfra, Anil Ambani and a few ADAG board members from the capital markets for two years. SEBI also debarred Indian citizens and NRIs from investing in P-Notes to thwart such dubious transactions and the money laundering opportunities P-Notes afforded.[18]

Whither Anil?

Like Vijay Mallya, Anil's lavish lifestyle—helicopter rides to office, art and jewellery collections, the ₹400 crore ($84 million) luxury yacht he gifted his wife, socializing with

Bollywood stars and reports of him building a house to rival Mukesh Ambani's 'Antilla'—worked to his disadvantage when ADAG's performance deteriorated. Mukesh Ambani too leads an equal if not more extravagant life, but understandably does not attract as much censure, courtesy his helming one of India's most profitable corporates.

In 2008, The *New York Times* published a detailed profile of Mukesh Ambani. The column ended with the columnist Anand Giridharadas asking the RIL chairman about his 'intelligence agency' in New Delhi encompassing lobbyists and spies who reportedly collected data about 'the vulnerabilities of the powerful; about the minutiae of bureaucrats' schedules, about the activities of their competitors'. Mukesh said that these activities were overseen by his brother before the split and, with a belly laugh, added that 'We de-merged all of that.' The column stated Anil Ambani's spokesperson refused to comment.[19]

Soon after, Anil sued Mukesh for defamation, claiming ₹10,000 crore ($2.30 billion) in damages. Lawsuits were slapped against Indian and international media outlets including The *Economic Times*, The *Financial Express*, *Hindustan Times*, *NDTV*, The Wire, BloombergQuint and The *Financial Times*, besides politicians and journalists for critiquing ADAG's performance, RCom's sale of telecom assets to Jio and the Rafale deal. Scroll reported that, in 2018 alone, ADAG had filed twenty-eight cases in the Ahmedabad court, of which the damages claimed in sixteen cases amounted to ₹80,500 crore ($11.8 billion).[20] The perception of Anil's strong sense of entitlement is underscored by his lavish style coupled with the tendency to initiate legal action against his critics.

The collapse of IL&FS, in which Anil Ambani had no role to play, and the Yes Bank crisis, for which ADAG was partially responsible, precipitated ADAG's crises.

Is it the end of the road for Anil Ambani, who turned sixty-two in 2021?

In the Mahabharata, the Pandavas—who spent twelve years in exile and a year in agyatvasa or incognito after losing the game of dice to their cousins—reclaim their kingdom after a bloody war. A combination of high-risk appetite and extraneous events led to Anil battling multiple crises—the 'gas wars', 2G spectrum allocation, the Rafale deal, Jio's telecom foray, the Pluri case, the Yes Bank fiasco, the collapse of IL&FS—while attempting to build ADAG into an enterprise that could rival RIL.

As of 2021, RCom's debt resolution is underway, while there appears to be some progress in moderating the indebtedness and divesting Reliance Infrastructure, Reliance Power and Reliance Home Finance. Though the 1959-born Anil may not be written off yet, whether he is likely to create the big bang impact of his heydays remains to be seen.

Will Anil Ambani emerge victorious in what appears to be his final expedition of settling ADAG's liabilities and establishing himself as a successful tycoon? Or will he fade into obscurity?

The outcome will be of interest to ADAG's stakeholders, politicians and the public.

Part 4: Icarus Entrepreneurship

Chapter 20

Knives Out

It appears to be the end of the road for *Unfinished Business*'s three living protagonists—Vijay Mallya, Naresh Goyal and Anil Ambani. Barring RInfra, all listed entities of the ADAG Group have filed for bankruptcy. Naresh Goyal has not publicly announced his association with any business enterprise since his ouster from Jet Airways, while Mallya is fighting extradition from the UK to India.

The protagonists of this narrative do share interesting characteristics. They were empire builders who built memorable brands and whose enterprises garnered sizeable market shares. They leveraged their proximity to the political establishment, lenders and equity investors to raise millions of dollars. Yet, they stumbled. What caused their enterprises to collapse?

Scale versus Sustainability

VGS, Goyal and Anil did not oversee a single business that generated adequate cash to finance their empire building expeditions. Mallya had a controlling stake in the UB Group, a cash cow. However, this was inadequate to finance Kingfisher Airlines, the RCB and Force India F1 teams, and his flamboyant lifestyle.

These entrepreneurs, consciously or unconsciously, prioritized scale over sustainability. Becoming market leaders in their respective industries was more alluring to the quartet than the onerous chore of nurturing an enterprise to become operationally and financially sustainable. VGS and Anil helmed conglomerates, none of whose constituents generated meaningful and consistent profits that were adequate to repay liabilities and pay dividends. Mallya and Goyal attempted to operate full-service airlines whose ticket prices were comparable to those of low-cost carriers. They committed other strategic errors that aggravated their airlines' untenable pricing.

Mallya acquired Air Deccan to work around the government's 5/20 rule, launched Kingfisher's international routes amidst the 2007-08 global financial crisis, and subsequently wound-up Kingfisher Red (the rebranded Air Deccan), the budget arm of his airline. With Kingfisher Airlines having to shelve its international routes, the ₹1,000 crore ($242 million) debt-funded Air Deccan acquisition proved to be pointless.

Goyal acquired Air Sahara in March 2007 for ₹1450 crore ($351 million), which analysts opined was excessive although it was 35 per cent lower than his June 2006 offer of ₹2250 crore ($500 million). The Air Sahara acquisition shared two similarities with Mallya's Air Deccan acquisition. It was also predominantly debt-funded and occurred during the 2007-08 financial crisis. This acquisition only served to exacerbate Jet Airways' losses. VGS, Mallya and Anil were supposedly experts in finance. Goyal was a veteran of the airline industry. Yet, their enterprises were weakened by lax financial management.

All four enterprises were also propped up with political support. The quartet were politically well connected. Mallya and Anil were MPs. VGS was former Karnataka chief minister S.M. Krishna's son-in-law and a close friend of Congress politician D.K. Shivakumar. Goyal's prowess to shape policy and legislation to his benefit along with his ties with the underworld are legendary. Political connections enabled these entrepreneurs to cut through the bureaucratic red tape, secure quick regulatory approvals and raise vast sums of money, especially from public sector banks.

Fickle Friends

Political proximity was neither the exclusive domain of the quartet nor the sole reason for their downfall. Numerous others like G.D. Birla, JRD Tata, Dhirubhai Ambani, Mukesh Ambani and Gautam Adani have cultivated and leveraged on their political connections to grow their corporate fiefdoms. RIL and the Adani Group owe their meteoric rise thus far to impeccable project execution skills and political savvy of Mukesh Ambani and Gautam Adani.

Politicians being fair weather friends, and the independence of the much-maligned Indian regulators and judiciary, contributed to the premature end to the entrepreneurial journeys of VGS, Mallya, Goyal and Anil Ambani. On the shoulders of these men who had access to better training, wider connections and more wealth than most Indians lies the responsibility of running their businesses aground.

Propelled by the paraffin wings of debt and political connections, enterprises helmed by Anil, Goyal, Mallya and VGS became market leaders. But this 'Icarus Entrepreneurship' that facilitated the rapid ascent of ADAG, Jet Airways, Kingfisher Airlines and CDEL dissipated when scorched by the heat of meeting contractual liabilities, generating a fair return for investors, and overcoming regulatory and legal hurdles.

The operating environment, specifically lenders, mutual funds, equity investors, credit rating agencies and regulators, did play a role in the failures of CDEL, Jet Airways, Kingfisher Airlines and ADAG.

Dubious Due Diligence

Loans extended by banks and bonds subscribed by retail and institutional investors like mutual funds and insurance companies are the two major sources of debt financing for corporates. Financing extended by venture capital and private equity firms, whose risk appetite is higher than those of banks and mutual funds, usually comprises both debt and equity. Bank loans are the largest source of financing for Indian corporates. Yet, lax due diligence and credit underwriting has resulted in recurring accumulation of non-performing assets and government bailouts.

The financials of CDEL, Jet Airways, Kingfisher Airlines, and ADAG were always shaky. These companies' financial disclosures are testimony to this fact. Yet, these companies had no difficulty in raising money from both public and private sector banks to finance their losses, capital expenditures and even acquisitions. The banks never asked or were not successful in getting VGS, Mallya, Goyal and Anil to bring in additional equity to moderate the risks of their companies' growing indebtedness. Their political connections enabled them to borrow vast sums of money and, in Mallya's case, even convert debt to equity at terms detrimental to public sector banks.

Private sector banks, too, lent to these fundamentally unsustainable enterprises. The lure of higher interest and fees blinded them to the risk of default. Yes Bank's CEO, Rana Kapoor, also engaged in fraud by requiring high risk borrowers to divert a part of his bank's lending to his personal investment vehicles.[1]

'Directed lending' practices prevalent in public sector banks has contributed to an apathetic appraisal culture. In private sector banks, the compensation structure rewards employees for loan growth as opposed to the quality of loans they originate. There is no provision to claw back bonuses if loans turn sour due to wilful underwriting lapses. The prevailing compensation structure perversely incentivizes decision makers at banks to disburse loans to high risk borrowers.

Bank deposits are the preferred source of investment for middle-class Indians due to the trust they continue to repose in the system and limited financial literacy. Indian politicians and the managements of several public and private sector banks have failed in their fiduciary duty to depositors, whose monies are a stable and significant source of funding for the banks.

"No, he's not our founder. He's just a great man who took every loan we had on offer!"

Cartoon: Ravikanth Nandula. This cartoon was originally published in The Hindu BusinessLine. *Reproduced with permission.*

Not just banks, but also mutual funds reneged on their fiduciary duties. In the aftermath of the IL&FS collapse in October 2018, liquidity had dried up. Highly indebted companies found it difficult to borrow further. Promoters of such entities pledged their shares with mutual funds and NBFCs to raise debt. It is commonly believed that promoters availing loans by pledging their holdings started after the IL&FS collapse. However, Anil had started borrowing by offering his holdings as collateral since FY2015, while VGS began borrowing against CDEL shares from FY2017.

Debt mutual funds including but not limited to Franklin Templeton, Bank of India AXA, Aditya Birla Sun Life, Reliance Mutual and IDBI Mutual, lent against promoters' shares. In certain cases like Yes Bank, the money was diverted to promoters and unlisted companies they owned, even as the listed companies failed to report the extent of pledged promoters' stake, which is a regulatory requirement.

Pitfalls of Promoter Financing

Mutual funds lending against promoters' holdings of listed companies was imprudent for three reasons. First, the companies against whose shares mutual funds had lent were already highly indebted. They were struggling to service the existing debt; their cash flows were clearly inadequate to service the incremental debt that the mutual funds were lending. Second, the prices of the shares against which the mutual funds lent were declining and the prospect of share price appreciation appeared bleak. The dividend yield of these shares was quite modest, with CDEL and R-Power paying zero dividends. The only year during which R-Power paid dividends was FY2016. Hence, the mutual funds had lent against depreciating assets that generated little or no dividend income. Third, the mandate of mutual funds is to 'invest' in bonds issued by companies with adequate debt servicing ability, unless its mandate is to explicitly invest in junk debt. By 'lending' to promoters against shares that consistently generated capital losses and minimal dividends, mutual funds had abused the trust their investors had reposed in them.

Moral Hazard in IPOs

As the promoters of companies borrowed recklessly, shareholders as the co-owners remained mute witnesses. This illustrates low investor awareness and the still nascent state of investor activism in India. Yet another example of investor ignorance is the premium

Figure 1: The Premium IPO Investors Pay versus Their Stake

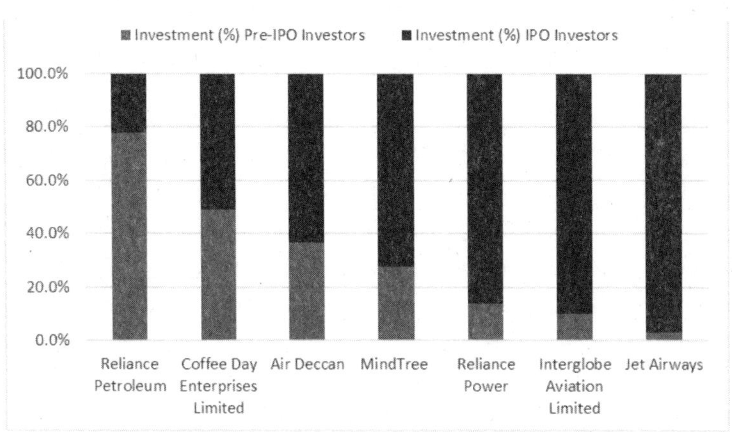

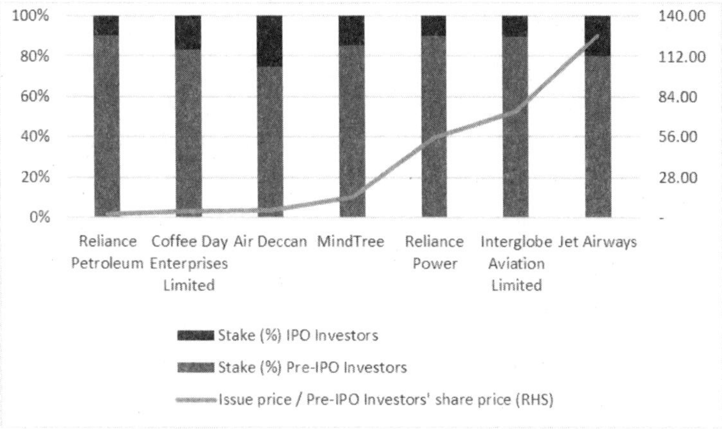

Source: IPO Prospectus & author calculations

Listed Indian corporates and FIs seldom divulge adequate information for regulators and analysts to make timely assessments of their operating performance. Listed entities in ASEAN, in contrast, provide a deck along with their interim and annual results that encapsulates their operating performance. Quarterly results published by listed entities in India obfuscate more than they reveal. This is because only the profit and loss account or income statement is reported along with select balance sheets and almost no cash flow metrics.

The reporting of RIL, one of India's most valuable companies by market capitalization, has become more opaque. Brokerages, including BNP Paribas, JP Morgan and Edelweiss, observed that RIL had stopped reporting 'capitalized expenses (JioMart), payments to InvITs (infrastructure investment trusts) from Jio Platforms Ltd (JPL), segment level retail revenues and EBITDA, and gross refining margins (GRM)' at its flagship crude oil refining division from the third quarter of FY2021. 'Transparency levels are falling across businesses,' opined Edelweiss.[3]

One reason why financial reporting in India does not compare favourably with other Asian countries is the piecemeal approach to upgrading disclosures. The last major improvement was made in 2019, when the ministry of corporate affairs eliminated the distinction between operating and financial leases and required lessors to report all leases on the balance sheet. Operating leases were previously reported off balance sheets, a practice that understated an entity's liabilities. The change in lease accounting is aligned with global best practices.

In October 2018, the GoI set up the National Financial Reporting Authority (NFRA) to oversee auditing and accounting standards. It is imperative that NFRA, in conjunction with the Institute of Chartered Accountants of India (ICAI) and the ministry of corporate affairs, issues a set of comprehensive directives that align Indian accounting standards and reporting with global best practices. Companies and FIs must be provided adequate time and training to adopt the new accounting standards and disclosure norms. Timely and transparent disclosures may act as a catalyst for the growth in Indian bond markets and facilitate better price discovery of equities and bonds; they are a prerequisite for thorough underwriting and appropriate credit ratings.

Kickstarting India's Corporate Bond Market

Bond markets have long been a stable and reliable source of long-term financing for government, corporates and FIs. They provide an alternate source of funding to bank financing by bringing together borrowers who need long-term financing and investors like pension funds and insurance companies that seek long-term investment avenues.[4] Listing bonds enables investors or bond holders to sell their investments ahead of the contractual maturity date, thereby enhancing the instrument's liquidity. A thriving and liquid bond market enables borrowers to diversify their funding sources. Banks also benefit as corporate dependence on banks for debt is lower and so is the banks' tenor mismatch, which arises from banks typically borrowing short- to medium-term and lending long-term.

Notwithstanding these advantages, India's corporate bond market is much smaller than in other developed and developing countries. India's ratio of outstanding corporate bonds to GDP at 17.16 per cent is lower than in Brazil (99.05 per cent), China (18.86 per cent), Malaysia (44.40 per cent), Singapore (34.02 per cent), South Korea (74.30 per cent) and the US (123.47 per cent).[5] The 0.005 per cent stamp duty on issue of securities (debt and equities), illiquidity premium, investment bankers and CRA fees may add up to 2 per cent to interest payments on bonds, resulting in borrowers preferring to avail bank loans.[6] The illiquidity premium arises from the longer tenor of bonds and limited trading in the secondary markets.

Regulations rightly stipulate that pension funds and insurance companies that are traditionally the largest investors in long-dated debt may invest in securities with the highest domestic credit ratings—AAA and AA. Though RBI approved the use of credit default swaps (CDS) in 2011, no clarity has yet been provided on the 'netting' of mark-to-market positions against the same counterparty for capital adequacy and exposure norms.[7] A CDS is a contract under which the seller of the contract will compensate the buyer should a bond issuer or borrower default, in return for an upfront fee known as premium; a CDS is akin to risk insurance. When a lender buys a CDS, default risk is hedged as the CDS seller will compensate the lender in the event of a non-payment. However, neither the government nor the private sector has created an agency that writes or sells CDS contracts.[8]

Hypothetically, had CDEL, Jet Airways, Kingfisher Airlines and ADAG raised debt both through bank loans and rated and listed bonds in India's well-developed bond markets, there would have been early warning signals aplenty. First, sustained poor financial performance would have resulted in bond prices falling and, hence, bond yields rising. Bankers, too, would have been forced to increase interest rates on loans, forcing the borrowers to rethink their expansion plans. Second, as CDEL, Jet Airways, Kingfisher Airlines and ADAG were generating inadequate cash flows to repay their debts, refinancing bonds would have been difficult. Banks would have been subject to regulatory censure and negative press had they extended loans to refinance bonds of poor credit quality. When refinancing maturing debt becomes difficult, raising new debt is out of the question. Had the quartet been so convinced of their projects' viability, they would have had to inject additional equity into their companies. Third, CDS premia would have skyrocketed, instilling reluctance even among risk-seeking bond investors. Fourth, investors and the media would have picked up sustained incongruities between yields, CDS premia and credit ratings, forcing CRAs to be more agile in their decisions.

Enhancing the Reliability of Credit Ratings

A vibrant bond market may enhance the timeliness of CRAs' rating actions. Reforms are, however, necessary to improve the reliability of credit ratings in India. Personal and anecdotal experience indicate that the quality of analysis among Indian CRAs is as rigorous as their global counterparts. However, the robustness of domestic ratings is limited by multiple factors, including opaque corporate reporting, conflicts of interest arising from borrowers paying for credit ratings, the failure of domestic CRAs to adopt global best practices and the crowded and intensely competitive industry structure.

Globally, it is the issuers or borrowers who compensate CRAs. The debt issuer or borrower pays the CRAs to avail a credit rating. The conflict of interest inherent in this remuneration structure is often attributed to the CRAs' delayed and indefensible rating decisions. An issuer paying a CRA is akin to students directly paying examiners to grade their exams.

Investor or lender pay and regulator pay models are alternate CRA compensation structures. In the US, between 1971 and mid-1974, S&P charged investors, while Moody's charged issuers. Research indicates that Moody's ratings were higher than S&P's during this period.[9] A 'regulator' pay model is not financially sustainable, feasible or desirable. The regulator would have to get involved in the nitty-gritty of new credit rating mandates and periodic surveillance exercises. Also, the potential for CRAs assigning more optimistic ratings to state-owned enterprises exists.

SEBI, undeterred by the lack of precedence, may consider creating a regulatory sandbox to experiment with the 'stakeholder pay' model. In a stakeholder pay model, regulators, lenders, investors and stock exchanges form a corpus to compensate CRAs, thereby reducing the conflict of interest inherent in the issuer pay model. The mode of mandating CRAs to assign ratings to specific debt issuances to minimize, if not eliminate, conflicts of interest needs to be explored.[10]

Both domestic and international CRAs have been guilty of lapses in judgement. The overtly optimistic credit ratings assigned by international CRAs ahead of the Asian Financial Crisis (1999), to Enron (2001), to mortgage-backed securities backed by sub-prime mortgages (2007-08) and to the Hong Kong-headquartered

Noble Group (2015), among others, caused billions of dollars of losses to lenders and equity investors alike. In India, the accuracy of credit ratings and the timeliness of ratings actions drew considerable flak in the case of CRB Capital (1996), IL&FS (2018), Dewan Housing Finance Limited (2019) and Essel Group (2019). This is a non-exhaustive list.

Domestic CRAs have failed to adopt global best practices and update their methodology to reflect country-specific ground realities. For example, CARE, ICRA and India Ratings were not wrong in assigning 'AAA' to IL&FS despite its weak financials, had they assigned both a standalone rating and a supported credit rating. IL&FS's standalone credit rating would have been non-investment grade reflecting its track record of losses, dividends paid from reserves and opaque disclosures. The supported rating would have reflected the strength of the shareholders and their willingness to ensure IL&FS did not default on debt servicing, a premise CRAs were obliged to confirm with shareholders at least annually. IL&FS was after all entirely owned by a formidable array of domestic and international institutional investors including LIC, HDFC, SBI, Central Bank of India, Orix Corporation and Abu Dhabi Investment Authority prior to its collapse.

Domestic CRAs have not ensured that their ratings better reflect ground realities. Several promoters, including VGS, Anil and Essel Group's Subash Chandra, had pledged their holdings to raise debt. Domestic CRAs are yet to update their methodologies to reflect the risks stemming from the promoters' weakening stake in their companies. International CRAs have started incorporating environmental, social and governance assessments in their ratings; domestic CRAs are yet to do so.

India's outstanding institutional debt, comprising corporates, financial institutions and government debt, at $4 trillion as of December 2020, is less than one-tenth of the US's outstanding debt of around $54 trillion.[11] It defies logic that there are seven SEBI-registered CRAs in India while the Securities and Exchange

Commission has designated nine CRAs as nationally recognized statistical rating organizations in the US. India's credit rating industry is among the most crowded and competitive in the world.

Sadly, some of the recommendations of the 2019 Standing Committee on Finance's report on 'Strengthening the Credit Rating Framework in the Country' serve to debilitate the robustness of credit ratings assigned by domestic CRAs. These recommendations include rotation of CRAs and increasing the number of CRAs in India! The committee recommended that CRAs be rotated every three years, despite the Department of Economic Affairs pointing out that this move may result in CRAs adopting a short-term view, that the incidence of rating shopping may increase, and that Argentina had discontinued the practice of rotating CRAs.[12]

Business-unfriendly Government Policies

The ratings industry is not the only one that is over-crowded and unhealthily competitive in India. Aviation is another such industry. The Tymms Committee in pre-independent India, G.S. Rajadhyaksha Committee (1953) and the Naresh Chandra Committee (2003) recommended that the government's role should be restricted to that of regulator in civil aviation and commercially sensible policies must be adopted for private airlines to thrive. Yet, successive governments have permitted numerous airlines to operate and compete on the basis of ticket fares, which has resulted in several airlines shutting shop, thousands losing their jobs and an accumulation of unpaid loans. Optimism triumphed experience in 2017; GoI repeated this mistake when it launched the regional connectivity scheme, UDAN. Nine airlines, including the state-owned Alliance Air and the two LCCs, IndiGo and SpiceJet, have been authorized to operate UDAN routes. Two airlines—Deccan Charters and Air Odisha—have already ceased operations.

Similarly, in the telecom sector, GoI has licensed over twenty operators since 2002, many of which have folded up or merged with larger players. The situation worsened when the Mukesh Ambani-controlled Reliance Jio unleashed a price war as part of its entry strategy in 2016. There were twelve telecom companies in India that year. Four years later, the number of players had halved to six, including the embattled state-owned enterprises BSNL and MTNL.

While the credit ratings industry requires highly skilled and knowledgeable personnel, airlines and telecoms are both capital and skill intensive. In India, governments across the political spectrum have ignored these ground realities and encouraged the evolution of over-crowded industries with disastrous consequences. The GoI further vitiated the business environment by levying high general and industry specific taxes. Corporate tax rates in India, though slashed from 35 per cent to 30 per cent in 2019, are still higher than the Asian average of 21.43 per cent and the global average of 23.65 per cent in 2021.[13] Industries such as airlines and telecommunications pay additional taxes.

High levies have resulted in Indian carriers paying much more for aviation turbine fuel (ATF) than some of their better-managed global counterparts. Between FY2010 and FY2019, Indian carriers spent a minimum of 23.6 per cent and a maximum of 54.9 per cent of revenue on ATF. As a percentage of revenues, ATF purchases ranged between 18.9 per cent and 40.7 per cent for Cathay Pacific, Singapore Airlines and Qantas. Both state-owned enterprises (BPCL, HPCL and IOC) and private enterprises (RIL, BP, Shell India, and Nayara Energy) sell ATF in India at government stipulated prices. The price sensitive nature of the Indian market limits airlines' flexibility to charge fares that ensure a reasonable return over costs.

Telecom levies, too, are on the higher side in India. According to the Cellular Operators Association of India, telecom levies in India range between 29 per cent and 32 per cent. This is significantly higher than the levies imposed in Pakistan (20.5–22 per cent), Sri Lanka (27.55 per cent), Bangladesh (25.95 per cent), China (11 per cent) and Malaysia (12.5 per cent). *Mint* aptly reported in November 2019, 'Ironically, Indian telecom operators, which offer the cheapest mobile data services in the world, pay more for airwaves than any of their global counterparts, an unsustainable situation that has proved ruinous to many . . . they pay 18% goods and services tax and also 3 per cent to 5 per cent of the adjusted gross revenue as spectrum usage charges and 8 per cent as license fees to the government. Effectively, for every ₹100 telcos receive from customers, ₹30 goes straight to the government's coffers.'[14]

Inefficiencies in tax administration and high tax rates have resulted in India's tax-to-GDP ratio lagging behind its Asian counterparts. This has resulted in high fiscal deficits, which the government has had to finance through borrowings. India has among the highest government debt-to-GDP ratios among investment grade sovereigns in Asia. The saving grace is that most of the sovereign borrowing is denominated in rupees, thereby enabling the country to use foreign exchange reserves for imports, especially crude oil. Higher sovereign indebtedness has fuelled inflation and driven interest rates upwards. Interest rates in India are higher than in most investment grade countries, resulting in sovereign, government-linked and corporate borrowers spending a lot more on debt servicing.

GoI must undertake a comprehensive evaluation of best practices around the globe to develop and strengthen institutions that support a fair and vibrant business environment. In addition to a CDS seller, the government must set up a public sector holding company like Temasek Holdings in Singapore or Khazanah Nasional Berhad in Malaysia; a mortgage corporation like Cagamas in Malaysia to promote home ownership and mortgage-backed securities, and a bad bank to resolve non-performing loans on an ongoing basis. It is only in 2021, after the economy was ravaged by Covid-19, that the government is considering setting

Figure 2: Low Taxe Revenues = High Debt

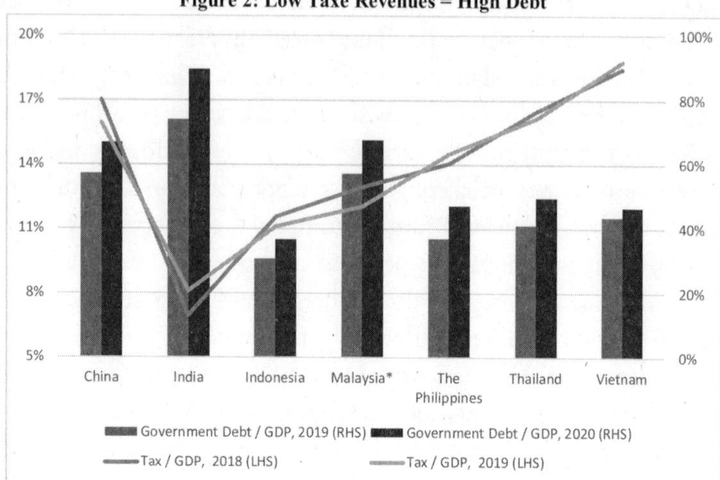

** Malaysia' tax to GDP data pertains to 2017 & 2018*
Source: Asian Development Bank & World Economic Outlook, April 2021

up a bad bank. It does not behove a nation that set up BSE, Asia's first organized stock exchange, and is one of the world's largest financial and real markets, to lag in learning and innovation.

Tackling Corporate Failures

Several factors contribute to failures in business in developed and developing countries, such as cyclical downturns, incorrect management decisions, product and service obsolescence and fraud. The collapse of the German payments processor Wirecard in 2020, and New York-headquartered hedge fund Archegos Capital and London-headquartered supply chain financier Greensill Capital in 2021 demonstrate that fraud and crony capitalism are not the exclusive hegemonies of developing countries. However, developed nations tend to do a better, though not a perfect job, in bringing wrongdoers to book and effecting systemic improvements necessary to reduce the recurrence of corporate lapses and frauds.

The strengthening of capitalization of US banks and certain banks in Europe after the global financial crisis supports this view.

The banks' latitude to overlook Archegos Capital's stratospheric leverage and the paltry fees they charged to render high risk prime brokerage services is an example of banks' lapses in developed countries. A more glaring lapse is that, of the mere forty-seven bankers imprisoned for their roles in the global financial crisis, only one was from the US. Twenty-five were domiciled in Iceland, eleven in Spain, seven in Ireland, and one each in Cyprus, Germany and Italy. The *Financial Times* observed, 'The US, ground zero for the financial crisis, has jailed just one banker for issues relating to the crisis. Former Credit Suisse trader Kareem Serageldin was sentenced to thirty months in prison for artificially inflating the price of subprime mortgages, a financial product at the very heart of Wall Street's unravelling.'[15]

The title of this book does not just signify the derailing of the once promising enterprises founded by VGS, Goyal, Mallya and Anil Ambani. *Unfinished Business* also refers to the long way the government of the world's largest democracy has to traverse to create a fair and invigorating business environment and ameliorate the quality of life for its 1.3 billion population.

Epilogue

The entrepreneurial careers of the three living protagonists of *Unfinished Business* appear to have come to a grinding halt. What has become of the organizations they lead? After all, among the first lessons students of business learn is that a private or public limited (liability) company is a distinct entity from its owners and shareholders. The liability of shareholders being limited to the extent of their committed share capital, the transferability of ownership through sale of equity stakes, and the separation of ownership and management enables limited companies to have a life of their own, independent of their shareholders. These features enable limited companies, along with appropriate support and effective management, to bounce back from crises.

Will the companies chronicled in *Unfinished Business* sink like Enron and Lehman Brothers or be resurrected like Apple and IBM? The trajectories of these companies after the protagonists ceased to lead them offer interesting insights.

Mixed Bag

Notwithstanding the fact that all of ADAG's listed entities, except RInfra, have filed for bankruptcy, the prospects for certain entities of the conglomerate do not appear too bleak. In September 2021, the Supreme Court upheld a ₹4600 crore ($612 million) arbitral award payable by Delhi Metro Rail Corporation to RInfra after a protracted nine-year legal battle.[1] Reliance Power has announced the sale of its equipment at the Samalkot power project to a Bangladesh-based power plant for ₹1500 crore ($200 million).[2]

Reliance Capital was unable to pay interest on the ₹2500 crore ($355 million) non-convertible debentures (NCDs) that the Employees Provident Fund Organisation—an arm of the government—had subscribed to since October 2019. The EPFO was desirous of initiating action against Reliance Capital under IBC 2016. However, RBI pre-empted EPFO's action by initiating corporate insolvency resolution process (CIRP) against the company in December 2021.[3]

Mumbai-based Authum Infrastructure emerged as the highest bidder for Reliance Home Finance (RHF) and Reliance Commercial Finance (RCF) in July 2021, about six months ahead of RBI initiating CIRP. Lenders to RHF and RCF have agreed to take a 80 per cent haircut and are likely to receive ₹4127 crore ($558 million) out of a combined debt of over ₹20,000 crore ($2.73 billion).[4, 5] Prominent financial groups such as Oaktree, JC Flowers & Co, Blackstone and Bain Capital have reportedly evinced interest in buying the viable subsidiaries and associates of Reliance Capital—Reliance General Insurance, Reliance Nippon Life Insurance, Reliance Health Insurance, Reliance Securities, Reliance Asset Reconstruction Company, and Indian Commodity Exchange.[6]

However, Authum's less-than-stellar credentials and performance are causes for concern. Alpana Dangi, who holds a 68.72 per cent stake in Authum, is married to Sanjay Dangi, a stockbroker whom SEBI banned a decade ago for collusion with promoters and share price manipulation.[7] Sanjay Dangi, who worked for RIL's Anand Jain, is now a non-executive director of Authum.[8]

Authum's assets and net worth fortuitously trebled—ahead of NCLT awarding it RHF and RCF—to ₹1968 crore ($266 million) and ₹1432 crore ($193 million) respectively. Its profit after tax touched a decennial peak of ₹135 crore ($18 million) in FY2021. The NBFC had reported losses in FY2019 and FY2020 and the second highest profit it reported since FY2011 was ₹8.35 crore ($1.25 million) in FY2017.[9] RHF's and RCF's total assets as of March 2021 was ₹14,898 crore ($2.01 billion) and ₹8240 crore ($1.11 billion) respectively.[10, 11] Lenders were willing to accept the bids of the NBFC whose assets are just 8.5 per cent of the combined assets of RHF and RCF and the track record of the key management personnel in executing such large acquisitions and effectively managing large NBFCs is not known.

Investor interest in the bankrupt Reliance Capital is a reflection of the low penetration of financial services in India that translates into favourable growth prospects for lenders and insurers, and the value investors perceive in certain components of Reliance Capital's business.

Dead End

Kingfisher Airlines, which at its peak operated sixty-nine aircraft, is now defunct. Lessors deregistered twelve aircraft leased to the bankrupt airline and leased or sold them to other airlines. Fifteen A320s that the airline had leased were damaged and consigned to scrapyards.[12] The service tax department to whom the airline owed ₹800 crore ($116 million) sold Mallya's luxury jet in 2018 for a paltry ₹34.80 crore ($5.05 million).[13]

Kingfisher's reported liabilities as of March 2013 was ₹15,731 crore ($2.87 billion). The Debt Recovery Tribunal sold shares of United Breweries to realize ₹5824.50 crore ($788 million).[14] Mallya's Kingfisher Villa in Goa was sold for just ₹52.25 crore ($7.10 million) in the ninth attempt; Kingfisher House in Mumbai fetched sightly over the reserve price of ₹73 crore ($11 million).[15,16]

Lenders tried to sell the controversial Kingfisher brand and trademarks twice in 2016. The ₹366.70 crore ($55 million) reserve price was not even one-tenth of the value at which it was pledged as a collateral for the loan; not a single bid was received.[17] In January 2022, a London court awarded UBS AG the right to repossess and sell Mallya's luxury townhouse overlooking Regent's Park.[18] Mallya, through Rose Capital, a British Virgin Island registered entity, had pledged the townhouse for a ₹200 crore ($37 million) five-year loan in 2012 to the Swiss Bank, UBS AG. The loan has not been repaid at its expiry in 2017 or subsequently.[19] Mallya and Rose Capital plan to contest the verdict.

Green Shoots

Jet Airways, which operated its last flight on 17 April 2019, has been grounded for over four years. Lenders agreed to a 95 per cent hair cut to their exposure and the new owner - the Kalrock-Jalan consortium is in the process of reviving the erstwhile market leader.

The government granted security clearance for Jet Airways to relaunch commercial operations in May 2022 and the airline conducted its test flight to and from the Hyderabad airport—a prerequisite to obtain an air operator certificate.[20] The airline started recruiting pilots in July 2022. It will be a bumpy ride for Jet Airways, though, with the world still grappling with the Covid-19 pandemic, the Tatas aggressively re-entering civil aviation with a formidable array of airlines (Air India, AirAsia India and Vistara), Akasa Air starting operations, and IndiGo having perfected the seemingly impossible mission of operating profitably in the cut-throat Indian aviation market.

CDEL's debt reduction after Malavika Hegde assumed charge as CEO has been impressive. The listed company's outstanding debt and lease liabilities reduced by 74 per cent from ₹7269 crore ($1.03 billion) in March 2019 to ₹2073 crore ($280 million) in March 2021 and further to ₹1861 crore ($249 million) in March 2022. According to the company's FY2021 annual report, asset sales generated ₹3,505 crore ($491 million) in FY2020 and

₹79 crore ($11 million) in FY2021.[21] The sale of Global Village Techparks to Blackstone at an enterprise value of ₹2700 crore ($364 million) accounted for 75 per cent of the cash inflow from asset divestments.[22] The Chennai-headquartered Shriram Credit Company acquired an 85.63 per cent stake in Way2Wealth securities for ₹56 crore ($7.5 million).[23] CDEL's consolidated cash, which reduced from ₹2367 crore ($491 million) in FY2019 to ₹47 crore ($6.3 million) in FY2021, also financed the debt reduction. By March 2022, CDEL's cash balance had inched up to a still modest to ₹53 crore ($7.1 million)

The need to streamline its unwieldly operations and the Covid-19 outbreak resulted in CCD cafés declining to 495 in FY2022 from 572 in FY2021 and 1752 in FY2019. Vending machines declined to 38,810 in FY2022 from 56,799 in FY2019. These measures resulted in consolidated expenses more than halving from ₹3740 crore ($543 million) in FY2019 to ₹1641 crore ($221 million) in FY2021. While CDEL reported a post-tax loss of ₹652 crore ($88 million in FY2021) vis-à-vis a profit of ₹1849 crore ($259.15 million) in FY2020, this loss narrowed to ₹131 crore ($17.53 million) in FY2022 However, loans that CDEL had on-lent to related entities more than doubled from ₹1032 crore ($150 million) in FY2019 to ₹2652 crore ($358 million) in FY2021 and remained at around this level in FY2022. The major recipient of these loans continues to be MACEL, whose outstanding borrowings from CDEL is ₹2289 crore ($309 million) in FY2021.[24]

The unlisted MACEL, as of 31 December 2021, has filed only its FY2020 annual report, as per which its debt has risen by 9 per cent from ₹4112 crore ($597 million) in FY2019 to ₹4471 crore ($627 million) in FY2020. MACEL's borrowings, like in past years, were on-lent as advances, which increased from ₹3795 crore ($551 million) in FY2019 to ₹4175 crore ($585 million) in FY2020. In other words, 93 per cent of MACEL's outstanding debt has been on-lent.

While the monies lent to VGS's parents has increased, the single largest recipient continues to be VGS, Malavika and their partnership, whose dues as of 31 March 2020 was ₹3391 crore ($492 million), which is 5 per cent higher than the outstanding as of 31 March 2019—₹3235 crore ($470 million). Loan outstanding with VGS, Malavika and the couple's partnership as of 31 March 2020 was a substantial 76 per cent of MACEL's debt though somewhat lower than the 83 per cent in March 2019.

CDEL's stake in its struggling logistics arm, SICAL Logistics, declined from 55.18 per cent in March 2019 to 34.09 per cent in March 2021. SICAL was admitted in corporate insolvency process in March 2021. As of January 2022, SICAL's lenders received four firm bids for acquisition in January 2022.[25]

CDEL is not out of the woods yet. The company generated losses in FY2021 and FY2022, primarily on account of its multiple businesses (excluding its café arm) making losses, SICAL's

Figure 1: Loans and Advances given by MACEL

iii) Balances with the related parties

Name of the Related party	Nature of Transaction	As on 31.03.2020	As on 31.03.2019
Late Sri S V Gangaiah Hegde	Loans/advances Given/(received)	4,85,27,061-00	2,31,42,061-00
Smt Vasanthi Hegde	Short term advances given	6,25,57,448-00	1,48,72,986-00
Gonibeedu Coffee Estates Private Limited	Advances received	31,90,27,475-00	171,58,86,935-00
Coffee Day Hotels & Resorts Private Limited	Advances received	136,95,79,785-00	-
Coffee Day Econ Private Limited	Advances received	103,20,47,841-00	-
Coffee Day Consolidations Private Limited	Long Term Advances given	30,68,50,395-00	36,42,20,118-00

LAVITHA & ASSOCIATES
Chartered Accountants
M.No 226473

Chethan Wood Processing Private Limited	Advances Given	10,20,65,407-00	10,00,19,407-00/
Devadarshini Info Technologies Private Limited	Long Term borrowings	62,28,80,897-00	91,81,58,509-00
Giri Vidyuth India Limited	Long Term Borrowings	370,00,00,000-00	-
GMDH Curing Works Private Limited	Advances given	9,75,84,501-00	-
GVBS Tech Park Private Limited	Advances given	8,22,300-00	-
Coffee day Natural Resources Private Ltd	Long term advances given	217,51,81,618-00	77,68,00,975-00
Rajagiri & Sankhan Estate Private Ltd	Long term advances Received	50,86,78,479-00	115,11,67,729-00
Sampigehutty Estate Private Ltd	Advances received Amounts payable	- 29,97,72,866-00	12,68,65,881-00 22,98,50,000-00
Kummergode Estate Limited	Advances given Advances received	9,74,37,077-00 -	- 93,04,95,160-00
Liquid Crystal India (P) Ltd	Advances given	9,39,64,103-00	9,39,64,103-00
Vaitarna timber trading Private Ltd	Long term advances given	68,42,67,604-00	67,40,78,859-00
Terra Firma (Solid Waste Management) Private Limited	Advances given	6,72,300-00	6,73,640-00
Chandrapore Estate Private Ltd	Long term advances given Long Term Advances received	41,78,49,905-00 -	- 120,86,21,492-00
Dark forest Furniture Company Private Ltd	Advances given	98,18,21,105-00	58,49,12,983-00
Kurkenmutty Estates Private Ltd	Long term advances given	188,98,46,257-00	118,17,05,412-00
Late Sri V G Siddhartha, Smt Malavika Hegde & partnership firm in which he/she is a partner	Long Term Advances	3390,55,95,871-00	3235,16,49,924-00

LAVITHA & ASSOCIATES Chartered Accountants M.No 220473

Source: Pages 29 to 31 of MACEL's FY2020 Annual Accounts

Figure 2: Key Financial Metrics of CDEL, its holding companies & MACEL

₹ Crore	Revenue		Post-tax Profit		Networth		Debt	
	FY2020	FY2021	FY2020	FY2021	FY2020	FY2021	FY2020	FY2021
CDEL (Listed Entity)	2,653	981	1,849	-652	4,938	3,896	3,691	2,004
Holding Companies	52	3	-18	-26	-659	-643	1,024	930
MACEL	3	3	-41	-19	-264	-284	4,471	4,489
CDEL Group	**2,708**	**987**	**1,790**	**-697**	**4,014**	**2,970**	**9,186**	**7,423**

Source: Annual reports of CDEL, MACEL & the four holding companies—Coffeeday Consolidations Private Limited, Devadarshini Info Technologies Private Limited, Gonibedu Coffee Estates Private Limited and Sivan Securities Private Limited.

bankruptcy, and the Covid-19 outbreak. At significant risk is the debt on the books of its holding companies and MACEL, all of which are incapable of independently servicing the debt. The holding companies and MACEL are predominantly loss-making shell companies.

Nevertheless, CDEL continues to feature among India's leading café chains. The food and beverage company emerging from its current crisis as a financially stable company that efficiently manages India's favourite café chain will be a fitting tribute to its visionary founder, VGS.

The income tax raids and S.M. Krishna shifting his allegiance to the BJP did not affect the relationship between VGS's and D.K. Shivakumar's families. The wedding of Shivakumar's daughter, Aishwarya, and VGS and Malavika Hegde's son, Amartya, was solemnized in February 2021.

Signing Off

The four entities covered in *Unfinished Business* share at least three commonalities. First, equity investors have experienced substantial erosion in their investments that they are unlikely to recoup. Second, lenders have undertaken sizeable haircuts. While CDEL has indeed performed a tremendous feat of slashing its debt to sustainable levels, lenders to SICAL Logistics may have to accept a haircut. Third, there has been a loss of livelihoods.

One may argue that these founder CEOs of listed companies have also witnessed an erosion in their net worth.

However, *Forbes'* estimates of net worth are subjective as they include the market values of the CEOs' holdings of listed companies and self-declarations of their liabilities and unlisted assets. The four protagonists may no longer feature in billionaire rankings, but there appears to be no deterioration in their standards of living, substantiating the frequent observation, 'In India, companies may fail. But the lifestyles of their founders almost never deteriorate'.

Figure 3: Protagonists' Networth

$ Million	Anil Ambani	Naresh Goyal	Vijay Mallya	V.G. Siddhartha
2006			1,000	
2007			1,500	
2008			1,200	
2009			1,000	
2010	13,700		1,400	
2011	8,800		1,000	
2012	7,800	600		
2013	5,200			
2014	5,000			
2015	4,000			1,150
2016	2,500			
2017	2,700			
2018	2,700			
2019	1,700			

Source: forbes.com

"He is a true rags to riches case! Rags for the banks, riches for himself!"

Cartoon: Ravikanth Nandula

Acknowledgements

Unfinished Business would have remained so but for the efforts of two people. My friend and literary agent, Suhail Mathur, CEO of The Book Bakers, suggested that I work on V.G. Siddhartha's biography and came up with the title. I am grateful to Deepthi Talwar, the commissioning editor, for being my sounding board and supporting my idea to broaden the scope of the book to the rise and fall of the four 'Icarus Entrepreneurs' and the resultant ripple effects.

When I began writing *Unfinished Business*, I set myself three goals. First, I decided, rather unrealistically, to eschew data. Second, I was determined to add a dash of humour to the narrative. Third, I wanted the book to be an objective and accessible account of the Indian business landscape during the first two decades of the twenty-first century.

I sadly failed to achieve my first goal; I guess my day job as a credit research analyst reared its head. The Gujarat Cooperative Milk Marketing Federation Ltd. (Amul) and *The Hindu BusinessLine* permitted me to use their topicals and cartoons free of cost and thus enabled me to achieve my second goal. I am thankful for their support. I am also thankful to Ravi Nandula of *The Hindu BusinessLine* for sketching two cartoons specifically for *Unfinished Business*.

My honest and meticulous reviewers, listed in alphabetical order, hopefully ensured that my third goal of objectivity was met. Arun Arumugam, Raghuvir Srinivasan, Raj Jayaram, Shankar

Parameshwaran, Shijo George, and Siddharth Vijayaraghavan highlighted errors, nudged me to reflect and, most importantly, urged me to simplify. I am particularly indebted to Mr R. Gopalakrishnan, retired director of Tata Sons and vice chairman of Hindustan Unilever, for writing the foreword and providing me with invaluable feedback.

Sir Isaac Newton once remarked that, 'If I have seen further, it is by standing on the shoulders of giants.' The authors and journalists listed in the Bibliography, who fearlessly covered these high-profile and controversial events often at great personal risk, are indeed the colossi whose work is the cornerstone of *Unfinished Business*.

Writing a book is, at times, a lonely task of which introspection is an inevitable outcome. I realize I have travelled some distance from being an introverted and self-effacing banker in 2004 to a self-assured finance professional–writer–translator in 2022. The master's in finance programme that I pursued at the London Business School, armed with scholarships awarded by the Tata and K.C. Mahindra Trusts, marked the beginning of this life-changing journey. Three people reposed much confidence and supported me during this transformative experience—Dr G.E. Dutta, Mr Dilip Samadar (Dilip uncle) and Mrs Kumkum Samadar (Kumkum aunty). My maiden India-focused non-fiction book—*Unfinished Business*—is dedicated to these loving people, whose unconditional affection and support I continue to be a grateful recipient of.

Notes

1 https://vedicastrology865894967.wordpress.com/2021/10/02/lord-venkateshwara-the-kaliyuga-varadaana/

2 'Vijay Mallya offers gold bricks for birthday in Tirupati', *The Hindu BusinessLine*, 19 December 2012.

3 'Anil Ambani treks to Tirumala', *The Hindu*, 31 May 2010.

4 'Vijay Mallya offers gold bricks for birthday in Tirupati', *The Hindu BusinessLine*, 19 December 2012.

5 FY2003 implies financial year ended 31 March 2003. The Indian financial year begins on April 1 and ends on March 31 of the subsequent year.

6 'GDP growth in 2012–13 worse than expected', Asit Ranjan Mishra, *Mint*, 1 February 2014.

7 '10 things you need to know about Sahara row', Shishir Asthana, *Business Standard*, 28 February 2014.

8 'Subrata Roy gets 4-week parole for mother's death', Dhananjay Mahapatra, The *Times of India*, 7 May 2016.

9 'Subrata Roy must pay ₹ 62,600 crore to stay out of jail: Regulator SEBI', Upamanyu Trivedi, Bloomberg, 20 November 2020.

10 'How Nirav Modi allegedly executed a $2 billion PNB fraud', Jeanette Rodrigues, Bloomberg, 16 February 2018.

11 'Mallya left India on March 2, Government tells court', Krishnadas Rajagopal, *The Hindu*, 9 March 2016.

12 'Truth behind how Vijay Mallya fled India', Kingshuk Nag, Dailyyo.in, 26 July 2017.
13 'UK court declares Vijay Mallya bankrupt for Indian banks to realise debt', *The Hindu*, 26 July 2021.
14 'What the break-up means', Alam Srinivas, *Outlook India*, 4 July 2005.
15 'After months of acrimony, an outbreak of brotherly love at Reliance', Knowledge@Wharton, 13 July 2005.

Part 1: Coffee King
Chapter 1: At the Netravati

1 'VG Siddhartha made a profit of Rs 2,858 cr from his Mindtree stake sale to L&T', *Business Today*, 20 March 2019.
2 'CDEL filing to BSE and NSE, Req. 30 — Approval to sell the equity shares held in Mindtree Limited', 18 March 2019.
3 CDEL Annual Report, 2019
4 Director General.
5 The emphasis is the author's. The writer of the letter meant possession.
6 'CCD owner's death: Kiran Shaw slams PE firm, Mahindra says business failure need not destroy self-esteem', The *Indian Express*, 1 August 2019.
7 Ibid
8 Ibid
9 'I-T Dept disputes Siddhartha's letter to CCD board alleging tax harassment', *Business Standard*, 30 July 2019.
10 'Death of a tycoon: What you should know', The *Economic Times*, 31 July 2019.
11 'I've failed, sorry to let you all down: VG Siddhartha's last letter found', The *Economic Times,* 30 July 2019
12 'Coffee Day Enterprises Limited: Ratings downgraded to [ICRA]D', downloaded from www.icra.in, 10 September 2019.

Chapter 2: Way to Wealth

1 'V.G. Siddhartha: The lord and master of coffee beans', Anshul Dhamija, *Fortune India*, 30 July 2019.
2 '"Entrepreneurs don't retire . . . they die": Secret diary of VG Siddhartha – Part 1', N. Mahalakshmi, *Outlook Business*, 5 August 2016.
3 'How the Marx-loving fluke entrepreneur became India's coffee king', Manu Balachandran, *Forbes*, 30 July 2019.
4 New India Assurance Limited, National Insurance Company Limited, United India Insurance Company Limited and Oriental Insurance Company Limited.
5 RBI Bulletin, June 2020.
6 '"Entrepreneurs don't retire . . . they die": Secret diary of VG Siddhartha – Part 1', N. Mahalakshmi, *Outlook Business*, 5 August 2016.
7 'VG Siddhartha: From coffee to cyber cafes and beyond', M.D. Riti, The Rediff Business Special, 3 July 2000.

Chapter 3: The Rise

1 The World Bank Commodity Markets data downloaded from https://www.worldbank.org/en/research/commodity-markets.
2 'India: Macroeconomics and Political Economy 1964–1991', Vijay Joshi and I.M.D. Little, Comparative Macroeconomic Studies, The World Bank, Washington D.C., 1994.
3 'The long road to the 1991 economic crisis', Ankit Mital, *Mint*, 8 July 2016.
4 'Remembering V.G. Siddhartha', Allen Mendoca, *Man's World* India, 21 November 2019.
5 'How Infosys became the darling of investors', Ravindra Sonavane and Varun Sood, *Mint*, 12 June 2018.
6 https://www.worldbank.org/en/research/commodity-markets.

7 '"One can't be an entrepreneur without taking calculated risks": Secret diary of VG Siddhartha – Part 2', N. Mahalakshmi, *Outlook Business*, 5 August 2016.
8 ₹1.50 crore was approximately $463,000 in 1995.
9 ₹50 lakh was around $154,000.
10 Ibid.
11 Ibid.
12 'Tech-savvy Siddhartha got many a tech winner going', Raghu Krishnan, The *Economic Times*, 31 July 2019.
13 ₹10 crore was approximately $2.32 million in 1999.
14 Ibid.
15 'Here's how much VG Siddhartha made as profit from Mindtree after investing Rs 340 crore', *CNBC TV18*, 19 March 2019.
16 Mindtree Limited, Integrated Annual Report 2018–19.
17 'For CCD's VG Siddhartha, brewing fortunes is second nature', *Business Standard*, 10 February 2019.
18 'Coffee king on Amazon trail for furniture biz', The *Times of India*, 8 August 2011.

Chapter 4: The Listing

1 'Sandal, vandals and a scandal', *Financial Express*, 23 March 2003.
2 '"Govt, not Rajkumar family, paid ransom": Ex-DGP', The *Times of India*, 22 November 2000.
3 'Defamation case against former Karnataka top cop dismissed', Shubham Ghosh, https://www.oneindia.com/bengaluru/defamation-case-against-former-karnataka-top-cop-dismissed-1531688.html, 29 September 2014.
4 'KKR-led consortium to invest in Coffee Day Resorts', from media.kkr.com, 30 March 2010.
5 George Anders, *Merchants of Debt: KKR and the Mortgaging of American Business*, (Beard Books, US, 2002).

6 Anita Raghavan, *The Billionaire's Apprentice*, (Grand Central Publishing, US, 2015).
7 George Anders, *Merchants of Debt: KKR and the Mortgaging of American Business*, (Beard Books, US, 2002).
8 'Café Coffee Day group to take control of Sical' Baiju Kalesh and P. Manoj, *Mint*, 14 November 2010.
9 Ibid.
10 The INR depreciated vis-à-vis the USD during the six years ending 31 March 2015. Though net worth increased in INR terms, it had declined in USD terms.
11 'Coffee Day Enterprises shares slump 18% on market debut', Ami Shah and Swaraj Singh Dhanjai, *Mint*, 3 November 2015.
12 Ibid.
13 Ibid.
14 https://www.chittorgarh.com/ipo/indigo_ipo/492/, accessed on 17 October 2020.

Chapter 5: The Meltdown

1 Personal interview with Bala Naidu.
2 'I-T raids on DK Shivakumar: BJP wins perception battle; hits 2 election-bound states with one stroke', T.S. Sudhir, Firstpost, 3 August 2017.
3 'History of "resort politics" in India', sutori.com.
4 'I-T raids on DK Shivakumar: BJP wins perception battle; hits 2 election-bound states with one stroke', T.S. Sudhir, Firstpost, 3 August 2017.
5 IL&FS subsidiary NTADCL dragged to the appellate tribunal; AIDQUA steps up the pressure on Tirupur water project woes', Sucheta Dalal, moneylife.in, 17 July 2019.
6 'Revealed: SFIO interim report blows the lid off the extent of fraud in IL&FS', Tarun Sharma, moneycontrol.com, 4 December 2018.

7 IL&FS saga tells us that the experts cannot be trusted', Anil Dharker, The *Times of India*, 6 October 2018.
8 'IFIN ex-CEO Bawa says LIC didn't back Piramal's IL&FS bid', Rashmi Rajput, The *Economic Times*, 15 July 2019.
9 'RBI asks shareholders to rescue IL&FS', Ridhima Saxena, BloombergQuint, 28 September 2018.
10 'IL&FS gets only Rs 5.47 lakh from rights issue as large shareholders stay away', M Saraswathy, www.moneycontrol.com, 31 October 2018.
11 'Government takes control of IL&FS', The *Economic Times*, 1 October 2018.
12 'IL&FS Scam: ED Arrests Arun Saha and K Ramchand in Money-Laundering Probe', *MoneyLife*, 20 June 2019.
13 'Former IL&FS chairman Ravi Parthasarathy arrested by Chennai police', Dev Chatterjee, *Business Standard*, 12 June 2021.
14 'Ex-IL&FS chairman Ravi Parthasarathy dies from prolonged illness: Report, *Business Standard*, 27 April 2022

Chapter 6: The Jewel in the Crown

1 'The inside story of the Mindtree shakedown', Sundeep Khanna and Varun Sood, *Mint*, 5 April 2019.
2 'MindTree IPO price fixed at Rs 425/share', *Business Standard*, 19 January 2013.
3 Mindtree Consulting Limited, Red Herring Prospectus, 29 January 2007.
4 Mindtree Limited, Annual Report, FY2018.
5 'L&T Infotech seeks to acquire stake in Mindtree', Arijit Barman, Raghu Krishnan and Priyanka Sangani, The *Economic Times*, 21 January 2019.
6 'Tax department stops VG Siddhartha's plans to sell stake in Mindtree', BloombergQuint, 26 January 2019.
7 'How VG Siddhartha is freeing up pledged Mindtree shares', Bloomberg Quint, 22 March 2019.

8 An escrow account is a bank account in which a trustee oversees the monies arising out of an asset sale. The buyer in the transaction is legally required to deposit the purchase consideration in the escrow account. The seller has no access to the account till legal due diligence and pre-requisites to transaction completion are completed.
9 'Mindtree says had detected irregularities by VG Siddhartha in disclosures', *Business Standard*, 19 March 2019.
10 https://twitter.com/skilledinodisha/status/1107297314811449344?lang=hr.
11 https://twitter.com/skilledinodisha/status/1107299169415225345?ref_src=twsrc%5Etfw.
12 'Is L&T's open offer price for Mindtree good enough for investors?' Agam Vakil, BloombergQuint, 1 April 2019.
13 'Mandatory open offer: Did L&T breach 25% in Mindtree?' Venkatesh Ganesh, *The Hindu BusinessLine*, 28 May 2019.
14 'L&T gets CCI approval for its Mindtree takeover bid', Anirudh Laskar, *Mint*, 6 April 2019.
15 'What Nalanda's exit means for Mindtree', *Moneycontrol News*, 24 June 2019.

Chapter 7: Collateral Damage

1 The glossary provides definitions of algo-trading, high frequency trading, and co-location.
2 'Blowing the whistle on manipulation in NSE', Sucheta Dalal, moneylife.in, 19 June 2015.
3 'Cracking the NSE colocation controversy', Aarati Krishnan, *The Hindu BusinessLine*, 2 May 2019.
4 Ibid.
5 'SEBI fines NSE Rs 90 crore for violations in dark fibre case', BloombergQuint, 11 September 2015.
6 'Ajay Shah colluded to misuse NSE data for commercial purposes: SEBI', Jayshree P. Upadhyay, *Mint*, 2 May 2019.

7 'Cracking the NSE colocation controversy', Aarati Krishnan, *The Hindu BusinessLine*, 2 May 2019.
8 'CBI arrests ex-NSE chief Chitra after quizzing in co-location scam', Rajashekhar Jha, The *Times of India*, 7 March 2022
9 'Death of the coffee king: Power and money in corporate India', Henny Sender, *Nikkei Asian Review*, 26 May 2020.
10 'In seven years, 30 Congress leaders deserted party', Dibyendu Mondal, The *Sunday Guardian*, 18 July 2020.
11 'D.K. Shivakumar's troubles began with I-T raids in 2017', *The Hindu*, 3 September 2019.
12 '"Vendetta": DK Shivakumar On ₹ 75 crore disproportionate assets case', Arvind Gunasekar, Maya Sharma, *NDTV*, 5 October 2020.
13 'D.K. Shivakumar declares total assets of Rs 840 crore, a staggering jump from Rs 251 crore in 2013', The *New Indian Express*, 19 April 2018.
14 FY2018 and FY2019 annual reports of Coffeeday Consolidations Private Limited, Devadarshini Info Technologies Private Limited, Gonibedu Coffee Estates Private Limited and Sivan Securities Private Limited, downloaded from mca.gov.in.
15 'Probe reveals Coffee Day arms advanced ₹3,535 crore to Siddhartha's private arm', *The Hindu BusinessLine*, 24 July 2020.

Part 2: High-Flyers
Chapter 8: Take Off

1 R.M. Lala, *Beyond the Last Blue Mountain: A Life of J.R.D. Tata* (Penguin Random House India, New Delhi, 2017).
2 Ibid.
3 Ibid.
4 Air India annual reports downloaded from www.airindia.in.

5 'After 68 years, Tatas win back Air India with ₹18,000-crore bid', Jagriti Chandra, *The Hindu*, 8 October 2021.
6 'SIA won't be Tata Group's co-pilot in bid for Air India', Kala Vijayraghavan and Anirban Chowdhury, The *Economic Times*, 29 January 2021.

Chapter 9: Open Skies

1 'Government opens up the skies for private air taxies', Paranjoy Guha Thakurta, *India Today*, 15 May 1990.
2 'Valentine's day crash which shattered Bangalore', The *Times of India*, 22 May 2010.
3 'Madhavrao Scindia faces problems in aviation sector', Raj Chengappa, *India Today*, 30 July 1991.
4 'Government opens up the skies for private air taxis', Paranjoy Guha Thakurta, *India Today*, 15 May 1990.
5 'Fairgrowth Financial's executives own up to company's involvement in securities scam', *India Today*, 31 August 1992.
6 Josy Joseph, *A Feast of Vultures: The Hidden Business of Democracy in India* (HarperCollins Publishers India, New Delhi, 2016).
7 Ibid.
8 Ibid.
9 Ibid.
11 Ibid.
11 Ibid.

Chapter 10: Simply Fly

1 Air transport statistics for the year 1997–98 downloaded from https://dgca.gov.in/digigov-portal/.
2 'Didn't want to bribe our way into airline business: Tata', *India Today*, 15 November 2010.

3 'Jet thwarted Tata airline plan in '97: ex-aviation secy', *Hindustan Times*, 30 April 2012.
4 Jet Airways (India) Limited, Draft Red Herring Prospectus, January 2005.
5 'Jet Airways: Indian or foreign?' Rediff.com, 17 August 2001.
6 'Arun Shourie clips wings of Jet, Sahara', Diwakar, The *Times of India*, 5 February 2004.
7 'Adopting a revolutionary approach', Nilima Pathak, *Gulf News*, 8 April 2011.
8 Ibid.
9 'Air Deccan launches one rupee ticket for "common man",' *Outlook India*, 6 June 2005.
10 'R.K. Laxman the king of cartoons, and I', Captain Gopinath, The *Economic Times*, 2 February 2015.
11 Deccan Aviation Limited, Draft Red Herring Prospectus, 2006.
12 Air India Annual Report 2007-2008 downloaded from www.airindia.in.
13 Air Transport Statistics for the year 2003-04 downloaded from https://dgca.gov.in/digigov-portal/.
14 'Jet Airways IPO priced at Rs. 1100 per share', *Business Standard*, 28 February 2005.
15 'Air Deccan IPO ends on a feeble note', *Business Standard,* 14 February 2013.
16 'Air Deccan: IPO struggle reflects Indian overcapacity worries', *Aviation Strategy*, June 2006.
17 'Jet–Sahara deal: Reasons behind collapse of India's most high-profile aviation merger', Puja Mehra, *India Today*, 9 July 2006.
18 Ibid.
19 'Jet Airways in a row in the US', T.V. Parasuram, *Outlook India*, 4 June 2005.
20 Josy Joseph, *A Feast of Vultures: The Hidden Business of Democracy in India* (HarperCollins Publishers India, New Delhi, 2016).
21 Jet Airways annual report, FY2010.

Chapter 11: Overbooked

1. NEPC acquires Damania, 24 May 1995, www.flightglobal.com.
2. Fleet, personnel and financial statistics, www.dgca.gov.in, 2018-19.
3. Go Airlines (India) Limited, Draft Red Herring Prospectus, 13 May 2021, downloaded from www.sebi.gov.in
4. K. Giriprakash, *The Vijay Mallya Story*, (Penguin Books, India, 2014).
5. 'The flight and fall of Vijay Mallya', Venkatesha Babu, *India Today*, 27 March 2016.
6. Ibid.
7. Berkshire Hathaway chairman's letter to shareholders, 2007.
8. 'Dr. Vijay Mallya launches Kingfisher Airlines', www.businesswireindia.com, 9 May 2005.
9. 'What happened to Indian carrier Kingfisher Airlines?' Joanna Bailey, simpleflying.com, 23 August 2019.
10. '5/20: A rule that needs to be changed', Anjuli Bhargava, *Business Standard*, 18 May 2016.
11. 'Air Deccan rules out sale to beer billionaire', *Hindustan Times*, 8 May 2007.
12. 'Can this marriage work?' K.R. Balasubramanyam, *Business Today*, 27 January 2008.
13. 'Kingfisher goes international', Brendan Sobie, *Flight Global*, 4 August 2008.
14. Ibid.
15. 'Kingfisher launches international flight', *Financial Express*, 3 September 2008.
16. 'Kingfisher puts on hold new international flights', P.R. Sanjai, *Mint*, 12 October 2008.
17. 'Kingfisher, Mallya were not authorised to use brand valuation report to raise funds: Grant Thornton', *Business Today*, 16 October 2018.
18. Ibid.

19 Ibid.
20 'Gopinath continues to reduce his stake in Kingfisher Airlines', The *Economic Times*, 15 September 2009.
21 'Captain Gopinath quits Kingfisher board', *Business Standard*, 24 March 2010.
22 'Vijay Mallya cheated me of my dream', The Quint, 9 November 2020.
23 'Kingfisher Airlines: the beginning of the endgame?' Tamal Bandyopadhyay, *Mint*, 14 January 2013.
24 Kingfisher Airlines annual report, FY2011.
25 'Kingfisher Airlines: The beginning of the endgame?' Tamal Bandyopadhyay, *Mint*, 14 January 2013.
26 'Kingfisher to exit low-cost airline, shuts down Kingfisher Red', *Business Today*, 2 December 2011.
27 'Aviation regulator grounds Kingfisher on safety concerns', *The Hindu BusinessLine*, 12 October 2012.
28 'How not to run a service business: lessons from Kingfisher Airlines', Govindaraj Ethiraj, *Forbes India* blogs, 20 February 2012.
29 'Kingfisher getting fuel supply on cash & carry basis: IOC', *Business Standard*, 25 January 2013.
30 'Diageo acquires majority stake in United Spirits', P.R. Sanjai, Mihir Dalal, Deepti Chaudhary, *Mint*, 10 November 2012.
31 'Diageo gains control of United Spirits, raises stake to 55%', Mihir Dalal, *Mint*, 2 July 2014.
32 'Vijay Mallya quits as United Spirits chairman', P.R. Sanjai, *Mint*, 26 February 2016.
33 'The legacy of Raghuram Rajan', Anil Padmanabhan, *Mint*, 26 January 2016.
34 'Truth behind how Vijay Mallya fled India', Kingshuk Nag, dailyo.in, 26 July 2017.
35 'SBI moves Karnataka high court seeking Vijay Mallya's arrest', Sharan Poovanna and Suneera Tandon, *Mint*, 5 March 2016.
36 'Vijay Mallya left India on 2 March, Supreme Court told', Shreeja Sen and P.R. Sanjai, *Mint,* 10 March 2016.

37 'CBI arrests former IDBI chairman Yogesh Aggarwal and 8 others in Vijay Mallya loan default case: Sources', The *Economic Times*, 24 January 2017.
38 'Vijay Mallya to step down from United Breweries board, name successor', Kala Vijayraghavan, The *Economic Times*, 23 October 2017.
39 'Vijay Mallya used around 40 shell companies to siphon off more than Rs 100 crore abroad: report', *Business Today*, 9 May 2017.
40 'Extradition "stalled": Vijay Mallya seeks asylum?' Murali Krishnan and Prasun Sonwalkar, *Hindustan Times*, 6 October 2020.
41 'Why Covid-19 may impact extradition timeline of Vijay Mallya', *Financial Express*, 14 May 2020.
42 'Rs 3,600 crore recovered from Vijay Mallya till now, Rs 11,000 crore still pending', The *Free Press Journal*, 26 October 2020.
43 'House of debt—revisited', Ashish Gupta, Kush Shah and Prashant Kumar, Credit Suisse, 13 August 2013.
44 'Vijay Mallya drops out of billionaire ranks', Nazneen Karmali, *Forbes*, 25 October 2012.

Chapter 12: Holding Pattern

1 'Jet Airways: How Naresh Goyal lost the plot', Manu Balachandran, *Forbes India*, 18 April 2019.
2 'Retelling the Jet Airways saga. How mismanaged operation costs took down the airline Part 2', Satyendra Pandey, *India Infra Hub*, 20 July 2020.
3 'Etihad buys stake in India's Jet Airways amid protests', Naazneen Karmali, *Forbes*, 25 April 2013.
4 Ibid.
5 Ibid.
6 'The highs and lows of Naresh Goyal's turbulent time at Jet Airways' helm', Deborshi Chaki and Amrit Raj, *Mint*, 26 March 2019.

7 'Jet Airways chairman steps down in debt restructuring pact', Simon Mundy, The *Financial Times*, 25 March 2019.
8 'Ministry of Corporate Affairs moved a month ago to bar Naresh Goyal from leaving India', Rashmi Rajput, The *Economic Times*, 27 May 2019.
9 'Jet Airways crisis: Naresh Goyal withdraws from bidding after Etihad, TPG Capital threaten to walk out', *Business Today*, 16 April 2019.
10 List of creditors (version 9) updated till 3 October 2020, www.jetairways.com.
11 'CoC approves Kalrock Capital-Murari Jalan's plan to revive Jet Airways', Aneesh Phadnis and Subrata Panda, *Business Standard*, 17 October 2020.
12 'Financial creditors to take 95% haircut on Rs. 7,800 cr Jet Airways dues', Arindam Majumder, *Business Standard*, 1 July 2021.
13 'Disinvestments—A Historical Perspective', bsepsu.com.
14 'Naresh Chandra Committee report on the civil aviation sector', nishithdesai.com, 8 January 2004.
15 'Before Tatas buy Air India, a look at 5 bad decisions that led to national carrier's downfall', *India Today* Web Desk, 21 June 2017.
16 'Air India puts more than 60 real estate assets under the hammer', Rhik Kundu, *Mint*, 16 August 2019.
17 'Air India stake sale: Govt 24% stake may have put investors off', The *Economic Times*, 4 June 2018.
18 'Budget 2021: Air India divestment to be concluded next fiscal', Rhik Kundu, *Mint*, 1 February 2021.
19 'Meet Ajay Singh, SpiceJet's white knight and Team Modi's slogan writer', *Hindustan Times*, 17 January 2015.
20 'CBI court discharges Maran brothers in illegal telephone exchange scam', The *Indian Express*, 14 March 2018.
21 'Top 10 Highest Paid CEO in India, 2021', https://theenterpriseworld.com/top-10-highest-paid-ceo-in-india/.

22 'Marans made a bad call with SpiceJet', Arindam Mukherjee, *Outlook India*, 20 April 2015.

23 'Co-founder Ajay Singh may be SpiceJet's white knight', *Hindustan Times*, 18 December 2014.

24 'Sweet deals are made of this', Arindam Mukherjee, *Outlook India*, 15 June 2015.

25 'Tribunal rules in favour of SpiceJet in Rs 1,323-crore spat with Maran', BloombergQuint, 23 July 2018.

26 'Relief for SpiceJet: Supreme Court stays Delhi HC order on payment of Rs 243 crore to Kalanithi Maran', Moneycontrol News, 6 November 2020.

27 Deepak Patel, 'Former SC Judge PV Reddi to mediate SpiceJet-Kalanithi Maran spat', *Business Standard*, 7 September 2022.

28 https://eliteaviations.com/news/2022/07/31/spicejet-flights-limited-in-light-of-safety-issues-airlinegeeks-com

29 'DGCA to deregister two more SpiceJet aircraft on lessor's request', Deepak Patel, *Business Standard*, 28 August 2022.

30 'The world's top airline stock is SpiceJet, with 124% advance', Anurag Kotoky and Santanu Chakraborty, BloombergQuint, 27 June 2017.

31 Deccan Aviation Limited, Draft Red Herring Prospectus, 2006 downloaded from sebi.gov.in.

32 'How Rahul Bhatia found IndiGo gold', Cuckoo Paul, *Forbes*, 3 November 2010.

33 'Secret of IndiGo's consistent profits: What makes it prosper despite a troubled industry', The *Economic Times*, 28 April 2015.

34 'IndiGo pays Rs 2.1 crore to SEBI, settles case of allegedly violating noms', The *Indian Express*, 10 February 2021.

35 Read full text of IndiGo co-founder Rakesh Gangwal's letter to SEBI, cnbctv18.com, 19 July 2019.

36 'Why IndiGo's promoters fell out and how the upcoming EGM can settle the dispute', Yaruqhullah Khan, moneycontrol.com, 9 December 2021.
37 Ibid

Chapter 13: Air Pockets

1 Petroleum Planning & Analysis Cell, Ministry of Petroleum & Natural Gas, Government of India.
2 'India's corporate bond market: Issues in market microstructure', Reserve Bank of India Bulletin, January 2019.
3 'New ATF pricing method on cards; airlines eye relief,' The *Economic Times*, 30 August 2022.
4 'Excise duty on jet fuel cut from 14% to 11% in relief for airlines', Gireesh Chandra Prasad, *Mint*, 10 October 2018.
5 'Not quite flying: Why the Modi govt's UDAN scheme is struggling', Sai Manish, *Business Standard*, 5 February 2020.
6 Ibid.
7 List of RCS Routes Commenced Under RCS-UDAN 1.0, 2.0, 3.0, & 4.0 (As on 29 November 2021), downloaded from https://www.aai.aero/en/rcs-udan.
8 'All you wanted to know about International UDAN', Anand Kalyanaraman, *The Hindu BusinessLine*, 22 October 2018.
9 '4 years on, UDAN plan struggles to exit turbulence', Rhik Kundu, *Mint*, 19 February 2021.
10 dgca.gov.in.

Part 3: The Financial Whiz
Chapter 14: The Patriarch's Demise

1 'Dhirubhai: Larger than life, even in death', *Financial Express*, 8 July 2002.
2 Hamish MacDonald, *The Polyester Prince: The Rise of Dhirubhai Ambani* (Allen & Unwin, Australia, 1999).

3 Ibid.
4 Ibid.
5 A large building divided into many separate tenements, offering inexpensive and basic accommodation.
6 Ibid.
7 Ibid.
8 Ibid.
9 Hamish MacDonald, *The Polyester Prince: The Rise of Dhirubhai Ambani* (Allen & Unwin, Australia, 1999).
10 'I am an Indian citizen. I was born and raised here: Nusli Wadia', *India Today*, 31 August 1989.
11 Hamish MacDonald, *The Polyester Prince: The Rise of Dhirubhai Ambani* (Allen & Unwin, Australia, 1999).
12 Ibid.
13 'Mukesh, Anil Ambani face tough task of steering Reliance empire into ultra-ambitious future', Vivek Law, Sheela Raval and Sandeep Unnithan, *India Today*, 7 July 2002.
14 Hamish MacDonald, *The Polyester Prince: The Rise of Dhirubhai Ambani* (Allen & Unwin, Australia, 1999).
15 Annual reports of Reliance Industries Limited, FY1980 to FY1988, downloaded from https://www.ril.com/InvestorRelations/FinancialReporting.aspx.
16 'Reliance Industries stands accused in infringement of India's export-import laws', Prem Shankar Jha, *India Today*, 15 September 1986.
17 Ibid.
18 Hamish MacDonald, *The Polyester Prince: The Rise of Dhirubhai Ambani* (Allen & Unwin, Australia, 1999).
19 Ibid.
20 'Mukesh, Anil Ambani face tough task of steering Reliance empire into ultra-ambitious future', Vivek Law, Sheela Raval and Sandeep Unnithan, *India Today*, 7 July 2002.

Chapter 15: Ashwamedha Yagna

1 'The Reliance tussle', V. Sridhar and Anupama Katakam, *Frontline*, 14 January 2005.
2 Ibid.
3 'The house dad built', Alam Srinivas, *Outlook India*, 6 December 2004.
4 Ibid.
5 Ibid.
6 'Caught in the cross heirs, Alam Srinivas, *Outlook India*, 13 December 2004.
7 Certain members of Parliament alleged that RIL had issued fake share certificates.
8 Ibid.
9 'Mukesh got 12% stake in Infocomm as sweat equity', Kausik Datta, Rediff.com,10 December 2004.
10 'Mukesh gives up 12% equity in Infocomm', *Outlook India*, 23 December 2004.
11 'The house dad built', Alam Srinivas, *Outlook India*, 6 December 2004.
12 'An empire split', Anupama Katakam, *Frontline*, 15 July 2005.
13 'Ambanis seal deal, finally', *Business Standard*, 19 June 2005.
14 'What the break-up means', Alam Srinivas, *Outlook India*, 4 July 2005.
15 'After months of acrimony, an outbreak of brotherly love at Reliance', Knowledge@Wharton, 13 July 2005.
16 'An empire split', Anupama Katakam, *Frontline*, 15 July 2005.
17 'Ambanis bid goodbye to staff', *Financial Express*, 20 June 2005.
18 Ibid.
19 Ibid.
20 'Anil Ambani forms new group', *Hindustan Times*, 20 June 2005.
21 'RIL completes allotment of shares of four new entities', *Outlook India*, 5 February 2006.

22 'Reliance Petroleum is the world's 13th biggest in '06', *Financial Express*, 24 December 2006.
23 stats.arrepim.com, World Billionaire Lists.
24 Reliance Communications Limited, Annual Report, 2006-07.
25 'Brothers in arms, misappropriating a fortune—the full version', Neeraj Monga and Varun Raj, Veritas Investment Research, 18 July 2011.
26 The $ value of Paytm's IPO is lower than that of Coal India due to exchange rate depreciation. The exchange rates in 2010 and 2021 were ₹45.73/$ and ₹73.33/$ respectively.
27 '10 years after RPower listing: Busting many myths', K.S. Badri Narayanan, 9 February 2018.

Chapter 16: Kurukshetra

1 'MTN, RCom end talks; go separate ways', Baju Kallesh, *Mint*, 19 July 2008.
2 'Three years on, Ambani brothers keep bickering', The *Economic Times*, 17 June 2008.
3 'Anil Ambani's AGM statement: complete text', *Mint*, 28 July 2009.
4 'Gas Wars: Crony Capitalism and the Ambanis', Paranjoy Guha Thakurta and Subir Ghosh, AuthorsUpFront, 1 January 2014.
5 'Ambani vs. Ambani: A dispute over natural gas price flares up', Knowledge@Wharton, 10 September 2009.
6 'Full statement by Reliance Industries', The *Economic Times*, 11 October 2009.
7 'Timeline: Key dates in Ambani brothers' dispute', *Hindustan Times*, 23 May 2010.
8 'Ambanis scrap non-compete agreements', Bhuma Shrivastava, Satish John, Baiju Kalesh and Utpal Bhaskar, *Mint*, 24 May 2010.
9 'Reliance Power to give back Dadri land to UP govt, which will return it to the farmers', *Hindustan Times*, 18 January 2005.

10 Reliance Power Limited, Annual Reports, FY2012 to FY2020.
11 Reliance Power Limited, Draft Red Herring Prospectus, 3 October 2007.
12 'Govt aided RIL in gas contract, lost money: CAG', Anupama Airy, *Hindustan Times*, 13 June 2011.
13 'Reliance, DGH, oil ministry in the firing line', Utpal Bhaskar and Sahil Makkar, *Mint*, 9 September 2011.
14 'United States became fourth-largest crude oil supplier to India in 2020: Report', Sanjeev Choudhary, The *Economic Times*, 9 July 2021.
15 'Gas pricing reform in India: Implications for the Indian gas landscape', Anupama Sen, Oxford Institute for Energy Studies, April 2015.
16 'Making a mockery of domestic gas pricing', Surya P. Sethi, *The Hindu*, 18 January 2013.
17 'Reliance Industries, BP withdraw gas price arbitration against government', Sanjeev Choudhary, The *Economic Times*, 23 June 2017.
18 'Reliance exits shale gas business in US', *Mint*, 9 November 2021.
19 Ibid.
20 'CAG report provides breather to RIL', Anand Kalyanaraman, *The Hindu BusinessLine*, 12 March 2018.
21 'Standing committee report summary: Stressed/non-performing assets in gas based power plants', Prachee Mishra, *PRS Legislative Research*, 30 January 2019.
22 'RIL, BP start production at Asia's deepest gas field', Kalpana Pathak, *Mint*, 18 December 2020.

Chapter 17: Lakshagriha

1 Arvind Subramanian, *Of Counsel: The Challenges of the Modi–Jaitley Economy* (Penguin Viking, New Delhi, 2018).
2 'House of debt, Indian financial sector review', Ashish Gupta, Kush Shah and Prashant Kumar, Credit Suisse

Equity Research, 2 August 2012, 13 August 2013, and 21 October 2015.

3 'Reliance Group says it is not the most indebted conglomerate', P.R. Sanjai and Mobis Philipose, *Mint*, 8 June 2016.

4 'Not violated any license norms with Swan stake: Rcom', *Mint*, 13 February 2011.

5 'Zero loss R.I.P.', *The Hindu*, 9 August 2012.

6 'Cabinet sets Rs 14,000 cr as reserve price for 2G spectrum', FirstPost, 4 August 2012.

7 'As 2G scam verdict is announced, questions remain about Anil Ambani's "memory loss"', The Wire, 20 December 2017.

8 Ibid

9 Ibid

10 '2G scam verdict: A Raja, Kanimozhi, others acquitted', *The Hindu BusinessLine*, 9 January 2018.

Chapter 18: Chausar

1 'How and why Anil Ambani bought into the Pipavav fire sale', P.R. Sanjai and Ashish K. Mishra, *Mint*, 12 March 2015.

2 Ibid.

3 'Narendra Modi government shortlists Larsen & Toubro, Pipavav for Rs 60,000 crore submarine contract', Huma Siddiqui, The *Financial Express*, 12 March 2015.

4 'Rafale deal: The Anil Ambani connection', Sandeep Unnithan, *India Today*, 7 October 2018.

5 'Air Force declines to share details on the Rafale Deal', The *New Indian Express*, 5 February 2017.

6 'Reliance Defence will get 3% of Rs. 30,000 crore Rafale offset', The *Economic Times*, 15 October 2018.

7 'Reliance has 10% offset in Rafale, in talks with 100 firms: Dassault CEO', AFP, 12 October 2018.

8 'Reliance Defence corners offset contracts worth ₹21,000 crore on Rafale deal', Amrita Nair Ghaswalla, *The Hindu BusinessLine*, 12 January 2018.

9 'Reliance Defence eyes Rs 300 billion offset from Dassault deal', Palak Shah, The *Economic Times*, 28 February 2017.
10 'EXCLUSIVE: 1st full details of Rafale's €4-billion make-in-India & offsets plan', livefistdefence.com, 13 March 2018.
11 'Rafale deal: Understanding the controversy', The Wire, 23 August 2018, https://www.youtube.com/watch?v=GcJRXmYWXW0.
12 'Rafale deal: The Anil Ambani connection', Sandeep Unnithan, *India Today*, 7 October 2018.
13 'Rafale judgment: Government moves supreme court seeking correction in para that makes reference to CAG report, PAC', Bloomberg Quint, 15 December 2018.
14 'Rafale documents not stolen, petitioners used photocopies: Attorney General K.K. Venugopal', *The Hindu*, 9 March 2019.
15 'Rafale deal: Chronology of events', *The Hindu BusinessLine*, 10 March 2019.
16 'Rafale deal: SC crashes hopes for court-monitored probe, political row takes flight on Justice Joseph's note', Aneesha Mathur, *India Today*, 15 November 2019.
17 'CAG Report Summary: Capital Acquisition in Indian Air Force', Vinayak Krishnan, *PRS Legislative Research*, 26 February 2019.
18 'Decoding the CAG report on Rafale fighter jet deal in 10 points', *Hindustan Times*, 13 February 2019.

Chapter 19: Agyatvasa?

1 'Cancel broadband spectrum held by Reliance: CAG draft report', *Outlook India*, 29 June 2014.
2 'The creation of a mobile juggernaut', Kiran Stacey and Simon Mundy, The *Financial Times*, 10 February 2018.
3 Ibid.
4 Ibid.
5 Ibid.

6 'How India's banks ran up a $7 billion phone bill', Andy Mukherjee, BloombergQuint, 4 February 2019.
7 'Ericsson calls for Ambani to be jailed over non-payment of fees', Simon Mundy, The *Financial Times*, 5 January 2019.
8 'China bank files insolvency case against Rcom', Rajesh Kurup, *The Hindu BusinessLine*, 9 January 2018.
9 'Ericsson dues settlement row: Anil Ambani, RCom guilty of contempt of court rules SC', Krishnadas Rajagopal, *The Hindu*, 19 February 2019.
10 CARE Ratings reports on Reliance Capital dated 24 March 2017, 14 April 2017, 14 July 2017, 26 December 2017, 18 January 2018, 8 October 2018, 6 March 2019, 18 April 2019, 18 May 2019, 6 July 2019, 24 August 2019 and 20 September 2019.
11 'Anil Ambani vs Chinese banks: Court case exposes stunning decline', Benjamin Parkin, The *Financial Times*, 17 March 2020.
12 'Anil Ambani tells UK court he leads "disciplined" lifestyle', *The Hindu*, 26 September 2020.
13 'Anil Ambani vs Chinese banks: Court case exposes stunning decline', Benjamin Parkin, The *Financial Times*, 17 March 2020.
14 Reliance Capital Annual Report, FY2020.
15 'Yes Bank takes possession of ADAG's Mumbai headquarter', Gopika Gopakumar, *Mint*, 29 July 2020.
16 'Sale of pledged shares by L&T Finance, Edelweiss illegal: Reliance Group', *Business Standard*, 9 February 2019.
17 'Anil Ambani, an FII Investor?', Vidya Ram, *The Hindu BusinessLine*, 10 June 2012.
18 'Why has SEBI barred NRIs and Indians from P-Notes', Lokeshwari S.K., *The Hindu BusinessLine*, 26 April 2017.
19 'Indian to the core, and an oligarch', Anand Giridharadas, The *New York Times*, 15 June 2008.
20 'Anil Ambani's defamation blitz', Vijayta Lalwani, Scroll.in, 25 November 2018.

Chapter 20: Knives Out

1 'Huge scam in YES Bank for many years, says Enforcement Directorate', Shrimi Choudhary, *Business Standard*, 26 May 2020.
2 If the IPO share price is 56 times the average pre-IPO price, the premium is one less at 55.
3 'Analysts raise transparency concerns at Reliance Industries and its units', Kalpana Pathak, *Mint*, 12 February 2021.
4 africanbondmarkets.org.
5 'India's corporate bond market: Issues in market microstructure', Reserve Bank of India Bulletin, 10 January 2019.
6 'Here is what Modi govt should do to lift-off Indian bond market', The *Economic Times*, 6 February 2018.
7 'Get going, fast, on the bond market', ET Editorials, The *Economic Times*, 27 July 2020.
8 'Focus on credit default swaps to address insolvency stress', Ajoy Nath Jha, *Mint*, 12 May 2020.
9 'Who should be paying for the credit rating of bonds?' The *Economic Times*, 25 February 2019.
10 'Improving outcomes for the financial system through credit rating agencies—Part 2', Nandini Vijayaraghavan and Deepti George, https://www.dvara.com/blog/2019/12/19/improving-outcomes-for-the-financial-system-through-credit-rating-agencies-part-2/, 19 December 2019.
11 'Global debt monitor', Emre Tiftik and Khadija Mahmood, Institute of International Finance, 17 February 2021.
12 'Strengthening the credit rating framework in the country', Standing Committee on Finance 2018-19, Sixteenth Lok Sabha.
13 Corporate tax rates for 2011–2021, KPMG https://home.kpmg/xx/en/home/services/tax/tax-tools-and-resources/tax-rates-online/corporate-tax-rates-table.html.
14 'High levies, low tariffs double whammy for the telecom industry', Navadha Pandey, *Mint*, 14 November 2019.

15 'Who went to jail for their role in the financial crisis?' Laura Noonan, Cale Tilford, Richard Milne, Ian Mount and Peter Wise, The *Financial Times*, 20 September 2018.

Epilogue

1 'Reliance Infra set to get Rs 4,600 crore arbitration award from Delhi Metro Rail Corp', Samanwaya Rautray, The *Economic Times*, 10 September 2021.
2 'RPower to sell Samalkot project equipment to cut debt', Suresh P. Iyengar, *The Hindu BusinessLine*, 28 June 2021.
3 'Reliance Capital defaulted in paying Rs 535 crore interest on EPFO's NCD investment of Rs 2,500 crore: Govt', www.moneylife.in, 14 December 2021.
4 'Reliance Home Finance resolution: lenders zero in on a potential winner', Vishwanath Nair, BloombergQuint, 16 June 2021.
5 'Reliance Commercial Finance debt holders okay sale to Authum Investment', Joel Rebello, The *Economic Times*, 10 December 2021.
6 'Anil Ambani's financial empire goes under the hammer', Dev Chatterjee, *Nikkei Asia*, 14 January 2022.
7 Authum Investment and Infrastructure Limited, Annual Report, FY2021.
8 'Top bidder for Reliance Home Fin wife of once banned investor Sanjay Dangi', Anand Adhikari, *Business Today*, 18 June 2021.
9 Authum Investment and Infrastructure Limited, Annual Reports, FY2012 to FY2021.
10 Reliance Home Finance, Annual Report, FY2021.
11 Reliance Commercial Finance, Annual Report, FY2021.
12 'Kingfisher Airlines 15 leased planes may land in scrapyards', Saurabh Sinha, The *Times of India*, 8 April 2013.
13 'Finally, service tax department sells Vijay Mallya luxury jet for a paltry Rs 35 crore', The *Economic Times*, 1 July 2018.

14 'Debt Recovery Tribunal sells Rs 5,800 crore of Mallya's United Breweries shares for PSBs', The *Economic Times*, 24 June 2021.
15 'Vijay Mallya's Kingfisher House sold for just Rs 52 crore in 9th attempt', Munish Chandra Pandey, *India Today*, 15 August 2021.
16 'Kingfisher Villa finally sold, businessman Sachiin Joshi picks up Vijay Mallya's erstwhile party pad', *India Today*, 8 April 2017.
17 'No takers for brand Kingfisher, trademarks', *The Hindu BusinessLine*, 30 April 2016.
18 'Vijay Mallya loses battle to keep London home', Naomi Canton, The *Times of India*, 19 January 2022.
19 'UK judge reserves judgment on whether Vijay Mallya is to be evicted from posh London home', Naomi Canton, The *Times of India*, 11 January 2022.
20 'Home ministry grants security clearance to Jet Airways', The *Economic Times*, 8 May 2022.
21 Coffee Day Enterprises Limited, Annual Reports, FY2019 to FY2021.
22 'Coffee Day's sale of tech park to Blackstone through', K.R. Balasubramanyam, The *Economic Times*, 18 March 2020.
23 'Coffee Day to sell 85.6% stake in Way2Wealth to Shriram Credit Co', *The Hindu BusinessLine*, 20 November 2020.
24 Coffee Day Enterprises Limited, Annual Reports, FY2019 to FY2021.
25 'Coffee Day Enterprises promoted Sical Logistics received four firm bids under insolvency proceedings', Sangita Mehta, The *Economic Times*, 12 January 2022.

Glossary

Algorithmic trading or algo-trading	Algo-trading uses a computer program that follows a defined set of instructions (an algorithm) to place a trade. The trade, in theory, can generate profits at a speed and frequency that is impossible for a human trader to replicate. The defined sets of instructions are based on timing, price, quantity or any mathematical model. Algo-traders frequently employ high frequency trading (HFT) technology. While it provides advantages, such as faster execution time and reduced costs, and is more systematic by ruling out the impact of human emotions on trading activities, algo-trading can also exacerbate the market's negative tendencies by causing flash crashes and immediate loss of liquidity.
Amortisation	An accounting technique used to periodically lower the book value of a loan or intangible assets (software, brands and goodwill, etc.) over a period of time. Amortisation, applied to intangible assets, is similar to depreciation.

Bankruptcy	A court order that stipulates how an insolvent person/entity will pay off their creditors and/or sell off their assets to settle their liabilities.
BJP	Bhartiya Janata Party. It was founded in 1980 and led by Narendra Modi since 2014.
Bonus issue	Free allocation of shares to the existing shareholders of a company. A 1:5 bonus issue implies that shareholders are allotted five shares for every share they own.
BSE	Bombay Stock Exchange.
CBI	Central Bureau of Investigation.
CFO	Cash flow from operations. It is the cash an entity generates from its core business after taxes.
Co-location	Locating computers owned by HFT firms and proprietary traders in the same premises where a stock exchange's computer servers are housed. This enables HFT firms to access stock prices a split second before the rest of the investing public. Co-location has become a lucrative business for exchanges, which charge HFT firms millions of dollars for the privilege of 'low-latency access'. Latency is the time that elapses from the moment a signal is sent to its receipt. Since lower latency equals faster speed, high frequency traders spend heavily to obtain the fastest computer hardware, software and data lines so as to execute orders as speedily as possible and gain a competitive edge in trading.

Conglomerate	An entity comprising multiple and, sometimes, unrelated businesses. Conglomerates oversee multiple businesses. The holding / parent company's earnings mostly comprise dividends paid by their constituent companies.
CRA	Credit Rating Agency.
Crore	An Indian unit of measurement equal to 10 million.
Debt	Money borrowed by one party from another. There are multiple types of debt, including bank loans, bonds, non-convertible debentures, corporate fixed deposits, bank fixed deposits, etc.
Debt/EBITDA ratio	Debt expressed as a multiple of earnings before interest, taxes, depreciation and amortisation of an entity. The higher the ratio, the greater an entity's indebtedness and financial risk.
Debt/Equity ratio	Debt expressed as a multiple of shareholders' equity, also referred to as balance sheet leverage. It denotes the share of borrowings vis-à-vis shareholders' equity in financing an entity's assets. The higher the ratio, the greater an entity's indebtedness and financial risk.
Depreciation	An accounting method of allocating the cost of tangible or physical assets over their useful lives. Depreciation represents how much of an asset's value has been used up.
DGCA	Directorate General of Civil Aviation. It's a government entity that regulates civil aviation in India.

Dividend	Distribution of a fraction of an entity's earnings to its shareholders as determined periodically by the board of directors.
EBITDA	Earnings before interest, taxes, depreciation and amortisation. This is a measure of the company's operating performance before payment of interest and taxes.
Equity	Also referred to as shareholders' equity, it represents the money that will be returned to an entity's shareholders after all assets were to be liquidated to repay all liabilities.
FI	Financial Institutions. These include banks, insurance companies, non-banking finance companies and mutual funds.
Free cash flows	Cash generated by an entity, defined as CFO minus interest and lease expenses minus capital expenditure minus dividends. CFO – Interest – Lease expenses – Capital Expenditure - Dividends
FSC	Full-Service Carrier. It refers to the airlines that typically offer passengers in-flight entertainment, checked baggage, meals, beverages and comforts such as blankets and pillows. Usually, the seats have more recline than those of budget airlines. Hence FSCs' price their ticket higher than budget airlines.
GIC	General Insurance Corporation of India. It is the state-owned monopoly reinsurer in the domestic market.
GFC	Global Financial Crisis of 2007–08.
GoI	Government of India.

High frequency trading or HFT	A method of trading that uses powerful computer programs to transact a large number of orders in fractions of a second. Typically, the traders with the fastest execution speeds are more profitable than traders with slower execution speeds. While HFT may enhance market liquidity, it is criticised for allowing larger traders, who usually have access to co-location facilities, to gain an upper hand in trading.
Holding company	A company that usually does not conduct any business but owns stakes in one or more entities, whose businesses it oversees. Dividends form the bulk of holding companies' revenues.
Insolvency	A state of financial distress in which a person/entity is unable to meet their operating expenses and settle contractual liabilities in a timely manner. A person/entity is deemed insolvent when their liabilities exceed their assets.
IBC/IBC 2016	Insolvency and Bankruptcy Code. This is India's bankruptcy law which outlines separate insolvency resolution processes for individuals, companies and partnership firms.
INC	Indian National Congress, aka Congress. Founded in 1885 and currently led by Mallikarjun Kharge.
Interest	An amount the lender charges the borrower and is a percentage of the principal or amount loaned.

IL&FS	Infrastructure Leasing and Financial Services.
IPO	Initial Public Offering. This is the process of listing the shares of a company on a stock exchange by selling its shares to the public comprising retail and institutional investors like banks, mutual funds, insurance companies, provident fund trusts, etc.
L&T	Larsen & Toubro. It is India's largest engineering conglomerate.
Lakh	An Indian unit of measurement equal to 100,000.
LC	Letter of Credit. It is a type of short-term credit extended by banks to facilitate businesses to purchase goods on credit. If the buyer is unable to pay the seller a whole or part of the purchase consideration on time, the bank will make good the shortfall.
LCC	Low-Cost Carrier, aka budget airlines.
Lease	A contract through which the owner of the asset or lessor rents it to the user or lessee. Indian companies used leases to keep their liabilities off the balance sheet till 2019 when a change in accounting rules made it mandatory to include leases as on-balance sheet liabilities.
NBFC	Non-banking Finance Company.
NCLT	National Companies Law Tribunal that was established under the Companies Act 2013 and constituted on 1 June 2016 is a quasi-judicial body that adjudicates for the insolvency resolution process of companies and limited liability partnerships under IBC 2016.

NCLAT	National Companies Law Appellate Tribunal. It is a body that adjudicates appeals to NCLT decisions. NCLAT decisions may be further appealed at the Supreme Court of India.
NDA	National Democratic Alliance. It is a coalition of political parties founded in 1998 and led by the BJP.
Net debt/EBITDA	Debt minus cash expressed as a multiple of a company's EBITDA.
Net lease adjusted debt/EBITDA	Debt plus lease liabilities minus cash expressed as a multiple of a company's EBITDA. Higher the net debt and net lease adjusted debt to EBITDA ratios, greater the financial risk a company is exposed to.
Net worth	A company's assets minus liabilities. An alternate definition is the sum of equity capital plus cumulative profits earned minus cumulative dividends paid since incorporation.
NRI	Non-Resident Indian.
NSE	National Stock Exchange.
OFCD	Optionally Fully Convertible Debentures. It is debt securities that investors have the option to convert to equity at dates/periods and prices specified at the time of issue.
PAT	Profit after tax, also referred to as net income. This is an indicator of an entity's profitability and is calculated as sales minus cost of goods sold, selling, general and administrative expenses, operating expenses, depreciation, amortisation, interest and taxes.

PNB	Punjab National Bank. It is a listed bank in which GoI has a majority stake.
RAW	Research & Analysis Wing, India's foreign intelligence agency.
RBI	Reserve Bank of India, India's central bank.
SEBI	Securities and Exchange Board of India, the capital markets regulator in India.
Shareholder	Also referred to as a common shareholder or stockholder, this is a retail or institutional investor who owns at least one share of an entity's stock, which is known as equity. Shareholders are an entity's owners, whose return on investment comprises dividends and appreciation in share values. Conversely, they earn losses when an entity is unable to pay dividends and / or share prices decline. In a liquidation scenario, lenders and preference shareholders have precedence over common shareholders, who may be left with nothing.
UTI	Unit Trust of India.
UPA	United Progressive Alliance. This is a coalition of political parties founded in 2004 and led by the Indian National Congress.
Working capital	A measure of a company's liquidity defined as the difference between current assets (cash, receivables, inventories) and current liabilities (payables, debt falling due within a year, tax payable within a year).

Source: Investopedia and author's definitions